DeVIANCe+ CRIME

THEORY, RESEARCH AND POLICY

Walter S. DeKeseredy University of Ontario Institute of Technology

Desmond Ellis York University

Shahid Alvi University of Ontario Institute of Technology

Deviance and Crime: Theory, Research and Policy, Third Edition

Copyright © 2005
       Matthew Bender & Company, Inc., a member of the LexisNexis Group

Phone 877-374-2919
Web Site www.lexisnexis.com/anderson/criminaljustice

Library of Congress Cataloging-in-Publication Data

DeKeseredy, Walter S., 1959-
    Deviance and crime : theory, research and policy / Walter S. DeKeseredy, Desmond Ellis,
    Shahid Alvi.–3rd ed.
      p. cm.
    Includes bibliographical references and index.
    ISBN 1-58360-549-5 (softbound)
    1. Crime. 2. Deviant behavior. 3. Criminology. I. Ellis, Desmond. II. Alvi, Shahid. III. Title.
HV6025.D354 2005
364.3--dc22   2005003540

Cover design by Tin Box Studio, Inc./Cincinnati, Ohio

EDITOR   Ellen S. Boyne
ACQUISITIONS EDITOR   Michael C. Braswell

Dedication

For Andrea, Pat, and Steven DeKeseredy, Eva Jantz,
and the late Michael D. Smith
—WSD

For Benjamin
—DE

For Pamela, Megan, and Erin
—SA

Preface

This book was supposed to be the third edition of *The Wrong Stuff: An Introduction to the Sociological Study of Deviance*. However, constructive suggestions made by Michael C. Braswell (our close friend and Acquisitions Editor) and some anonymous reviewers influenced us to change the title and to focus on theories, research, and policies omitted from the first two editions of *The Wrong Stuff*. Despite the new title and the inclusion of new scholarly work, the primary objective of this book is the same: to introduce students to the sociological study of deviance, crime, and social control. This involves a two-step process. The first step is to show the influence of classical and general sociological theories on five major, contemporary theoretical perspectives. The second step is to apply these five perspectives to substantive topics such as woman abuse, corporate crime, and homicide.

The five theoretical perspectives covered include strain, social control, interactionist, ecological, and critical perspectives. They are regarded as standard theoretical perspectives because each one is well established in the sociology of deviance, crime, and social control. Most sociologists who study these topics either use one of them or some combination of elements borrowed from more than one. This does not mean, however, that all sociologists who study deviance, crime, and social control would place any given theoretical perspective under the same general title we selected. Here, as elsewhere, there is a lot of room for differences in judgment.

We also provide a comprehensive, highly intelligible overview of sociological research on five substantive topics. Of course, we could have covered many more, and several other texts do. However, we limited our focus to only five—not because we think others are unimportant or of little social consequence. Rather, we decided to replace the standard "cafeteria concept"—covering a little bit of many kinds of topics—with the concept of *table d'hôte*, presenting a few selected offerings. These are limited in number, so that each topic can be covered in some depth, an approach we believe necessary for acquiring more than superficial knowledge of it.

It cannot be emphasized enough that we wanted to avoid what Walter DeKeseredy and Martin D. Schwartz refer to in their book *Contemporary Criminology* as the "immunization factor of crime theory." That is, you read about theory in one or two chapters and are now immunized and never have to read about it again. Again, in *Deviance and Crime*, we always return to theories when covering substantive topics like homicide and woman abuse. Rather than just describe the extent and distribution of these problems, we also show how different theories explain them. This is a highly effective way of showing students that there is more than one way to explain any type of deviance, crime, or method of social control.

What is to be done about deviance, crime, and social control? Of course, there are many conflicting answers to this question, all of which are informed by theories. In this book, we provide some example of policies derived from the above five major theoretical perspectives. As stated in Chapter 8, none of the theories reviewed in this text have a monopoly on any particular solution. For example, because strain theorists and critical theorists are deeply concerned about the criminogenic consequences of inequality, it is not surprising that both groups propose policies aimed at reducing this problem. Moreover, just because critical theorists call for a transition to a socialist feminist society does not mean that they disregard criminal justice reform, an issue that is also of central concern to conservative scholars.

Definitions, research, theories, and policies are described in a way that will make the sociological study of deviance, crime, and social control "come alive." For example, whenever possible, we provide real-life anecdotes to illustrate complex issues. Sometimes, these anecdotes are about our own lives. Some scholars may claim that this approach is unorthodox, but it is how many of us learn. Indeed, all of us have either directly or indirectly experienced crime, deviance, and social control. These aren't "things that only happen to other people."

While we try to be as fair as possible, this is not a "value-free" book. For example, with its decidedly sociological orientation, it sees a smaller role for biological and psychological theories of deviance and crime. Moreover, *Deviance and Crime* devotes attention to theorists and topics that are often ignored or given superficial treatment in other texts. In particular, critical criminological theories are given considerable attention here. Still, the strengths and weaknesses of the critical offerings reviewed are noted.

Each chapter attempts to engage and involve the reader in a dialog with the authors, with her/himself, with other students, and with the people quoted or referred to in this text. To achieve this goal, discussion questions, problem–solving scenarios, suggested readings, and online resources are included at the end of every chapter. Further, *Deviance and Crime* is accompanied by an instructor's manual and PowerPoint presentations for each chapter. We hope instructors and students will find these supplements useful and we look forward to hearing their feedback.

In his groundbreaking book *Confronting Crime: An American Challenge*, Elliott Currie (1985:vii) correctly points out that "[m]ost books about social questions are, to a much greater extent than is usually recognized, the products of collective effort." The same can be said about this one. Each of us has always been keenly interested in deviance, crime, and social control, and we wanted to co-author a book such as this for years. However, if it were not for the encouragement and support of Michael C. Braswell, Ellen Boyne, and other staff at Lexis Nexis Anderson Publishing, this project would not have come to fruition. *Deviance and Crime* was a long time coming and we deeply appreciate these colleagues' patience and guidance. Special thanks also go to Emily Troshynski, who devoted long hours to copy editing each chapter.

As always, our families helped us in immeasurable ways. Our intimate partners, parents, and children were always there to cheer us up and to remind us that there is more to life than sociology. Our loved ones also play key roles in the ongoing attempt to make people and communities safer and kinder.

It is often said that being a professor is one of the best jobs in the world. We couldn't agree more. In addition to having considerable control over our labor, we have greatly benefited from the comments, criticisms, lessons, and encouragement provided by the following people: Bruce Arrigo, Bernard Auchter, Gregg Barak, Raquel Bergen, Jennifer Blank, Mickey Braswell, Michelle Brown, Henry Brownstein, Susan Caringella-MacDonald, Meda Chesney-Lind, Kim Cook, Francis Cullen, Dawn Currie, Joseph Donnermyer, Bonnie Fisher, David Friedrichs, Carole Garrison, Alberto Godenzi, Colin Goff, Judith Grant, Mandy Hall, Mark Hamm, Ron Hinch, Carolyn Joseph, Victor Kappeler, Michael Kimmel, Mary Koss, Michael Lynch, Brian MacLean, MaDonna Maidment, Lorraine Halinka Malcoe, Rick Matthews, Ken Mentor, James Messerschmidt, Jody Miller, Karen Miller-Potter, Dragan Milovanovic, Stephen Muzzatti, Tim Newburn, Patrik Olsson, Barbara Perry, Ruth Peterson, Gary Potter, Claire Renzetti, McKenzie Rogness, Leora Rosen, Greg Saville, Martin D. Schwartz, Aysan Sev'er, Peter St. Jean, Betsy Stanko, Kenneth Tunnell, Thomas VanderVen, and Jock Young. Because many of these people disagree with one another, we assume full responsibility for the material presented in this book.

Last, but certainly not least, we thank the support staff at the University of Ontario Institute of Technology's (UOIT) Faculty of Social Science. Emma Aquilino and Christina Vanderlee went out of their way to help us write *Deviance and Crime*, and we will never forget their patience and good humor. Note, too, that many UOIT students contributed to the completion of this book by providing us with feedback on drafts of chapters.

Contents

Chapter 3
Woman Abuse   87

The laundry list of unacceptable conduct varies with the age and status of the person compiling it (Smith & Pollack, 1997:25).

CHAPTER 1

DEFINITIONS OF DEVIANCE AND CRIME

British criminologist Colin Sumner (1994:ix) argues that deviance is "a field of sociology that has died." Further, some prominent U.S. sociologists, such as Joel Best (2004), suggest that academics are finding the concept of "deviance" increasingly less valuable as time goes on (Schwartz & Maume, 2003). From our standpoint and that of many other sociologists, nothing can be further from the truth. Gibbs's (1981:483) claim still holds true today: "If publications and course enrollments are the criteria, no sociological subject rivals the popularity of deviance." For example, until recently, close to 650 York University undergraduates consistently enrolled in *one* of Desmond Ellis's classes on this topic. Moreover, the Sociology of Deviance or Deviant Behavior is taught in every North American sociology department, and it generally attracts high or higher enrollments from nonmajors as from sociology majors (Schwartz & Maume, 2003). Similarly, as you read this chapter, criminology courses taught at North American institutions of higher learning collectively draw thousands of students.

Not surprisingly, the mass media attracts a much bigger audience interested in hearing, reading, and seeing both fictional and nonfictional stories about the "dark side" of society. Think about how many people routinely watch television shows like *NYPD Blue, The John Walsh Show, CSI Miami, Law and Order, The Sopranos*, and so on. Further, much of North Americans' everyday conversation, regardless of whether it occurs at home, in the workplace, bars, classrooms, at sporting events, and so on, includes stories about friends, relatives, celebrities,

1

athletes, politicians, and others who did the "wrong stuff" (Ellis & DeKeseredy, 1996), as well as debates about what is to be done about these "outsiders" behaviors, beliefs, and attitudes (Becker, 1973).

There are several reasons why so many people are interested in what they regard to be deviant or criminal behavior. For example, across North America, thousands of students want to be agents of social control (e.g., police officers) and believe that a social scientific understanding of crime and deviance will help them achieve their career goals. Then, of course, there are those who "have a special affinity" for these subjects because of their personal experiences as victims or perpetrators of crime. Another group gravitates to the topics covered in this book and elsewhere because they "offer the promise of excitement or the exotic" (Adler & Adler, 1997:1). Regardless of what motivates people to learn about deviance and crime, before they can effectively study these topics, they first have to define them (Thio, 2004).

The main objective of this chapter is to sensitize you to the fact that there is substantial disagreement within the academic community and among policymakers and the general public over what behaviors, conditions (e.g., physical attributes), and people should and should not be designated as deviant or criminal. In the discussion that follows, we critically review three major ways of defining crime and deviance: (1) normative conceptions; (2) the societal reaction/labeling approach; and (3) the critical approach.[1] It is to normative conceptions that we turn first.

Normative Conceptions of Deviance

Prior to the 1960s, almost every sociologist adhered to normative or objective conceptions of deviance and crime, which basically assert that they are rule-breaking behaviors (Gibbs, 1981). Supporters of normative conceptions assume that in any given group, these rules or social norms are given; they exist, and group members uphold them. Group members who violate these objective standards or norms, are deviants, their rule violations constitute deviance. Thus, same-sex marriages violate the social norms of some people, including President George W. Bush,[2] and are therefore defined as deviant by them. Jumping ahead in a line to buy tickets for a rock concert, telling lies, body piercing, and using profanity at a dinner party for your grandmother are all deviant behaviors because they violate social norms.[3]

Legal norms are backed up by the coercive power of the government and constitute a subset of social norms. Often, but by no means invariably, legal norms regulate behaviors thought to be either most harmful to society and/or threaten its major values. Thus, murder is a crime because if everyone did it, either to get what they wanted or in retaliation for a harm done to them (e.g., adultery), life would soon become "brutish and short." Moreover, murder challenges the value of respect for life. Murder, then, is a crime because it violates legal norms. Still, just because some behaviors violate legal norms and are therefore criminal does not mean that they violate the social norms of a large number of individuals. Consider recreational marijuana use. Many people sharply oppose criminalizing this activity, as well as the government's punitive response to physically ill persons (e.g., those afflicted with AIDS) who smoke marijuana to alleviate their pain and/or to stimulate their appetite. Therefore, some sociologists, such as Hagan (1994), contend that it is essential to categorize violations of legal norms as either **consensus** or **conflict** crimes.

Murder is an example of a consensus crime. It is a behavior that many legal theorists who like to use Latin refer to as *male in se*, or bad in and of itself. Murder, rape, kidnapping, and robbery constitute consensus crimes because members of all or most social groups share norms and values that legally prohibit these forms of conduct, and that impose the most severe penalties on those who violate laws relating to them (Hagan, 1994). Generally speaking, the more harmful the criminal conduct is perceived to be, the greater the consensus and the more severe the punishment. Thus, murder is punished more severely than shoplifting because more members of society agree that it is more harmful to society, as well as one of the most serious forms of wrongful conduct in which a person may engage.

Often referred to as *mala prohibita* (bad because they are prohibited), the characteristic feature of conflict crimes is normative disagreement or conflict. People are divided as to whether prostitution, marijuana use, the consumption of pornography, and so on should be called crimes and therefore liable to punishment by the state. Note, too, that many sociologists and criminologists refer to certain conflict crimes like prostitution and drug dealing as "victimless crimes" that do not involve a clear-cut victim or offender. Instead, they are seen as:

> the exchange between willing partners of strongly desired goods and services. The "offense" in such a situation, then, consists of a consensual transaction—one person gives or sells another person something he or she wants (Schur, 1974:6).

According to Hagan (1994), there are two other types of norm violations that, although not regulated by criminal law, are still subject to official social control. Hagan refers to the first type as **social deviations**. These are statutes that attempt to control conditions and activities such as mental illness, pollution, corporate price-fixing, and false advertising. The second type is referred to as **social diversions**, and they include what Hagan regards as "lifestyle variations," such as body piercing and membership in the Macintosh Society. Members of the Macintosh Society spend their lives dressed entirely in rubber. There is no law or government regulation against being a rubber fetishist, and it is fair to conclude that most people would react to such a person "with no more than a mixture of amusement and amazement. . . ." (Hagan, 1994:18).

Critique of Normative Definitions

No doubt, you have detected several problems with the normative approaches identified here. For example, if there is widespread agreement that killing is wrong, then why in March 2003 was there considerable popular support in the United States for President Bush's decision to declare war on Iraq? People knew that many innocent lives would be lost, and at the time of writing this chapter, the Iraq Body Count Project (2003) estimated that there were at least 5,531 reported civilian deaths in this war, which, according to many critics, is still going on as this book goes to press. Further, if most people believe that murder should result in severe punishment, why, then, weren't the U.S. federal government and the soldiers who acted on its behalf in Iraq convicted of this crime?

Another point to consider is that if most members of our society share norms and values that legally prohibit sexual assault, why do survey data show that annually at least 28 percent of Canadian women experience one or more types of such victimization in college dating relationships (Schwartz & DeKeseredy, 1997)? To make matters worse, this figure is an underestimate because many sexual assault survivors do not report their experiences in surveys due to factors such as embarrassment, fear of reprisal, and the reluctance to recall traumatic memories (DeKeseredy & Schwartz, 1998a; Kennedy & Dutton, 1989; Schwartz, 2000; Smith, 1987).

Some people also question whether prostitution, illicit drug use (e.g., ingesting heroin and/or marijuana), and drug dealing are really victimless crimes (Brownmiller, 1975; DeKeseredy, 2000a; Hodgson, 1997). Indeed, more than 25 recent North American studies found alarmingly high levels of violence against street prostitutes (Farley & Kelly, 2000). For example, of the 130 San Francisco street workers who participated in Farley and Barkan's (1998) study, 82 percent reported being physically assaulted during the course of their work, and 68 percent stated that they were raped. Indoor prostitution is not much safer. Consider Raphael and Shapiro's (2004) Chicago study, which found that 50 percent of the female escort service workers they interviewed reported forced sex. Raphael and Shapiro also discovered that 51.2 percent of women who worked as exotic dancers were threatened with a weapon, and one-third of women who had sex for money in their own residences experienced at least one type of sexual assault (e.g., threatened rape, fingers or objects inserted vaginally, etc.). In Box 1.1, one of Miller and Schwartz's (1995) respondents provides a terrifying example of what happens to female sex trade workers during a "bad date."[4]

Box 1.1
An Example of a "Bad Date"

Well, a girlfriend brought a date over to a friend's house where we was stayin' . . . And, uh, she was gonna go out with him but instead he saw me and he wanted to date me. Ok, so I said yeah. And, uh, we went back and got in his car, and as we was leavin' he pulled a knife out and stuck it to my throat with one hand and drove with the other on . . . And he drove me all the way to ***, and on the way here, he stopped on the side of the freeway and he tied my hands behind my back, and tied my feet together, and put a thing around my mouth so I couldn't scream or nothing' no more. And, uh, after that, we got to *** in this field and he put a rope around my neck and tied it to the steering wheel. He blacked both of my eyes, he busted two ribs, and busted up my back real bad. He beat me for like four hours. And he was gonna kill me, if it weren't for my friend havin' his—the color of his car and stuff was and all that, he would've killed me I think. And then he gave me twenty dollars and put me out in the field. Told me to find my own way back.

Source: Miller, J. & Schwartz, M.D. (1995). "Rape Myths and Violence against Prostitutes." *Deviant Behavior: An Interdisciplinary Journal*, 16, 1-23.

Illicit drug use and drug dealing are considered by many people to be, like prostitution, victimless crimes. For an undetermined number of people who engage in these activities, such as those who infrequently smoke or sell marijuana at parties, this may be the case. However, peddling drugs can be extremely dangerous work, as discovered by a dealer interviewed by Elijah Anderson (1999). His name is John, and he was shot in the stomach in an altercation that took place during "a misunderstood drug deal." Consequently, as some people say on the streets of Philadelphia, John is now "carrying around a bag and will be for the rest of his life. He is now about twenty-seven" (1999:285).

Drug dealing not only harms many dealers. It also has numerous "undesirable consequences" for communities (Meier & Geis, 1997). For example, people living near drug dealers and their transactions are often victimized by fatal or nonfatal acts of random violence (Anderson, 1999). As Currie (1993:9) reminds us in his description of "the American nightmare" that occurred in the 1990s and is still going on in many inner-city communities today:

To anyone observing the state of America's cities in the 1990s, it seems devastatingly obvious that we have failed to make much headway against the drug crisis. Americans liv-

ing in the worst-hit neighborhoods still face the reality of dealers on their doorstep and shots in the night; many fear for their
lives, or their children's lives, and sense that their communities have slid downward into a permanent state of terror
and disintegration. Even those fortunate enough to live in better neighborhoods cannot pick up a newspaper or watch the
news without confronting story after story about the toll of
drugs and drug-related violence on communities and families.
For most of us, the drug plague seems to have settled in,
become a routine feature of an increasingly frightening and
bewildering urban landscape.

If drug dealing hurts many neighborhoods, the same can be said
about illicit drug use. Would you like to live in a public housing community like the one described below by one of DeKeseredy, Alvi,
Schwartz, and Tomaszewski's (2003:20) respondents?

> We are four houses together so they are all single moms.
> And no husbands or boyfriends. So it's peaceful. But when I
> used to live across the street in 1290, just across the street, side
> doors across, these people used to sit in the backyard and
> smoke drugs. And I did tell [Housing Authority] about it. They
> used to smoke drugs. You used to smell it. In the summer I
> used to have to shut my windows in the back because the smell
> of marijuana would come in. Yeah. It was hard for me because
> [for my daughter], the only place for me where she could play
> was in my backyard. I got the little up and down swing and
> little things for her to play—a little car. You know, a little area
> for her to play. Well, with these new people moving there and
> smoking and having drinking, and fights! Always fights! A
> fight with a wife and you can hear at one, two o'clock in the
> morning and shutting doors and screaming and things like
> that. Really bad drugs smoke. Right there it was drugs.
> Smoke, and alcohol.

Needless to say, excessive consumption of illicit drugs—or any drug
(e.g., tobacco) for that matter—can also harm users in the following ways:

- It can interfere with the building and development of
  satisfying social and personal relationships.

- It precludes many people from finding meaningful employment and can reduce work productivity.

- It involves major health risks, such as acquiring HIV
  through needle sharing.

- It leads some people to commit crimes (e.g., vandalism,
  theft) they otherwise would not have done if they were
  sober (Meier & Geiss, 1997:103).

Hence, just because a critical mass of people think that a lifestyle, behavior, or condition is not deviant does not mean that it is not harmful. Further, there are many real harms done to individuals, communities, and society at large that rarely are designated as deviant or criminal. For example, in 1999, the DuPont company dumped 55,000 pounds of ammonium perfluorooctanoate (C8) in the Ohio River and released another 31,250 pounds of C8 into the air during 2000. C8 is a detergent-like material used to prevent resins from forming into large particles during the production of Teflon-related coatings (Hawthorne, 2003). As described in Box 1.2, although the dumping of C8 causes considerable harm to people and the environment, at the time of writing this chapter, this chemical was not regulated by the U.S. federal government, and West Virginia government officials claimed that C8 levels in drinking water were safe. Thus, since the 1960s, cases such as this have led many sociologists to challenge normative conceptions of deviance and to offer alternative approaches. Referred to as societal reaction/labeling definitions, these offerings assert that deviance and crime are labels that are not "in" behavior but are external to it.

Box 1.2
Internal Warnings: Industry Memos Show DuPont Knew for Decades That a Chemical Used to Make Teflon is Polluting Workers and Neighbors

Little Hocking, Ohio—Kenny Taggart always volunteered for blood drives at the DuPont plant across the Ohio River, where he spent most of his adult life mixing chemicals used to make Teflon anti-stick coatings.

When Taggart stopped by the plant's medical office in the early 1980s to offer another pint, the nurse shook her head and turned him away. His name was on a list of employees whose blood was contaminated with ammonium perfluorooctanoate, a chemical known within the company as C8.

Taggart didn't know much about C8, but DuPont did.

Company scientists issued internal warnings about the chemical as early as 1961, according to DuPont records filed last year with a West Virginia court. Medical studies conducted in the 1970s and '80s by DuPont and 3M, chief supplier of the chemical, showed that C8 builds up in human blood, doesn't break down in the environment and might cause serious health problems, including liver damage, reproductive and developmental defects and cancer.

DuPont records also show the company has known for at least two decades that C8 contamination extends beyond workers at its Washington Works plant west of Parkersburg, W.Va., where the chemical has been used since 1951 to help keep Teflon and related coatings from clumping as they are manufactured.

As the warning signs about C8 mounted at DuPont, few people outside the company were told, including thousands of people in the surrounding river valley who drink and breathe the chemical everyday, according to internal documents and interviews with local officials.

Box 1.2, *continued*

> Government officials didn't know much, either. Like thousands of other chemicals used by industry, C8 is not regulated by the federal government. But that could change soon.
>
> Amid growing concerns about the persistence of C8 in humans and its potential health effects, the U.S. Environmental Protection Agency launched an investigation in September to determine a national standard for the chemical. A decision is expected later this year.
>
> The agency took action after 3M provided research showing that millions of Americans likely have been exposed to the chemical. The studies detected low levels of C8 across the nation in human blood and in foods such as apples, bread, green beans and ground beef.
>
> EPA scientists still are trying to determine how C8 spreads in the environment and what it can do to humans.
>
> Under pressure from the EPA to contain C8 and a related chemical used in Scotchgard, 3M announced in May 2000 that it would stop making them. DuPont know makes C8 at one of its own plants.
>
> "Who knows how much C8 I've still got in my blood," said Taggart, 62, who retired from DuPont nine years ago but still drinks C8-contaminated ware at his home in Little Hocking. "It can't be good. If it was, the good Lord would have put it in your body when he made you.

Source: Hawthorne, M. (2003, February 16). "Internal Warnings: Industry Memos Show DuPont Knew for Decades That a Chemical Used to Make Teflon is Polluting Workers and Neighbors." *The Columbus Dispatch*, A1, A8-A9. Reprinted with permission from *The Columbus Dispatch*.

Societal Reaction/Labeling Definitions

At the start of all of his lectures on defining deviance and crime, Walter DeKeseredy asks students, "How many of you have never committed a crime?" At best, less than a handful of people raise their hands. Then he asks, "How many of you who committed one or more crimes were never arrested?" Again, very few raise their hands. What do these responses tell you? Well, the answer to the first question supports those who contend that deviance and crime are normative. In other words, as Gabor (1994) reminds us, "everybody does it." How many people do you know have done one or more of the following? Chances are that you know quite a few and perhaps you did some of them too:

- Made inflated insurance claims following a fire or theft.

- Driven while legally impaired by alcohol in a manner endangering others.

- Used prohibited drugs or abused prescription drugs.

- Failed to inform a store, customer, or bank of a financial error in our favor.

- Engaged in dishonest business practices.

- Failed to make truthful declarations at a border crossing.

- Destroyed or damaged property maliciously.

- Physically struck another person intentionally.

- Exhibited disorderly conduct in public (e.g., urinating in public).

- Illegally copied computer software, music, or videos.

- Abused the environment through dumping trash in an inappropriate place or by some other means.

- Violated the human rights of others through sexual harassment or discrimination on the basis of race, disability, age, or sexual orientation.

- Demonstrated cruelty to animals or hunted without a permit out of season, or in excess of that permitted by law (Gabor, 1994:7-8).

Even those we trust to protect our safety, such as police officers, frequently break the law or violate ethical standards. We could provide an even longer list of people Friedrichs (2004a) refers to as "trusted criminals," such as corporate executives who engage in price-fixing, false advertising, and the illegal dumping of toxic chemicals. However, a key point to consider here is that deviance and crime are not rare behaviors or conditions. Rather, they are widespread in North America and elsewhere. In fact, regardless of where you live and how kind and "respectable" members of your community are, you will always find people engaging in behaviors that violate norms and laws (DeKeseredy & Schwartz, 1996).

Consider Glen Ridge, New Jersey, "an affluent, idyllic suburb, the kind of town that exemplifies the American Dream" (Random House, 2003:2). If you went there for a visit, your first impression would probably be similar to that described below by journalist Bernard Lefkowitz (1997:5-6):

> My first mental snapshot: Glen Ridge was a squeaky-clean, manicured town that liked to display its affluence by dressing its high school graduates in dinner jackets and gowns. What impressed me most was the orderliness of the place. The streets, the lawns, the houses—everything seemed in proportion. There were no excesses of bad taste, no evidence of neglect or disrepair.

As is often said, looks can be deceiving. For example, in March 1989, something went terribly wrong in "paradise" (Random House, 2003). Thirteen male athletic students who attended Glen Ridge High School (actor Tom Cruise's alma mater) lured a mentally disabled girl into a basement where four of them raped her with a baseball bat and a broomstick while the others looked on. To make matters worse, it was weeks before anyone reported this crime to the police and years before the boys went to trial. Four of them were eventually convicted of various crimes. However, one was convicted only of a third-degree conspiracy charge and received a sentence of three years of probation and 200 hours of community service. The other three were granted bail and remained free until their appeals were decided, which at that time were estimated to take five or six years.

This would not likely happen to a poor African American arrested for allegedly committing similar crimes. Rather, as Lefkowitz (1997:487) points out:

> Most likely he wouldn't have been able to come up with the bail money when he was arrested. He would have to spend months, maybe years, locked up waiting to go to trial or to cop a plea. He wouldn't have been represented by the best legal talent that money could buy. He would have been represented by an underpaid public defender with a huge caseload. After he was convicted of first-degree sexual assault, he probably would have been jailed immediately.

By allowing the three white affluent boys out on bail, the judge, as pointed out by Ron Scott, a reporter for the New York CBS television station, told the Glen Ridge community and the rest of the United States that "If you're white, it's all right" (cited in Lefkowitz, 1997:487). Perhaps this also helps explain why so few students in DeKeseredy's criminology and deviance classes said that they were arrested for committing crimes.[5] Obviously, many were not caught and/or there was no negative societal reaction to their crimes. Indeed, as proponents of the societal reaction/labeling perspective point out, no act is inherently deviant or criminal. Rather, deviance and crime are labels, and there is nothing automatic about the relation between violating social or legal norms and being labeled criminal or deviant.

There is *nothing* inherently criminal? Not murder or rape? What could these scholars be thinking? Let us return to the Glen Ridge gang rape. Although the offenders clearly committed what sociologists like Hagan (1994) refer to as "consensus crimes," the community stood by the boys and attacked the media for covering the case. Further, a boy of color who witnessed the rape and reported it to the authorities was ostracized by his peers. Moreover, the judge made it explicit that he "didn't want to lock up all-American boys and throw away the key" (Lefkowitz, 1997:486).

The Glen Ridge rapists also engaged in less serious forms of what many would consider deviant behavior and were not officially or informally sanctioned for their conduct. For example, Kevin Scherzer would frequently stroke his penis during classes, even in front of teachers and students. According to Lefkowitz (1997:167), "Such odd behavior over such a long time. And no one in authority seemed able to stop it—or acted as if they were even aware that it was going on." Given these examples, perhaps, now, arguments made by labeling theorists such as Howard Becker (1973:9) make sense:

> [S]ocial groups create deviance by making the rules whose infraction constitutes deviance, and by applying those rules to particular people and labeling them as outsiders. For this point of view, deviance is not a quality of the act the person commits, but rather a consequence of the application by others of rules and sanctions to an "offender." The deviant is one to whom that label has successfully been applied; deviant behavior is behavior that people so label.

Clearly, in the case of Scherzer, subjective processes of interpreting and assigning meaning to his behavior were at work. He fondled himself in front of others, which is a violation of the law; however, his behavior was not defined as such, and he was never punished. Instead, Scherzer was not required to receive psychological treatment, was able to continue to attend classes, played on the football team, and was selected as co-captain (Lefkowitz, 1997).

In sum, then, subscribers to the societal reaction/labeling approach contend that definitions of deviance and crime should direct attention to the interactions between the rule-breakers and rule-makers instead of just to the rule-breakers alone. Basically, to be designated as deviant or criminal, all that counts according to these scholars is what reaction you get from people around you. As stated earlier in this chapter, although both affluent and disenfranchised people commit violent crimes (sometimes in different contexts and for different reasons), there are significant differences in the social and legal responses to their actions. This is just what Jeffrey Reiman (2004) was talking about when he chose the title for one of his books: *The Rich Get Richer and the Poor Get Prison*.

Sometimes, too, labeling someone a deviant or criminal can lead to more rule-breaking behavior or to what Lemert (1951) refers to as career or secondary deviance. As stated earlier, it would be hard to find someone who has never broken the law or committed a deviant act. Again, everybody does it (Gabor, 1994). When we do this, we are committing an act of **primary deviance**. Primary deviations are those that are "rationalized or otherwise dealt with as functions of a socially acceptable role" (Lemert, 2000). Moreover, the causes of primary deviance are random, varied, and have an insignificant impact on the perpetrators. For example, in the college town Athens, Ohio (home to Ohio University), it is not uncommon to see students drinking excessively in bars, and often their "partying" goes unnoticed because it is regarded by many as a legitimate part of college life. In addition, their relations with teachers and peers are typically not affected by such behavior.

However, suppose a student starts to get drunk everyday in a particular bar and is eventually banned because of his obnoxious behavior (e.g., swearing at customers). He goes to another bar and is soon banned from that place as well. On top of experiencing this type of social exclusion, the student starts to receive bad grades because his excessive drinking causes him to miss classes and submit assignments after the required deadline. Eventually, he becomes bitter and starts drinking even more, either at bars that allow him entry or at home. To make matters worse, because he spends a substantial amount of money on "booze," he is unable to pay his tuition and rent, which causes him to leave school. Lacking a college degree, he can't find a meaningful job and thus resorts to selling drugs to pay for his binges. Following a few arrests, he gradually comes to see himself as a failure, a drunk, and a criminal. He is now a secondary deviant because he self-identifies with the negative labels bestowed upon him.

This is a person who began drinking heavily for several reasons, such as school-related stress, peer pressure, or to overcome his fear of interacting with women to whom he is attracted. Now his drinking is "a means of defense, attack or adjustment to the overt and covert problems created by the societal reaction to it" (Lemert, 2000:23). Developed by Lemert (1951, 2000), this societal reaction approach is described in Figure 1.1.

Chambliss's (1973) participant observation study provides another example of how negative societal reactions can lead to career or secondary deviance. For two years, he observed two groups of high school students: the Saints and the Roughnecks. Over this time period, Chambliss made two key observations. First, the rate of delinquency in both groups was roughly equal. Second, whereas not one Saint was arrested for the various delinquent and criminal activities (truancy, dangerous driving, vandalism, petty theft) in which they engaged, the Roughnecks were constantly in trouble with the police and community.

Some years after they graduated from high school, Chambliss returned to try to find out what happened to members of both groups, which led to an important finding. Members of each group had followed the careers predicted for them by the police and community. Most of the Saints were recruited to colleges and universities, while most of the Roughnecks went to prison. How did this come about? Why were the Saints and Roughnecks morally/legally differentiated from each other when their rate of delinquency was similar?

Figure 1.1
Lemert's Societal Reaction Model

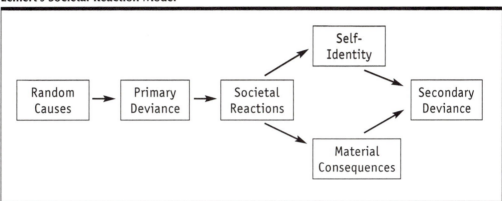

The major cause of this differentiation is differences in the reactions of the community and the police to the delinquencies of members of the two groups. The delinquencies of the Saints were interpreted by the police as "high spirits," as behaviors they would grow out of as they progressed toward becoming doctors, lawyers, teachers, and accountants. Police interpreted Roughneck delinquencies in quite another way.

The invitational edge of Lemert's model stops short of inviting us to inquire into the reasons behind differences in police power to define. In Chambliss's study, social class differences explain differential police definitions and reactions. For example, Roughneck members came from lower-class homes, while the Saints had middle-class parents. The socioeconomic status of the family was used by the police as a vehicle or medium for interpreting and reacting to similar behavior. The police were also aware of the fact that influential and knowledgeable middle-class parents are much more likely to effectively challenge legal definitions and police reactions than are uneducated, powerless lower-class parents. Ultimately, then, control over legal institutions by the middle-class explains why the police react to middle- and lower-class delinquencies in different ways.

Clearly, the police in Chambliss's study defined similar Saint and Roughneck behaviors in different ways. However, the police's definition of behavior as criminally deviant was also influenced by differences in the social power possessed by members of different social classes. As described in Figure 1.2, Chambliss's contribution moves beyond Lemert's (1951, 2000) offering and tells us much about the linkage between social class, societal reactions, and career outcomes. Perhaps you can detect some similarities between Chambliss's findings and events that occurred in Glen Ridge. Indeed, social class had a lot to do with how the judge and other members of the community reacted to the perpetrators of the gang rape.

Figure 1.2
The Saints and the Roughnecks

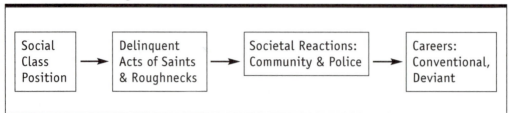

Power derived from being socially and economically privileged also accounts in large part for why companies like DuPont are rarely held accountable for their deviant or criminal actions (Reiman, 2004). Of course, there are exceptions to this common societal reaction. For example, in late June 2003, the Federal Energy Regulatory Commission issued what they called a "death penalty" to the Houston-based Enron Corporation, barring this company from competitively selling electricity and natural gas in the United States after finding that it manipulated Western states' power markets in 2001. Still, harsh sentences are very rare because corporate deviants have high educational levels and occupational prestige that creates a "status shield" protecting them from harsh sentences given to "common" criminals. Further, many judges come from the same social class background and have the same high standing the community. Hence, they identify with affluent offenders (Rosoff, Pontell & Tillman, 2001).

In addition to social class, gender and race can affect whether one will be defined as deviant or criminal and/or end up being a career deviant or criminal. Recall what the CBS television reporter had to say about the judge's reaction to the Glen Ridge rapists' behavior? As prominent African-American scholar, theologian, and activist Cornell West (2001:xxv) reminds us in some of his recollections of negative societal reactions that have harmed him and his son, "race matters" (despite President George W. Bush's ongoing attempt to create a "color-blind society"):

> Years ago, while driving from New York to teach at Williams College, I was stopped on fake charges of trafficking cocaine. When I told the police officer I was a professor of religion, he replied, "Yeh, and I'm the Flying Nun. Let's go, nigger." I was stopped three times in my first ten days in Princeton for driving too slowly on a residential street with a speed limit of twenty-five miles per hour. (And my son, Clifton, already has similar memories at the tender age of fifteen.) Needless to say, these incidents are dwarfed by those like Rodney King's beating. . . .

What happened to West was by no means an isolated incident. In fact, several recent studies show that throughout many parts of the United States white drivers are less likely to be stopped by the police than are African-American and Latino drivers (Walker, 2000). For example, in San Diego, although African Americans constitute only 8 percent of the city's population ages 15 years and older, 12 percent of all traffic stops involved African-American drivers (Berjarano, 2001). Similarly, a recent study conducted in Columbus, Ohio, found that African-American drivers are more likely than whites to be stopped by the police. Further, in the same city, African-American drivers are almost twice as likely to be searched as white drivers, and Latino drivers are four times as likely to be searched (Ferenchik, 2003). Consider, too, that results generated by a national representative sample show that African-American and Hispanic drivers are significantly less likely to report that police had a legitimate reason for stopping them and were significantly less likely to report that the police "acted properly" (Lundman & Kaufman, 2003).[6]

Obviously, despite serious attempts by federal, state, and local governments to end racial profiling,[7] this problem continues to plague many people, especially those of color at airports. Consider the case described in Box 1.3. This event occurred in 1999 and more like it have been documented since September 11, 2001. Ostensibly to prevent more planes from flying into buildings or being hijacked, approximately 67 percent of the people subjected to personal searches upon entering the United States are people of color (American Civil Liberties Union, 2002). In addition to violating civil liberties, this approach fails to consider people such as Timothy McVeigh. Recall that in 1995, the young, white McVeigh bombed the Oklahoma City federal building. Close to 170 innocent people were killed, including 19 babies. It is also important to note that thousands of young, white male neo-Nazis are scattered throughout the United States, and they threaten the physical and psychological well-being of U.S. citizens on a daily basis (Perry, 2001, 2003a). Such men, who go so far as to produce violent racist video games (see Box 1.4) are rarely targeted. How often are young, white males subjected to searches like the one described in Box 1.3?

Box 1.3
An Example of Racial Profiling at U.S. Airports

In 1999, the ACLU filed a complaint with the Customs Service on behalf of Yvette Bradley, an African-American advertising executive who suffered a humiliating search by Customs officers after returning from a vacation in Jamaica. Bradley said that as she and her sister arrived in Newark Airport last April from a vacation in Jamaica, they, and most of the other black women on the flight, were singled out for searches by Customs agents. She was directed to a room where an officer ran her hands and fingers over every area of her body including her breasts and, through her underwear, the inner and outer labia of her vagina. No contraband was found.

Source: American Civil Liberties Union (2002). "Racial Practices: Racial Profiling." Available at: http://www.aclu.org/PolicePractices

Box 1.4
Racist Groups Using Computer Gaming to Promote Violence Against Blacks, Latinos, and Jews

On Martin Luther King Day [2002], Resistance Records, a distributor of racist, anti-Semitic "White Power" music began to advertise *Ethnic Cleansing*, a CD-ROM-based computer game whose object is to kill "subhumans"—i.e., Blacks and Latinos—and their "masters," the Jews, who are portrayed as the personification of evil. The ads said, "Celebrate Martin Luther King Day with a virtual Race War!" Resistance Records is owned by the National Alliance, the largest and most active neo-Nazi organization in the United States.

Patterned after popular mainstream video games such as *Quake* and *Doom*, the game turns racially motivated violence into "entertainment." Racists and anti-Semites are clearly trying to spread their hate-filled vision to a wider, computer-savvy, younger audience through the violent body-strewn world of shoot-'em-up computer games while hoping to make some money along the way.

The premise of *Ethnic Cleansing* is that a city—clearly New York—has been destroyed by gangs of "sub-humans" controlled by Jews who are led by the "end boss" lurking in the subterranean "Lair of the Beast." Plans for world domination are seen in the subway, along with a map of "problem" areas in the U.S. and a sign reading "Diversity, It's Good for Jews."

The player (who can choose to dress in KKK robes or as a Skinhead) roams the streets and subways murdering "predatory sub-humans" and their Jewish "masters," thereby "saving the white world. During the game monkey and ape sounds are heard when Blacks are killed, poncho-wearing Latinos say "I'll take a siesta now!" or "Ay carumba!" while "Oy vey!" rings out when Jewish characters are killed. The game has a high level of background detail and various National Alliance signs and posters appear throughout while racist rock blares on the soundtrack.

At the end, the player confronts the "end boss," a rocket launcher-wielding Ariel Sharon, who hurls insults such as: "Oy vey! Can you shoot no better than that?"; "We have destroyed your culture!"; and "We silenced Henry Ford." When Sharon dies, he coughs out "Filthy White dog, you have destroyed thousands of years of planning."

Source: Anti-Defamation League (2002). "Racist Groups Using Computer Gaming to Promote Violence against Blacks, Latinos and Jews." Available at: http:www.adl.org/videogames/default.asp

It should be noted in passing that the former leader of the racist National Alliance, Willam Pierce, wrote *The Turner Diaries*, a hate-filled book that heavily influenced Timothy McVeigh. Certainly, many people, especially those who are Jewish, African-American, and Latino, would find games like that described in Box 1.4, *The Turner Diaries*, and people who produce these media major threats to their homeland security. Yet, in our own domestic and international journeys, we have never seen white people at airports searched for such products. Even more alarming is that the racist behaviors described here are not the practices of "a few misguided individuals" (Alvi, 2003). Rather, they are part of an "institutionalized system of advantage benefiting whites in subtle as well as blatant ways" (Tatum, 1997).

Again, gender also influences whether a person or group will be labeled deviant or criminal. Let us provide a crude example based on personal experience before summarizing some relevant sociological research on this problem. In late August 2003, Walter DeKeseredy went to Ohio University's Alden Library to pay a brief visit to a colleague that worked there. Because he was entitled to a coffee break and desired some fresh air, this man asked DeKeseredy to sit outside with him for a few minutes. Shortly after they sat on a bench, a young woman with a short top and tight jeans walked by them. The colleague then whispered to DeKeseredy, "Look at that woman dressed like a whore. Would you allow your daughter to walk around like that?" Although it was a very humid day, this man felt that the young female student was deviant because, from his standpoint, "good girls" don't' dress like that. In other words, he argued that she violated one of the major types of **gender norms** described in Table 1.1.

The norms identified in Table 1.1 contribute to keeping a woman "in her place" (Schur, 1984). Moreover, stigmatizing women who violate one or more of these norms can help groups of men rationalize their own deviant or criminal behaviors. Consider male college students who sexually assault female acquaintances or dating partners. If they belong to all-male patriarchal peer groups, these subcultures often reinforce abusive men's beliefs in the moral validity of sexual assault under certain conditions. For example, some men experience guilt and shame after sexually assaulting women (DeKeseredy, 1988a; Godenzi, Schwartz & DeKeseredy, 2001). The belief that they did something wrong, however, may disappear after learning group-based justifications for the abuse that identify their victims as legitimate objects of predatory attacks. After hearing from their peers that the women they abused were "pickups" or "gold diggers," men can convince themselves that they are not deviant and are normal, respectable students (Kanin, 1967; Schwartz & DeKeseredy, 1997).

Keep in mind, too, that the law is often used to stigmatize or punish females who violate some of the gender norms described in Table 1.1. For example, in the United States, girls are much more likely to be arrested and convicted for **status offenses** than are boys, even though they there is no empirical evidence of greater female involvement in status offenses (Chesney-Lind & Pasko, 2004; Figueira-McDonough, 1985). Status offenses are those that, if engaged in by adults, would not be officially designated as crimes (Boritch, 1997). Further, status offenses permit the arrest of youths for many behaviors that challenge parental domination and control, including running away, truancy, incorrigibility, and violations of liquor laws.

Table 1.1
Gender Norms and Female Deviance

Major Category of Norms	Typical "Offenses" and Deviance "Labels"
1. Presentation of Self	
a. Emotions	Too little emotion ("cold," "calculating," "masculine"); or too much emotion ("hysterical"); or various wrong emotions (different types of mental illness)
b. Nonverbal Communication	"Masculine" gestures, postures, use of space, touching, etc.
c. Appearance	"Plain," "unattractive," "masculine," "overweight," "fat," "old," "drab," "poorly made up"; or "overly made up," "flashy," "cheap"
d. Speech and Interaction	"Unladylike," "bossy," "competitive," "aggressive"; or "timid," "mousy," "nonentity"
2. Marriage/Maternity	
a. Marital	"Spinster," "old maid"; or "unmarried," "divorcee," "widow"; or "unwed mother"; or sleeps around
b. Maternity	Voluntary childlessness ("selfish"); or abortion ("killer"); or "unwed" motherhood; or "unmaternal," "unfit mother," etc.
3. Sexuality	
a. Behavior	"Oversexed," "nymphomaniac," "promiscuous," "loose," "cheap," "whore"; or "cock-teaser," "cold," "frigid"
b. Orientation	"Butch," "dyke," "queer," etc.
4. Occupational Choice	In a "man's" job, "tough," "aggressive," "castrating," "ball-buster," etc.
5. "Deviance Norms"	Norm-violation "inappropriate" for females (e.g., armed robber, political revolutionary)

Source: Schur, E.M. (1984:53). *Labeling Women Deviant: Gender, Stigma, and Social Control.* Philadelphia: Temple University Press.

The differential implementation of the law addressed here is a prime example of "the sexual double standard" (Chesney-Lind & Pasko, 2004). Note, too, that girls are far more likely to be given custodial dispositions than boys for status offenses, which are used to punish them for "unfeminine" behavior (Boritch, 1997; DeKeseredy, 2000a). In fact, in the United States, some see status offenses as being basically "buffer charges for suspected sexuality when applied to girls" (Chesney-Lind, 1997:65). Criminal justice officials, like many parents and teachers, tend to view sex as "ruining" girls but enhancing boys

(Orenstein, 1994). Even today, many parents who define themselves as pro-feminist or who oppose sexism still feel uncomfortable "tampering" with some sexual double standards and "do not want their children becoming misfits" (Chesney-Lind & Pasko, 2004; Katz, 1979:24).

Some men are also labeled deviant or sanctioned for not conforming to certain gender norms. For example, in North America and elsewhere (e.g., Australia), men are strongly encouraged to live up to the principles of **hegemonic masculinity** (Connell, 1995). In the United States, this type of masculinity is best exemplified by movie actors such as Arnold Schwarzenegger (now Governor of California), Vin Diesel, or Clint Eastwood. Most men are brought up to aspire to be like them and other "tough guys." They are, among other things, expected to: avoid all things feminine, restrict their emotions severely, show toughness and aggression, exhibit self-reliance, strive for achievement and status, exhibit nonrelational attitudes toward sexuality, and actively engage in homophobia (Levant, 1994; Schwartz & DeKeseredy, 1997). If men and boys don't live up to these ideals, they risk being labeled a "fag" or "sissy," and the fear of being labeled as such can promote men to engage in violent behavior.

For example, to avoid being labeled a "fag," some college men who belong to hypermasculine subcultures or other heterosexual, all-male peer groups use force or date rape drugs to "work a yes" out of women who do not want to have sex with them (Sanday, 1990). Such behavior proves to themselves and others that they have "genital potency"—that they are heavily involved in heterosexuality (Godenzi, Schwartz & DeKeseredy, 2001; Messerschmidt, 2000). Forcing women into sexual acts, then, for some men becomes an act of compliance with norms by men who are "committed to a conventional line of action, and . . . therefore committed to conformity" (Hirschi, 1969:21).

Of course, there are men who reject hegemonic masculinity, such as members of the gay community, which makes them even more vulnerable to stigmatization and to the violent consequences of refusing to "be a man" (Perry, 2003b). Let us turn, for example, to one of the terrifying experiences of hate crime victim William Hassel (1992). He was attacked at knifepoint by two male teenagers, and below is a vivid description of how they punished him for taking on what they defined as a deviant identity:

> They made me address them as "Sir." They made me beg them to be made into a real woman. They threatened to castrate me. They threatened to emasculate me. They called me "Queer," Faggot." One of them urinated on me. They threatened me with sodomy.

As Collins (2000), Perry (2003a), and other scholars remind us, sometimes the intersection of race, class, and gender shape being labeled criminal or deviant. Consider gay men of color. They experience multiple forms of discrimination in society at large and are, according to one gay black man living in the far west side of Columbus, Ohio, an "invisible and a double minority even within the gay community" (cited in Williams, 2004:B3). Another gay man of color living in the same city told *Columbus Dispatch* reporter Sherri Williams (2004:B3) that "he's been ignored by bartenders and waiters at gay-owned bars and restaurants similar to the way blacks were during the Jim Crow segregation era."

What Collins (2000:69) refers to as "intersecting oppressions of race, class, gender, and sexuality" also affect women of color. For example, Dumas (1980) found that African-American female executives are often treated as "mammies" by their white colleagues and are penalized if they don't seem to be kind, warm, and nurturing. Moreover, many women of color never seem to be able to achieve "goodness" and are frequently "assaulted with a variety of negative images" (Gilkes, 1983:294; Perry, 2003b), such as the following listed by Harris (1982:4):

> Called Matriarch, Emasculator and Hot Momma. Sometimes Sister, Pretty Baby, Auntie, Mammy and Girl. Called Unwed Mother, Welfare Recipient and Inner City Consumer. The Black American Woman has had to admit that while nobody know the troubles she saw, everybody, his brother and his dog felt qualified to explain her, even to herself.

Critique of the Societal Reaction/Labeling Approach

Societal reaction/labeling approaches sensitize us to the subjective nature of defining deviance and crime. Still, they have been roundly criticized by sociologists and criminologists from the political right to the political left. For example, conservative critics typically question the empirical validity of this approach and contend that the notion of secondary deviation has not been scientifically verified (Curran & Renzetti, 2001). For example, many people become career deviants or criminals without ever having been subject to negative societal reactions. Consider terrorists, such as those who committed unforgettable atrocities in New York City and other parts of the United States (e.g., the Pentagon) on September 11, 2001. Labeling had nothing to do with their actions. Rather, the choice to join a terrorist network and to kill thousands of people was directly shaped by their commitment to political, religious, or social values or ideals (Bell, 1979; Ellis, 1987; Rapaport, 1984). More than this, terrorists, as individuals, are often secret deviants. No label is applied to them because generally they remain unknown. In short, a definition that ignores terrorists and focuses on societal reactions to them cannot generate an adequate perspective on, or theory, of career terrorism.

This criticism is part of another, more general one. As subjective offerings, societal reaction/labeling approaches divert attention away from a socially and sociologically significant set of questions. These have to do with explaining why, in any given society, some groups are more likely to engage in terrorist activities than others, why rates of terrorism vary across societies and in the same society in different historical periods, and why countries themselves vary in their commitment to terrorism. The explanation entailed by a subjective definition leads one to conclude that only one factor—different government reactions—explains all these variations (Ellis, 1987).

Another common criticism is that the proponents of the societal reaction/labeling approach is that it portrays individuals as simply passive beings during the stigmatization process (Curran & Renzetti, 2001). Many people, in fact, reject labels and do not go on to become career deviants. For example, we know several prominent criminologists who at one time in their lives were in serious conflict with the law and are now teaching at major institutions of higher learning. Further, during his last year of high school, Walter DeKeseredy's guidance counselor told him, "You are not a good student and are destined for failure at university. Perhaps you should consider becoming a laborer or going to technical school." Obviously, DeKeseredy resisted the counselor's label and become a productive academic. Hence, many people often overcome stigma (Curran & Renzetti, 2001; Prus, 1975; Rogers & Buffalo, 1974).

Some people, too, value deviant labels and even seek them (Akers, 1968, Currie, 1993). For example, unemployed women living in impoverished inner-city communities are denied legitimate means of attaining status (DeKeseredy & Schwartz, 1996). With its street reputation as the most dangerous drug, heroin bestows on its users a reputation as the most serious outlaws. A number of bored and alienated women are finding this reputation attractive (Rosenbaum, 1981). Similarly, some girls join gangs because they believe that the deviant labels associated with gang membership are symbols of accomplishment and status (Curran & Renzetti, 2001). As one of Miller's (2001) respondents told her, "I felt like, yeah now I'm going to be cool, I'm gonna be Miss Thang in the gang and walk around Miss Bad Butt. Nobody can mess with me because I am in a gang."

Some of the basic arguments of the societal reaction/labeling approach were adopted by left-wing or **critical criminologists.** Critical criminologists view the major sources of crime as the class, ethnic, and patriarchal relations that control our society. Further, they reject as solutions to crime and deviance short-term measures such as tougher laws, increased incarceration, counseling therapy, and the like. Rather, these scholars regard major structural and cultural changes within society as essential steps to reducing criminality.[8]

Although heavily influenced by scholars such as Becker (1973), critical criminologists argue that societal reaction/labeling perspectives do not explicitly address the broader structural and cultural forces that influence police officers, judges, and other agents of social control (e.g., teachers, psychiatrists, etc.) to label people criminal or deviant. Taylor, Walton, and Young (1973:168-169), for example, argue that subjectivist approaches do not "lay bare the structured inequalities in power and process which underpin processes whereby laws are created and enforced." Related to this argument is another criticism from critical criminologists. Because labeling/societal reaction theorists often are uninterested in broader political and economic factors, they focus too much on societal reactions to "exotic" people or behaviors, such as nudists, prostitution, and illicit drug use (Liazos, 1972). Hence, the "the everyday oppression at affects a large number of persons" receives selective inattention (Davis & Stasz, 1990:46). Some examples of such oppression are poverty and unemployment, which are topics of central concern to critical criminologists.

The Critical Approach

Critical criminologists emphasize the political nature of crime and deviance (Muncie, 2001), and like societal reaction/labeling theorists, are sharply opposed to legalistic definitions of crime (DeKeseredy & Schwartz, 1996). They argue that the law is a tool used by powerful social groups to promote and protect their interests, and that definitions of crime favor those in privileged economic and political positions. As Matthews (2003a:35) reminds us in his recent essay on "crony capitalism,"[9] "political connections between elites can serve to facilitate forms of harmful deviance," and these linkages help powerful people who threaten our physical, economic, psychological, and environmental well-being avoid punishment and other forms of stigmatization. Consider the corporate crimes described in Chapter 5. Why is it that most people who commit them rarely, if ever, receive prison sentences (Reiman, 2004)? Similarly, why is DuPont still able to commit the harms described earlier in this chapter, while poor people caught committing drug offenses typically end up in prison and are sentenced to an average of seven years behind bars in the United States (Chambliss, 2001)?[10]

These are important questions that critical criminologists try to answer, and they want to broaden definitions of crime and deviance to include serious damage done to the environment by corporations, as well as other harms done by economic and political elites that are not typically considered illegitimate (e.g., false advertising). Critical criminologists also call for criminalizing: violations of human rights; poverty; unemployment caused by moving corporations to developing countries; inadequate social services (e.g., substandard housing, day care, education, and medical care), and state terrorism (Lynch, Michalowski & Groves, 2000; Schwendinger & Schwendinger, 2001). Of course, as stated before, some powerful people who commit these or other "crimes of the powerful" are investigated or indicted on criminal charges (Pearce, 1976). Take, for example, Martha Stewart and some high-ranking executives at corporations like WorldCom, Tyco, Adelphia, Qwest, and Rite Aid (Friedrichs, 2003). However, as critical criminologists often point out, corporate offenders, politicians who violate criminal or regulatory laws, and other "trusted criminals" are "seldom subject to the kinds of punishments we accept as routine for street offenders" (Friedrichs, 2004a; Lynch, Michalowski & Groves, 2000:63).

Another point to consider is that in this day and age of globalization, U.S. corporations based in developing nations promote lax regulatory laws in these countries, which is why many people living there are forced to work in sweat shops and are frequently injured or killed in the workplace due to unsafe working conditions. Few politicians, however, ever dare to call these and other negative consequences of privatization and deregulations "crimes" (Lynch, Michalowski & Groves, 2000). Furthermore, there appears to be next to no political will to curtail harmful corporate and political conduct in developing nations, the United States, and elsewhere through "serious and meaningful regulation" (Matthews, 2003a; Matthews & Kauzlarich, 2000).

Critique of the Critical Approach

Critical criminologists are fundamentally concerned with analyzing how power shapes definitions of crime and deviance, and they have played a key role in sensitizing us to how the law is used to create many crimes of the powerless and few crimes of the socially and economically privileged (Lynch, Michalowski & Groves, 2000). Nevertheless, there are those on the left and right who find very broad definitions to be problematic. Bohm (1982), for example, is a critical criminologist, but suggests that sweeping accounts may be too broad or vague. Turk (1975:41) refers to this broad scope as encompassing "everything but the kitchen sink." Then there are more conservative critics who claim that broad critical definitions are simply political agendas rather than valid scientific contributions.

Tappan is one such critic and he argued that:

> the rebel may enjoy a veritable orgy of delight in damning as criminal anyone he pleases; one imagines that some expert would thus consign to the criminal classes any successful capitalistic businessman. . . . The result may be fine indoctrination or catharsis achieved through blustering broadsides against the existing system. It is not criminology. It is not social science (1947:44-45).

Tappan and others who share his perspective want a definition of crime to include only people convicted of an offense, something sharply opposed by both societal reaction/labeling and critical scholars (DeKeseredy & Schwartz, 1996).

Many critical criminologists respond to this criticism by stating that regardless of whether they are officially defined as crimes, economically, socially, environmentally, and physically injurious acts committed by elites are just as, if not more, important as those committed by powerless people (Lynch, Michalowski & Groves, 2000). Further, the law's bias cannot be adequately examined "unless we compare those things that are illegal with similar forms of social injury that are not" (Michalowski, 1985:317).

Summary

The sociology of deviance and crime is characterized by a variety of definitions, three of which were described in this chapter. All of them have limitations and, regardless of which one you prefer, choosing the one that best suits you is a "primal sociological act or decision" (Ellis, 1987:210). For example, how one defines deviance or crime helps determine his or her method of gathering data, as well as the type of theory that is used in the collection, analysis, or interpretation of research findings. So, if you are influenced by normative definitions, you will divide people into rule-breakers and conformists and try to determine how they differ. On the other hand, if you are driven by societal reaction/labeling accounts, you will be more concerned with the processes by which people come to be designated as criminal or deviant. Finally, if you are a critical criminologist, you are probably more interested in how broader political, economic, and social forces influence what is and what is not considered criminal or deviant. Further, you are likely to view many behaviors as criminal or deviant not considered as such by criminal law (DeKeseredy & Schwartz, 1996).

Notes

[1]   There are, of course, many other definitions of deviance, including the cross-cultural approach (Sellin, 1938) and the statistical definition (Wilkins, 1964). See Henry and Lanier (2001) for discussions of key offerings not reviewed here.

[2]   See President Bush's 215th State of the Union Address (January 22, 2004).

[3]   As Pitts (2003:126) points out, some conservative journalists, politicians, and other mainstream commentators see the recent increase in tattooing, scarring, and piercing as "a new social problem of delinquency, sickness and perversion."

[4]   See the special issue of *Violence Against Women* (Volume 10, Number 2, 2004) for a collection of recent articles on violence in the sex trade industry.

[5]   DeKeseredy taught at Ohio University from January 2001 to June 2004 and never had more than six African-American students in any of his sociology or criminology classes.

[6]   Titled *Contacts between Police and the Public: Findings from the 1999 National Survey*, the data gathered from the national sample were collected as part of the annual National Crime Victimization Survey (Langan, Greenfield, Smith, Durose & Levin, 2001). The results briefly summarized here are based on citizen self-reports of their experiences with the police rather than police reports.

[7]   For example, in 2000, the Mayor of Columbus, Ohio, ordered police to record traffic stops and undergo training to avoid racial profiling. Moreover, the mayor "beefed up" the Internal Affairs Bureau and added video cameras in police cars. Columbus police are also required to list the race of each driver based on their perceptions, record the sex of each driver and where stops occurred, and record the reason for the stop and whether the driver was arrested, searched, or given a warning. However, the researchers who conducted the Columbus study briefly described here found that there is no way to determine whether police officers correctly filled out forms (Ferenchik, 2003).

[8]   This is a modified version of Young's (1988) definition of radical criminology.

[9]   Here, crony capitalism refers to "tightly interwoven, political and corporate interests and connections, where family ties, political relationships, and money serve to facilitate the accumulation of wealth for selected insiders. It is a system where one class of citizens takes risks, and another makes profits" (Matthews, 2003a:36).

[10]   Sixty percent of federal and 30 percent of all state inmates are sentenced for drug violations. Moreover, more than 36 percent of all prisoners sentenced for drug offenses are not serious criminals, have no current or prior offenses, have never served time before, and are "low level drug offenders" (Chambliss, 2001).

Discussion Questions

1. What are the differences between social and legal norms?

2. What are the key limitations of normative definitions of crime and deviance?

3. How do class, race, and gender influence how people come to be labeled deviant or criminal?

4. What is the difference between primary and secondary deviance?

5. Why do critical criminologists call for broad definitions of crime?

6. What are the major criticisms of the critical approach to defining crime?

Problem-Solving Scenarios

1. Get together with several other students and provide concrete examples of how people are labeled criminal or deviant based on their sex, class, or race/ethnicity.

2. Generate a group discussion on the ways in which the media contribute to popular definitions of crime and deviance.

3. In a group, discuss effective ways of influencing policymakers to adopt a critical criminological definition of crime.

4. Identify specific examples of situations in which you were defined as deviant because of your behavior, appearance, or group membership.

5. How would you train police officers to stop stereotyping certain groups as most likely to be involved in criminal or deviant activities?

Suggested Readings

Becker, H. (1973). *Outsiders: Studies in the Sociological Study of Deviance.* New York: Free Press.

> A classic book on the how the societal reaction/labeling approach contributes to a rich sociological understanding of deviance and crime.

Henry, S. & M. Lanier (eds.). (2001). *What is crime? Controversies Over the Nature of Crime and What to Do About It*. Lanham, MD: Roman & Littlefield.

> This book provides an excellent overview of various sociological definitions of crime and deviance.

Lynch, M.J., R. Michalowski & W.B. Groves (2000). *The New Primer in Radical Criminology: Critical Perspectives on Crime, Power and Identity*, 3rd edition. Monsey, NJ: Criminal Justice Press.

> The authors provide an in-depth account of the critical conception of crime.

Mann, C.R. (1993). *Unequal Justice: A Question of Color*. Bloomington: Indiana University Press.

> This widely read and cited book includes a comprehensive analysis of how race influences the ways in which people are treated by the U.S. criminal justice system.

Schur, E.M. (1984). *Labeling Women Deviant: Gender, Stigma and Social Control*. Philadelphia: Temple University Press.

> This book describes the various ways in which women are defined as deviant.

Online Resources

1. **Deviance and Criminology**
   http://ryoung001.homestead.com/Deviance.html
   Created by Robert G. Young, this web site has several links to definitions of deviance.

2. **Paul's Crime and Justice Page on Corporate Deviance**
   http://www.paulsjusticepage.com/elite-deviance.htm
   Developed and maintained by Eastern Michigan University criminologist Paul Leighton, various links on crimes of the powerful are included in this widely used web site.

3. **Critical Criminology Division of the American Society of Criminology**
   http://www.critcrim.org
   This web site includes a variety of critical criminology links, including those dealing with definitional issues covered in this chapter.

4. **Cecil Greek's CJ Links**
   http://www.criminology.fsu.edu/cj.html
   This web site is ranked by many criminologists as one of the best electronic resources on issues of key concern to those interested in the sociological study of deviance and crime.

Theory, whether we realize it or not, is a fundamental part of our everyday lives. We all draw on theory to make our lives safer, simpler, and less uncertain, although we rarely stop to think that this is what we are doing (Curran & Renzetti, 2001:1).

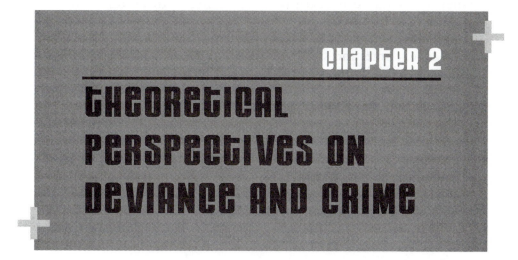

CHAPTER 2

THEORETICAL PERSPECTIVES ON DEVIANCE AND CRIME

Thus far, we have concentrated on sociological answers to one important question: What is deviance and crime? The next question is one that, over the years, has concerned researchers like us more than any other: Why do people commit deviant or criminal acts? Similarly, the general public is always eager to know why people such as Martha Stewart break the law or violate social norms. Unfortunately, despite access to generations of exhaustive research and deep thought, few social scientists would be so bold as to state that they can easily answer this question. Further, if anyone does claim to have the definitive answer, most other sociologists and criminologists would quickly find fault with it (DeKeseredy & Schwartz, 1996). Note, too, that people who attend the annual meetings of the American Society of Criminology intending to discover from the most prominent scholars in the field the current thinking on the major causes of crime usually encounter:

> something akin to the Tower of Babel. They will not be offered one answer but a series of competing and contradictory visions of the nature of man, deviation, and the social order. Very typically, they will be informed that their questions cannot even be discussed because they are not correctly phrased: they must first reconstruct their problem so that it can be placed with others in one of the master theories of deviance (Downes & Rock, 2003:1).

Our experience dictates that students, too, find the "smorgasbord of theories" presented in textbooks as diverse, confusing, and partisan (DeKeseredy & Schwartz, 1996), and most of them are overwhelmed by the constantly growing number of theorists' names and perspectives they are required to learn (Curran & Renzetti, 2001). In this book, rather than briefly describe every theory we know, we cover a broad range of the most widely read and cited sociological perspectives on deviance, crime, and social control. The theories reviewed here and in subsequent chapters are grouped under five general headings: strain, social control, interactionist, ecological, and critical. Because elements or parts of one perspective are combined with elements of others, these groupings only roughly separate the five perspectives from each other. Still, they are sufficiently different from one another to warrant their groupings under the headings indicated above. However, before describing and evaluating these contributions, it is first necessary to define the term **theory** and explain the value of developing the **sociological imagination** (Mills, 1959).

What is a Theory?

Theories of deviance and crime are like opinions: most people have them (Lilly, Cullen & Ball, 2002). For example, at the time of writing this chapter, many people from different walks of life offered their own accounts of why Martha Stewart's involvement in insider trading. Walter DeKeseredy's mortgage broker told him that "arrogance drove her to it," while others, including journalists and legal experts, attributed her behavior primarily to greed, as stated by a newspaper editor in Box 2.1. Of course, other reasons for her illicit business practices were and continue to be offered. Nevertheless, the most important point to consider here is that most of these "theories" are grounded in personal experiences or what people see, hear, or read in the media (Cote, 2002). On the other hand, for people who make a living out of studying deviance and crime, theory construction is a much more complex process and is heavily grounded in scientific research. More specifically, following Curran and Renzetti's thinking (2001:2), a theory is defined here as "a set of interconnected statements or propositions that explain how two or more events or factors are related to one another."

Box 2.1
Costly Lies: Martha Stewart was Brought Down by Greed and Deception

Whether motivated by simple greed or a misguided belief that the rules somehow didn't apply to a person of her wealth and power, domestic diva Martha Stewart took advantage of insider information to sell 3,928 shares of ImClone stock on Dec. 21, 2001, before its market price tanked. Then she lied to cover up the misdeed.

In the end, the combination of her lies and the truth reluctantly told by two women close to her brought Stewart to the threshold of federal prison.

Ann Armstrong, Stewart's assistant, broke down on the witness stand as she told the court that Stewart had altered the log of a phone message from her broker warning her that ImClone executive Sam Waksal was dumping his stock. Stewart had second thoughts and had Armstrong restore the original text, but the incident created an almost insurmountable situation for defense attorneys. Their client knew what she had done was wrong and her inclination to alter the paper trail, even though reconsidered, showed guilty knowledge.

Then there was the celebrated Martha quote, "Isn't it nice to have brokers who tell you these things?"

Mariana Pasternak, Stewart's close friend and traveling companion, let the cat out of the bag during her trial testimony, alluding to a telephone contact from Merrill Lynch broker Peter Bacanovic's office. Although she tried to rebag the cat, claiming that the thought might have been hers based on other things she heard Stewart say, nobody was buying.

Stewart's lawyers tried to discredit 28-year-old assistant Douglas Faneuil during two days of intense cross-examination. But his testimony that Bacanovic had ordered him to tell Martha about ImClone held up.

According to some reports, Stewart was offered a no-jail deal in exchange for pleading guilty to one of the four charges of which she ultimately was found guilty, but she turned down the deal.

Barring a successful appeal, which most court watchers consider a long shot, Stewart will probably do some jail time but nothing close to the 20-year maximum allowable. She brings a clean record to the pre-sentence investigation and the label "convicted felon" to any future business dealings.

To what extent Stewart's conviction will affect her company and affiliations with others is an open question. Stewart, at 62, is tough, smart and likely to stage a comeback, even after incarceration. And, of course, she'll still be wealthy.

Stewart joins the ranks of Richard Nixon and other famous figures brought down not by the crime but the cover up.

Another little-mentioned but important lesson from Stewart's conviction: Don't lie to federal agents. Unlike state authorities, who must advise suspects of their rights, FBI agents and investigators from the Securities and Exchange Commission operate under different rules. Lying to them, even during what might appear to be a casual conversation, is a federal crime.

Ask Martha Stewart.

Source: Sheller, G. (2004, March 11). "Costly Lies: Martha Stewart Was Brought Down by Greed and Deception." *Columbus Dispatch*, A10. Reprinted with permission from *The Columbus Dispatch*.

In addition to serving as conceptual tools that help us make sense of data, theories are practical. For example, to cure AIDS, researchers must first identify the cause of this deadly disease. In fact, almost every policy or strategy developed to prevent or control crime is derived from some theory or theories (Akers, 1997; DeKeseredy, 2000a). Still, some theories are better than others. Further, every theory described in this book and other criminology and deviance texts has limitations. There is no "pat explanation" of deviance or crime and what we have, then, are "bad, good, and better theories" (Curran & Renzetti, 2001:5).

The Sociological Imagination

Prior to the twentieth century, most theories of deviance and crime located the causes of these problems inside the individual. Biological, psychological, or supernatural forces—not social factors—were seen as driving people to violate social and legal norms (Lilly, Cullen & Ball, 2002). Today, most criminologists see crime and deviance as social products, but some social scientists and many politicians are still heavily influenced by individualistic theories developed prior to the twentieth century. For example, guided by assertions made by the eighteenth-century "fathers" (e.g., Jeremy Bentham) of the **classical school of criminology** (see Box 2.2),[1] Gottfredson and Hirschi's (1990) general theory of crime contends that people who have low self-control are most likely to engage in deviant or criminal activities. Other examples of contemporary theories informed by classical thinkers will be provided in subsequent sections of this book. One major reason why most of the arguments presented in Box 2.2 are currently held in high regard by neo-conservative politicians, journalists, and corporate executives is that they serve their political and economic interests. For example, the notion that criminals are egoistic, rational, and calculating individuals:

> makes it easier to blame the offender for all aspects of crime, rather than share some of that blame with society for creating conditions that force some people into crime. If it is an individual's decision to commit crime, then he or she is morally responsible and deserves to be punished. The great advantage of this reasoning is that we do not have to do anything other than punish while the individual is in our control. Thus, rehabilitation and skill training are no longer a part of what a prison must do. In addition, we do not have to engage in expensive social programs to improve conditions that create crime, nor do we have to engage in more expensive social reform. An assumption that individuals make fully rational decisions to engage in criminal behavior can save a lot of money (Williams & McShane, 1994:23).

Box 2.2
The Major Points of the Classical School of Criminology

1. Supernatural forces do not drive people to commit crime.

2. Human beings are innately egoistic and have free will. Moreover, people are seen as making rational, calculated choices to maximize pleasure and minimize pain.

3. All people have equal rights and should be treated accordingly by the law.

4. Crime is a moral offense against society.

5. Punishment should be proportional to the crime.

6. Punishment should be swift and certain and used only to deter people from harming others.

7. Capital punishment should be avoided because it is an evil that is worse than the evil of the crime itself.

If only a small number of people committed crimes, it would be easy to accept the argument that crime is mainly a property of the individual. The truth is, though, that most offenders are not motivated by Satan, nor are they mentally or physically defective. Consider wife beating. It is estimated that less than 10 percent of all incidents of such violence are caused by mental disorders, and psychological perspectives cannot explain the other 90 percent (DeKeseredy, 2005; Gelles & Straus, 1988). Note, too, that data presented throughout this text and elsewhere show that the United States is the most violent country in the advanced industrial world; an alarmingly high number of other crimes (e.g., theft) are committed everyday (Messner & Rosenfeld, 2001). Further, as pointed out in Chapter 5, corporate crimes like those committed by Martha Stewart are not rare. Rather, they are *endemic*, that is, a constant and permanent feature of North American life.

Therefore, sociologists ask, given the widespread (endemic) nature of deviance and crime, how can we maintain that these problems are acts committed by "sick" or pathological individuals? Even if this were the case, one would have to spend a great deal of time examining the social structure of a country that produces more sick or pathological individuals than the rest of the world. Because the United States has astoundingly high rates of crime, individualistic perspectives have little to offer in explaining its rate of crime.

Instead, we need to develop what C. Wright Mills (1959) refers to as the **sociological imagination**, which calls for an understanding of the ways in which **personal troubles** are related to **public issues**. Personal troubles are just what you might think. If you are a poor inner-city youth who cannot afford new clothes or to go out on a date with a woman, you have a problem and have to deal with it. You may need a loan from friends or other types of social support. Many people, however, such as a sizeable portion of adolescent drug dealers, are suffering from the same type of personal problem at the same time. If 100 boys have similar experiences in one year in the same city or town, each one of them has a personal problem (or personal troubles). At the same time, though, Mills would argue that there is something about broader structural or cultural forces (for instance, high rates of unemployment caused by transnational corporations moving operations to developing countries to pay lower salaries) that influence so many boys who have experienced inner-city poverty to deal drugs (Anderson, 1999; DeKeseredy, Alvi, Schwartz & Tomaszewski, 2003). To look beyond the personal troubles of one or two young drug dealers and see the broader problem of poverty and its causes is to posses the sociological imagination.

Applied to the study of crime, the sociological imagination shows that North American society is structured to promote criminal activities. Chesney-Lind and Pasko (2004:176) provide an excellent example of how the sociological imagination can be applied to the study of female crime in the United States. They state that:

> If we are to respond to the challenge of girls' and women's crime, we must seek solutions that are based on the real causes of women's offenses, not on myths fostered by misinformation. We must understand how gender and race shape and eliminate choices for girls, how they injure (intentionally or not), and how they ultimately create very different features for youths who are born female in a country that promises equality yet all too frequently falls short of that dream. We must also confront the fact that the United States has the highest rates of child poverty in the industrialized world (Donziger, 1996:215), and we must understand the ways in which this economic marginalization has directly affected girls and their mothers. Only with these understandings finally in mind can we imagine real solutions to the terrible problems of violence and crime in women's lives.

Now that we have provided you with a rationale for analyzing deviance and crime sociologically, we can move on to reviewing five sociological schools of thought that have had a major impact on contemporary studies of deviance and crime.

Strain Perspectives

Strain theories possess the sociological imagination. Rather than viewing deviance and crime as functions of some deficiency in the individual, they assert that they are products of America's social structure.

In other words, there is something in the social forces generated by society that propels or drives people into violating social or legal norms. The impulse to do so comes from outside rather than inside people. Strain is not something that everyone in society equally shares. Some people suffer more strain than others. This is why, these theorists argue, some parts of society have more crime than others: they have more strain. Before reviewing contemporary strain theories, it is necessary to examine Emile Durkheim's writings on crime, deviance, and social control because they heavily influenced the development of modern strain perspectives.

Strain Theories: The Influence of Emile Durkheim

Four ideas are central to Durkheim's sociology. First, human beings are essentially egoistic. Their wants always exceed the means available to satisfy them. Because they are exclusively interested in satisfying their own individual wants and will do anything to satisfy wants that are always increasing, it is not possible to have a stable society composed solely of rampant egoists. They will routinely rob, deceive, and kill each other to satisfy escalating psychological and material wants. Imagine what society would be like if it were composed solely not of patient, trouble-free Maytag repairmen, but only of infants whose every psychological and material want must be instantly and continuously satisfied without regard to the wants or needs of others.

Second, the basis of social order is shared values and norms. That is to say, egoism is effectively regulated only among interacting individuals who believe that life ought to be preserved, who believe in honesty, trust, and so on. **Moral regulation**, then, is the basis of a relatively peaceful, orderly society. In such a society, these rules are obeyed because they are right and not because of the material benefits such obedience may confer.

Third, in more or less obvious ways, most, if not all, regularly recurring activities, as varied as religious worship, sports, crime, and work continue to exist in society because they contribute to the stability of society. They are, in other words, **functional** or good for society as a whole, which is why they continue to exist.

Fourth, society can be viewed as an organism made up of interdependent parts in equilibrium. Change one part and you change other parts. The direction of change is usually toward restoring stability or dealing with disturbances caused by social change. As crime and social control are both regularly recurring, interdependent activities, each must be studied in relation to the other if we wish to obtain an adequate sociological understanding of either. The centrality of the above ideas for Durkheim's functional theory of crime and social control is clearly evident in his treatment of crime in *Rules of Sociological Method* (1950/1895) and of **anomie** in *Division of Labour in Society* (1952/1893) and *Suicide* (1951/1897).

Behavior that is defined as criminal is a regularly recurring feature of all known societies that have criminal laws. This indicates that crime is a normal feature of life. Crime is normal and keeps recurring in these societies because it is functional for them. That is to say, it makes a positive contribution to social life. More specifically, a certain amount of crime—not too little and not too much—is functional for society and keeps it healthy. Thus, criminals draw members of society together by providing a target for their self-righteous moral indignation. Crimes like those committed by Martha Stewart remind the "good guys" that they are good and morally praiseworthy and therefore different from the "bad guys." In the process, norms and values are reinforced, and their shared character is emphasized.

Anomie or **normlessness** is central to Durkheim's work on crime. In his theory, he uses the concept of anomie in two different ways. In *Rules*, anomie is associated with social change and refers to the economy. An anomic or pathological economy increases egoistic behavior because it "frees individuals from the moderating action of (moral) regulation" and places the individual "in a state of war with every other." In *Suicide*, anomie refers to an agitated state of mind induced by the fact that the norms or rules that formerly regulated behavior are no longer appropriate to changed circumstances.

Anomie in the first usage is a characteristic feature of industrialized societies. An industrialized economy provides a context in which egoistic behavior flourishes. Individuals use any means, not just proper or morally appropriate means, in attempting to satisfy their wants. At the same time, and partly as a consequence of industrialization, people become more individualized. The society-wide, shared moral system that, in pre-industrial societies used to be able to effectively regulate egoistic behavior, is no longer capable of doing so. Industrialization, in other words, has weakened the hold of the "collective consciousness," the hold of widely shared values and norms. In this formulation of anomie, the economy, social control, and deviance are interrelated.

Anomie in the second or social psychological sense also results from normlessness. This means that the norms and values held by the individual are no longer appropriate to changed circumstances. Thus, economic crises *and* periods of prosperity are characterized by high rates of suicide. In the rapidly changed circumstances created by industrialization, normally operative regulatory influences become ineffective. Individuals experience societal weakness in this respect as deregulation. Made weary, despondent, and angry at themselves by experiencing a lack of any relationship between their changed economic circumstances and the regulatory power of existing values and norms, they commit suicide. Anomie, in both senses then, is associated with psychological stress or strain.

Durkheim's **functionalist** approach is subject to a number of criticisms. For example, some criminologists fault Durkheim for viewing people's aspirations as egoistic, contending instead that such behavior is learned (DeKeseredy & Schwartz, 1996). Further, some critical criminologists find his approach too biological and inherently conservative (Taylor, Walton & Young, 1973). Still, many criminologists view Durkheim as an important resource for developing their own work. Even some critical criminologists argue that much of Durkheim's work can be of great value "to help specify a realistic set of socialist goals" (Pearce, 1989:10). Regardless of how one views Durkheim's contributions, they heavily influenced contemporary strain perspectives such as Robert K. Merton's (1938) anomie theory.

Merton's Anomie Theory

Unquestionably, Merton's anomie theory has strongly influenced contemporary sociological analyses of deviance and crime. In fact, his (1938) paper, "Social Structure and Anomie," is still one of the most widely read and cited sociological articles. Merton strongly opposed individualistic explanations of crime, such as those heavily driven by the writings of conservative seventeenth-century English philosopher Thomas Hobbes and psychoanalyst Sigmund Freud. These theories view crime as a function of human nature and prevailed in the 1930s. Merton made explicit his strong opposition to the Hobbesian-Freudian position:

> There persists a notable tendency in sociological theory to attribute the malfunctioning of social structure primarily to those of man's imperious biological drives which are not adequately restrained by social control. In this view, the social order is solely a device for "impulse management" and the social processing" of tensions. These impulses, which break through social control, be it noted, are held to be biologically derived. Nonconformity is assumed to be rooted in original nature. Conformity is by implication the result of a utilitarian calculus or unreasoned conditioning. This point of view, whatever its other deficiencies, clearly begs one question. It provides no basis for determining the non-biological conditions which induce deviations from prescribed patterns of conduct (1938:672).

According to Merton, to understand why people engage in deviant or criminal activities, we must critically examine the wider structure of North American society. And, because he did not view crime as a function of human nature, Merton reconceptualized Durkheim's original discussion of anomie accordingly. For example, Durkheim suggested that anomie is the result of an epidemic (a sudden acute breakdown), while Merton saw anomie as endemic (a regular feature of society). He defined anomie as a feeling of strain experienced by individuals who are socialized by the media, their family, and schools to believe that the "American Dream" is theirs to realize, but for whom ethnic origin or lower-class position means a denial of equal access to the legitimate educational and occupational opportunities necessary for the achievement of a lifestyle that will enable them to buy expensive commodities such as a BMW, a home theater system, or a luxurious suburban home.

In Merton's account, then, the disjunction between the norms and values that make up the American Dream and social structure, the unequal distribution of educational and employment opportunities, causes deviance by inducing strain in individuals. Consider the Puerto Rican drug dealers who participated in Bourgois's (1995) East Harlem study. They are not "exotic others." Rather, they were "made in America," and:

> [l]ike most other people in the United States, drug dealers and street criminals are scrambling to obtain their piece of the pie as fast as possible. In fact, in their pursuit of success they are even following the minute details of the classical yankee model for upward mobility. They are aggressively pursuing careers as private entrepreneurs; they take risks, work hard, and pray for good luck. They are the ultimate rugged individualists braving an unpredictable frontier where fortune, fame, and destruction are all just around the corner, and where the enemy is ruthlessly hunted down and shot (1995:326).

In technologically well-developed capitalist countries like the United States, the source of strain identified by Merton is not likely to diminish for two reasons. First, advertising and other agents of socialization (e.g., parents and teachers) continuously nourish the "American Dream." Second, inequality provides the motivational energy for capitalistic enterprise. This means that the disjunction referred to by Merton is likely to be an enduring attribute of capitalistic societies, if not a defining characteristic of them (DeKeseredy, Alvi, Schwartz & Tomaszewski, 2003; Young, 1999). Figure 2.1 describes Merton's anomie perspective.

Cohen's Theory of Delinquent Boys

For Albert Cohen (1955), Merton's anomie theory was an important one because it accounted for the social distribution of deviance and crime. More specifically, it explained why lower-class boys were more likely to become delinquent. They experienced more strain than did middle-class boys. At the same time, he felt that the theory could be improved by making a number of changes and additions. First, Merton seemed to regard deviance and crime as rational, instrumental kinds of activities. This may not be true for the expressive, destructive behavior of delinquents. Consider what Walter DeKeseredy and his friend witnessed one afternoon in a bar in Athens, Ohio, in May 2002. Two "well lubricated" Ohio University freshmen decided to "have some fun" and, in front of at least 20 witnesses, went outside and destroyed two young trees located near the bar entrance. Needless to say, they didn't do this for money.

Figure 2.1
Merton's Anomie Theory

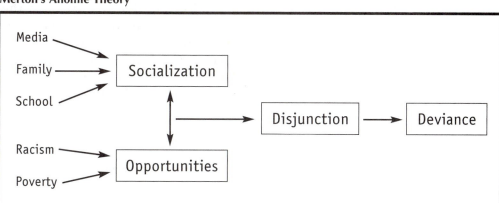

Second, much delinquency is group activity (Warr, 2002), but Merton focused on the individual as deviant or criminal. Third, it is not enough to say simply that strain causes norm-violating behavior. The way in which lower-class boys create a collective or group solution to the problem of societally induced strain must also be specified. Finally, the psychological mechanism that enables boys to accept values opposed to those "American Dream" values they once believed in and shared with the rest of society must be identified.

In Cohen's (1955) theory, strain results from status frustration. All adolescents are assumed to be motivated by the quest for status, perhaps mainly from their peers. They also believe that the proper way to achieve status is by using legitimate means, and the school is the major site for status acquisition. Still, not all students are equally successful in achieving high social and/or academic status in school. For example, because of their class (family) background, working- and lower-class students are, for motivational and technical reasons, not in as good a position as middle-class males to satisfy their striving for status.

Socially and academically then, middle-class students do better than less privileged ones in meeting the expectations of their middle-class teachers who use "middle-class measuring rods" to assess their students' performance. This results in greater status frustration and, hence, psychological strain for working- and lower-class male students. They react by inverting middle-class values. So, if teachers value property, punctuality, manners, and courtesy, the students value lateness, dishonesty, and vandalism.

Students whose strivings for status are frustrated tend to flock together and share their experiences and inverted values. Behavior that is consistent with these inverted values, that is, delinquent behavior, becomes a way of achieving status in their group—their delinquent group. In this way, the delinquent subculture helps solve the problem of status frustration. Figure 2.2 describes Cohen's theory.

Cohen's theory makes several important contributions to a sociological understanding of deviance and crime. First, it extends the work of Merton by identifying the *mechanism* (**reaction formation**) that translates strain into delinquency. Second, his theory explains the *emergence* of the delinquent subculture. Third, it explains the *distribution* of the delinquent subculture (e.g., it tells why lower- and working-class boys are more likely to create delinquent subcultures).

Figure 2.2
Cohen's Theory of Delinquent Boys

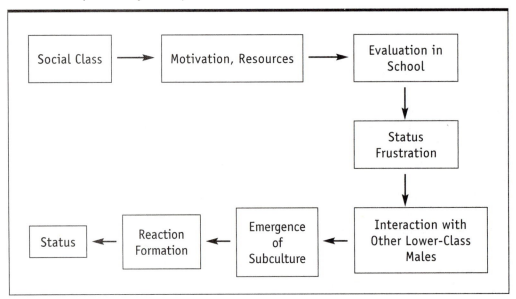

Cloward and Ohlin's Differential Opportunity Theory

Building upon the work of both Merton and Cohen, Cloward and Ohlin (1960) accepted the idea that strain was associated with deviance/crime but claimed that Cohen's extension of Merton's theory suffered from three major limitations. First, Cohen overemphasized the role of the school. For many urban lower- and working-class boys, school is not all that relevant and being rejected by school authorities is not all that important. Much more important to street-corner kids was success in the market place; to make a lot of money was the societal goal they valued the most. The status frustration they experienced most vividly was generated by the feeling that the closest they would come to achieving such a goal would be in obtaining a full-time, poorly paid job—if they were lucky.

Second, Cohen failed to see that delinquent subcultures are not all the same. Instead, there are three main types of delinquent subcultures, all of which emerge depending on the types of opportunities available in working-class neighborhoods. These are the **criminal subculture**, the **conflict subculture**, and the **retreatist subculture**. Third, the emergence of one or other of these subcultures is dependent not simply on differential access to *legitimate* (educational or occupational) opportunities, as Merton and Cohen assumed, but also on differential access to *illegitimate* opportunities. In cities (or parts of them) where juveniles had the opportunity of becoming involved with established adult criminal rackets of one kind or another (burglary, fencing stolen property, and so on) criminal subcultures are likely to emerge.[2] Where these opportunities do not exist, juveniles form conflict gangs, and where neither legitimate nor illegitimate opportunities are available, drug-oriented (retreatist) subcultures emerge.[3] Figure 2.3 describes Cloward and Ohlin's differential opportunity theory.

Figure 2.2
Cloward and Ohlin's Differential Opportunity Theory

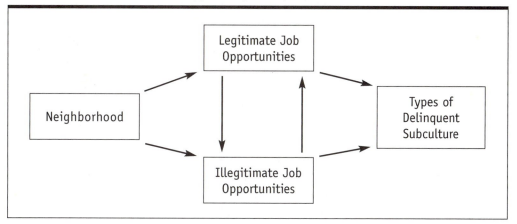

Cloward and Ohlin were extremely important in the history of criminological theory, in that perhaps no other theory was responsible for generating so much government funding for social programs. The logic was simple: money was better spent on prevention than on cure, and if the problem was a lack of legitimate opportunity structures, then the solution was to increase these opportunities (DeKeseredy & Schwartz, 1996). Under President Kennedy, and especially President Johnson with his "War on Poverty" in the 1960s, a wide variety of programs were instituted to deal with educational deficiencies and job training. Under what Curran and Renzetti (2001) call President Reagan's "War on the Poor" in the 1980s, those programs that were not earlier eliminated by President Nixon were terminated. As Vold, Bernard, and Snipes (1998:169) point out, "Although billions of dollars were spent on these programs, the only clear result seems to have been the massive political resistance that was generated against this attempt to extend opportunities to people without them."

Agnew's General Strain Theory

According to Robert Agnew (1992, 2000), strain theories developed by Merton, Cohen, and Cloward and Ohlin do not receive much empirical support because they have a narrow conception of strain. He argues that there are two other types of strain besides the disjunction between goals and means discussed previously. The first type results from the "actual or anticipated removal (loss) of positively valued stimuli from an individual" (1992:57). Such strain might occur when an intimate relationship is terminated, when one loses a job, or when one's parents take away privileges such as playing computer games (Lilly, Cullen & Ball, 2002). The second type of strain identified by Agnew (1992:58) is generated by the "actual or anticipated presentation of negative or noxious stimuli." Examples of these situations include exposure to family violence, being picked on in school, or experiencing some type of traumatic event such as an automobile accident (Curran & Renzetti, 2001). These types of strain and those stemming from failing to achieve positively valued goals, according to Agnew (2000:109), "make us feel bad" and "we might engage in crime to end the bad treatment we are experiencing. For example, we might steal to get the money we want, or we might attack people to stop them from harassing us."

Still, not all adaptations to strain are deviant or criminal. Rather, breaking the law or violating social norms is contingent upon what Agnew refers to as **conditioning factors**, such as the availability of social support, relationships with delinquent peers, a person's self-esteem and intelligence, and so on. For example, "Individuals are more likely to steal when there are no police or teachers around and valuable objects are within reach" (2000:109).

Agnew's theory was tested many times, mostly using self-report data gathered from youths attending school and living with their families.[4] There is consistent evidence that exposure to strain increases the likelihood of deviant or criminal behavior (Lilly, Cullen & Ball, 2002). However, there is little support for Agnew's hypothesized role of conditioning factors, and this may be a function of the types of methods and data analysis procedures used by those who tested his theory (Curran & Renzetti, 2001).

Women's Liberation/Emancipation Theories of Female Crime[5]

Perhaps you already know that the strain theories covered so far in this chapter don't say anything about girl or women offenders. In fact, "A long-standing deficiency of most strain theories is their neglect of the gender issue" (Hackler, 1994:198). To address this problem, in 1975, Freda Adler and Rita Simon separately published two important books that are outgrowths of strain and opportunity theories. Unlike Cohen (1955) and others who argued that women are "naturally inhibited from committing crime, Adler (1975) and Simon (1975) argued that women lacked opportunities to break the law, and if given such opportunities, they would act just like men. Adler and Simon were among the "first wave of women" of their generation to do criminological research and to help legitimate serious research on female crime and punishment (Faith, 1993).

Adler (1975:16) analyzed FBI arrest statistics and found that between 1960 and 1972:

- the number of women arrested for robbery increased by 277 percent, while the male rate rose 169 percent;

- the female embezzlement arrest rate increased 280 percent compared with a 50 percent increase for men;

- the female larceny arrest rate rose by 303 percent compared to an 82 percent increase for men; and

- the number of women arrest for burglary increased by 168 percent, while the male rate rose by 63 percent.

What accounted for the above increase in female crime rates? Adler argued that while the women's liberation movement opened up new roles for women in the military, education, business, and politics, it was also opening up new roles for women in crime, which had been historically dominated by men. According to Adler (1975:13):

But women, like men, do not live by bread alone. Almost every other aspect of their life has been similarly altered. The changing status of women as it affects family, marriage, employment and social position has been well documented by all types of sociologists. But there is a curious hiatus: the movement for full equity has a darker side which has been slighted even by the scientific community. . . .

In the same way that women are demanding equal opportunity in fields of legitimate endeavor, a similar number of determined women are forcing their way into the world of major crimes.

Girls are not exempt from Adler's liberation/emancipation thesis. She argued that the women's movement seems to be "having a twofold influence on juvenile crimes" (1975:95). She stated:

Girls are involved in more drinking, stealing, gang activity, and fighting—behavior in keeping with their adoption of male roles. We also find increases in the total number of female deviancies. The departure from the safety of traditional female roles and the testing of uncertain alternative roles coincide with the turmoil of adolescence creating criminogenic risk factors, which are bound to create this increase. These considerations help explain the fact that between 1960 and 1972 national arrests for major crimes show a jump for boys of 82 percent—for girls, 306 percent (1975:95).

What Adler (1975:13) refers to as the "shady aspect of liberation" is also a major part of Simon's (1975) theory. However, Simon departs from Adler by arguing that the increase in female crime is limited mainly to property offenses and that violent female crime has decreased. Further, Simon attributed the decrease in female violence to feminism, which makes women "feel more liberated physically, emotionally, and legally" and decreases their frustration and anger. Consequently, their desire to kill male objects of their anger or frustration on whom they are dependent (e.g., lovers, husbands, and cohabiting partners) declines (1975:40). Simon also predicted that female emancipation will contribute to an increase in female white-collar crime for the following reasons:

As women become more liberated from hearth and home and become involved in full-time jobs, they are more likely to engage in the types of crime for which their occupations provide them with the greatest opportunities. Furthermore . . . as a function of both expanded consciousness, as well as occupational opportunities, women's participation role and involvement in crime are expected to *change* and *increase* (1975:1, emphasis in original).

Simon's opportunities theory of female crime is described in Figure 2.3.

Figure 2.3
Simon's Opportunities Model of Female Crime

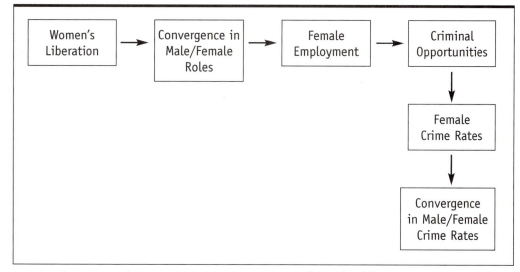

As Curran and Renzetti (2001:126) remind us, the liberation/emancipation theories described here should be commended for forcing "a contemporary reassessment of the relationship between sex and participation in criminal activity." Still, these perspectives have major problems. First, they are based on police statistics, which are not accurate indicators of the extent of crimes committed by men and women. Police statistics only tell us about the number of offenses that police officers officially deem to be criminal, and many illicit activities never come to their attention or are ignored. Second, the number of females arrested in Adler's (1975) sample was so low to begin with that a small rise translated into major changes in percentage terms (Chesney-Lind & Shelden, 1992). For whatever reason, in comparing male and female arrest rates, Adler (1975) did not control for the absolute base numbers from which the rates of increase were calculated. Thus, the rate changes she reports in her book *Sisters in Crime* are exaggerated (Curran & Renzetti, 2001).

Another example is warranted here. If, hypothetically, the absolute base number of U.S. women who committed homicide was two in 2003 and rose to four in 2004, one could argue that the female homicide rate rose by an alarming 100 percent. On the other hand, if the absolute number of males who committed homicide in 2003 were 750 and rose to 1,000 in 2004, the male rate would appear to be markedly lower than the female rate change. Clearly, as Curran and Renzetti (2001:126) remind us, "if we look only at percent changes without taking into account these major absolute base differences, we end up with a very distorted picture of men's and women's involvement in crime."

There are several other widely cited problems with the theories offered by Adler and Simon;[6] however, their popularity, at least in the minds of much of the general public, as well as many conservative politicians and journalists is undiminished (Chesney-Lind & Pasko, 2004; DeKeseredy, 2000a). Indeed, today, it is not unusual to read newspaper stories similar to this one that appeared on December 23, 1992, in *The Washington Post*: "Delinquent Girls Achieving a Violent Equality in DC" (Lewis, 1992). Note, too, that several academics have recently "recycled" the work of Adler and Simon (Chesney-Lind & Pasko, 2004). For example, based on their analysis of New York City arrest data, Baskin, Sommers, and Fagan (1993:406) argue that "the growing drug markets and a marked disappearance of males" interact with other factors in poor inner-city communities "to create social and economic opportunity structures open to women's increasing participation in violent crime." Next, we review another widely read and cited recent example of what Chesney-Lind (1989:20) refers to as "essentially a not-too-subtle variation of the . . . 'liberation hypothesis'": power-control theory.

Power-Control Theory[7]

Described in Figure 2.4, and often referred to as either a feminist or social control theory, the power-control theory developed by Hagan, Gillis, and Simpson (1987) and Hagan (1989) attempts to answer the question: "What differences do the relative class positions of husbands *and* wives in the workplace make for gender variations in parental control and delinquent behavior of adolescents" (1987:789)? They argue that there will be lower rates of female delinquency in a family where the father is controlling, and more equal male and female rates of delinquency when parental power is equalized.

Figure 2.4
Power-Control Theory

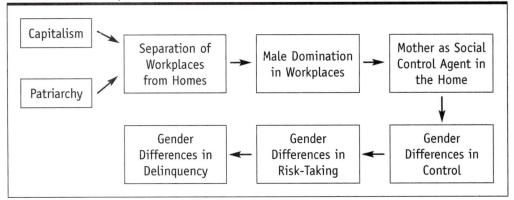

Delinquency is, according to Hagan, a type of risk-taking behavior. It is fun, liberating, and gives youths the "chance to pursue publicly some of the pleasures that are symbolic of adult male status outside the family" (1989:152-153). However, boys are more willing to take such risks than are girls because they are supervised less closely and punished less severely by their parents. Thus, the "taste for such risk-taking is channeled along sexually stratified lines" (Hagan, 1989:154). Thus, we need to focus on the relationship between the family and the work force.

Hagan, Gillis, and Simpson (1987) contend that parents' positions of power in the workplace are reproduced at home and affect the probability of their children committing delinquent acts. These theorists identify two general types of family structure based on parents' power in the workplace. The first type is **patriarchal**. It consists of a husband who works outside the home and in a position of authority and a wife who is delegated responsibility for socializing and controlling the children. Such families are typically working-class and "socially reproduce daughters who focus their futures around domestic labor and consumption as contrasted with sons who are prepared for participation in direct production" (1987:791). In these families, male children are encouraged to take risks because this prepares them for participation in the labor force, while females are closely supervised and are expected to grow up and be like their mothers and to avoid risk-taking behavior.

The second type of family structure identified by Hagan, Gillis, and Simpson (1987) is **egalitarian**. In egalitarian families, husbands and wives work outside the home in positions of authority. An egalitarian family "socially reproduces daughters who are prepared along with sons to join the production sphere" (1987:792). Further, both sons and daughters are inclined to engage in risk-taking activities, such as delinquency.

Although there is some empirical support for power-control theory and the elaborated version of it (see McCarthy, Hagan & Woodward, 1999), there are several key problems with this perspective. For example, having a job does not necessarily mean that a woman has equal power at home. While a growing number of men "help" around the house, most married working women have to do all of the cooking, cleaning, and child care, and most of them lack equal decision-making power (Alvi, DeKeseredy & Ellis, 2000). Moreover, many middle- and upper-class women are beaten, psychologically abused, and sexually assaulted by their husbands or cohabiting partners (Beirne & Messerschmidt, 1995; DeKeseredy & MacLeod, 1997; Finkelhor & Yllo, 1985).

In addition to neglecting the fact that a place in the paid marketplace does not automatically translate into power at home, Hagan and his colleagues ignore the influence of the following important variables: social class, negative parental sanctions, peer group influence, and the role of the school (Chesney-Lind & Shelden, 1998). However, from a feminist standpoint, "the worst problem of all" is that power-control theory is a variation of the "women's liberation/emancipation-leads-to crime" theories previously reviewed in this chapter (DeKeseredy & Schwartz, 1996). Of course, Hagan (1989) and Hagan, Gillis, and Simpson (1987) do not explicitly state that women's liberation causes female crime. Still, they strongly suggest that "mother's liberation" in joining the paid labor force causes daughters to commit crimes. There is an obvious problem with this: there has been a major increase in the number of women in the paid workforce over the past several decades, with no corresponding increase in female delinquency (Chesney-Lind & Pasko, 2004). Rather, major *decreases* in self-reports of serious female delinquency are evident during this time period (Chesney-Lind & Belknap, 2002).

Evaluation of Strain Theories

On top of making important contributions to the sociological study of deviance and crime, strain theories are very much "alive and kicking" (Curran & Renzetti, 2001). Three contributions stand out. First, in emphasizing strain, attention is being drawn to an important class of variables (subjective states) that mediate the relationship between social position (e.g., social class) and rule-breaking behavior. Strain is a subjective state that motivates or pushes individuals to break rules they were taught to accept and believe in. Moreover, it provides a subjective basis upon which countercultural ideologies can build. This expands the theoretical uses to which strain theory can be put.

Second, by conceiving of deviation as a solution to the problem of strain or frustration, strain theories encourage us to view delinquency or deviation as more rational than we might imagine if we only focused on the behavior itself. Thus, even seemingly senseless acts as vandalism may be a means to an end, perhaps a way of solving the problem of status frustration induced by school teachers by doing something that increases one's standing in the eyes of other members of the group (Ellis, 1987).

Third, a more recent formulation of strain theory addresses more than just one type of strain and more types of adaptations. Finally, strain theories contributed to the development of a wide variety of sociological explanations, ranging from Durkheimian to left realist accounts (see DeKeseredy, Alvi, Schwartz & Tomaszewski, 2003; Young, 1999). Strain theories are also subject to a variety of criticisms. Four of the most salient of these are their consensual assumptions, their emphasis on the motivations of deviants/criminals rather than the reactions of rule enforcers, and the selective inattention given to women and girls in conflict with the law. Box 2.3 provides a more detailed critique of the gender-blind nature of three types of strain theory.[8]

Consider, too, that the strain theories reviewed here do not address offenses such as those committed by Martha Stewart. Are they applicable to corporate crime and other crimes of the powerful? Some scholars (e.g., Snider, 1993) contend that they are not. However, as described in Chapter 5, some criminologists, such as Box (1983), Friedrichs (2004a), and Passas (1990), offer a novel challenge to this criticism and offer strain theories of corporate misconduct.

Box 2.3
The Gender-Blind Nature of Strain Theories

What do strain theories have to say about female delinquents and adult offenders? So far, the answer to this question is not much. . . . Consider Merton's theory. In the United States, women's aspirations appear to be the same as men's. Men and women are socialized to desire things such as nice clothes, a suburban home, luxurious vacations, and perhaps an expensive car. Martha Stewart certainly desires these things. Nevertheless, many women are excluded from the paid work force, and those who do find jobs are "concentrated overwhelmingly at the lower levels of the occupational hierarchy in terms of wages and salary, status and authority" (Ehrenreich, 2001; Messerschmidt, 1993:125). Furthermore, although there is a growing number of female executives, managers, and administrators, further examination shows that they tend to hold low-status positions (for example, personnel, research, affirmative action) within these occupations (Alvi et al., 2000).

Because of gender discrimination, a large number of women do not have the same legitimate opportunities as men to achieve their material goals. According to Merton's theory, these women should experience more strain than men and therefore commit more crime than men. A large body of mainstream and feminist research reveals that this is not the case. Women are clearly not more criminal than men, a fact that seriously challenges anomie theory (Chesney-Lind & Pasko, 2004). Anomie theory still may be of some value here, however. Although economic marginalization has not made women more criminal than men, it may very well explain the kinds of crime that women *do* commit (emphasis in original). The bulk of women's crimes tend to be petty property offenses such as shoplifting, passing bad checks, fraud, and whatever else people who cannot earn enough money to make ends meet might be tempted to try in order to pick up a few extra dollars (Stanko, 2001).

Source: DeKeseredy, W.S. & M.D. Schwartz (1996). *Contemporary Criminology*. Belmont, CA: Wadsworth, p. 216.

Social Control Theories

Social Control Theories: The Influence of Thomas Hobbes

Contemporary social control theories are heavily influenced by Hobbes's seventeenth-century writings on social control.[9] His theory has three core ideas. First, human beings are assumed to be egoistic. This means that they will rely on any means of satisfying their own wants and, in the process, will be quite indifferent to the welfare of others. Second, because egoism is natural in humans, it does not need to be explained. What needs to be explained is the "unnatural" behavior of human beings who conform with human-made rules regulating rampantly egoistic behavior. Third, social control is a response to deviance and crime, and coercive forms of social control can effectively regulate deviance.

Hobbes's theory of social control answers the following question: Given that human beings are essentially egoistic and if left to themselves will routinely use force and/or fraud to get what they want, how is social order possible? The answer is: because people conform with rules/norms regulating the use of force and fraud. But why are norms able to elicit conformity? Durkheim, you may recall, answered this question by saying that widely shared social norms, those that are essential for orderly social life, are characterized by a moral aspect. Individuals conform with them because, as Martha Stewart would say, "It is a good thing." Conformity is the right thing to do; it is what one *ought* to do, regardless of whether gains or losses are incurred in the process. Hobbes's answer is very different. Conformity with norms is a matter of prudence, a matter of calculation. In any given social situation, individuals will weigh the positive and negative consequences of conformity and deviance and behave accordingly. For Hobbes then, conformity is a matter of rational choice.

Hobbes answered the "How is social order possible?" question by emphasizing fear of consequences. In contrast to people's pre-civilized, civil-war "natural condition," social life in a civilized society would be regulated by an all-powerful sovereign (state) that would be in a position to punish deviations from rules that prohibited reliance on force and/or fraud in satisfying wants. Without the backing of the threat of punishment, values and norms were not capable of effectively regulating the rampant egoism of the human being. Conversely, people would curb their naturally given egoistic inclinations if the costs made contingent upon rule transgressions were made high enough. For Hobbes, then, the absence of effective social controls accounted for the recurring *expression* of egoistic, deviant forms of behavior. This idea is taken up and elaborated by a number of sociologists referred to collectively as social control theorists. Here, we focus on three of the most widely known and cited contemporary social control perspectives: (1) Hirschi's (1969) social bond theory, (2) the "broken windows" thesis developed by Wilson and Kelling (1982) and modified by Kelling and Coles (1997), and (3) Braithwaite's (1989) reintegrative shaming perspective.

Hirschi's Social Bond Theory

Described in Figure 2.5, Hirschi's social control theory is partly grounded in what he calls "the Hobbesian question," which is, "Why *do* men obey the rules of society?" (1969:10, emphasis in original). His answer is that most people obey rules because their strong **social bond** to conventional society stops them from breaking the law. Stated in reverse, "delinquent acts result when an individual's bond to society is weak or broken" (1969:16). Hirschi contends that the social bond has four elements: attachment, commitment, involvement, and belief.

Figure 2.5
Hirschi's Social Bond Theory

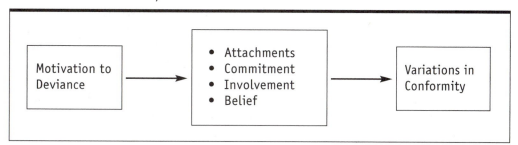

The first element, **attachment,** refers to the degree to which people have close emotional ties to conventional others, such as parents, teachers, and friends. The more we are attached to these significant others, the more we tend to take their feelings, wishes, and expectations into account, which, in turn, inhibits deviant or criminal behavior. However, the lonely person, the one with few or no attachments to conventional others, is less likely to respect the norms that are important to others.

Although people may have few friends or no relatives, they may still remain largely conformist because they have a strong **commitment** to the conventional social order or a "stake in conformity" (Toby, 1957). Suppose one of the reasons why an individual is lonely is that he or she spends all his or her time in the quest for profit. Much that is acquired, all the time and effort invested in getting rich and acquiring material goods, may be jeopardized if he or she engages in deviant acts and is discovered doing so.

Involvement refers to the amount of time one spends doing conventional or legitimate activities, such as studying, working, or volunteering. An individual who is lonely because she or he spends all of her or his time working at a legitimate job is thus doubly controlled. Being successful, she or he has acquired a great stake in conformity. Being so busy, she or he does not have the time to enjoy riding a motorcycle, let alone to join the Hell's Angels.

The fourth element of the social bond, **belief,** refers to an acceptance of conventional norms and values. Because they believe that obeying the law is the proper or right thing to do, many people do not break the law. However, those who beliefs are less strongly held feel less obliged to conform with societal rules and/or laws. According to Hirschi, "The less a person believes he should obey the rules, the more likely he is to violate them" (1969:26).

Many criminologists find Hirschi's perspective appealing because it is easy to test. Arguably the most discussed and tested criminological theory (Akers, 1997), it has received considerable empirical support, although studies have been far from unanimous in supporting this theory.[10] Overall, it seems best suited for explaining less serious (e.g., nonviolent) types of delinquent behavior. Studies of more serious forms of delinquency and adult criminality are less likely to support Hirschi's theory (DeKeseredy & Schwartz, 1996; West, 1984).

Much more problematic to feminist criminologists (e.g., Chesney-Lind & Pasko, 2004) is Hirschi's dismissal of women's experiences. Although his empirical work on social bond theory involved collecting self-report survey data from female high school students, he excluded their responses from his statistical analysis. In his book *Causes of Delinquency*, Hirschi states in a footnote that "in the analysis that follows the 'non-negro' becomes 'white," and the girls disappear" (1969:35-36). However, subsequent tests of his theory have included females, and some argue that Hirschi's theory does a better job of explaining female delinquency than male delinquency (Jensen, 1990; Krohn & Massey, 1980). But what about people like Martha Stewart? Can social bond theory be applied to corporate crime? The answer is yes, as will be pointed out in Chapter 5.

The "Broken Windows" Thesis[11]

According to Miller (2001:2), "If there were a Hall of Fame for influential public-policy ideas, then the 'broken windows' thesis would probably have its own exhibit." First developed in the early 1980s by James Q. Wilson and George L. Kelling (1982), and more recently revised by Kelling and Coles (1997), this perspective contends that neighborhood physical and social disorganization (e.g., graffiti, litter, drinking in parks, etc.) leads to more serious crime because these problems give prospective offenders the impression that no one cares about what goes on in their community. According to Kelling, "Just as a broken window left untended is a sign that nobody cares and leads to more damage and vandalism, so disorderly behavior left untended is a sign that nobody cares and leads to more serious crime" (cited in Nifong, 1999:8).

There is no strong empirical support for the assertion that disorder left unchecked, directly causes crime (DeKeseredy, Alvi, Schwartz & Tomaszewski, 2003; Miller, 2001; Sampson & Raudenbush, 2001). Even James Q. Wilson, cofounder of the "broken windows" thesis, admitted at the 2000 annual meeting of the American Political Science Association that, "It is only a theory." He also told *The New York Times*, "God knows what the truth is" (cited in Miller, 2001:7). George Kelling also admits that the "broken windows" theory has not been supported using sophisticated quantitative methods:

> Broken windows remains a hypothesis which has a lot of support in the form of anecdotes and case studies . . . My evidence for this continues to be the constant, repeated contact I have with citizens and communities. I don't care where you go, citizens believe that there's this link . . . that every time you start to restore order, crime goes down (cited in Miller, 2001:7).

In addition to lacking empirical support and constituting little more than an attempt to garner support from liberal voters (Harcourt, 1998), the "broken windows" thesis suffers from what British critical criminologist Jock Young (1999:130) refers to as the cosmetic fallacy, which:

> conceives of crime as a superficial problem of society, skin deep, which can be dealt with using the appropriate ointment, rather than as any chronic ailment of society as a whole. It engenders a cosmetic criminology which views crime as a blemish which suitable treatment can remove from a body which is, itself, otherwise healthy and in little need of reconstruction. Such criminology *distances* itself from the core institutions and proffers technical, piecemeal solutions. It, thus, reverses causality; crime causes problems for society rather than society causes the problem of crime (emphasis in original).

Reintegrative Shaming Perspective

John Braithwaite asserts that his "theory of reintegrative shaming explains compliance with the law by moralizing qualities of social control rather than by its repressive qualities" (1989:9). Described in Figure 2.6, Braithwaite's social control perspective is heavily but selectively influenced by Durkheim, but he does not share Durkheim's assumption about the egoistic nature of human beings. Still, Braithwaite accepts and cites Durkheim's emphasis on the moral-reductive effects of punishments and the significance of attachment to others as the basis of effective social control. Finally, like Durkheim, he also believes that repressive social control (e.g., shaming by stigmatizing) is not only ineffective, but also morally wrong.

Unlike some other social control theorists, such as Hirschi (1969) and Wilson (1985), Braithwaite does not assume that human beings are, or behave as if they were, "amoral calculators." Rather, he regards humans as moral actors capable of making choices. Their morality is learned, and the choices they make are made "against a background of societal pressures mediated by *shaming*" (1989:9, emphasis added). The shaming reactions a society makes in responding to individuals who make criminal choices are more likely to control crime effectively if the "human dignity" of these people is accepted rather than denied.

Almost all social theorists agree that conformity with social and legal norms is the result of informal processes of social control by parents, teachers, friends, neighbors, coworkers, and so on (Ellis & DeKeseredy, 1996). Their approval and disapproval, and their ability to impose external sanctions (criticism, reprimands, gossip) and internal sanctions (guilt, shame) are what induce most of us to behave in conformist ways most of the time. In fact, most deterrence studies show that perceived certainty and severity of formal sanctions (such as arrest and imprisonment) are not key determinants of conformity (Miller & Simpson, 1991; Paternoster, 1987). However, the guilt, shame, and fear associated with such sanctions—what have been called the "indirect costs" of these sanctions—seem to be effective deterrents.

Braithwaite argues that shaming can be **reintegrative**, or **stigmatizing** and **repressive**. Reintegrative shaming involves "expressions of community disapproval [that] are followed by gestures of reacceptance into the community of law-abiding citizens" (1989:55). **Disintegrative shaming** is "counterproductive" (Curran & Renzetti, 2001) and involves "stigmatizing expressions of a community by creating a class of outcasts" (Braithwaite, 1989:55). This form of shaming is unforgiving, segregates the offender from the community, and affixes a stigmatizing, stereotypical **master status**[12] from which he or she cannot easily escape. These master labels influence all, or most, reactions to "drug addicts and child molesters." In sharp contrast, reintegrative shaming is not stigmatizing. Rather, it is forgiving and is meant to reintegrate the offender into the conventional community.

Disintegrative shaming is not merely less effective in controlling crime; it actually increases crime because the process of creating stigmatized outcasts provides individuals who commit crimes with justifications for rejecting their rejecters and their laws. By way of contrast, reintegrative shaming does not reject and segregate the offender. It focuses on his or her behavior and keeps him or her in contact with the law-abiding persons whose laws were violated. Reintegrative shaming, according to Braithwaite, is more effective in controlling crime because "shame is more deterring when administered by persons who continue to be of importance to us" (1989:25). Thus, the core of effective deterrence is not the severity of sanctions but their "social embeddedness."

The family constitutes a model or paradigm of social embeddedness and is also the primary inculcator of guilt and shame through the processes of socialization and social control. Family socialization helps inculcate social norms whose violation induces a sense of guilt or shame. Actual violations of family norms by children are controlled by reintegrative social control processes. However, family socialization and social control do not guarantee self-regulation. For example, the closer the criminal justice system and the community control systems that supplement informal social controls approximate a "family model of punishment" (reintegrative shaming), the lower the crime rate will be.

Braithwaite contends that reintegrative shaming is most likely to be found in "communitarian" societies characterized by family-like patterns of interdependence, mutual assistance, trust, and commitment to the group. Braithwaite asserts that contemporary Japanese society is a prime example of such a society; however, he is cognizant of the fact that Japanese norms and culture cannot simply be transferred to other societies such as the United States, which still seems strongly committed to outcasting people who engage in deviant or criminal acts. For Braithwaite, then, it is not surprising that the United States has so much crime.

Braithwaite's perspective is seen by some criminologists as enriching "labeling theory by illuminating not only that shaming (or labeling) varies in its nature and effects but also why this variation ultimately is contingent on the society in which shaming takes place" (Lilly, Cullen & Ball, 2002:122). Certainly, his theory has garnered considerable attention from the international criminology community, and it has major implications for policy and practice. Still, at this point in time, Braithwaite's contribution has not been subject to much empirical scrutiny.

Evaluation of Social Control Theories

There are other social control theories that could have been reviewed here, such as Tittle's (1995, 1999) control-balance theory and Gottfredson and Hirschi's (1990) self-control perspective. Space limitations preclude describing these and other contributions; however, a key point to consider is that by taking deviance and crime for granted and formulating theories that explain conformity (Why are most people not deviant?), they offer a novel challenge to other theoretical perspectives. Consider, too, that some control theories, such as Hirschi's (1969) have generated considerable research and have strong empirical support. Still, control theories are often criticized for neglecting the motivation or push toward rule-breaking, and except for a few accounts (e.g., Colvin, 2000; Godenzi, Schwartz & DeKeseredy, 2001), "remain largely silent on how issues of power and inequality influence the quality and impact of social control" (Lilly, Cullen & Ball, 2002:104).

Figure 2.6

Braithwaite's Reintegrative Shaming Perspective

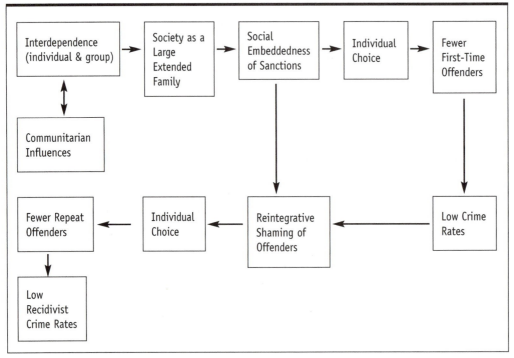

Interactionist Perspectives

Interactionist Perspectives: The Influence of George Herbert Mead

The interactionist perspectives reviewed here, in Chapter 1, and in other parts of this book are derived from **symbolic interactionist theory**, a major sociological school of thought developed by University of Chicago scholar George Herbert Mead (1934). Central to symbolic interactionism as a distinctive theoretical perspective are the following core ideas. First, the Hobbesian problem of social order is redefined as a cognitive one. Whereas Hobbes and Durkheim had answered the question, "How is society possible?" by identifying the social control of rampant egoism as a necessary condition, the answer given by Mead (1934) and other symbolic interactionists emphasizes shared meanings. They argue that:

> human actions are best understood in terms of the meaning that those actions have for the actors, rather than in terms of pre-existing biological, psychological, or social conditions. These meanings are to some extent created by the individual, but primarily they are derived from intimate personal inter-actions with people (Vold, Bernard & Snipes, 1998:219).

Second, according to Mead, via the process of socialization, human beings gradually learn the meanings, the descriptions and evaluations that constitute their symbolic universe. Central to this process is the emergence of the social self or "self-as-object-to-itself." Socialized individuals, individuals in whom this kind of self has emerged, have acquired the ability to describe and evaluate themselves in the same way that others describe and evaluate them. The source of the social self, then, is the reaction of others. We tend to see ourselves as other see us. Moreover, the way we see ourselves influences the way we behave. Usually, individuals tend to behave in ways that are consistent with their self-images.

Third, while the metaphor of multi-player games such as ice hockey, football, or baseball may be applied to symbolic interaction and society, Mead's game has one very important and distinctive property: in the course of interacting with each other, self-images and the rules of the game may be changed. New self-images and rules may be created, some rules applied, and other's not. Simply examining the game's rules as they appear in the rule book will not tell you very much about how the game is actually played or about the course of the game. Games like ice hockey have an emergent quality to them, and the process of emergence must be studied directly. The game's structure, its rules, and its competitive values should be taken into account, but the primary focus of analysis is the process of symbolic interaction. The large, many-player game called society emerges out of, and can be changed by, the symbolic interaction that takes place among individuals in such small-scale settings as homes, schools, workplaces, churches, and so on.

Most sociologists who adopt a social psychological, symbolic interactionist approach to the study of deviant and/or criminal social behavior in these settings work with a set of sensitizing concepts bequeathed them by Mead. These include interaction, symbols, meanings, process, emergence, and self-concept. A few have borrowed concepts formulated by other theorists, and some have tried to combine Mead's micro-sociological approach with a macro-sociological one.

In Chapter 1, we briefly described one type of interactionist theory that has been applied to the study of crime and deviance: the societal reaction/labeling perspective. There, we said that societal reaction/labeling theorists want to develop a sociological understanding of how people and behaviors come to be designated as criminal or deviant. This is very different from wanting to describe the causes of crime. Recall that for scholars such as Howard Becker (1973), nothing is inherently deviant or criminal. Rather, crime is a social construct or a label attached to a behavior during the course of social interaction between rule-makers and rule-breakers. Here, we introduce you to one major variant of the interactionist perspective: Sutherland's differential association theory.

Differential Association Theory

As originally formulated by Sutherland (1947) and later revised by Sutherland and Cressey (1966), differential association theory is an interactionist account of both conformity and deviation. However, because of its inclusion of motives, its emphasis on the original or random causes of deviance/crime, and its acceptance of the traditional notion that social control is caused by deviance instead of vise versa, differential association theory differs from the interactionist accounts reviewed in Chapter 1. At the same time, the differential association and societal reaction/labeling accounts are similar to each other in the centrality given by each to symbolic interaction and how individuals define situations.

Also central to both accounts is their opposition to a conception of deviation as an expression of individual biological (e.g., body types) or psychological (e.g., psychopath) pathology. Instead, Sutherland and Cressey (1966) define both conformity and deviation as forms of learned behavior. Both are outcomes of ordinary, everyday, normal processes of learning that occur when individuals interact with each other.

The societal context for learning in complex, industrialized societies such as Canada and the United States is characterized by differential social organization. This means that North Americans grow up and live in communities composed of groups holding conflicting values, norms, and attitudes toward obeying and disobeying the law. Because individuals are usually members of different groups holding conflicting values, they are routinely subjected to a variety of cross-pressures regarding conformity and deviance in general and law-abiding and law-violating behavior in particular.

According to Sutherland and Cressey, differential association theory represents an attempt to explain both conformity and deviation. More specifically, it "purports to explain the criminal and noncriminal behavior of individual persons" who are members of a number of groups supporting conflicting definitions of law-abiding and law-violating behavior. Their theory is also a process theory, a theory of "the processes by which persons become criminals" and conformists (1966:80).

Differential association theory is easy to follow and includes the following nine propositions:

- Criminal behavior is learned.

- Criminal behavior is learned in interaction with other persons in a process of communication.

- The principal part of the learning of criminal behavior occurs within intimate personal groups.

- When criminal behavior is learned, the learning includes (1) techniques of committing the crime, which are sometimes very complicated and other times very simple, and (2) the specific direction of motives, drives, rationalizations, and attitudes.

- The specific direction of motives and drives is learned from definitions of the legal codes as favorable or unfavorable.

- A person becomes delinquent because of an excess of definitions favorable to the violation of law over definitions unfavorable to the violation of law.

- Differential associations may vary in frequency, duration, priority, and intensity.

- The process of learning criminal behavior by association with criminal and anticriminal patterns involves all of the mechanisms that are involved in any other learning.

- Although criminal behavior is an expression of general needs and values, it is not explained by those general needs and values, because noncriminal behavior is an expression of the same needs and values (Sutherland, 1947:6-8).

The point, then, behind the term **differential association** is that everyone is exposed to definitions in favor of deviance/crime and conformity, but that things are not equal. As suggested, frequent exposure to ideas, long-term exposure, early exposure, and definitions that come from people who the person holds in high regard all help to push a person in one direction or another.

Evaluation of Differential Association Theory

A theory designed to explain both conformity and deviance is worthy and rare. Also of some importance is the fact that the differential association perspective is based on valid and useful cultural-conflict assumptions regarding the nature of contemporary capitalist societies such as the United States and Canada. Further, it can be applied to crimes of the powerful as well as to those that occur on the street and in other social settings. Still, this theory is very difficult to test (Curran & Renzetti, 2001). Not surprisingly, other scholars disagree, and some tested hypotheses were derived from it.[13] Moreover, several criminologists revised Sutherland's work and have developed what are referred to as social learning theories of crime and deviance (e.g., Akers, 1973, 1998; Burgess & Akers, 1966).

Although differential association theory had a major impact on the study of crime and deviance, it is subject to several criticisms. For example, in its original form, it neglects a very important source of definitions, the mass media (Glaser, 1956). However, in fairness to Sutherland, the media, especially television and video games, were not as influential in people's everyday lives when he constructed his theory as they are today (Curran & Renzetti, 2001). Consider, too, that differential association theory is criticized for diverting attention away from a problem of great significance for sociologists interested in the study of deviance and crime. This problem has to do with why, in the first place, some normal learned behaviors are defined as crimes (e.g., street gambling) while others, such as fraudulent business practices, are not (Ellis, 1987; Vold, 1979).

Ecological Perspectives

Like Janus, the Roman god of beginnings and doorways, the University of Chicago's Department of Sociology had two faces. One face was **ethnographic** and observed and described the real and subjectively lived experiences of people like hobos and delinquents. Students were also encouraged to do similar research. Consider what Robert Park told young University of Chicago sociologists 80 years ago:

> You have been told to go grubbing in the library, thereby accumulating a mass of notes and a liberal coating of grime . . . one thing more is needful: first hand observation. Go and sit in the lounges of the luxury hotels and on the doorsteps of the flophouses; sit on the Gold Coast settees and on the slum shakedowns; sit in Orchestra Hall and in the Star and Garter Burlesk (quoted in Hagan, 1993:189).

Ethnographic studies provide rich and interesting information on rule-breakers and rule-makers that can't be uncovered using statistical techniques. Further, **human agency**—human beings choosing, deciding, and doing within a set of constraints—figures prominently in them.

The other face of the University of Chicago's Sociology Department was ecological, one that observed and described the city of Chicago—how it grew, and the impact of its growth and its other attributes on Chicago's crime and delinquency. Human agency disappeared, and instead of "jumping into" (i.e., choosing) criminal and delinquent activities, criminals and delinquents appeared to be "pushed into them from behind," and the city changed. It is this other ecological face that we shall focus on here.

Ecological Perspectives: The Influence of the Chicago School

Robert Park was one of the founding "fathers" of the **Chicago School**, which is also known as the **Ecological School** or the **School of Human Ecology** (Curran & Renzetti, 2001). He was a "newspaper reporter-turned-sociologist" (Lilly, Cullen & Ball, 2002), and he spent a great deal of time in the 1920s with his colleagues investigating and describing social conditions in the city of Chicago. He also used plant society—the life, death, and distribution of plants—as a metaphor for human society. For him, plant societies were analogous to human societies. He said that the city:

> may be regarded as a functional unit in which the relations among individuals that compose it are determined, not merely by the city's physical structure, nor even by the formal regulations of a local government, but rather by the direct and indirect interaction of individuals upon one another (1925:2).

Park and his colleagues Burgess and McKenzie (1925/1967) co-edited *The City,* which featured Burgess's (1925/1967) widely read and cited **concentric zone theory**. It contends that cities expand out from their center in a pattern of concentric zones or rings, as depicted in Figure 2.7. The first zone is referred to as "The Loop" or central business district, and the others are described below by Burgess (1925/1967:50):

> Encircling the downtown area that is normally an area of transition, which is being invaded by business and light manufacture (II). A third area (III) is inhabited by the workers in industries who have escaped the area of deterioration (II) but who desire to live within easy access of their work. Beyond

this zone is the "residential area" (IV) of high-class apartment buildings or of exclusive "restricted" districts of single-family dwellings. Still further out beyond the city limits is the commuters' zone (V)—suburban areas or satellite cities—within a thirty- to sixty-minute ride of the central business district.

Figure 2.7
Burgess' Concentric Zone Theory

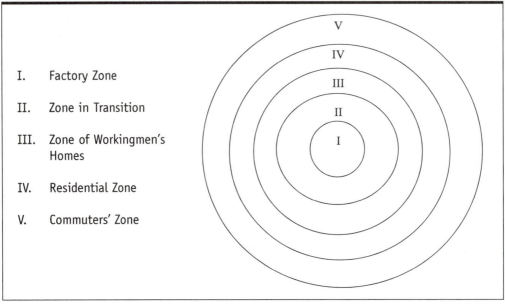

I.   Factory Zone

II.   Zone in Transition

III. Zone of Workingmen's Homes

IV.   Residential Zone

V.   Commuters' Zone

Source: Burgess, E.W. (1925/1967). "The Growth of the City." In R.E. Park, E.W. Burgess & R.D. McKenzie (eds.), *The City* (p. 51). Chicago: University of Chicago Press.

The above theory influenced the study of many types of deviance (Curran & Renzetti, 2001). However, it was Shaw and McKay (1942) who were the first to empirically assess whether it was a "fruitful approach to the study of crime" (Lilly, Cullen & Ball, 2002:35). It is to their theoretical contribution that we now turn.

The Criminogenic Zone of Transition

Fourteen years after the publication of *The City*, University of Chicago sociologists Shaw and McKay applied the concentric zone theory to the problems of explaining city-wide differences in juvenile delinquency rates as measured by police and court statistics. These official or government data revealed that the communities with the highest rates were all located in a part of the city called the **zone of transition**, which was the area surrounding the central business district that formed the central core of the city.

As stated above by Burgess (1925/1967), the primary cause of transition in this zone was the invasion by expanding or new established businesses and factories. When houses were vacated, they were allowed to deteriorate because their owners expected them to be bought up and converted to business and industrial use. As housing conditions deteriorated, rents were lowered, which increased the proportion of the most disadvantaged groups who became residents in the community. Those who already lived there and could afford to move out did so. Thus, as members of some visible minority or new immigrant groups moved out, members of other groups moved in and took their places. Regardless of the national origins of zone of transition residents (e.g., African-American, Hispanic, Irish, Polish, Italian), delinquency rates in the zone of transition remained the highest in the city of Chicago.

A detailed analysis of the records of juvenile delinquents revealed that a very high proportion of them were detached from the conventional institutions of their communities. In other words, they were detached from families, schools, churches, police, youth clubs, Boy Scouts, and so on. The ability of these institutions to control juveniles was, for this reason, greatly weakened. Because the population was so transient, with established residents leaving and newcomers arriving all the time, informal patterns of social control by neighbors and friends were also impaired. In short, communities in the zone of transition were in a condition of **social disorganization**. Social disorganization was the major cause, detachment from conventional institutions was the mechanism, and ineffective social control was the process that resulted in the highest delinquency rates being found in the zones of transition. The Shaw/McKay social disorganization theory influenced recent ecological perspectives reviewed in the next section and this perspective is described in Figure 2.8.

Figure 2.8
Shaw and McKay's Social Disorganization Theory

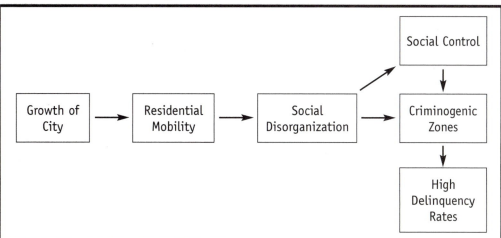

The New Chicago School[14]

Robert Park and Shaw and McKay may be "long gone" (Sampson, 2002), but there is clearly still a major interest in ecological perspectives on crime and deviance. For example, described in Figure 2.9, DeKeseredy, Alvi, Schwartz, and Tomaszewski (2003) developed and tested a social disorganization/collective efficacy model of crime in public housing that can be traced to the sociological writings of Park and Burgess and Shaw and McKay. Models like this one have in common the notion that urban ecological variables (e.g., neighborhood structural density)[15] influence crime and delinquency via their impact on formal and informal processes of social control (Ellis & DeKeseredy, 1996). The relationship between these factors is presented more parsimoniously in the human ecology process model offered in Figure 2.10, which takes both social disorganization and **collective efficacy** into account.

Figure 2.9

DeKeseredy et al.'s Social Disorganization/Collective Efficacy Model of Crime in Public Housing

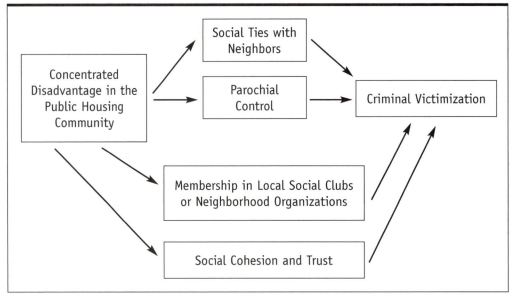

Source: DeKeseredy, W.S., S. Alvi, M.D. Schwartz & E.A. Tomaszewski (2003). *Under Siege: Poverty and Crime in a Public Housing Community.* Lanham, MD: Lexington Books, p. 85.

In the center of Figure 2.10 is what R.B. Taylor (2001:128) refers to as a "constellation of processes": social disorganization and its antithesis—collective efficacy. There are many definitions of social disorganization. Here it is defined as "the inability of a community structure to realize the common values of its residents and maintain effective controls" (Sampson & Groves, 1989:777). Perhaps the most important of these controls are private, parochial, and public control (Bursik & Grasmick, 1993a; Piquero, 1999; Sampson, Morenoff & Earls, 1999; Sampson, Raudenbush & Earls, 1997, 1998). There are a variety of reasons why these controls are missing in socially disorganized communities,[16] but it is an underlying argument of models such as those presented in Figure 2.9 that they *are* missing.

Figure 2.10
Human Ecology Process Model

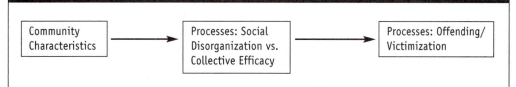

Source: Taylor, R.B. (2001). "The Ecology of Crime, Fear, and Delinquency: Social Disorganization versus Social Efficacy." In R. Paternoster & R. Bachman (eds.), *Explaining Criminals and Crime* (pp. 124-139). Los Angeles: Roxbury.

Private control "occurs when parents care and effectively socialize their children, and when neighbors care about and are influenced by the opinions of others" (Paternoster & Bachman, 2001:121). Thus, the family itself provides a measure of control over the potential delinquencies of its members.

Parochial control occurs "when neighbors watch and supervise other children in the community, when they question strangers who enter the neighborhood, and when schools are effectively used as the focal point of community activities" (Paternoster & Bachman, 2001:121). In effect, here we are dealing with a variation of the timeless notion that "it takes a village to raise a child." For example, when parents know the parents of their children's peers, they can watch the children's behaviors in different social contexts, talk to other parents about their children, and create social norms (Coleman, 1990; Furstenberg et al., 1999). Further, this type of "structural and normative adult-child closure" provides children with social support, gives parents information, and fosters informal social control (Sampson, Morenoff & Earls, 1999; Sandefur & Laumann, 1998).

Public control refers to "the capacity of the neighborhood to successfully secure goods and services from larger political entities (for example, city government) that will directly affect them" (Paternoster & Bachman, 2001:121). By definition, the entire concept of "broken windows" discussed earlier in this chapter presumes that a city will allow abandoned buildings to remain in certain neighborhoods, abandoned and burned-out cars to remain on the streets, garbage to pile up, and many city ordinances to remain unenforced (Kelling & Coles, 1997; Wilson & Kelling, 1982). Some neighborhoods seem to be much better than others at convincing the government to take care of these problems (Velez, 2001). There is much reason to believe that neighborhoods abandoned by the city government will have much more fear of crime, if not actual increases in crime itself (Alvi, Schwartz, DeKeseredy & Maume, 2001).

Again, the above three controls are missing in socially disorganized communities, and these areas are characterized by particular problems identified by Taylor (2001b:128):

> [R]esidents do not get along with one another; residents do not belong to local organizations geared to bettering the community and thus cannot work together effectively to address common problems; residents hold different values about what is and what is not acceptable behavior on the street; and residents are unlikely to interfere when they see other youths or adults engaged in wrongdoing.

Generally, high crime rates are more likely to be found in urban neighborhoods characterized by anonymity, weak social ties with neighbors, and diminished control over people's behavior (Sampson, Squires & Zhou, 2001).

In contrast, a neighborhood characterized by a high level of collective efficacy is one where a "central goal is the desire of community residents to live in safe and orderly environments that are free of predatory crime, especially interpersonal violence" (Sampson, Raudenbush & Earls, 1997:918). According to proponents of the New Chicago School, in communities where collective efficacy is high, neighbors interact with one another, residents can count on their neighbors for various types of social support such as childcare, people intervene to prevent teenagers from engaging in delinquent acts, and neighborhood leaders struggle to obtain funding from governments and local businesses to help improve neighborhood conditions.

Typically, communities high in collective efficacy are better off than public housing communities such as those studied by DeKeseredy, Schwartz, Alvi, and Tomaszewski (2003). Note, too, that Sampson and his colleagues (1997) found that in Chicago neighborhoods where concentrated poverty was high, collective efficacy was low, which is why they had higher rates of crime. Thus, collective efficacy functions as an important intermediary between concentrated poverty and crime. In fact, Sampson and colleagues' (1997) data show that collective efficacy—not race or poverty—was the greatest single predictor of violent crime.

However, it is important to note that collective efficacy does not completely mediate the relationship between a community's structural characteristics and crime. For example, Sampson and his colleagues (1997) found that, after controlling for collective efficacy, concentrated disadvantage still exerted independent effects on violent crime. This is why Taylor (2001b) calls for the slightly revised model described in Figure 2.11.

Figure 2.11
Revised Human Ecology Process Model

Source: Taylor, R.B. (2001). "The Ecology of Crime, Fear, and Delinquency: Social Disorganization versus Social Efficacy." In R. Paternoster & R. Bachman (eds.), *Explaining Criminals and Crime* (pp. 124-139). Los Angeles: Roxbury.

Evaluation of Ecological Theories

The ecological models reviewed here have had a major influence on criminology and will continue to do so. Further, they have been "the touchstones for prevention programs for well over fifty years" (Taylor, 2001:134). However, several key issues need to be addressed in future theoretical work. For example, thus far, members of the New Chicago School, such as Robert Sampson, have not explicitly addressed the fact that collective efficacy can take different shapes and forms (DeKeseredy, Alvi, Schwartz & Tomaszewski, 2003). According to St. Jean (1998), definitions of "the common good" of a neighborhood may vary among residents in different contexts or situations. If we consider social cohesion and trust for instance, many poor public housing residents may feel that the police are oppressive and are more likely to target them and their neighbors for wrongdoing than those in more affluent areas. So, in addition to counting on their neighbors to help them care for their children, they may be able to rely on them to hide from the police if they are being investigated for some sort of criminal activity.

Critical Perspectives

Critical criminology was defined in Chapter 1 as a school of thought that views the major sources of crime as the class, ethnic, and patriarchal relations that control our society. Of course, there are other definitions, and there are many types of critical criminology. Still, one thing most, if not all, modern critical perspectives have in common is that they have roots in the writings of Karl Marx (Schwartz & Hatty, 2003). Thus, prior to reviewing three important types of critical criminological theory, it is first necessary to address the influence of his work.

Critical Theories: The Influence of Karl Marx

According to his friend and colleague, Friedrich Engels, Karl Marx was above all a fighter, a revolutionist.[17] He was also a great preacher and scholar, and for Marx, these roles were inseparable. As a warrior-scholar-preacher, his achievements are great. Still, not included among these achievements is a systematic theory of crime and deviance. In view of this generally accepted conclusion, it may be surprising to discover a number of contemporary sociologists whose sole claim to immortality is a Marxist theory of these very phenomena. Our surprise decreases, however, when we learn that their theories were influenced not by Marx's sparse and scattered references to crime, but by his general class conflict theory of social change (Matthews, 2003b).[18] Specifically, Marx's general theory helps them understand the relation between the economy, class conflict, and three problems of major interest to sociologists who study deviance and crime: (1) the causes of deviance and crime, (2) the origins of law, and (3) the functions of law.

Marx's General Theory

One important goal of Marx's general sociological theory is to provide a scholarly account of, and help bring into being, the economic and political conditions necessary for individuals to rediscover and actualize their essential selves. **Capitalism**, with its major class division and antagonistic class relations, its inequality, and its exploitation of both human labor and nature in the interests of capital accumulation, dehumanizes, alienates, and "denatures' human beings. **Socialism**, characterized by the abolition of private property, and thus of the inequality based upon its differential possession, and by the replacement of a highly developed division of labor with a system in which each individual performs a variety of occupational and other social roles, will return to individuals the feeling of being free, or joy in labor, of being integrated with nature and with their fellows (Marx, 1844/1963). Socialism would actualize Marx's image of human beings, while capitalism negated this image. Marx's general theory is an attempt to replace the latter social formation by the former one by showing how history made such a transformation inevitable.

The starting point of Marx's general **materialist** theory is the premise that "man must be in a position to live (obtain food, clothing, shelter) in order to be able to make history" (Marx & Engels, 1846/1939:7). This premise is the basis for Marx's materialist account of class formation, class conflict, and revolutionary change under a historically specific set of circumstances. A materialist account is one that explains human nature, the origins and functions of ideologies, class formations, and class conflict by pointing to the economy, to real people at work, earning a living under historically specific economic arrangements.[19]

Marx's general theory is a historical materialist one, which may be stated as follows: scarcity motivates human labor. For much of human beings' early history, their labor did not produce goals and services beyond the essential requirements of consumption. An improvement in human skills, knowledge, materials, and social organization helped human labor produce a surplus beyond the needs of immediate consumption. In pre-capitalist or "tributary societies," rulers (the state) used force or its threat to take the surplus away from those who helped produce it. With the political fragmentation of European societies and the rise of a mercantile class, an autonomous economic realm emerged, alongside the state. State laws guaranteeing the right to private property helped merchants appropriate the surplus legally, returning some of it in the form of taxes to the state. Gradually, mercantilism was replaced by capitalism.

Capitalists were those who owned the instruments of production. They legally appropriated most of the surplus and used much of it to achieve even greater surpluses in the future (**capital accumulation**). The state benefited from this by obtaining increased revenues. In return, it coordinated capitalist activities and interests, and created and enforced laws (e.g., law of contract) supportive of capitalism. What the workers and capitalists thought about their respective situations in life and their relation to each other was determined by where each group stood in relation to the means of production. In addition, capitalists rely on the state and on their control over both communications and the instruments of production to conceal from the **proletariat** (those who do not own the instruments of production) the real material reasons for their alienated and oppressed situation in life. Ideological forms of consciousness (**false consciousness**) are disseminated by capitalists, and capitalist ideologies justify capitalism to capitalists and workers alike.

Ownership and nonownership of the instruments of production divide society into two major social groupings: capitalists and workers. As a result of contradictions endemic to capitalism, capitalists become their own gravediggers.[20] For example, by massing workers in factories, they facilitated worker communication and consciousness of class. With the development of class consciousness, conflicts between workers and individual capitalists were transformed into class conflicts between workers and capitalists generally.

Capitalists, Marx predicted, would not voluntarily relinquish control of an economic system that generated massive inequality in wealth and standard of living. They would be willing to use force to prevent social change. For their part, the workers would come to see revolutionary violence as being the only way of creating a radically transformed, more egalitarian socialist society. The workers would win. In winning, they would also liberate the capitalists.

Today, as noted by Schwartz and Hatty (2003:x), "Although few critical criminologists would identify as Marxists, all critical theorists share in common a concern with class, or at least the economic structure of society, and the manner in which the inequalities of modern capitalist society influence crime." Consider, too, that some critical criminologists argue, rightfully so, that given the rapidly increasing gap between the "haves and have nots, Marxism remains as relevant as ever for analyzing crime, criminal justice, and the role of the state" (Russell, 2002:113). It is to one group of critical theorists who are still heavily influenced by Marxist theory that we now turn.

Left Realism[21]

Left realists, like other critical criminologists, view poverty as a powerful determinant of muggings, armed robbery, sexual assault, wife-beating, and so on. However, most poor people do not commit these crimes. This is why left realists contend that relative poverty rather than **absolute poverty** is the key to understanding crime in socially and economically disenfranchised inner-city communities (DeKeseredy, Alvi, Schwartz & Tomaszewski, 2003; Lea & Young, 1984; Young, 1999). Absolute poverty refers to a family or person's inability to buy basic necessities (e.g., food, shelter, and clothing), while relative poverty is defined in relation to a society's mean or median income. Thus, if your income is at the bottom of the income distribution, you are poor regardless of your absolute income (Devine & Wright, 1993).

According to left realists, it is not the inability to buy a high-definition television or other "glittering prizes of capitalism" that motivates people to commit crime. Rather, it is a "lethal combination" of **relative deprivation** and individualism (Young, 1999). For example, poverty experienced as unfair (relative deprivation when compared to someone else) breeds discontent (Lea & Young, 1984). Individualism leads such discontent to foster "Hobbesian jungles" of the urban poor (Young, 1999), a "universe where human beings live side by side but not as human beings" (Hobsbawm, 1994:341). Crime, then, is an unjust individualistic "solution" to the "experience of injustice" (Young, 1998). However, it is important to note that experienced injustice, combined with an individualistic solution, occurs throughout society (Young, 1999). Crime is certainly not "ghetto-specific" (Wilson, 1996). After all, many affluent people use illicit drugs, beat their wives, and sexually assault their dating partners. Still, because of structural changes (e.g., deindustrialization, the North American Free Trade Agreement, and transnational corporations moving operations to developing countries to use cheap labor), many poor ghetto residents cannot find work and thus have little reason to refrain from criminal activity. This is a key reason why interpersonal violence, drug dealing, illicit drug use, and other crimes occur with greater frequency in ghettos, barrios, and slums (DeKeseredy, Alvi, Schwartz & Tomaszewski, 2003, Wilson, 1996).

Left realists also argue that people who lack legitimate means of solving the problem of relative deprivation may come into contact with other frustrated disenfranchised people to form subcultures, which, in turn, encourage and legitimate criminal behaviors. For example, receiving respect from peers is highly valued among ghetto adolescents who are denied status in mainstream, middle-class society. However, respect and status is often granted by inner-city subcultures when one is willing to be violent, such as using an assault rifle (DeKeseredy & Schwartz, 2005; Messerschmidt, 1993).

A cautionary note about ghetto-based criminal subcultures is required here. We maintain that they should not be construed as "somehow alien to the wider culture" (Young, 1999:86), which is what **culture of poverty theorists** such as Lewis (1966) and Banfield (1974) do. The truth is that they, like most North Americans, want to achieve the American Dream and its related status but lack the legitimate means to do so (Messner & Rosenfeld, 2001). Recall the Puerto Rican drug dealers Bourgois (1995) studied in East Harlem, New York City. In fact, criminal subcultures like this one are "based on all-American notions of work as an area of rugged individualism and competition and sanctioned by a film industry that carries the message of didactic violence. . . ." (Young, 1999:87).

Evaluation of Left Realist Theory

Left realist theory contributes to a rich sociological understanding of deviance and crime in contemporary capitalist societies. Nevertheless, it is criticized on several grounds, especially by feminist scholars. For example, although left realism embraces elements of radical and socialist feminism, as evident in their empirical work on violence against women (e.g., Jones, MacLean & Young, 1986), there is no attempt to theorize women's experiences of crime as suspects, offenders, defendants, and inmates (Carlen, 1992). The issues of why women's offenses are distinct from men's and the sexist nature of the criminal justice system are also often given short shrift. These are valid criticisms because left realists' theoretical work on the relationship between gender and violence has focused mainly on male-to-female victimization in domestic/household settings and in public places. Still, their analysis of this major problem is deemed by some critics to be problematic because they have not developed and tested theories of male patriarchal domination and control over women (DeKeseredy, 1996a; DeKeseredy & Schwartz, 1991). This is likely to change soon as we are seeing new left realist literature that addresses this concern (Mooney, 2000).

Take, for example, Young's recent attempt to explain the relationship between relative deprivation, individualism, "macho" subcultural dynamics, and violence against women. Seen as a result of exclusion and inclusion, he argues (1999:13-14) that this form of woman abuse:

> can be caused by relative deprivation and by clashes among individuals demanding equality and others resisting them. Where both relative deprivation and individualism occur together, as in the macho culture of lower class, young unemployed males when confronting the demands for equality for women, often in poorly paid yet steady employment, one would expect a particularly high rate of conflict, often resulting in the preference for setting up home separately and the preponderance of single mothers. Indeed, this latter group has the highest rates of violence against them, usually from ex-partners.[22]

Left realists are also criticized for not explaining crimes of the powerful, such as corporate crime, white-collar crime, and political crime (Henry, 1999). In its current form, left realist theory cannot do so because it is restricted to interpersonal relations between economically and socially disenfranchised individuals (Pearce & Tombs, 1992). This is not to say, however, that left realists only advance what Henry (1999:138-139) refers to as a "narrow, common-sense concept of crime" that excludes "hidden victims of the structurally powerful." If this is the case, then why do left realists John Lea and Jock Young (1984) contend that working-class people are victimized from all directions and that a "double thrust" against both street crime and "suite crime" is necessary? Further, left realism "notes that the more vulnerable a person is economically and socially the more likely it is that both working class and white collar crime will occur against them; that one sort of crime tends to compound another as does one social problem another" (Young, 1986:23-24).

Although some criminologists (e.g., Gottfredson & Hirschi, 1990) have tried, to the best of our knowledge, no one has developed a theory that can adequately explain *all* types of crime. If this is a major shortcoming, then the theoretical work of many who attack left realists for devoting most of their attention to crimes of the powerless should also be considered flawed. For example, most of the people who criticize left realists for ignoring crimes of the powerful do exactly the opposite: only look at crimes of the structurally powerful but not crimes of the "truly disadvantaged" (Wilson, 1987). This, too, is a one-sided narrow approach, and it inhibits the development of progressive alternative policies aimed at curbing predatory street crime, woman abuse, and other crimes that plague poor inner-city areas.

There are several other criticisms of left realist theory, and because they are well documented elsewhere,[23] they will not be repeated here. Many more new ones are likely to emerge, too, given that left realists are constantly modifying their theoretical contributions in accordance with rapid changes now occurring in advanced capitalist societies.

Feminist Theories[24]

Many critical criminologists, especially those who generated theories of deviance, crime, and social control in the 1970s and early 1980s, relied on Marxist analyses of capitalist society.[25] For the most part, these scholars took a "gender-blind" approach to explaining rule-breaking behaviors and societal reactions to them (Gelsthorpe & Morris, 1988). Of course, this criticism can just as easily be directed against most of the other theories reviewed in this chapter and other sources (DeKeseredy & Schwartz, 1996). One major exception to this tendency is research on woman abuse (see Chapter 3). Feminist contributions are clearly evident in theoretical literature on male-to-female harms. In fact, much of feminist criminology today is still mainly concerned with the victimization of women. However, there is a rapidly growing body of theoretical work on topics such as female gangs, prostitution, and gender inequality in the law and criminal justice system. Before reviewing several feminist theories of deviance and crime, it is first necessary to define feminism.

Feminism is defined here as "a set of theories about women's oppression *and* a set of strategies for change (Daly & Chesney-Lind, 1988:502, emphasis in original). Contrary to popular belief, the goal of feminist criminologists is "not to push men out so as to pull women in, but rather to **gender** the study of crime and criminal justice" (Renzetti, 1993:232). The following five elements of feminist thought distinguish it from theories that misrepresent gender and feminism:

- Gender is not a natural fact but a complex social, historical, and cultural product; it is related to, but not simply derived from, biological sex differences and reproductive capacities.

- Gender and gender relations order social life and social institutions in fundamental ways.

- Gender relations and constructs of masculinity and femininity are not symmetrical but are based on an organizing principle of men's superiority to and social and political dominance over women.

- Systems of knowledge reflect men's view of the natural and social world; the production of knowledge is gendered.

- Women should be at the center of intellectual inquiry, not peripheral, invisible, or appendages to men (Daly & Chesney-Lind, 1988:504).

Further, as briefly described in Chapter 1, feminist scholars attempt to address how the intersection of race, class, and gender shape women's involvement in rule-breaking activities and societal reactions to their appearance or behavior (Miller, 2003; Schwartz & Milovanovic, 1996).

Neither feminism nor criminology is a monolithic enterprise, which is why some scholars assert that a feminist criminology does not exist (Daly & Chesney-Lind, 1988). So, scholars use a variety of feminist theories to explain a variety of crimes and techniques of social control. There are at least eight types of feminist theory (Tong, 1998), each of which takes a distinct approach to understanding gender issues, asks different types of questions, and offers different theories of crime and its control. Nevertheless, the four theories most often discussed in criminological literature are: (1) **liberal feminism**, (2) **Marxist feminism**, (3) **radical feminism**, and (4) **socialist feminism**. These perspectives are briefly described by Daly and Chesney-Lind (1988:537-538) in Box 2.4.

Box 2.4
Four Types of Feminist Theory

Liberal Feminist

Causes of gender inequality: Not stated explicitly, but assumed to stem from societal inhibitions on women's full exposure to and participation in intellectual inquiry (reading and writing), physical education (competitive sports and physical fitness), and other activities in the public sphere.

Process of gender formation: Socialization into gender roles; psychological theories such as social learning, cognitive development, or schema used.

Strategies for social change: Removal of all obstacles to women's access to education, paid employment, political activity, and other public social institutions; enabling women to participate equally with men in the public sphere; emphasis on legal change.

Key concepts: Socialization, sex (or gender) roles, equal opportunity, equal treatment of men and women, equal rights.

Marxist Feminist

Causes of gender inequality: Derived from hierarchical relations of control with the rise of private property and its inheritance by men. Class relations are primary; gender relations, secondary.

Process of gender formation: Not stated explicitly in early works, but implicitly in a master-slave relationship applied to husband and wife. Some twentieth-century arguments draw from psychoanalytic theories.

Box 2.4, *continued*

> *Strategies for social change*: In the transformation from a capitalist to a demo-cratic socialist society, bringing women fully into economic production, socializing housework and child care, abolition of marriage and sexual relations founded on notions of private property, eradication of working-class economic subordination.
>
> *Key concepts*: Capitalist oppression and working-class resistance, women as a "sex class" or a reserve army of labor for capital, husbands' exploitation of wives' labor.

Radical Feminist

> *Causes of gender inequality*: Needs or desires of men to control women's sexual-ity and reproductive potential. Patriarchy—a set of social relations in which individual men and men as a group control—predating the rise of private property; "ownership" of women the precursor to ownership of territory. Some arguments assume a biological basis for men's needs or desires to control women.
>
> *Process of gender formation*: Power relations between men and women structure socialization processes in which boys and men view themselves as superior to and as having a right to control girls and women. Gender power relations amplified and rein-forced by heterosexual sexuality (male-defined). Psychological and psychoanalytic the-ories used.
>
> *Strategies for social change*: Overthrowing patriarchal relations, devising meth-ods of biological reproduction to permit women's sexual autonomy, creating women-centered social institutions (and women-only organizations). In strategies for change, dealing explicitly with the oppressive nature of sexual and familial relations for women and with their link to relations in the public sphere. Eradication of women's social subordination without obliterating gender difference. A new offshoot of radi-cal feminism (or perhaps an amalgam of liberal and radical feminism)—cultural fem-inism—celebrates gender differences, especially women's special capacities or talents, but does not situate gender differences in the framework of power differences.
>
> *Key Concepts*: Patriarchy, women's oppression, men's control of women's bodies and minds, heterosexism.

Socialist Feminism

> *Causes of Gender Inequality*: Flexible combination of radical and Marxist feminist cat-egories, i.e., universal male domination and historically specific political-economic rela-tions, respectively. Focus on gender, class, and racial relations of domination, in which sexuality (including reproduction) and labor (paid and unpaid) are linked. Differs from Marxist feminism in that both class and gender relations are viewed as primary.
>
> *Process of gender formation*: Similar to radical feminism, but with greater empha-sis on making psychological or psychoanalytical arguments historically and cultur-ally specific and on analyzing women's agency and resistance.
>
> *Strategies for social change*: Amalgam of Marxist and radical feminist strategies; simultaneous focus on transforming patriarchal and capitalist class relations (includes similar relations in self-defined socialist or communist societies).
>
> *Key Concepts*: Capitalist patriarchy, women's subordination and resistance to men; men's exploitation and control of women's labor and sexuality.

Source: Daly, K. & M. Chesney-Lind (1988). "Feminism and Criminology." *Justice Quarterly*, 5, 497-538. Reprinted with permission.

Feminist theorists, then, offer an alternative way of thinking (Vold, Bernard & Snipes, 1998). Consider Chesney-Lind and Pasko's (2004:28) theory. Below, they describe a perspective that focuses on how poverty, unemployment, and family violence propel girls into property crimes, prostitution, and drugs:

> Young women, a large number of whom are on the run from sexual abuse and parental neglect, are forced by the very statutes designed to protect them into the lives of escaped convicts. Unable to enroll in school or to take a job to support themselves because they fear detection, young female runaways are forced into the streets. Here they engage in panhandling, petty theft, and occasional prostitution to survive. Young women in conflict with their parents (often for legitimate reasons) may actually be forced by present laws into petty criminal activity, prostitution and drug use.

There, are of course, other feminist theories of deviance, crime, and social control, and they are described in subsequent chapters of this book. Again, it should also be noted that some theories reviewed earlier in this chapter, such as those developed by Adler (1975), Simon (1975), and Hagan, Gillis, and Simpson (1987), are considered by several criminologists to be liberal feminist perspectives.

Evaluation of Feminist Theories

Feminist theories have made many important contributions to the study of problems discussed throughout this text. Further, feminist theorists and researchers alike have had a major impact on criminal justice policy (Lilly, Cullen & Ball, 2002). Consider that, due in large part to the efforts of feminist scholars, police departments and other agents of social control are no longer simply ignoring the plight of battered and sexually abused women. Still, because feminist criminological work challenges conservative "male-centered" ways of understanding deviance, crime, and social control, it is constantly challenged and often ridiculed by conservative students, practitioners, and academics "who incorrectly reduce" feminists' criticisms of gender-blind theories and research to "an attack on the sex of the researcher" (Flavin, 2004:36). Another common conservative attack on feminist scholarship is that it offers little more than single-factor explanations driven by a political agenda instead of "value-free" scientific thought (Fekete, 1994).

As Miller (2003), among many others, points out, these are not legitimate criticisms. After all, social scientific methods, theories, and policies in general are not value-free (DeKeseredy, 1996b; Harding,

1987). Further, although *some* feminists claim that patriarchy is the direct source of women's victimization or offending, the bulk of the recent feminist literature on women's experiences with crime does not view patriarchy as the only determinant. In fact, many feminists are among the most critical of single-factor explanations of female victimization or rule-breaking.[26]

Feminist theoretical work on crime has also been critiqued by feminists and other critical scholars. In fact, as Miller (2003:22) reminds us, "some of the most important critiques of feminist criminology have come from debates *among* feminists. . . ." (emphasis in original). For example, the influence of class and race/ethnicity has not received the attention it deserves, given that the experiences of poor females and women of color are often distinct from women who are economically privileged or of European descent. Consider women living in public housing. They report rates of male violence that are much higher than those uncovered by surveys of the general population (DeKeseredy, Alvi, Renzetti & Schwartz, 2004).

Another criticism offered by some feminist criminologists is that much of feminist criminology "focuses narrowly" on women's victimization (Miller, 2003), which gives "the false impression that women have only been victims, they have never successfully fought back, that women cannot be effective social agents on behalf of themselves or others" (Harding, 1987:5) These and other feminist critiques are being addressed and, as described in other sections of this book, feminists have developed and are developing perspectives that take into account many factors that propel women into crime and that spawn their victimization. For example, as stated in Chapter 3, DeKeseredy and Schwartz's (2002) theory of woman abuse in public housing integrates insights from male peer support theory with feminist perspectives on male-to-female victimization and theoretical work on how broader economic changes shape crime in centers of concentrated urban disadvantage.

Masculinities Theories[27]

Feminist theories have been fundamental to the development of **masculinities theories** of crime (Gardiner, 2005; Messerschmidt, 2005). Like feminist scholars, masculinities theorists put gender at the forefront of their analyses and contend that for many men, crime or deviance is the only perceived available technique of expressing and validating their masculinity. Consider youth gang violence, a topic to be addressed in greater detail in Chapter 7. This behavior is a serious threat to many poor communities and is committed primarily by groups of young men. Still, most boys do not belong to violent gangs. Those who do are socially and economically marginalized youths who experience status frustration caused by their inability to accomplish masculinity at school through academic achievement, participation in sports, and involvement in extracurricular activities (Cohen, 1955; Messerschmidt, 1993).

This problem plagues both whites and minorities. As Cohen (1955) pointed out decades ago, some youths try to deal with this problem by seeking extra help from teachers, while others quit school and come into contact with other "dropouts" who share their frustration. A subculture soon emerges that grants members status based on accomplishing gender identification through violence and other illegitimate means. However, some dropouts avoid gang participation because they construct their masculinity through such behaviors as legitimately working.

Still, for many young men living in inner-city or rural communities damaged by deindustrialization, the frustration spawned by the inability to accomplish masculinity in the school setting is exacerbated by their failure to find a steady, well-paying job, which is another important theme that emerges from the extant literature on masculinities and gangs. These men are hit with a "double whammy" that puts them at even greater risk of teaming up with others to create a subculture that promotes, expresses, and validates masculinity through violent means (Hagedorn, 1988; Messerschmidt, 1993). In communities damaged by deindustrialization, there is also "a greater proportion of peer groups that subscribe to violent macho ideals" (Schwendinger & Schwendinger, 1983:205).

Then there are young men who are hit with a "triple whammy" (DeKeseredy & Schwartz, 2005). They are not only failures in school and unable to find a job, but also people of color who face institutional racism on a daily basis (Perkins, 1987; Shelden, Tracy & Brown, 2001), especially if they live in public housing complexes. An example of how public housing contributes to social and economic exclusion is provided below by a Chicago-based employer interviewed by William Julius Wilson (1996:116). The man felt that people who lived in public housing would jeopardize his financial status:

> I necessarily can't tell from looking at an address whether someone's from Cabrini Green or not, but if I could tell, I don't think that I'd want to hire them. Because it reflects on your credibility. If you came here with this survey, and you were from one of those neighborhoods, I don't know if I'd want to answer your questions. I'd wonder about your credibility.

In sum, then, many inner-city African-American young men are denied masculine status in three ways: through the inability to succeed in school, a lack of meaningful jobs, and the racism and stereotypes of their neighborhoods (DeKeseredy & Schwartz, 2005). Many Hispanic and Asian young men experience similar problems. Thus, it is not surprising that members of these socially marginalized ethnic groups compose most of the street gangs in the United States (Klein, 2002). Nevertheless, it cannot be emphasized enough that social factors—not skin color or biological makeup—contribute to a higher concentration of these people in violent youth gangs. These are young men who are most likely to go to schools that lack adequate financial and human resources, who live in neighborhoods plagued by concentrated urban poverty, and who are unable to find jobs in a society brutalized by major structural transformations, such as the shift from a manufacturing to a service-based economy (DeKeseredy, Alvi, Schwartz & Tomaszewski, 2003; Kazemipur & Halli, 2000; Wilson, 1996; Zielenbach, 2000).

In a section dedicated to briefly surveying the theoretical literature on masculinities, it is only possible to go into depth in one area of men's crime. There many more areas in which masculinities play a role in facilitating men's violations of criminal law.[28] In fact, there are various forms of masculinities (Connell, 1995; Hatty, 2000), which helps explain the wide range of responses to contemporary crises facing men.

Among these other arenas is hate crime. Following Connell (1987), Perry (2003b) argues that a great deal of racist and homophobic violence (e.g., "gay bashing") can be traced to the desire of white men to assert their superiority and dominance as well as to their desire to "prove the very essence of their masculinity: heterosexuality" (p. 158). She asserts that many men do not view such violence as breaking a cultural norm (on violence) as much as affirming a "culturally approved hegemonic masculinity: aggression, domination, and heterosexuality" (p. 158). Of course, men engage in masculinist discourse to justify and allow their own violence in many areas (DeKeseredy & Schwartz, 2005).

Evaluation of Masculinities Theories[29]

Many theories attempt to identify which offender characteristics best predict criminal conduct, but the single best determinant of who commits beatings, homicide, bank robberies, rapes, and so on is whether the offender is male (Schwartz & Hatty, 2003). Why are most offenders men? As argued by masculinities theorists (e.g., Polk, 2003), it has little to do with their biological makeup or with factors identified by evolutionary psychologists (e.g., Daly & Wilson, 1988).[30] Clearly, as masculinities theorists remind us, for many men, crime is, under certain situations, the only perceived available technique of expressing and validating masculinity.

However, masculinities theories developed so far have several key limitations. For example, the theory of gang violence described here, like other perspectives on the connection between masculinities and crime, requires more in-depth analyses of complex factors related to race/ethnicity (DeKeseredy & Schwartz, 2005). Related to this shortcoming is that, to the best of our knowledge, not one systematic study on how masculinities contribute to date rape in the African-American community has been conducted.[31] Similarly, Messerschmidt (1997:17) appears to be the only criminologist guided by the work of masculinities theorists who examined "the historical and/or contemporary construction of varieties of whiteness and their relation to crime."[32]

Additional criticisms and suggestions for new directions in theoretical work could easily be suggested here and will be in the near future, because there is a growing interest in the relationship between masculinities and crime as demonstrated by a series of important books published since the early 1990s. Even so, "masculinities are not the whole story" about crime. Obviously, there are many other sources of crime and deviance covered in this chapter and elsewhere. Nevertheless, these social problems and attempts to curb them cannot adequately be understood without an in-depth understanding of masculinities (DeKeseredy & Schwartz, 2005; Messerschmidt, 2005).

Summary

In this chapter, we described and evaluated major sociological perspectives on deviance and crime that fall under these headings: strain, social control, interactionist, ecological, and critical. We could have easily reviewed more theories, but again, our intent was to cover the most widely read and cited accounts. Some theories excluded from this chapter are covered in subsequent ones because they are directly relevant to topics such as woman abuse, corporate crime, and drugs. Further, we identify whether they are variants of strain, social control, or other perspectives covered here.

Hopefully, now, you will have some appreciation for the variety of ways in which people can answer the question, "Why did Martha Stewart engage in insider trading?" Indeed, as Downes and Rock (2003:2-3) remind us:

> [T]he sociology of crime and deviance contains not one vision but many. It is a collection of different and rather independent theories. Each theory has its own history; it tends to be supported by a long train of arguments that reach into the foundational ideas of philosophy and politics; it discloses a number of distinct opportunities for explaining and manipulating crime and deviant behavior; and, in the main, its assertions will be put in such a discrete language that they resist immediate comparison with rival arguments.

What is to be done about the "lack of unison" described in this chapter and elsewhere (Downes & Rock, 2003)? Well, it is not likely to be minimized or overcome in the near future. Nevertheless, we are currently seeing a growing number of sociologists who contend that the study of deviance and crime should be interdisciplinary in nature. Consider criminologist Gregg Barak (1998), who has attempted to combine the knowledge provided by biology, psychology, sociology, law, and economics with the interdisciplinary studies of mass media, public policy, culture, gender, and ethnicity.

It is beyond the scope of this chapter to describe fully an interdisciplinary theoretical approach to explaining or studying one or more types of deviance or crime. In fact, we could write an entire book on this topic. Still, it is important to note that there are sociologists who appreciate the strengths of different "knowledges" within their own discipline and we are starting to see rapid growth in the number of integrated theories of crime, deviance, and social control (e.g., Barak, 1998; Messner, Krohn & Liska, 1990). For example, to explain separation/divorce sexual assault (an issue to be addressed in Chapter 3), DeKeseredy, Rogness, and Schwartz (2004) created a feminist/male peer support model that brings together several bodies of knowledge. In subsequent chapters, we will describe and evaluate integrated theories like this one and make explicit the schools of thought that influenced them.

Notes

[1]   The list of points included in this box is informed by summaries provided by DeKeseredy and Schwartz (1996); Taylor, Walton, and Young (1973); Vold, Bernard, and Snipes (1998); and Williams and McShane (1994).

[2]   Movie fans can find examples of the criminal subculture in popular films such as *Goodfellas*, *A Bronx Tale*, and *Once Upon a Time in America*.

[3]   Of course, not all of those whom Cloward and Ohlin refer to as "double failures" become drunks or drug addicts, but they are more likely to end up this way than other lower-class youths. Becoming an addict depends heavily on the presence of older drug users who can teach youths how to use and acquire drugs.

[4]   See Lilly, Cullen, and Ball (2002) for studies that tested Agnew's theory.

[5]   This section includes modified sections of work published previously by DeKeseredy (2000a).

[6]   See Chesney-Lind and Pasko (2004) and DeKeseredy (2000a) for more in-depth critiques of these perspectives.

[7]   This section includes modified sections of work published previously by DeKeseredy (2000a).

[8]   Box 2.3 is a modified version of a section of work published previously by DeKeseredy and Schwartz (1996).

[9]   See his books *De Cive* (1642) and *Leviathan* (1651).

[10]   See Curran and Renzetti (2001) for a review of studies that support and refute Hirschi's theory.

[11]   This section includes revised sections of work published previously by DeKeseredy, Alvi, Schwartz, and Tomaszewski (2003).

[12]   Following Curran and Renzetti (2001:174), master status is defined here as "a status that takes precedence over all other statuses or characteristics of the individual."

[13]   See Curran and Renzetti (2001) for a review of studies that tested differential association theory.

[14]   This section includes revised sections of work published previously by DeKeseredy, Alvi, Schwartz, and Tomaszewski (2003).

[15]   Neighborhood structural density is a function of the amount of apartments and other multi-family residences (Figlio, Hakim & Rengert, 1986; Sampson, 1986).

[16]   Informed by Hunter (1974, 1985), Bursik and Grasmick (1993a) argued that population instability and heterogeneity influenced the rate of neighborhood crime through these types of social control.

[17]   See Engels's (1963) eulogy delivered at Marx's funeral.

[18]   See, for example, Taylor, Walton, and Young (1973).

[19]   In this connection, Marx (1844/1963:181) argues, "In direct contrast to German (Hegelian) philosophy which descends from heaven to earth, here we ascend from earth to heaven. That is to say, we do not set out from what men imagine, conceive, nor from men as narrated, thought of, or imagined, conceived, in order to arrive at men in the flesh. We set out from real, active men and on the basis of their real life (labor) process, we demonstrate the development of the ideological reflexes and echoes of this life process."

[20]   On page 53 of *The Communist Manifesto* (1872/1959), Marx notes, "But not only has the bourgeoisie forged the weapons that bring death to itself; it has also called into the existence the men who are to wield those weapons, the working class."

[21]   This section includes sections of work published previously by DeKeseredy (2003).

[22]   As described in Chapter 3, some theories of woman abuse include similar arguments.

[23]   For more detailed critiques of left realism, see DeKeseredy (1996a); Henry (1999); Matthews and Young (1992); Michalowski (1991); Ruggiero (1992); Schwartz and DeKeseredy (1991); Sim, Scraton, and Gordon (1987); and Taylor (1992).

[24]   Parts of this section include revised versions of material published previously by DeKeseredy (2000a).

[25]   Major examples of widely read and cited critical theories that ignored gender during this time period are those offered by Chambliss (1975), Gordon (1971), Greenberg (1983), and Taylor, Walton, and Young (1973).

[26]   For example, see Messerschmidt (1993), Miller (1994), and Renzetti (1994).

[27]   This section includes modified sections of work published previously by DeKeseredy and Schwartz (2005).

[28]   See DeKeseredy and Schwartz (2005) and Messerschmidt (2005) for more in-depth reviews of the extant literature on masculinities and crime.

[29]   Parts of this section include revised sections of work published previously by DeKeseredy and Schwartz (2005).

[30]   Evolutionary psychologists claim that male violence is the result of competition for sexual access to women. Yet, men kill not only men, but also women. See Kimmel (2000) and Polk (2003) for more criticisms of the evolutionary theory of male violence.

[31]   At the time of writing this chapter, however, there was a recent study of dating violence, including sexual assault, among African-American youths (West & Rose, 2000). Further, some researchers (e.g., Bell & Mattis, 2000) have examined the linkage between African-American manhood and violence against women.

[32]   In Chapter 1 of his book titled *Crime as Structured Action: Gender, Race, Class and Crime in the Making*, he argues that "during reconstruction and its immediate aftermath, lynching was a response to the perceived erosion of white male dominance and was an attempt to recreate what white supremacist men imagined to be a lost status of unchallenged white masculine supremacy" (1997:16).

Discussion Questions

1. What is a theory, and what is the practical value of theory?

2. What is the value of the sociological imagination?

3. What is the difference between Merton's anomie theory and Cohen's perspective on delinquent boys?

4. Identify the ways in which contemporary social control theories were influenced by the writings of Thomas Hobbes.

5. What is the difference between liberal and radical feminism?

6. What are some of the limitations of masculinities theories?

7. In your opinion, which theory examined in this chapter best explains Martha Stewart's criminal behavior?

Problem-Solving Scenarios

1. Generate a group discussion on the practical value of developing a theory of violent youth gang activities.

2. When you watch television or read the newspapers over the next week, keep a record of stories that include elements of the theoretical work described in this chapter.

3. Identify one or more of the theories reviewed here that best explain your own involvement in deviant or criminal activities.

4. In a group, apply a theory that you and your peers feel best explains a recent major criminal event that occurred in your community.

5. Get together with several students and try to develop a theory of drug use that includes elements of at least three different theories described in this chapter.

Suggested Readings

Barak, G. (1998). *Integrating Criminologies*. Boston: Allyn & Bacon.

> This is, as the author points out, a "nontraditional criminology textbook." It is one of the few texts specifically designed to facilitate an integrative, interdisciplinary theoretical understanding of crime, deviance, and social control.

Downes, D. & P. Rock (2003). *Understanding Deviance: A Guide to the Sociology of Crime and Rule-breaking,* 4th ed. Oxford, NY: Oxford University Press.

> The authors offer an excellent and fair guide to the major sociological theories of deviance and crime. Unlike most U.S. theory texts, this book devotes a considerable amount of attention to *both* North American and British contributions.

Lilly, R.J., F.T. Cullen & R.A. Ball (2002). *Criminological Theory: Context and Consequences,* 3rd ed. Thousand Oaks, CA: Sage.

> This book provides one of the most in-depth overviews of criminological theories and devotes considerable attention to their practical applications.

Rubington, E. & M.S. Weinberg (eds.) (2005). *Deviance: The Interactionist Perspective,* 9th ed. Boston: Allyn & Bacon.

> This book is perhaps the most widely read collection of essays on the interactionist approach to the study of deviance, crime, and social control.

Schwartz, M.D. & S.E. Hatty (eds.) (2003). *Controversies in Critical Criminology.* Cincinnati: Anderson.

> Composed of original essays, this book provides students and faculty alike with a highly intelligible introduction to major critical criminological schools of thought, including left realist, feminist, and masculinities theories.

Taylor, I., P. Walton & J. Young (1973). *The New Criminology.* London: Routledge & Kegan Paul.

> Considered by most critical criminologists to be a classic, this book offers an in-depth appraisal of a wide range of sociological theories of deviance and crime from a Marxist perspective.

Online Resources

1. **Crim Theory: Criminology Theory Links on the Web**
   http://www.criminology.fsu.edu/crimtheory/theorylinks.htm
   This site includes links to many important sites on theories of deviance, crime, and social control. It also includes links to sites on specific crime and deviance theorists created by Florida State University students.

2. **CrimeTheory.com**
   http://www.crimetheory.com/
   Created by Ohio University sociologist Bruce Hoffman, this site is an excellent teaching and learning resource for students and faculty interested in theories of deviance, crime, and social control.

3. **Crime and Deviance**
   http://www.hewett.norfolk.sch.uk/curric/soc/crime/crim.htm
   Developed and maintained by the Hewett School's Department of Sociology, this site is especially useful for students and others seeking highly intelligible introductions to theoretical work done on deviance and crime in both North America and the United Kingdom. The Crime and Deviance Theory Map located at this site is a very useful guide to many of the theories examined in this chapter.

And I mean the one night he'd come
home and pull a double barrel and cock
both barrels and said he was going to
kill me. And it was like, wait a minute
here, you know, it was two o'clock in
the morning. I was sound asleep and I
got up at four and go to work. But he'd
always keep pressuring me, "If you leave
me, I'll find you. I'll kill you. If you
leave me, I'll find you, I'll kill you."

CHAPTER 3
WOMAN ABUSE

While beginning to write this chapter in October 2004, many, if not most, U.S. citizens publicly expressed their well-founded fear of experiencing another large-scale terrorist attack. Note, too, that at that time, a federal election was about to take place and both Democrats and Republicans were claiming that their respective leaders (John Kerry and George W. Bush) were the ones who could best prevent another event like that which occurred on September 11, 2001, from ever happening again. Relatively little attention, however, was devoted to the ongoing harms done to women like the one quoted at the beginning of this chapter. Interviewed by Walter DeKeseredy in rural Ohio, she and many U.S. females routinely experience another major variant of terrorism—"patriarchal terrorism" (Johnson, 1995). Yet, to the best of our knowledge, none of the presidential candidates presented an in-depth plan to lower the alarmingly high rates of abuse inflicted on women by their current or former male partners.[1] Further, none of the journalists who moderated the three televised presidential debates held during the month of October 2004 asked John Kerry and President Bush what they intended to do to help reduce the extent of wife beating, rape, and other terrifying examples of "not the way to love" (Fitzpatrick & Halliday, 1992).

In September of 2004, the *Las Vegas Sun* ran a story about a woman who was killed by her estranged husband directly in front of police officers. The police report of the incident indicated that while officers had a driver pulled over for a traffic violation, they heard a car honking and its driver screaming. Then they witnessed the front-seat passenger, later identified as the driver's ex-husband, Carlos Ortiz, grab the woman's hair, pull her head toward his lap, raise a gun, and shoot her. The woman, Maria Ortiz, was pronounced dead at the scene. The couple's daughter was in the back seat of the car during the killing.

Maria Ortiz had obtained a restraining order against her estranged husband in the month prior. The couple had a history of custody and child support battles, and in July 2001, Carlos Ortiz had been arrested for allegedly punching Maria Ortiz and threatening her with a gun. He also had a record of other domestic violence charges (Lawson, 2004).

How many more times do we have to read stories about lethal terrorism like this before politicians and the rest of society decide to declare a "war on woman abuse"?

Data presented in this chapter show that "deadly deeds"[2] such as the one described in Box 3.1 are far more common than attacks from groups led by people like Osama bin Ladin. Note, too, that U.S. citizens' intense fear of attacks by strangers on the streets is highly exaggerated. Small proportions of them are robbed, mugged, or killed by unknown predatory offenders, and their pain and suffering should not be trivialized, but what sociologists Richard Gelles and Murray Straus (1998:18) stated close to 20 years ago still holds true today: women "are more likely to be physically assaulted, beaten, and killed . . . at the hands of a loved one than anyplace else, or by anyone in society."

Many people find this hard to believe because they were socialized to view intimate heterosexual relationships as sources of love and safe refuges from the pains inflicted by the outside world (DeKeseredy, 2005; Duffy & Momirov, 1997). Others do not see woman abuse as a social problem because they have never indirectly or directly experienced it. Unfortunately, few male-female relationships are conflict-free, and many are plagued by harms that few of us can imagine. A key objective of this chapter is to describe the extent and distribution of various types of woman abuse in intimate heterosexual relationships. Widely read and cited theories will also be reviewed, but it is first necessary to define woman abuse.

What is Woman Abuse?[3]

A review of the extant social scientific literature on male-to-female assaults in relationships such as marriage/cohabitation and dating reveals considerable disagreement about what injurious acts should be included in a definition of woman abuse. For example, many North American researchers, policymakers, journalists, and members of the general public focus only on murder, physical attacks (e.g., beatings and kicks), or sexual assaults involving forced penetration. Psychological, verbal, spiritual, and economic abuse are deleted from their formulations because grouping these assaults with physically injurious behaviors is seen as muddying "the water so much that it might be impossible to determine what causes abuse" (Gelles & Cornell, 1985:23).

Others oppose broad definitions for different reasons. Consider Fekete (1994:60), who asserts that the Canadian national survey on woman abuse in dating (CNS),[4] a large-scale study that used a broad definition of woman abuse, was ideologically driven and specifically designed to show "that different heterosexual interactions are all variants of the same tree." Similarly, Gilbert (1994) argues that path-breaking U.S. sexual assault surveys done by Koss, Gidycz, and Wisniewski (1987) and by Russell (1982, 1984) are guilty of "definitional stretching," artificially inflating the rates of sexual abuse that do not coincide with "reasonable" women's attitudes and experiences.

On the other hand, like us, a growing number of researchers and government agencies contend that woman abuse is multidimensional in nature and that definitions, theories, and research should recognize that many women's lives rest on a "continuum of unsafety" (Stanko, 1990). Indeed, psychological or emotional abuse can be more painful than physical and sexual violence, and some women simultaneously experience different types of abuse. For example, in January 2004, Walter DeKeseredy was in the process of conducting an exploratory study of separation/divorce sexual assault in rural Ohio.[5] Of the 20 women interviewed at that time, only 20 percent experienced just one type of nonsexual abuse (e.g., physical, economic, psychological, etc.) (DeKeseredy & Joseph, in press). Mary is one of DeKeseredy's respondents; below is an account of what happened to her during the process of leaving her violent male partner:

> He had taken my car for about a day and I was, you know, by the time he finally returned it and everything, I was taking him back home, back to his mom's house and he tried to wreck the car. It was snowing; real bad weather and he tried to wreck the car and everything. I got angry with him and I think I slapped him. He said something and I said, "It is over. It is completely over." You know and he just, he just started punching me in the face and just clawing my face and punching my face and everything.

Box 3.1
Examples of Psychological Abuse

Yelling

Insulting the partner

Swearing at one's partner or calling him or her names

Belittling or ridiculing the partner; insulting the partner

Belittling or berating one's partner in front of other people

Putting down the partner's physical appearance or intellect

Saying things to upset or frighten one's partner; acting indifferently to one's partner's feelings

Making one's partner do humiliating or demeaning things

Demanding obedience to whims

Ordering the partner around/treating him or her like a servant

Becoming angry when chores are not done when wanted or as wanted

Acting jealous and suspicious of the partner's friends and social contacts

Putting down one's partner's friends and/or family

Monitoring the partner's time and whereabouts

Monitoring one's partner's telephone calls or e-mail contact

Stomping out of a room during an argument or heated discussion

Sulking and refusing to talk about an issue

Making decisions that affect both people or the family without consulting one's partner or without reaching agreement with one's partner

Withholding affection

Threatening to leave the relationship

Doing something to spite one's partner

Withholding resources such as money

Refusing to share in housework or childcare

Restricting the partner's usage of the telephone and/or car

Not allowing one's partner to leave the home alone

Telling one's partner his or her feelings are irrational or crazy

Turning other people against one's partner

Blaming the partner for one's problems and/or one's violent behavior

Preventing the partner from working or attending school

Preventing the partner from socializing with friends and/or seeing his or her family

Preventing the partner from seeking medical care or other types of help

Throwing objects (but not at the partner)

Hitting or kicking a wall, furniture, doors, etc.

Shaking a finger or fist at one's partner

Making threatening gestures or faces

Threatening to destroy or destroying personal property belonging to one's partner

Threatening to use physical or sexual aggression against one's partner

Driving dangerously while one's partner is in the car as a conscious intentional act to scare or intimidate

Using the partner's children to threaten them (e.g., threatening to kidnap)

Threatening violence against the partner's children, family, friends, or pets

Source: Mouradian, V.E. (2004). *Abuse in Intimate Relationships: Defining the Multiple Dimensions and Terms* [Online]. Available: www.vawprevention.org/research/defining/sthml

Consider, also, the voice of an abused Canadian woman interviewed by MacLeod (1987:12). She experienced some of the psychologically abusive behaviors listed in Box 3.1:

> The thing that's most hurting for me is the way he makes me feel so dirty, so filthy. He treats me like a dog, worse even. He tells me I'm ugly and worthless. He spits on me. It's not enough to hit me and kick me. He spits on me. Sometimes I think the hitting is better than being made to feel so low.

Broad definitions of woman abuse are necessary not only because they address the fact that women experience a wide range of highly injurious assaults, but also because they seriously affect how data survey data are gathered and the quality and quantity of social support services for women abused in intimate heterosexual relationships. For example, most North American crime surveys, especially those done by government agencies, such as the U.S. Justice Department and the Centers for Disease Control and Prevention, define sexual and physical violence in narrow legalistic terms. Consider the U.S. national Violence Against Women Survey (VAWS). This study used a narrow definition of sexual assault restricted to what VAWS researchers define as "rape," and thus excluded a broad range of harmful experiences experienced by many women. Note their five questions listed below[6] (Tjaden & Thoennes, 2000:6):

- Has a man or boy ever made you have sex by using force or threatening to harm you or someone close to you? Just so there is no mistake, by sex we mean putting his penis in your vagina.

- Has anyone, male or female, ever made you have oral sex by using force or threat of force? Just so there is no mistake, by oral sex we mean that a man or boy put his penis in your mouth or someone, male or female, penetrated your vagina or anus with their mouth.

- Has anyone ever made you have anal sex by using force or threat of force? Just so there is no mistake, by anal sex we mean that a man or boy put his penis in your anus.

- Has anyone, male or female, ever put fingers or objects in your vagina or anus against your will or by using force or threats?

- Has anyone, male or female, ever *attempted* to make you have vaginal, oral, or anal sex against your will but intercourse or penetration did not occur (emphasis in original)?

Respondents who answered "yes" to these questions were then asked whether their perpetrator was a current or ex-marital partner, a male or female live-in partner, a relative, "someone else they knew," or a stranger. Note that the incidence (percentage of women who stated that they were victims in the past year) and prevalence (percentage of women who were victimized in their lifetime) rates of intimate partner rape generated by these questions are very low (0.2 and 7.7%, respectively) compared to those uncovered by other sexual assault studies such as the CNS. Recall from reading Chapter 1 that CNS researchers found that annually 28 percent of Canadian women experience one or more types of sexual assault in college dating relationships (Schwartz & DeKeseredy, 1997).

The VAWS figures are much lower because the behaviorally specific questions used in this study excluded sexual assaults when victims were drunk or high, or when they were unable to give consent (Bachar & Koss, 2001). This is not a minor concern for a sizeable portion of sexual assault survivors. Consider the harm done to a rural Ohio woman while she was under the influence of a potent drug that her ex-partner slipped into her drink:

> I agreed to meet with him to discuss visitation and child support for our daughter and I wanted to go to a public place after everything he had done because it wasn't just sexual, it was mental, physical. And I showed up there. I had a couple friends who were sitting throughout keeping an eye on me. Ordered the drink, got up to use the bathroom, drank my drink and that was pretty much the last thing I remember until the next morning when I woke up with a killer headache and my daughter crying in her crib. That's what woke me up. I looked over. He was in bed next to me. I was actually—I had strangulation marks around my neck. I had marks around my wrists and an open wound on my face and he had obviously had sex. You know a woman can tell that thing. And I, I asked him straight up what happened and he goes, "Ah, well you got drunk." And I said, "How do I get drunk on one drink?" I've been drinking since, you know, you know. I don't make it a normal habit, but one drink is not enough to put someone in that kind of situation (cited in DeKeseredy & Joseph, in press:6-7).

Also excluded from the VAWS are "economic threats" resulting in unwanted sexual relations and "blackmail rapes" that are said to be common in Australia (Russell, 1990). Note the following incident "Mrs. Brown" described to Russell (1990:338). Just because there was no threat or actual use of force does not mean that her experiences were not terrifying, and she clearly labels what her first husband did as rape:

> The worst raping occasion was the morning I awoke in labor
> with my first child. The hospital I was booked into was a
> thirty-minute drive away, and this being the first time I had
> undergone childbirth. I had no idea of how close I was to giv-
> ing birth, or what was to happen to me next. I labored at home
> for a few hours until perhaps 11:00 A.M., and then said to my
> ex-husband that I thought we better go to the hospital. The
> pains were acute and I was panicking that I would not be able
> to bear them. He looked at me, and said, "Oh, all right. But
> we'd better have a screw first, because it'll be a week before
> you're home again." I couldn't believe it, even of him. "Please,
> W., take me to the hospital," I begged as another contraction
> stormed across my body. "Not until we have a screw," he
> insisted. I wept, I cried, I pleaded, but he wouldn't budge. The
> pleading went on until midday, by which time I was frantic
> to get nursing help. He stood adamant with his arms crossed,
> a smirk on his face, and jiggling the car keys as a bribe. In the
> end I submitted. It took two minutes, then we dressed and
> drove to the hospital. The baby was born five hours later.

If the VAWS included behaviors like this, unwanted sex "out of a
sense of obligation" (Bergen, 1996), sexual relations stemming from ex-
partner's threats of fight for sole custody of children, and other acts that
do not involve the use of or threats of force, again, it would have produced a higher rate of sexual assault. The fact that the VAWS was presented to respondents as a "crime study" also contributed to low
sexual assault rates, as well as to an incidence (1.3%) rate of intimate
partner physical assault that is much lower than most of the North
American wife abuse incidence figures presented in Table 3.1. Crime surveys create a set of "demand characteristics" and unless respondents
clearly label acts as criminal in their own mind, they tend not to report
them (Koss, 1996; Schwartz, 2000; Straus, 1998). If people do not think
of an intimate partner's violence as "criminal," they may not report it
in such a survey. In fact, close to 83 percent of marital violence incidents
are not reported in contexts in which the research emphasis is on criminal assault and victimization (Mihalic & Elliot, 1997).

Low rates of physical and sexual violence such as those uncovered
by the VAWS constitute a major problem for at least three reasons. First,
many policymakers only listen to large numbers (DeKeseredy, 1995;
Smith, 1994). Unfortunately, if government officials are led by some
survey researchers using narrow definitions to believe that violence
against women is not a statistically significant issue, they are not
likely to devote sufficient resources to prevent and control one of
North America's most pressing social problems (Jiwani, 2000). Second,
narrow definitions tend to create a "hierarchy of abuse based on seriousness" (Kelly, 1987). Just because the law does not define as abu-

Table 3.1
North American Wife Abuse Surveys

Description of Surveys					Abuse Rates			
Survey	Survey Location & Date	Sample Description	Interview Mode	Measure of Abuse	Abuse Past Year (%)	Severe Abuse Past Year (%)	Abuse Ever (%)	Severe Abuse Ever (%)
Straus et al. (1981)	U.S. National 1975	2,143 married or cohabiting men and women	Face-to-face	CTS (aggregate)[a]	12.1	3.8	–	–
Schulman (1979)	Kentucky 1979	1,793 presently or formerly married and cohabiting men and women	Phone	CTS[b]	10.0	4.1	21.0	8.7
Straus & Gelles (1986)	U.S. National 1985	3,520 presently or formerly married or cohabiting men and women	Phone	CTS (aggregate)	11.3	3.0	–	–
Brinkerhoff & Lupri (1988)	Calgary 1981	526 men and women	Face-to-face and self-administered questionnaire	CTS (men only)[c]	24.5	10.8	–	–
Kennedy & Dutton (1989)	Alberta 1987 women	1,045 men and and women	Face-to-face (aggregate) and phone	CTS	11.2	2.3	–	–
Lupri (1990)	Canada National 1986	1,530 married or cohabiting men and women	Face-to-face and mail questionnaire	CTS (men only)	17.8	10.1	–	–
Smith (1986)	Toronto 1985	315 women aged 18-55	Phone	CTS/open questions and 1 supplementary question	10.8	–	18.1	7.3
Smith (1987)	Toronto 1987	604 presently or formerly married or cohabiting women	Phone	CTS & 3 supplementary questions	14.4[d]	5.1	36.4[e]	11.3
Statistics Canada (1993)	Canada National 1993	12,300 women 18 years of age and older	Phone	CTS[f]	3.0	–	29.0	–

[a] Men-as-aggressors and women-as-victims from different couples.
[b] Women-as-victims.
[c] Men-as-aggressors.
[d] Past year rates based on CTS alone.
[e] Abuse ever rates based on CTS (25.0, 7.8) plus supplementary questions.
[f] Includes a sexual assault item.

sive incident as serious does not mean that legal definitions coincide with women's real-life feelings and experiences. For example, in 33 American states, men who rape their wives are exempt from prosecution in some situations (Bergen, 1996; Rogness, 2003), even though marital rape causes major pain and suffering. In these states, a husband is not prosecuted if his partner is vulnerable or cannot consent because she is psychologically impaired, unconscious, or asleep (Mahoney & Williams, 1998). This can include administering substances that inhibit a woman's ability to resist unwanted sex. Further, in some states, such as Ohio, it is not illegal to rape a spouse with objects other than a penis, such as bottles or gun barrels (Rogness, 2003; Schwartz, 2002).

The second major problem with narrow definitions is that if a survivor's partner's brutal conduct does not coincide with what researchers, criminal justice officials, politicians, or the general public refers to as abuse or violence, she may be left in a "twilight zone" in which she knows that she has been abused but cannot define or categorize it in a way that would help her (Duffy & Momirov, 1997). As stated by one of Walter DeKeseredy's rural Ohio interviewees who was harmed by separation/divorce sexual assault, "I don't sit around and share. I keep it to myself. . . . I'm not one to sit around and talk about what's happened."

Third, narrow definitions exacerbate the problem of underreporting (DeKeseredy, Rogness & Schwartz, 2004; Smith, 1994). As stated before, if people are asked questions based on narrow, legal criteria, researchers will elicit data underestimating the amount of abuse experienced by their respondents (Schwartz, 2000). Consequently, the scientific credibility of an entire survey is "put into jeopardy, for one cannot know if those women who disclosed having been abused are representative of all victims in the sample" (Smith, 1994:110).

For the above reasons, woman abuse is broadly defined here as any intentional physical, sexual, or psychological male assault on current or former intimate female partner. Of course, as stated previously, there are other highly injurious behaviors worthy of attention, such as economic and spiritual abuse. Nevertheless, due in part to space limitations and in part to the shortage of research on these harms, this chapter focuses mainly on physical, sexual, and psychological abuse. Although we present incidence and prevalence rates on each type of abuse, it is important to note that many women simultaneously experience two or more variants of the deviant or criminal acts addressed here. Consider the Canadian case described in Box 3.2. Like many other women who want to leave, are trying to leave, or who have left abusive or extremely possessive marital/cohabiting partners, Ann was physically, psychologically, and sexually abused by a man who was "fanatically determined" not to let her go (Russell, 1990). Fortunately, Ann did not end up becoming a victim of **intimate femicide**, a type of murder addressed in the next section of this chapter.

Box 3.2
An Example of the Multidimensional Nature of Woman Abuse

One of Ann's attempts to leave resulted in her being taken for a ride to a remote nature conservation area, some hours' drive north of Toronto. Rob's stated goal was reconciliation. Ann had gone along with his offer because she took it to be genuine. The ride was not smooth, because Ann did not immediately give in to Rob's reconciliation request. This was quite unlike Ann. Previously she would have readily given in to whatever Rob wanted. Ann was generally obedient, but on that hot and humid summer day, she did not immediately comply. Ann complained and asked Rob to treat her better. For her resistance, Rob's revenge was quite merciless. He stopped the van in the middle of the road, dragged Ann out into the bush, and violently raped her. The brush was sticky, and they were in the middle of the wilderness.

The rape was only the beginning of hours of torture that Rob inflicted on Ann. He ripped off all her clothes, jumped into his van, and started to drive away. Ann chased the van, totally exposed while he drove ahead watching her anguish from the rear-view mirror. Ann ran for seven miles. "It was a marshy area, the road was full of slithery things; he knew that I was deadly afraid of slithery things! I was hysterical." When Ann collapsed from her ordeal of the rape, coupled with her fear of the bush land and heat exhaustion, Rob picked up her nude body, drove back into the city, and dumped her on the front lawn of her parents' home.

Source: Sev'er, A. (2002:99-100). *Fleeing the House of Horrors: Women Who Have Left Abusive Partners.* Toronto: University of Toronto Press.

The Extent and Distribution of Intimate Femicide

The term *femicide* is two centuries old and was first used in John Corry's (1801) book *A Satirical View of London at the Commencement of the Nineteenth Century* to signify "the killing of a woman" (Russell, 2001). There are various types of femicide, but intimate femicide is one of the most common variants. It refers to the murder of women by their current or former male partners. What is the extent of this problem? In the United States, the most recent national U.S. data that answer this question come from Supplementary Homicide Report (SHR) information submitted to the Federal Bureau of Investigation (FBI)[7] and analyzed by the U.S. Bureau of Justice Statistics (2004). Because longitudinal data provide a more stable basis for drawing conclusions, most of the intimate femicide data presented in this section cover more than a single year.

Figure 3.1 presents data on the proportion of all intimate homicides for the years 1976 to 2002. What clearly stands out is that female homicide victims are much more likely than male victims to be killed by an intimate partner. In fact, in recent years, close to one-third of all female victims were killed by an intimate. Still, as described in Figure 3.2, the number of white and black wives/ex-wives killed by intimates has dropped considerably after 1993, which could be attributed in part to improved social services, declining rates of marriage, and increased public awareness about family violence (Browne & Williams, 1993; Dugan, Nagin & Rosenfeld, 1999; Rosenfeld, 2000). Figure 3.2 also shows that the intimate homicide rate for white girlfriends was the same in 2002 as it was in 1976. This, too, could be partially the result of declining rates in marriage.

Figure 3.1
Proportion of all Homicides Involving Intimates by Gender of Victim, 1976-2002

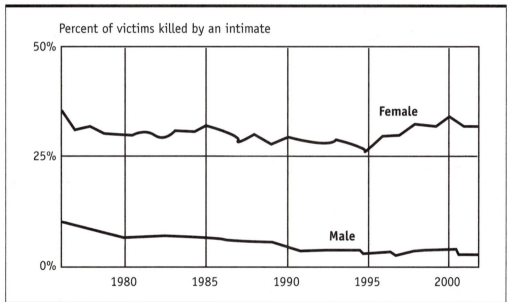

Source: U.S. Bureau of Justice Statistics (2004). *Homicide Trends in the U.S.: Intimate Homicide.* Washington, D.C.: Author, p. 3.

Data presented in Figure 3.2 and Table 3.2 tell us little, if anything, about separation, which is an intimate relationship that poses a major risk to women. In fact, this marital status category is nowhere to be found in the data thus far presented here. This is a major concern, given that in 16 percent of the cases of intimate femicide that occurred in Ontario, Canada, between 1974 and 1994, the victims were separated from their legal spouses (Gartner, Dawson & Crawford, 2001). Furthermore, throughout Canada, Wilson and Daly (1994) found that compared to co-residing couples, separation entails a sixfold increase in homicide risk for women. Some U.S. research also shows that separation is a key risk factor of intimate femicide.[8] Imagine, then, what the graph presented in Figure 3.3 would look like if it included a specific category of women who wanted to separate, tried to separate, or have separated from male partners.

Figure 3.2
Intimate Homicide Rate by Race, Gender, and Relationship, 1976-2002

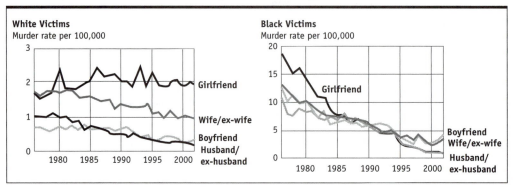

Source: U.S. Bureau of Justice Statistics (2004). *Homicide Trends in the U.S.: Intimate Homicide.* Washington, DC: Author, p. 5.

Table 3.2
Homicides by Relationship and Weapon Type, 1990-2002

Relationship of victim to offender	Total	Gun	Knife	Blunt object	Force	Other weapon
Husband	100%	70%	26%	2%	1%	2%
Ex-husband	100	87	9	1	0	2
Wife	100	68	14	5	9	4
Ex-wife	100	78	12	2	6	2
Boyfriend	100	46	45	3	3	3
Girlfriend	100	57	19	5	14	5

Source: U.S. Bureau of Justice Statistics (2004). *Homicide Trends in the U.S.: Intimate Homicide.* Washington, DC: Author, p. 7.

Not surprisingly, as described in Table 3.2, U.S. victims of intimate femicide are more likely to be killed by guns than by other weapons or by force. Moreover, data presented in Table 3.3 show that women under 18 years of age and who are 60 or older are at the lowest risk of being murdered by intimates, and African-American women are murdered at a rate more than three times higher than white women. Further, in 2002, Alaska had the highest rate of intimate femicide, followed by Louisiana and New Mexico (Victim Policy Center, 2004).

Figure 3.3
Homicides of Intimates by Relationship of Victim to Offender, 1976-2002

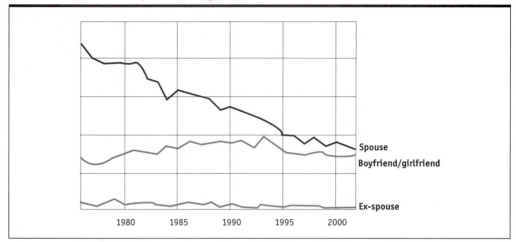

Source: U.S. Bureau of Justice Statistics. (2004). *Homicide Trends in the U.S.: Intimate Homicide*. Washington, DC: Author, p. 4.

Table 3.3
Percent of All Murders by Intimates, 1976-2002

	Male victims	Female victims
Under 18	1%	6%
18-24	2	29
25-29	5	37
30-34	7	41
35-39	8	43
40-44	10	41
45-49	10	40
50-59	10	32
60+	7	20

Source: U.S. Bureau of Justice Statistics. (2004). *Homicide Trends in the U.S.: Intimate Homicide*. Washington, DC: Author, p. 3.

Nonlethal Forms of Woman Abuse in Intimate Heterosexual Relationships

Many women are victimized in nonlethal ways by men within intimate relationships each year. Table 3.1 presents North American survey wife abuse data generated by various renditions of the Conflict Tactics Scale (CTS),[9] which is the most common measure of collecting family violence data. Most of the findings included in this table reveal that annually at least 11 percent of U.S. and Canadian married/cohabiting women are physically abused by male partners. A much higher number of women in these family/household settings experience psychological abuse. For example, a survey of impoverished minority women living in Minnesota found that 64 percent of the respondents experienced psychological abuse in the past year (Alvi, Schwartz, DeKeseredy & Bachaus, 2005).

Although, it receives less empirical and theoretical attention than physical violence in marriage/cohabitation, male-to-female sexual assault in these relationships is also a statistically significant problem in the United States and elsewhere. For example, several studies show that eight to 14 percent of women are victimized by this harm in their lifetime (Finkelhor & Yllo, 1985; Russell, 1990; Tjaden & Thoennes, 2000). Further, many women are at high risk of being sexually assaulted during and after separation/divorce, a harm examined in greater detail later on in this chapter.

Data presented thus far in this section group cohabitants and legally married people into one category. This is problematic because abuse is not spread equally among these groups. For example, Brownridge and Halli's (2001) review of 14 studies (eight done in the United States, five in Canada, and one in New Zealand) reveals "quite dramatic" differences in violence rates obtained from married persons and cohabitants. In fact, they found that typically, the rate of violence for the latter exceeds that of the former by two times, but the difference can be greater than four times. Cohabiting women are also more likely to experience more severe types of violence than their married counterparts. Similarly, cohabiting women are much more likely to be sexually assaulted than married women.

For example, presented in Table 3.4, data generated by Finkelhor and Yllo's (1985) Boston survey show that cohabiting women reported a rate of forced sex that is more than six times higher than the rate for married women. Separated/divorced women reported an even higher rate. Unfortunately, this survey did not include women who did not have children between the ages of six and 14 living with them. If such women participated in the study, chances are that all of the rates of sexual assault presented in Table 3.4 would be higher.

If cohabiting women report higher rates of nonlethal physical and sexual assault than married women, the same can be said about women who want to leave, are in the process of leaving, or who have left their male partners. For example, U.S. researchers Fleury, Sullivan, and Bybee (2000) found that more than one-third (36%, $n = 49$) of the women ($n=135$) who participated in their longitudinal study were physically attacked by a male ex-partner during a two-year period. Further, data generated by the redesigned National Crime Victimization Survey reveal that separated women were assaulted three times more than divorced women and close to 25 times more than married women (Bachman & Saltzman, 1995).

Table 3.4
Rates of Forced Sex in Marriage by Current Marital Status

Marital Status	% Reporting Forced Sex	N
Married	3	224
Separated/divorced	25	76
Cohabiting	20	5
Cohabiting, now separated	23	13
Widowed	14	7
P<.001		

Source: Finkelhor, D. & K. Yllo (1985). *License to Rape: Sexual Abuse of Wives.* New York: Holt, Rinehart and Winston, p. 205.

U.S. data on the incidence and prevalence of separation/divorce sexual assault may not be plentiful, but the limited amount available show that just before, during, and after terminating a relationship with a spouse/cohabitant are risky times. For example:

- Eight percent of the wife rape survivors in Russell's (1990) survey were assaulted after their marriages ended, and 7 percent were raped just before separation.

- Seventeen percent of the divorced women interviewed by Kurz (1995) reported that their ex-husbands forced them to have sex.

- Twenty percent of the 40 wife-rape survivors interviewed by Bergen (1996) were raped after separation/divorce.

- Two-thirds of the women in Finkelhor and Yllo's (1985) interview sample (n=50) were raped in the last days of a relationship, either after previous separations or when they were trying to leave a relationship.

A more recent and much larger study—the VAWS—also examined whether sexual and physical assault is more likely to occur following separation/divorce from either spouses or cohabitants. Unlike most other woman abuse surveys cited here, the VAWS provides more accurate data on the timing of assaults because it asked respondents to report whether their victimization occurred before, after, or both before and after the relationship was terminated. Conducting surveys that simply identify through statistical means that women who are separated from their spouses or cohabiting partners report higher rates of assault does not tell us whether abuse caused estrangement or if abuse started during or after breakups (DeKeseredy, Rogness & Schwartz, 2004). Still the relationship between separation/divorce and assaults identified by other studies is "more than coincidental" (Hardesty, 2002).

Based on their findings, VAWS researchers Tjaden and Thoennes (2000) contend that most physical and sexual assaults of women occur in ongoing rather than terminated relationships. Although surprising, at first glance their data support their claim because only 6.3 percent of the rape victims and 4.2 percent of the physical assault victims stated that their partners' attacks started after they broke up with them. Still, these figures should be viewed with caution because, as Tjaden and Thoennes (2000:38) state:

> It is not possible to ascertain from the data whether violence occurring before the relationship ended was linked to threats about leaving the relationship. It is also unclear whether women who said they were victimized before and after the relationship ended experienced more severe violence at the time of separation. Finally, it is important to note that when a relationship ends is a matter of interpretation rather than objective reality. Some women may have equated the end of the relationship with when they or their partner first started talking about leaving the relationship, whereas others may have equated it with the formal dissolution of a marriage.

The above points are well-taken, given that the preliminary results of a study of separation/divorce sexual assault in rural Ohio show that more than one-half of the women (55%) said that they were attacked when they wanted to leave, which supports Mahoney's (1991) assertion that numerous assaults are actually attacks on separation itself. Scores of men have a "fanatical determination" not to let their spouses or live-in partners go (Russell, 1990). This is also evident during the process of leaving, with 35 percent of the sample reporting that they were victimized at that time. A slightly higher percentage (40%) experienced sexual assaults after they left (DeKeseredy & Joseph, in press). Clearly, more research is needed on the timing of separation/divorce sexual assault and other issues related to this problem.

By now it should be clear that women do not have to be living with men in order to be abused by them. Research on male-female dating relationships also supports this claim. For example, using the CTS, White and Koss's (1991) national U.S. survey of college students found that, since age 14, 37 percent of the men in their sample reported having physically abused a dating partner during the year before the study, while 32 percent of their female respondents reported being victimized during the same time period. Sexual assaults in United State college dating are also common, as demonstrated by what is still considered by many to be the best survey on this topic conducted so far. Administered to a national representative sample consisting of 6,159 students, Koss, Gidycz, and Wisniewski's (1987) survey found that:

- 15 percent of the women reported that their most serious sexual victimization since the age of 14 had been a completed rape, while another 12.1 percent reported that their most serious victimization during the same time period was attempted but uncompleted sexual intercourse.

- In the year before the survey, 207 women had experienced a total of 353 rapes.

- In the year before the survey, 96 different men perpetrated 187 rapes.

Koss and her colleagues are not the only researchers who have uncovered alarmingly high rates of sexual assault in United States college dating relationships.[10] Although different methodologies, definitions, questions, and sampling procedures have produced rather different results, most U.S. research has found incidence and prevalence rates that range between 15 and 25 percent.[11] Not surprisingly, too, the rates of psychological abuse in post-secondary school are even higher, with estimates ranging from 77 to 87 percent in a one-year period (Mahoney, Williams & West, 2001).

Risk Factors

What is to be done about the alarming rates of physical, sexual, and psychological abuse presented in this chapter? Before we and others dedicated to enhancing women's quality of life can answer this question, it is first necessary to identify the key sources or **risk factors** associated with lethal and nonlethal forms of woman abuse (Jasinski, 2001). Risk factors are typically defined in the social scientific woman abuse literature as attributes of a couple, victim, or perpetrator that are associated with an increased probability of male-to-female victimization (Hotaling & Sugarman, 1986). They may be causes, co-occurrences, or consequences of abuse (Smith, 1990a).

Thus far, we pointed out that those who want to leave, are trying to leave, or who have left male partners report higher rates than do married women. So do cohabiting women. Poor, immigrant, and minority women are also at higher risk than members of the general population.[12] Below are some other key risk factors associated with lethal and/or non-lethal variants of woman abuse:

- Alcohol abuse and binge drinking (DeKeseredy & Joseph, in press; Kantor & Jasinski, 1998).

- Men's adherence to the **ideology of familial patriarchy,** which is a discourse that supports the abuse of women who violate the ideals of male power and control over women in intimate relationships (DeKeseredy & Schwartz, 1998a). Relevant themes of this ideology are an insistence on women's obedience, respect, loyalty, dependency, sexual access, and sexual fidelity (Barrett & McIntosh, 1982; Dobash & Dobash, 1979; Pateman, 1988; Smith, 1990b).

- **Male peer support,** which refers to "the attachments to male peers and the resources that these men provide which encourage and legitimate woman abuse" (DeKeseredy, 1990:130).

- Male consumption of pornography (Bergen, 1996; DeKeseredy & Schwartz, 1998a; Russell, 1990).

- Age. Most studies show that young men (age 16 to 24) are the most abusive (Barnett, Miller-Perrin & Perrin, 2005).

Theories of Woman Abuse

Only a few social scientific areas of inquiry have moved so far and so fast as the study of male-to-female victimization. Only 35 years ago, a comprehensive bibliography of North American sources on wife beating would fit on an index card (Schwartz & DeKeseredy, 1988). Today, hundreds of journal articles, scores of books, and several important journals specifically address a variety of forms of woman abuse. We now have rich empirical information and a wide variety of theories on woman abuse in a variety of relationships and social settings, making it clear that living in conditions of tyranny is a dangerous attack on women's psychological as well as physical health (Mattley & Schwartz, 1990).

There are at least 20 theories of woman abuse, and many more are currently being developed and tested. Certainly, we will not review all these contributions here. Instead, we present major arguments of some of the most widely used and cited contemporary theoretical perspectives that fall under the following categories: social learning theories, male peer support theories, feminist theories, routine activities theories, and integrated theories.

Social Learning Theories[13]

As stated in Chapter 2, differential association theory is an interactionist perspective that contributed to the development of social learning theories of crime and deviance. There are various types of social learning theories of woman abuse,[14] but all of them share one common argument: violence and aggression are not properties of the individual; rather, they are **learned behaviors**. The social learning perspective that is most often used to explain woman abuse in intimate relationships is what Levinson (1989) refers to as the **intergenerational transmission theory** (DeKeseredy & MacLeod, 1997). Briefly, proponents of this theory maintain that male children are more likely to grow up to assault female intimates if their parents abused them or if they observed their fathers assaulting their spouses. The case of "Craig," a violent husband, described below is an example of this learning process:

> I was a product of my mother being beaten up. I was also beaten up, whipped with a belt. I thought once that maybe my mother died to get out of that relationship with my father. I mean. I know she died of cancer, but . . . that's the ironic part. I remember wanting to dial the police when they were arguing, to protect her, and yet it's funny how I did the same thing as my father (quoted in Goldstein, 1977:10).

The intergenerational transmission theory has some empirical support[15] and is widely accepted in North American society. However, as Straus, Gelles, and Steinmetz (1981:122) point out, it is wrong to "put the whole burden of violence on what is learned in the family." Indeed, many, if not most, people raised in violent homes do not become wife beaters (Barnett, Miller-Perrin & Perrin, 2005). Consider the following statement made by a Scottish battered woman to Dobash and Dobash (1979:154), who asked her about how her violent husband's behavior affected her male children and their treatment of women:

> It's had the opposite effect on the boys. It's had the effect I'd hoped for. I used to say to them, "I've had to spend my time telling you this," that this wasn't the right thing for men to

> do, that they hadn't to treat a woman like that. They should
> treat a woman the way they'd like their own sisters to be
> treated, you know . . . So it did work, whether it was that or
> whether in their own inside they say to themselves, "Well, I'm
> not going to be like that. I've seen how my mother suffers. I'll
> not do that to any woman." I've tried to tell them, so I think
> it's worked. They're hard working, safe, look after their
> money. They're just normal blokes. They never have any
> trouble. They wouldn't hurt anybody. I mean, they're very hale
> and hearty boys, and they're well brought up. So I've won, you
> know, I feel a great—I've a great satisfaction in knowing
> that all the time I did spend trying to teach them the things
> that their father should have taught them, I've won in the end.

Thus, while many children's abusive fathers may be directly or indirectly teaching them to become wife beaters, their mothers may spend a substantial amount of time and effort teaching them that wife beating is wrong and that their future wives/cohabiting partners deserve to be treated with kindness, respect, and dignity. Children are not simply "hollow" beings who emulate whatever they see. Most of them have a sense of justice and fairness and are likely to regard wife beating as "bad" or "evil" (Dobash & Dobash, 1979).

This is not to say that the family is not a key "training ground" for woman abuse; however, people also learn to hurt female intimates from external sources such as their peers. It is to theories that address the influence of all-male social networks that we now turn.

Male Peer Support Theories

Woman abuse has many determinants or sources. Still, research shows that one of most significant of these determinants is male peer support, a problem defined in the risk factor section of this chapter. Close to 20 years ago, Walter DeKeseredy (1988a) developed the first male peer support model of woman abuse in university/college dating, and it is heavily informed by strain-subcultural theories reviewed in Chapter 2.

DeKeseredy's Male Peer Support Model

DeKeseredy (1988a) contends that many men experience various types of stress in dating relationships, ranging from sexual problems to challenges to their patriarchal authority. Some men try to deal with these problems themselves, while others turn to their male friends for advice, guidance, and various other kinds of social support. The resources provided by these peers may encourage and justify woman abuse under certain conditions. Further, male peer support can influence men to victimize their dating partners regardless of stress. DeKeseredy's model, as depicted in Figure 3.4, shows that dating relationship stress and male peer support increase the likelihood of abuse. Relationships are associated with stress that motivates men to seek support from their male friends. Such support increases the probability of sexual, physical, and psychological variants of woman abuse.

Figure 3.4
DeKeseredy's Male Peer Support Model

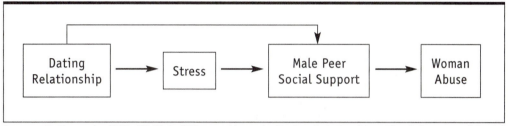

Source: DeKeseredy, W.S. (1988a). "Woman Abuse in Dating Relationships: The Relevance of Social Support Theory." *Journal of Family Violence*, 3, 1-13.

There is some support for DeKeseredy's model. For example, he (1988b) found that social ties with physically, sexually, and/or psychologically abusive peers is strongly related to dating abuse among men who experience high levels of life-events stress while dating. This finding supports a basic sociological argument promoted by differential association theorists (e.g., Sutherland, 1947) and other scholars: that the victimization of women is behavior that is socially learned in interaction with others (Scully, 1990). Nevertheless, DeKeseredy's model does not account for other explanatory variables, which is the main reason why he and his close friend and colleague Martin Schwartz developed a modified male peer support model of woman abuse in university/college dating.

The Modified Male Peer Support Model[16]

DeKeseredy and Schwartz (1993) criticized the model presented in Figure 3.4 for excluding four important variables: the ideology of familial and courtship patriarchy, alcohol consumption, membership in formal groups (e.g., fraternities), and the **absence of deterrence**. The last variable refers to the reluctance of various agents of social control (for example, campus administrators, police, security officers, etc.) to punish men who abuse female intimates. Together with the other three variables, this factor is included in their modified male peer support model, shown in Figure 3.5.

Figure 3.5
Modified Male Peer Support Model

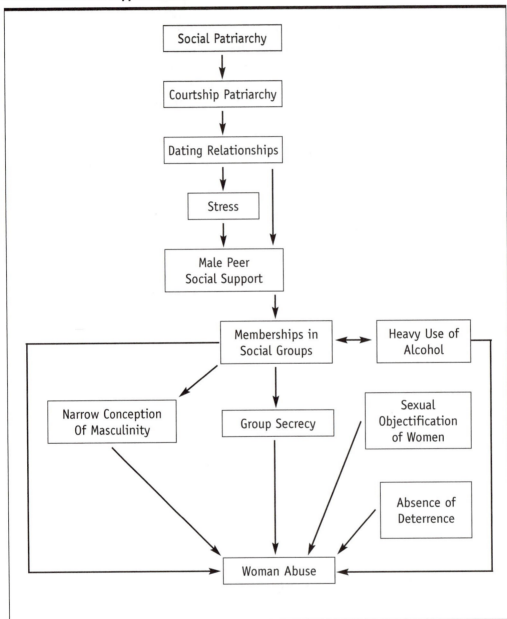

Source: DeKeseredy, W.S. & M.D. Schwartz (1993). "Male Peer Support and Woman Abuse: An Expansion of DeKeseredy's Model." *Sociological Spectrum*, 13, 393-413.

One of DeKeseredy and Schwartz's (1993) major criticisms of the earlier model is that it focuses only on individual behavior and does not recognize that such actions are smaller expressions of broader social forces. Thus, they added **social patriarchy** to the model, which generally refers to a set of beliefs in society suggesting that men should be in charge or in the various positions of leadership, power, and authority. Further, the somewhat different subsystem of **courtship patriarchy** was added, where ideals such as romanticism mean that relationships are handled differently than in more permanent relationships (Lloyd, 1991). In the early stages of a relationship, issues such as the connection between who paid for dinner and whether a man is "owed" sex can be rather different than later on.

Figure 3.4 also did not account for the effects of alcohol. Although few researchers would claim that there is a direct causal relationship (Hull & Bond, 1986), alcohol is related to woman abuse in many ways. For example, CNS data show that college men who drink two or more times a week and have male peers who support both psychological and physical abuse are nearly 10 times as likely to admit being sexual aggressors as men who have none of these traits (Schwartz, DeKeseredy, Tait & Alvi, 2001). Further, Schwartz and Pitts (1995) found that 17.1 percent of the U.S. college women in their sample reported a man having sexual intercourse with them when they couldn't resist because they were heavily under the influence of alcohol or other drugs. Alcohol is also used in contexts that support patriarchal conversations about women's sexuality and ways to control it, such as those held in "boys' nights out" in bars where men discuss the women in their lives (Hey, 1986; Schwartz & DeKeseredy, 1997).

Men receive pro-abuse social support in a variety of locations, but it is most common within social groups or settings such as fraternities, athletic teams, dormitory groups, business luncheons, workplaces, or other groupings. Here, men learn many things, including a **narrow conception of masculinity**. In other words, men learn that a "normal" heterosexual male is one who has the following stereotypical masculine attributes: clean-cut, handsome, athletic, wealthy, a high tolerance for alcohol, and sexual success with women. They also learn that they should not have effeminate physical and personality traits or take courses in disciplines regarded as the domains of women and homosexuals, such as nursing, social work, art, and music (Godenzi, Schwartz & DeKeseredy, 2001; Martin & Hummer, 1989).

Another thing men learn from their peers is the importance of **group secrecy**. Men are told that they should not reveal their friends' abusive actions to outsiders, such as the police or college administrators. In effect, group secrecy condones male abuse because these men are supported by the group and avoid any punishment. Further, they learn the sexual objectification of women, either informally in bar discussions and the like or through the actions of more organized groups such as fraternities, who may use women as "bait" to bring in new members, as adornments, or as servants at parties.

The final factor missing from Figure 3.4 is an absence of deterrence. Although male social networks may reward members for abusing women, a factor that allows this behavior to continue is a lack of punishment. While forcing sexual intercourse on a woman who has passed out from alcohol is a crime in most North American jurisdictions, it is unlikely that any male who does so will be prosecuted by criminal justice or university authorities.[17] Few people in the criminal justice system even consider it a crime to forcibly rape an acquaintance under any circumstance (DeKeseredy & Schwartz, 1996; Harney & Muehlenhard, 1991). It is a difficult task to convince men that it is wrong to rape women when it is not only fraternity brothers who sanction or reward such behavior; other students, parents, teachers, administrators, and the general public will all point out that the woman was drunk and therefore partly responsible.

Interestingly, few people would suggest that a woman who passes out from alcohol consumption in a bar shares responsibility for having her jacket or purse stolen or would argue against prosecuting the thief. Furthermore, if we knew that the thief had encouraged the victim to drink more so that she would not be able to resist his or her theft of the jacket and purse, we would be even more upset. However, when sex is involved, the facts are often seen as ambiguous and the moral waters muddied (Fenstermaker, 1989). Nor is it only in fairly minor cases that people are confused about blame and morality and therefore award men immunity from punishment; there will be no serious punishment on most campuses even in fairly serious cases such as gang rape.

DeKeseredy and Schwartz's modified male peer support model, albeit better than the original, has several limitations. Perhaps the most important one is that although each of the individual elements has been tested empirically, there has not yet been a test of the entire model. In fact, given its complexity, it very well may be that it has more value as a heuristic or teaching model than as a predictive model. In other words, its greatest strength may lie in summarizing the complex literature (a teaching model), rather than to isolate and predict which specific men on college campuses are most likely to abuse women.

Still, several hypotheses derived from this model have been tested. For example, Ageton (1983) found that more than 40 percent of the perpetrators of adolescent sexual assaults reported that their friends knew about their behavior and that virtually all approved of it or at least expressed indifference. Similarly, the CNS found a relationship between sexual abuse in college dating and two key variants of male peer support: (1) attachments to male peers who physically, sexually, and psychologically abuse their dating partners, and (2) friends who verbally encourage the physical, sexual, and psychological abuse of dates or girlfriends in certain situations, such as challenges to patriarchal authority (DeKeseredy & Kelly, 1995). Moreover, males who report physically, sexually, and psychologically abusing their dating partners are more likely to adhere to the ideology of familial patriarchy than those who do not report abusive behavior (DeKeseredy & Kelly, 1993).

Economic Exclusion/Male Peer Support Model[18]

Like affluent college students, impoverished men form "specialized relationships with one another" (Messerschmidt, 1993:110). Such close bonds, under certain conditions, also promote the abuse of women as a means of meeting "masculinity challenges," although these challenges are different from those encountered by college students (Messerschmidt, 2000). For example, men in public housing are more likely to physically assault their female partners than those who live in middle- and upper-class communities (DeKeseredy, Alvi, Schwartz, & Perry, 1999; Renzetti & Maier, 2002). To explain this problem, DeKeseredy and Schwartz (2002) offer an empirically informed economic exclusion/male peer support model, described in Figure 3.6.[19]

Briefly, DeKeseredy and Schwartz (2002) contend that recent major economic transformations (e.g., the shift from a manufacturing to a service-based economy) displace working-class men and women, who often end up in urban public housing or other "clusters of poverty" (Sernau, 2001).[20] Unable to support their families economically and live up to the culturally defined masculine role as breadwinner, socially and economically excluded men experience high levels of life-events stress because their "normal paths for personal power and prestige have been cut off" (Raphael, 2001a:703). For example, because they cannot afford to look after both their partners and their children, some women evict male intimates or "invert patriarchy" in other ways by making decisions for the household and having the lease and car in their names (Edin, 2000). Such actions are perceived by patriarchal men as "dramatic assaults" on their "sense of masculine dignity" (Bourgois, 1995:215).

Some men deal with stress caused by their partners' inversions of patriarchy by leaving them, while others use abuse as a means of sabotaging women's attempts to gain economic independence (Bourgois, 1995; Raphael, 2001b). Other men, however, turn to their male peers for advice and guidance on how to alleviate stress caused by female challenges to patriarchal authority. Large numbers of socially and economically excluded male peers in and around public housing view wife beating as legitimate means of repairing "damaged patriarchal masculinity" (Messerschmidt, 1993; Raphael, 2001a), and they often serve as role models because many of them beat their own intimate partners (DeKeseredy, Alvi, Schwartz & Tomaszewski, 2003).

Figure 3.6 is not a predictive model. Rather, like the one shown in Figure 3.5, it takes a heuristic perspective and does not attempt to isolate specific offenders. Still, unlike most woman abuse theories developed so far, it attempts to explain how broader economic changes (e.g., deindustrialization) that have occurred in recent decades contribute to one of North America's most pressing social problems. Further, this model calls for moving the experiences of those whom William Julius Wilson (1987) refers to as the "truly disadvantaged" to the center of empirical and theoretical work on the ways in which all-male social networks perpetuate and legitimate woman abuse (DeKeseredy & Schwartz, 1998c). To date, almost all male peer support theories focus exclusively on undergraduate members of patriarchal subcultures despite evidence showing that there are socially and economically disenfranchised male peer groups outside colleges that also use sexist or abusive means of doing masculinity (Anderson, 1999; Bourgois, 1995; Sinclair, 2002; Wilson, 1996).

Figure 3.6
Economic Exclusion/Male Peer Support Model

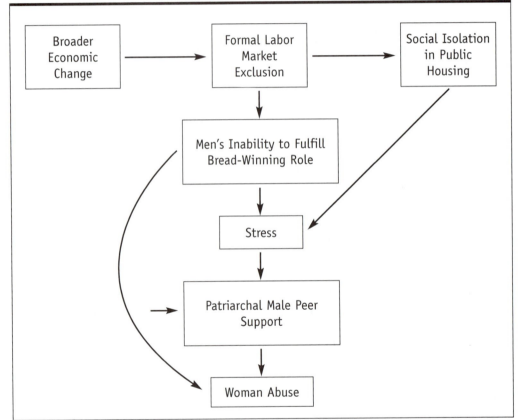

Source: DeKeseredy, W.S. & M.D. Schwartz (2002). "Theorizing Public Housing Woman Abuse as a Function of Economic Exclusion and Male Peer Support." *Women's Health and Urban Life*, 1, 26-45.

Although the economic exclusion/male peer support model fills several gaps in the literature on woman abuse, like any social scientific perspective, it can be improved. For example, consistent with the other male peer support theories reviewed here, it does not specifically address whether members of patriarchal male peer support groups are intentionally recruited into these alliances or whether they gravitate to such groups as a way of selectively attempting to sustain or receive support for their earlier acquired values and behavior. Further, it does not specify that men may interact with and be influenced by peers who live away from public housing. Another point to consider is that as with every other male peer support model, racial/ethnic variations in male peer support dynamics remain to be examined. DeKeseredy and Schwartz (2002) recognize these problems and hopefully, their future theoretical work on the relationship between economic factors, male peer support, and woman abuse in North American public housing will address these and other shortcomings.

Feminist Theories

Most theorists and researchers of woman abuse agree with Lewis Okun's (1986:100) assertion that feminism is "the most important theoretical approach to conjugal violence/woman abuse." However, of all the variants of feminist thought reviewed in Chapter 2 and elsewhere, it is radical feminism that has had the greatest impact on the sociological study of woman abuse.

Radical Feminism

Radical feminists contend that the most important set of social relations in any society is found in patriarchy. All other social relations, such as class, are secondary and originate from male-female relations (Beirne & Messerschmidt, 1991). Applied to woman abuse, radical feminist theory asserts that men engage in this behavior because they need or desire to control women (Daly & Chesney-Lind, 1988). The following statement made by British radical feminist Jill Radford (1987:43) exemplifies this perspective: "It is clear that men's violence is used to control women, not just in their own individual interests, but also in the interests of men as a sex class in the reproduction of heterosexuality and male supremacy."

In addition to explaining why men abuse female intimates, some radical feminists theorize the policing of male-to-female victimization. The police still, for the most part, do not take male violence against women as seriously as they do predatory street crime (Iovanni & Miller, 2001). In response to this problem and based on in-depth interviews with abused women, several radical feminists argue that instead of acting as a "value-free" agency of social control, the police organization is a "bastion of male authority and interest" that functions on behalf of men to maintain female subordination in intimate relationships (Edwards, 1989:31). One way in which the police achieve this goal is by taking a nonpunitive approach to men who victimize female partners.

Given what you read in Chapter 2, you probably know that radical feminist theories have been attacked both from the right and left, and criticisms presented in Chapter 2 are relevant here. For example, conservative scholars such as Dutton (1994), Gelles (1980), and Gelles and Cornell (1985) refer to radical feminist theories of woman abuse as single-factor explanations that have very little explanatory value in social science.[21] Radical feminist theories such as Radford's (1987) are also seen by some conservative social scientists as political agendas and as difficult to verify (Levinson, 1989). Feminist theorists have responded to these criticisms by showing how patriarchal forces together with other variables (for example, male peer support) contribute to female victimization. Furthermore, several large-scale surveys provide empirical support for radical feminist accounts of woman abuse, especially those that point to the ideology of familial patriarchy (DeKeseredy & Kelly, 1993; Smith, 1990b).

Again, as stated in Chapter 2, critiques of feminist theories such as those reviewed here have also come from feminist scholars. They call for more attention to be paid to how class and race/ethnicity are related to woman abuse. Of course, this criticism can be leveled against the overwhelming majority of woman abuse researchers of all political positions. Still, what remains a major problem for radical feminist theories is "the question of why, in a culture dominated by patriarchy, only a small percentage of men use violence against women" (Jasinski, 2001:13).

Routine Activities Theories

Routine activities theories are ecological perspectives on crime and deviance. To explain why so many college women are sexually assaulted, Schwartz and Pitts (1995) offer a feminist variant of routine activities theory, one that is heavily influenced by Cohen and Felson's (1979) work. Cohen and Felson (1979:590) define routine activities as "any recurrent and prevalent activities which provide for basic population and individual needs (e.g., working, schooling, leisure outings, shopping."

A Feminist Routine Activities Theory

Schwartz and Pitts's feminist routine activities theory of sexual assault integrates three concepts: routine activities, place, and lifestyle. They argue that a disproportionately high number of sexual assaults are committed on North American college campuses because **criminogenic convergences** are most likely to occur on them. A criminogenic convergence in this context means a male student who is motivated to assault a woman, the availability of suitable targets, and the absence of effective guardians who are willing to intervene.

The work of Schwartz and DeKeseredy (1997) and other researchers shows that colleges are characterized by the presence of male peer groups that encourage and legitimate the sexual exploitation of women,[22] especially those who are intoxicated. Male members of these social networks are much more likely than nonmembers to be motivated to sexually assault women (Godenzi, Schwartz & DeKeseredy, 2001). For example, several studies show that men who report having friends who support getting women drunk so that they cannot resist sexual advances are themselves likely to report using similar strategies (Boeringer, Shehan & Akers, 1991; Schwartz & Nogrady, 1996).

Schwartz and Pitts contend that two lifestyle factors increase women's "suitability" as targets of sexual assault. These are: (1) drinking to the point where they are unable to resist sexually predatory men, and (2) attending parties and social events frequented by a large number of potential offenders, such as members of pro-abuse subcultures (e.g., fraternities).[23]

So far, we have the convergence of motivated offenders and vulnerable victims. Their co-presence on campuses provides men with opportunities to engage in predatory sexual conduct. Nevertheless, opportunities for assaulting women do not necessarily translate into sexual aggression. Specifically, the differential process of effective guardianship mediates the effect of assault opportunities or actual assaults.

Several factors operate to make campuses "effective guardian-absent" locations. For example, as stated previously, many campus officials do not seriously sanction those who abuse women, even when they engage in extremely brutal behavior such as gang rape.[24] Even criminal justice personnel often disregard acquaintance and/or date rapes that occur in postsecondary school contexts. According to Harney and Muehlenhard (1991:5-6):

> [G]iven that police officers, jurors, attorneys, and judges, to name a few, rarely regard forced intercourse between acquaintances as rape, it is hardly surprising that women who have been forced by a male acquaintance to have sexual intercourse against their will, and men who have forced female acquaintances against their will, often do not regard these experiences as rape.

In sum, it is on college campuses that one is most likely to find the copresence of motivated male offenders, vulnerable or "suitable" victims, and the absence of effective guardians. This criminogenic convergence helps explain the relatively high rates of acquaintance and courtship rape in colleges.

Overall, Schwartz and Pitts's theory is supported by small- and large-scale surveys, including the CNS (Schwartz, DeKeseredy, Tait & Alvi, 2001). However, tests of their theory completed so far did not collect data on the absence or presence of effective guardians. Instead, empirical assessments of this perspective presume that the locations of their surveys—large universities—are "effective guardian absent." Nevertheless, several researchers and many victims/survivors would strongly agree with this presumption.

Despite this limitation, Schwartz and Pitts should be commended for offering a theory that is both logical and parsimonious (as it involves only three variables). Their perspective is also one of the very few attempts to address the "gender-blind" nature of previous routine activities theories, such as Cohen and Felson's (1979).

Integrated Theories

Although there are many theories of woman abuse, integrated perspectives are rare. So are theories of separation/divorce sexual assault. Similar to DeKeseredy and Schwartz's (2002) economic exclusion/male peer support model, DeKeseredy and colleagues' (2004) feminist/male peer support theory of sexual assault during and after separation/divorce brings together several bodies of knowledge partially in response to Jasinski's (2001) call for "acknowledging the existence of multiple risk factors" when doing theoretical work on woman abuse in general and following a growing trend among criminologists to develop integrated theories (e.g., Messner, Krohn & Liska, 1990).

A Feminist/Male Peer Support Model of Sexual Assault During and After Separation/Divorce[25]

Heavily informed by perspectives offered by DeKeseredy and Schwartz (1993, 2002), Ellis and DeKeseredy (1997), Rogness (2003), and Wilson and Daly (1992), the model presented in Figure 3.7 situates separation/divorce sexual assault within the larger context of societal patriarchy. North America is well known for being a continent characterized by gross gender inequity (Renzetti & Curran, 2000). As stated earlier in this chapter, in 33 U.S. states, under law, a man can be awarded conditional exemptions if he raped his wife (National Clearinghouse on Marital and Date Rape, 1998). Many more examples of patriarchal practices and discourses could easily be provided. Nevertheless, the most important point to consider is that a constant such as societal patriarchy cannot explain a variable such as changes in the frequency and severity of male sexual assaults on women who want to leave or who have left them (Ellis & DeKeseredy, 1997). In other words, if we live in a patriarchal society that promotes **male proprietariness**, why, then, do some men sexually assault during or after the exiting process, whereas most others do not? For instance, data generated by a number of researchers using patriarchal ideology scales of one kind or another indicate that there are variations in male proprietariness (DeKeseredy & Kelly, 1993; Smith, 1990b), which is "the tendency [of men] to think of women as sexual and reproductive "property" they can own and exchange" (Wilson & Daly, 1992:85). Proprietariness refers to "not just the emotional force of [the male's] own feelings of entitlement but to a more pervasive attitude [of ownership and control] toward social relationships [with intimate female partners]" (1992:85).

Figure 3.7
A Feminist/Male Peer Support Model of Societal Patriarchy Sexual Assault During and After Separation/Divorce

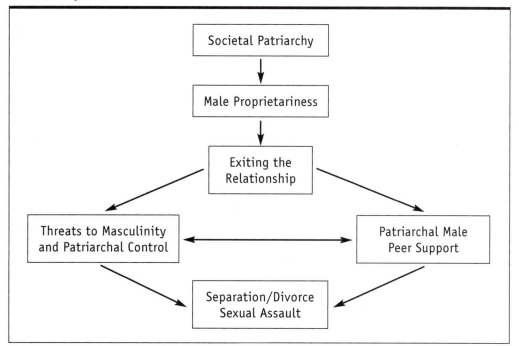

Source: DeKeseredy, W.S., M. Rogness & M.D. Schwartz (2004). "Separation/Divorce Sexual Assault: The Current State of Social Scientific Knowledge." *Aggression and Violent Behavior*, 9, 675-691.

Many women resist or eventually will resist their spouse/cohabiting partners' proprietariness in a variety of ways, such as arguing, protesting, and fighting back if they have been abused (Bergen, 1996; Ellis & DeKeseredy, 1997; Sev'er, 2002; Websdale, 1998). There are also many women, although the precise number is unknown, who defy men's control by exiting or trying to exit a relationship, and this may involve emotional separation, obtaining a separate residence, and/or starting or completing a legal separation/divorce. Emotional separation, a major predictor of a permanent end to a relationship, is defined by DeKeseredy and colleagues (2004) as a woman's denial or restriction of sexual relations and other intimate exchanges.[26] Emotionally exiting a relationship can be just as dangerous as physically or legally exiting one because it, too, increases the likelihood of male violence and sexual abuse (Kayser, 1993; Kirkwood, 1993; Notarius & Markman, 1993; Russell, 1990).

Regardless of how a woman does it, her attempt to exit or her successful departure from a sexist relationship challenges male proprietariness, but exiting alone cannot account for sexual assault. For example, as you know by now, many abusive patriarchal men have male friends with similar beliefs and values, and their peers reinforce the notion that women's exiting is a threat to a man's masculinity. Furthermore, many members of patriarchal peer groups view wife beating, rape, and other forms of male-to-female victimization as legitimate and effective means of "repairing damaged masculinity" (Messerschmidt, 1993). Not only do these men verbally and publicly state that sexual assault and other forms of abuse are legitimate means of maintaining patriarchal authority and control, they are also role models because they, too, are abusive to women.

In short, according to DeKeseredy and his colleagues (2004), patriarchal male peer support contributes to the perception of damaged masculinity and motivates sexually abusive men to "lash out against the women . . . they can no longer control" (Bourgois, 1995:214). Another point to consider is that if a patriarchal man's peers see him as a failure with women because his partner wants to leave or has left him, he is likely to be ridiculed because he "can't control his woman." Hence, like many college men who rape women, he is likely to sexually assault her to regain status among his peers. Similar to other men who rape female strangers, acquaintances, or dates, the sexual assaults committed by men during and after the process of separation/divorce may have much more to do with their need to sustain their status among their peers than either a need to satisfy their sexual desires or a longing to regain a loving relationship (Godenzi, Schwartz & DeKeseredy, 2001).

At this point in time, DeKeseredy et al.'s (2004) model serves as a building block for future theoretical construction. Obviously, there are other factors that contribute to separation/divorce sexual assault, such as male consumption of pornography (DeKeseredy & Joseph, in press; Russell, 1998), the contributions of formal and informal interventions (Ellis & DeKeseredy, 1997), and everyday life-events stress (Hardesty, 2002). Still, of the very limited theoretical work done so far on separation/divorce sexual assault,[27] the model shown in Figure 3.7 seems the most promising, and DeKeseredy and Joseph (in press) found some support for it using qualitative methods. Hopefully, this and other theories of separation/divorce sexual assault will be evaluated in the near future, using both quantitative and qualitative techniques.

Summary

This chapter shows that many intimate heterosexual relationships are not as safe and loving as many people think. Unfortunately, everyday, thousands of North American women are brutalized in many ways by their male dating, marital/cohabiting, and estranged partners. However, all women are not at equal risk of being abused. For example, those who are poor, cohabiting, or separated/divorced and belong to certain ethnic minority groups experience more victimization than women in other socioeconomic categories.

Why do men abuse female intimates? Here, we reviewed and evaluated several widely read and cited answers to this question, and we could have easily covered more. In fact, one could write an entire book on theories of woman abuse. Further, there are other variants of woman abuse in intimate relationships that occur in our society and that were not addressed here, such as lesbian battering.[28] Indeed, woman abuse is multidimensional in nature.

The good news, though, is that woman abuse is increasingly demanding the attention of social scientists and policymakers. For example, academic and government researchers are developing a substantial body of knowledge on the abusive behaviors addressed in this chapter. Moreover, as described in Chapter 8, they and others have created or proposed effective means of curbing woman abuse. Hopefully, you, too, will take part in the ongoing struggle to make women's lives safer.

Notes

[1] However, in fairness to John Kerry, he is the original cosponsor of the 1994 Violence Against Women Act and his wife, Teresa Heinz Kerry, had public conversations on domestic violence issues during the presidential campaign.

[2] This is the title of Silverman and Kennedy's (1993) book on homicide in Canada.

[3] This section includes revised sections of work published previously by DeKeseredy (2000b, 2005) and DeKeseredy, Alvi, Rogness, and Schwartz (2004).

[4] See DeKeseredy and Schwartz (1998a) for more in-depth information on the Canadian national survey and the data generated by it.

[5] See DeKeseredy and Joseph (in press) for more information on this study and the preliminary results.

[6] These questions were adapted from those used by the National Victims Center and the Crime Victims Research and Treatment Center (1992).

[7] The FBI's Uniform Crime Reporting Program (UCR) gathers basic information on serious crimes from participating police departments and records supplementary information about the circumstances of murder in its unpublished SHR (Victim Policy Center, 2004).

8   See Hardesty (2002) for an in-depth review of the empirical literature on "lethal separation assault."

9   The CTS was developed originally in the 1970s by Straus (1979) to study violence within families. Applied to the topic addressed here, this measure and the recently developed CTS2 (Straus, Hamby, Boney-McCoy & Sugarman, 1996) solicit information from men and women about the various tactics they used to resolve conflicts in their relationships. Most versions of the CTS consist of at least 18 items that measure three different ways of handling interpersonal conflict in intimate relationships: reasoning, verbal aggression (referred to by some researchers as psychological abuse), and violence. The CTS has been criticized on several grounds, including its inability to measure the contexts, meanings, and motives of violence (DeKeseredy & Schwartz, 1998b).

10   Fisher, Cullen, and Turner's (2000) recent National College Women Sexual Victimization Survey also shows that date rape is a major problem on U.S. college campuses.

11   See Barnett, Miller-Perrin, and Perrin (2005) and DeKeseredy and Schwartz (1998a) for in-depth reviews of the extant U.S. literature on sexual assault in college dating.

12   See Alvi, Schwartz, DeKeseredy, and Bachaus (2005) and DeKeseredy, Alvi, Schwartz, and Tomaszewski (2003) for in-depth reviews of the literature on the linkage between poverty, race/ethnicity, and woman abuse.

13   Parts of this section include modified sections of work published previously by DeKeseredy and MacLeod (1997).

14   See Barnett, Miller-Perrin, and Perrin (2005) for a detailed overview of the literature on social learning and woman abuse.

15   For example, see Ehrensaft, Cohen, Brown, Smailes, Chen, and Johnson's (2003) 20-year longitudinal, prospective study of intimate partner violence.

16   This section includes revised sections of work published previously by DeKeseredy and Schwartz (1993, 1996) and Schwartz and DeKeseredy (1997).

17   Similarly, university authorities are not likely to criminalize fraternity members who use graffiti to vandalize university property (Schaefer, 2004).

18   This section includes revised sections of work published previously by DeKeseredy and Schwartz (2002, 2005).

19   This model is a modified version of Sernau's (2001:24) web-of-exclusion model and is heavily informed by sociological perspectives offered by him, DeKeseredy and Schwartz (1993), Wilson (1996), and Young (1999).

20   A recent analysis of 2000 U.S. Census Bureau data (see Jargowsky, 2003), however, shows that the poor are becoming less concentrated in urban areas than they were prior to the 1990s. Still, in Washington, DC, Los Angeles, and San Diego, the percentage of people in high-poverty areas increased during this time.

21   Gelles (1980) and Gelles and Cornell (1985) were referring more specifically to the work of radical feminists Dobash and Dobash (1979).

22   See DeKeseredy and Schwartz (1998c) and Schwartz and DeKeseredy (1997) for in-depth reviews of the extant social scientific literature on male peer support and woman abuse on the college campus.

23   Some studies, such as Sanday's (1989), show that fraternity members are at much higher risk of engaging in sexual assault than are nonfraternity members.

[24] See Bohmer and Parrot (1993), DeKeseredy and Schwartz (1993), McMillen (1990), Schwartz (1991), and Schwartz and DeKeseredy (1997) for more detailed accounts of various social control agents' inadequate responses to the victims of date rape and other forms of sexual assault on campus.

[25] This section includes revised sections of an article published previously be DeKeseredy, Alvi, Rogness, and Schwartz (2004).

[26] This is a modified version of Ellis and DeKeseredy's (1997) definition of emotional separation.

[27] See DeKeseredy, Renzetti, and Schwartz (2004) for an in-depth review of the theoretical and empirical social scientific literature on separation/divorce sexual assault.

[28] See Mahoney, Williams, and West (2001) for a recent review of the social scientific literature on violence in lesbian relationships.

Discussion Questions

1. Do you agree that psychological abuse is just as, if not more, serious as physical violence? Why or why not?

2. Is woman abuse a major problem in your community? If so, why?

3. Why are poor women more likely to be abused than are middle- and upper-class women?

4. Why don't most men who grow up in abusive homes become wife beaters?

5. What are the limitations of the radical feminist perspective on woman abuse?

6. Are there other forms of pro-abuse male peer support you can think of that have been excluded from this chapter?

Problem-Solving Scenarios

1. How would you help a friend who told you that her male partner beat her?

2. In a group, discuss effective ways of preventing woman abuse on your campus.

3. In a group, identify the similarities and differences between the male peer support theories reviewed in this chapter.

4. What should be done to prevent separation/divorce abuse?

5. Generate a group discussion on what should or should not be included in a definition of woman abuse.

6. In a group, propose a plan to increase public awareness about woman abuse.

Suggested Readings

LaViolette, A.D. & O.W. Barnett (2000). *It Could Happen to Anyone: Why Battered Women Stay*. Thousand Oaks, CA: Sage.

> LaViolette and Barnett provide a comprehensive overview of the empirical, theoretical, and policy issues surrounding the question of why women remain in abusive relationships. Unlike many other books and articles that address this issue, this one constitutes a powerful challenge to explanations that blame women for their victimization.

DeKeseredy, W.S. & L. MacLeod (1997). *Woman Abuse: A Sociological Story*. Toronto: Harcourt Brace.

> This book offers an in-depth feminist analysis of the extent, distribution, and sources of woman abuse in intimate heterosexual relationships. The strengths and weaknesses of various policies designed to prevent and control this problem are also addressed.

Lefkowitz, B. (1997). *Our Guys: The Glen Ridge Rape and the Secret Life of the Perfect Suburb*. New York: Vintage Books.

> This book is about the 1989 gang rape of a mentally disabled high school girl in Glen Ridge, New Jersey. Thirteen boys lured this girl into a basement, and four of them raped her while the others observed this atrocity. This book reminds us that statistics reviewed in this chapter are intensely personal and document women's pain. The book is also relevant to the male peer support theories covered here.

Renzetti, C.M., J.L. Edleson & R.K. Bergen (eds.) (2001). *Sourcebook on Violence Against Women*. Thousand Oaks, CA: Sage.

> Edited by three of the world's leading experts on woman abuse, this book is the most comprehensive information source on this problem. It includes detailed analyses of conceptual, theoretical, methodological, and ethical issues surrounding various types of male-to-female victimization.

Schwartz, M.D. & W.S. DeKeseredy (1997). *Sexual Assault on the College Campus: The Role of Male Peer Support*. Thousand Oaks, CA: Sage.

This book includes a comprehensive analysis of the ways in which male peer support contributes to sexual assault on the college campus. Rich with theory, the book also includes a review of large-scale survey data gathered in the United States and Canada.

Online Resources

1. **Rape, Abuse & Incest National Network (RAINN)**
   http://www.rainn.org
   RAINN is the largest anti-sexual assault organization in the United States and it operates the National Sexual Assault Hotline. Links to statistics and other important resources are found on this site.

2. **California Coalition Against Sexual Assault (CALCASA)**
   http://www.calcasa.org
   Although based in Sacramento, California, CALCASA is heavily involved in many efforts to curb sexual assault and other forms of woman abuse across the United States. CALCASA also publishes reports and other documents that are useful for students, researchers, victims, and policymakers.

3. **U.S. Department of Justice – Office on Violence Against Women**
   http://www.ojp.usdoj.gov/vawo/
   This government site includes a wealth of information on woman abuse, including laws related to this problem and research publications.

4. **Ohio Domestic Violence Network (ODVN)**
   http://www.odvn.org
   The ODVN is an active and long-standing member of both the National Coalition Against Domestic Violence and the National Network to End Domestic Violence. This site provides students, activists, researchers, and others with comprehensive information on key issues covered in this chapter.

The average workplace murderer is likely to be unmarried, male and on the job at least 4 years. He has a grudge and knows exactly whom he wants to kill. Larry Hansel, for example, carried a 12-gauge shotgun to shoot co-workers in San Diego. He says he would do it again. (*USA Today*, July 15, 2004:1)

CHAPTER 4

HOMICIDE

The opening quotation in this chapter evokes a common image of a murderer. Cold, calculating, and unrepentant, murderers and homicide seem to defy explanation, except by resorting to statements about the perpetrator's "obvious" psychological problems or evil inclinations. Of all crimes, perhaps homicide makes us the most uneasy, incredulous, and angry. Indeed, most people would agree that homicide is among the most serious of all deviant and criminal behaviors, warranting the harshest punishments society can inflict. Intentionally taking the life of another person or persons would widely be regarded as a crime *mala in se*, which as you will recall from Chapter 1, refers to crimes over which there is consensus that the act is wrong in itself. Yet, as with many other types of deviant and criminal behaviors, the definition of homicide is the subject of some disagreement, and the issue is complicated by the fact that the phenomenon varies a great deal. These points will be taken up in the next section.

As you might guess, scholars also disagree over the causes of homicide. In this chapter, we will explore the nature, extent, and distribution of homicide in the United States and examine some of the most widely cited theories purporting to explain homicide. Before doing so, we need to take up the issue of definitions.

What is Homicide?

The most general definition of homicide is the taking of the life of another. At first glance, this appears to be a very simple and straight-forward approach to defining this crime. However, if we think carefully about this statement, several questions arise. One such question, for instance, is in relation to the time between a person's victimization and the time that they might die. For example, if a person seriously hurts another individual, but the victim does not die for a year, can the first person still be charged with murder? Some states still use the "year and a day rule" to determine the answer to this, in which the person in our hypothetical scenario could be charged with murder if the victim dies within one year and a day after the injuries were inflicted (but not one year and two days). Another controversy surrounds the use of the death penalty in the United States, in that many question whether the death penalty should be considered a form of unjustifiable homicide or whether it should belong to a category of "legally sanctioned" homi-cide. In addition, as Zahn and McCall (1999) point out, there have been historical periods in the United States in which abortion or infanticide have been defined as homicide, and other periods in which they have not. While these are important philosophical and legal issues (and also have consequences for understanding the accuracy of homicide data), they are not ones that we can take up here. Instead, we will simply define homicide as lethal interpersonal violent acts by a person with no legal mandate to use violence and where these behaviors are legally designated as criminal homicides (Gartner, 1995).

Categories of Homicide

Not all homicides are criminal acts, and within the legal definition described above, there are different types of homicide. For instance, Alvarez and Bachman (2003:11) point to three general categories of homicide that are recognized in the United States: excusable, justifiable, and criminal. Each of these categories is distinguished from one another by the degree of guilt of the perpetrator, with excusable homi-cide bearing the least and murder the most.

Excusable homicide refers to situations in which people are killed accidentally and in which there is limited negligence on the part of the perpetrator (such as when a person is accidentally killed during a hunting trip).

Justifiable homicide is considered a noncriminal murder in which an individual might have killed someone in self-defense or as a con-sequence of defending another person, or situations in which a police officer kills a felon while in the line of duty. Justifiable homicide is a legal grey area, given that serious questions arise for every case around issues such as whether the victim was likely to harm the defendant seriously before the latter killed the victim, or how certain we can be that a victim was likely to commit a serious criminal act before being killed himself or herself.

Criminal homicides are situations in which a human life is taken without justification or excuse. This category has several subcategories, depending on the jurisdiction, and includes types such as negligent homicide, reckless manslaughter, first-degree murder, second-degree murder, and felony murder.

Outside the scope of legal definitions, Alvarez and Bachman remind us that other classification schemes exist, with some scholars arguing that homicides can be distinguished on the basis of the "relational distance" between the participants (i.e., the degree to which participants know each other), or on the basis of whether homicides are expressive (e.g., committed out of passion, or rage) or instrumental (e.g., committed for a particular motive such as revenge or profit).

The Extent and Distribution of Homicide

Most criminologists would agree that data on homicide are among the most accurate crime data of all, primarily because unlike property crimes or even intimate and nonintimate assaults, the majority of homicides are reported or discovered by police (Fox & Piquero, 2003). In this section we will look at homicide trends in the United States, and will explore the extent to which homicide varies by various demographic indicators, such as age, sex, and geographic region.

Figure 4.1 shows the homicide victimization trend in the United States since the 1950s. As you can see from this graph, the mid-1960s witnessed the beginning of a sharp upward trend in homicide, in which the rate almost doubled. In 1980, the rate peaked again before falling slightly in 1984. Another upward trend characterized the late 1980s and peaked in 1991. Since then, the rate has been falling to its current level of approximately 5.6 per 100,000 people. Though this may be viewed as good news in some respects, the homicide rate in the United States still far exceeds that of other industrialized nations (Lane, 1999; Reiss & Roth, 1993). Only five countries (South Africa, Russia, Lithuania, Estonia, and Latvia) have higher rates (Fox, Levin & Quinet, 2005).

Figure 4.1
Homicide Rates USA: 1950-2002

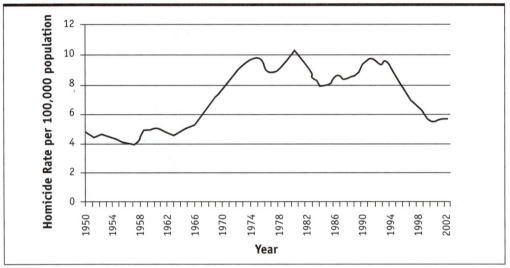

Source: Fox, J.A. & M.W. Zawitz (2004). "Homicide Trends in the United States" {Online}. Available at: http://www.ojp.usdoj.gov/bjs/homicide/homtrnd.htm#contents

These overall trends, particularly over the past 10 years, give rise to an important question: Why have homicide rates fallen? The answer to this question depends on the theoretical perspective one adopts (Blumstein, Rivara & Rosenfeld, 2000). Some scholars have argued that the falling rate reflects shifts in the age structure of U.S. society (fewer youths equals less homicide), while others have claimed that higher incarceration rates, better policing, fewer drug-related homicides, or better gun controls may have contributed to the decrease (Conklin, 2003). Some have even suggested that better emergency response times combined with more effective medical treatments for violence-induced trauma might be responsible for some of the decrease (Harris, Thomas, Fisher & Hirsch, 2002). Ongoing research has been unable to determine the precise answer to this question, and most criminologists agree that homicide rates have fallen as a result of a number of interrelated factors.

Aggregate homicide data are useful for observing overall trends, but they do not tell us much about the nature and characteristics of homicide. To gain a better picture of the contours of homicide, we need to examine how rates differ according to age, gender, and race.

Beginning with age, we can see that perpetrators of homicide are generally young: between the ages of 18 and 24, followed by young adults between the ages of 25 and 34 (see Figure 4.2). We would find a similar pattern if we examined the rates of victimization. If we look at the nature and dynamics of gender differences in Table 4.1, we find one of the most important differences: namely, that homicide victims and perpetrators are overwhelmingly male (Belknap, 2001) (also see Chapter 3 for more detailed information on the nature of homicide between intimates).

Figure 4.2
Homicide Victimization Rates per 100,000 Population by Age, USA, 1976-2002

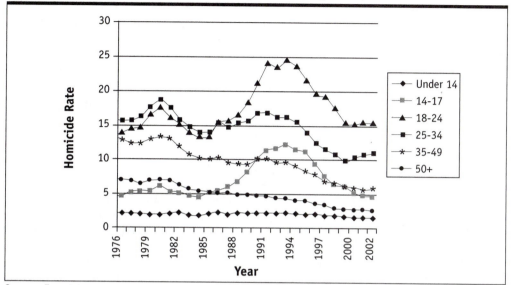

Source: Fox, J.A. & M.W. Zawitz (2004). "Homicide Trends in the United States" {Online}. Available at: http://www.ojp.usdoj.gov/bjs/homicide/homtrnd.htm#contents

Table 4.1
Homicide Type by Gender, USA, 1976-2002

	Victims		Offenders	
	Male	**Female**	**Male**	**Female**
All homicides	76.4%	23.6%	88.6%	11.4%
Victim/offender relationship				
Intimate	37.2%	62.8%	64.8%	35.2%
Family	52.0%	48.0%	70.3%	29.7%
Infanticide	54.5%	45.5%	61.6%	38.4%
Eldercide	58.2%	41.8%	85.4%	14.6%
Circumstances				
Felony murder	78.0%	22.0%	93.3%	6.7%
Sex-related	18.9%	81.1%	93.6%	6.4%
Drug-related	90.1%	9.9%	95.7%	4.3%
Gang-related	94.5%	5.5%	98.4%	1.6%
Argument	78.1%	21.9%	85.3%	14.7%
Workplace	78.6%	21.4%	91.4%	8.6%
Weapon				
Gun homicide	82.5%	17.5%	91.0%	9.0%
Arson	56.5%	43.5%	79.5%	20.5%
Poison	54.4%	45.6%	62.9%	37.1%
Multiple victims or offenders				
Multiple victims	62.8%	37.2%	93.5%	6.5%
Multiple offenders	85.5%	14.5%	91.8%	8.2%

Source: Fox, J.A. & M.W. Zawitz (2004). "Homicide Trends in the United States" {Online}. Available at: http://www.ojp.usdoj.gov/bjs/homicide/homtrnd.htm#contents

Box 4.1
Gender Differences in Homicide-Suicide

They love them to death, killing children and themselves to save them from a life of perceived misery, but women who commit murder and suicide rarely do so in anger.

"I'd be hard pressed to find a case of a woman committing murder-suicide in a rage," said Martin Daly, a professor of psychology at McMaster University. "Apart from the suicide, women are not equipped with the same kind of mentality of violent anger (as men)."

And while more men commit suicide after killing their wives, "it's rare for women to do that."

Yet murder-suicides by women have happened twice in Toronto in the past two weeks. In a case that gripped the city, Andrea Labbe killed her husband Brian Langer, daughter Zoe, 3, and then attempted to kill Brigitte, 2, before turning the knife on herself. Brigitte survived the Dec. 1 murder-suicide and Margot, 7 months, was unharmed.

On Sunday, police discovered two bodies—believed to be those of Leah Marie Mindach and her young son—in an east-end apartment. Police would not confirm their names yesterday, but Staff Inspector Jeff McGuire said the case is most likely a murder-suicide.

For those suffering from major depression and an ailing state of mind, murder and suicide are often the only relief from a miserable life for oneself and loved ones.

"It's a distorted view of love," said Dr. Michael Pare, vice-president of the General Practice Psychotherapy Association.

Among men there is often a spur of revenge, a sense of failure, or loss of control over a spouse. Men use more lethal methods, including guns.

Women may be pushed over the edge by the loss of a loved one or the desire to escape what they feel is an unhappy life. They tend to overdose, use suffocation or take poison.

And they only very rarely kill family members at the same time.

Research dating back 100 years involving more than 10,000 homicides in Toronto, Vancouver, Seattle and Buffalo found there hasn't been another case like the Labbe murder suicide, according to University of Toronto Centre of Criminology professor Rosemary Gartner.

"The Labbe case is extremely unusual," she added.

Regardless of its violent nature and the fact Labbe also killed her husband, "it could have been motivated by distorted love," Pare said of the incident, adding suicide is often impulsive, difficult to predict and rare even among patients with severe depression, "and very, very, very few commit murder-suicide."

"When someone is extremely depressed, the thought of suicide is a wonderful escape from pain," he said. "Suicide is the relief. Those who are depressed see suicide as a positive thing. And those who are suicidal can see murder as beneficial. They see life as horrible and are trying to help another person from living that life of horror."

A 1995 study "Familicide: The Killing of Spouse and Children" by Daly and colleagues Margo Wilson and Antonietta Daniele, found that although suicidal men chose to take their wives and children with them, suicidal women "almost never decide to 'rescue'" their husbands as well as their children.

"We hypothesize that this behavioural difference reflects a more general sex difference in proprietary constructions of the 'family,' with men feeling proprietary primarily about their wives and secondarily about their children, while women have strongly proprietary feeling about their children alone," the report noted.

Source: Ferenc, Leslie (2004). "Women Rarely Commit Murder-Suicide 'It's a Distorted View of Love.'" *Toronto Star*, December 14. Reprinted with permission.

Most homicides in the United States are intraracial (whites killing whites and blacks killing blacks). Moreover, in 2002, blacks were seven times more likely to commit homicide than whites, and six times more likely to be victimized by homicide. In addition, black victims were far more likely to be involved in drug-related homicides (see Table 4.2)

Table 4.2
Homicide Type by Race, 1976-2002

	Victims			Offenders		
	White	Black	Other	White	Black	Other
All homicides	51.1%	46.8%	2.1%	45.9%	52.1%	2.0%
Victim/offender relationship						
Intimate	56.2%	41.7%	2.2%	54.0%	43.9%	2.1%
Family	60.2%	37.4%	2.3%	58.8%	38.9%	2.2%
Infanticide	55.6%	41.9%	2.5%	55.0%	42.5%	2.5%
Eldercide	68.9%	29.6%	1.5%	53.9%	44.6%	1.6%
Circumstances						
Felony murder	55.0%	42.4%	2.5%	39.2%	59.2%	1.6%
Sex-related	67.1%	30.5%	2.4%	55.2%	42.9%	1.9%
Drug-related	37.0%	62.1%	.9%	33.5%	65.5%	1.1%
Gang-related	57.9%	38.7%	3.4%	54.3%	41.5%	4.2%
Argument	48.3%	49.7%	2.0%	46.5%	51.4%	2.1%
Workplace	85.2%	11.6%	3.2%	69.7%	27.3%	3.0%
Weapon						
Gun homicide	47.6%	50.6%	1.8%	42.3%	56.0%	1.7%
Arson	59.3%	37.8%	2.9%	55.5%	42.3%	2.2%
Poison	80.6%	17.1%	2.4%	78.8%	19.3%	1.9%
Multiple victims or offenders						
Multiple victims	64.1%	32.5%	3.3%	56.6%	40.1%	3.3%
Multiple offenders	55.3%	42.0%	2.7%	45.0%	52.6%	2.3%

Source: Fox, J.A. & M.W. Zawitz (2004). "Homicide Trends in the United States" {Online]. Available at: http://www.ojp.usdoj.gov/bjs/homicide/homtrnd.htm#contents

Racial differences in homicide rates in the United States have been the subject of much discussion because homicide is one of major reasons for differences in life expectancy between blacks and whites (Kposowa, 1999). As Wiersema (2001) states, official statistics indicate that:

> Approximately one-fifth of the difference between the life expectancies of black and white males is attributable to differences in homicide mortality. . . . Blacks are only 12% of the U.S. population, but they suffer nearly 50% of the homicide mortality. . . . For blacks between age 15 and 24 it was the leading cause of death and fourth for blacks of all ages and gen-

ders. . . . For black males 15-24 years, the homicide rate in 1991 was an astounding 158.9 per 100,000 population. . . . in a U.S. population whose rate was about 9 per 100,000.

In terms of the methods by which people are killed, it is clear that the weapon of choice in the United States is the handgun. Some proponents of gun ownership often argue that "guns don't kill people, people kill people." However, there is a strong positive relationship between gun availability and homicide rates. In fact, more than one-half (51%) of the homicides in the United States in 2002 were committed with a handgun, and "other guns" were used in another 16 percent (Fox & Zawitz, 2004).

In addition, Figure 4.2 suggests that over the past 25 years there has been a gradual decline in the percentage of homicides that result from "arguments" (though they still constitute the number-one set of circumstances in which homicide occurs), and an increase in the proportion of homicides for which the circumstances of the crime are unknown.

Figure 4.3
Homicide Victims by Circumstances, 1976-2002, USA

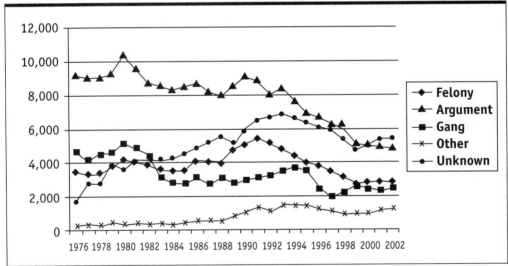

Source: Fox, J.A. & M.W. Zawitz (2004). "Homicide Trends in the United States" [Online]. Available at: http://www.ojp.usdoj.gov/bjs/homicide/homtrnd.htm#contents

Homicide also varies according to location. Although homicides have declined in large cities of more than one million people in the past decade, it is still mostly an urban crime (see Figure 4.4). On a larger geographical scale, homicide rates are persistently higher in the southern and western states than in the North (Cohen, 1998). However, some scholars have pointed out that the rates in mid-sized U.S. cities have not declined, and in many cases have increased—a trend they attribute to the inability of these communities to recover from the effects of massive economic restructuring and deindustrialization (Matthews, Maume & Miller, 2001). In a similar vein, when we examine the relationship between homicide and the socioeconomic conditions of local communities, we find reliably that homicide is more likely to occur in communities that are socially disorganized or suffer from social ills associated with poverty and concentrated disadvantage, including, but not limited to, factors such as underemployment and unemployment, low education, and low social control (Anderson, 1990; Peterson & Krivo, 1999; Wilson, 1996).

Figure 4.4
Percentage of Homicides by Size of City, USA, 2002

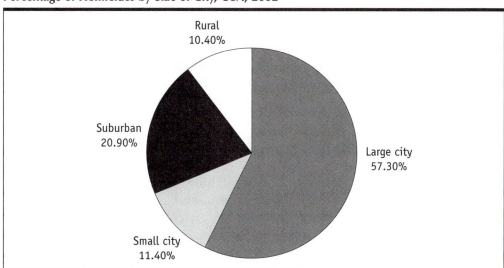

Source: Fox, J.A. & M.W. Zawitz (2004). "Homicide Trends in the United States" [Online]. Available at: http://www.ojp.usdoj.gov/bjs/homicide/homtrnd.htm#contents

Overall, this brief tour of the statistical landscape of homicide in the United States yields the following conclusions:

- Homicide rates vary considerably by age, gender, class position, and geographical location.

- The characteristics most likely to predict victims and perpetrators of homicide are young, male, belonging to a minority group, and living in socially and economically disadvantaged locations.

These data provide us with a sense of who commits homicide, who are victims, and the contexts within which homicides occur. We now turn to criminological explanations of *why* homicide happens.

Theories of Homicide

In this chapter we will examine theories that fall within the broader categories of theory discussed in Chapter 2. As a preface to our discussion, however, it is worth noting that for hundreds of years, perspectives on why people commit homicide were dominated by religious thinking. Such **demonological** perspectives (they really cannot be called theories because they are not falsifiable and fail to meet other criteria of a scientific theory) advance the notion that when people kill, they do so because they are possessed by evil spirits, or because they have been tempted by the devil. Today, such perspectives have been rejected by the scientific community, although there are still those who believe that demonology is the most valid explanation for the seemingly irrational nature of some criminal homicides. Despite these enduring beliefs, and following criminological scholars, we argue that "worldly" explanations based on scientific methodology and grounded in examining material conditions as well as human relationships are most likely to yield adequate explanations of homicide.

Rational Choice Theories

You will recall that classical criminology essentially argues that people have the capacity to make rational choices about their behavior. Thus, when they commit homicide they are deemed to have evaluated the "pros and cons" of doing their crime and, if caught, should be punished proportionally to the level of harm created by their crime. Given the centrality of deterrence to classical criminology, many argue that the death penalty also deters others from committing murder (Paternoster, 1991). There is, however, very little evidence that this is the case (Zimring & Hawkins, 1986).

One of the classical statements of the rational choice perspective is from economist Gary Becker (1968), who argues that the processes involved in choosing to commit crime are the same as the processes we might use to purchase consumer goods. Further, he contends that by examining and evaluating the relative costs and benefits to social institutions (the court system, police, prisons, etc.), victims, and offenders, we can come up with a rational "calculus" that enables us to determine what the nature of punishment should be. We can, he argues, "dispense with special theories of anomie, psychological inadequacies, or inheritance of special traits and simply extend the economist's usual analysis of choice" (Becker, 1968:170). Thus, in Becker's estimation, there is no need to analyze the *causes* of rational decisionmaking. It is simply enough to pursue models that help us to determine how to respond after someone has made the choice to kill.

A more recent variant of the rational choice perspective comes from the work of Cornish and Clarke (1986), who argue that any crime can be understood according to the following three principles:

1. Offenders try to benefit themselves through criminal behavior.

2. They make choices in the process of pursuing these benefits.

3. These choices are rational, and take into account available information, no matter what the quality of that information might be.

Cornish and Clarke attempt to go beyond the simple notion of "individuals making rational choices" to account for the role of broader factors in influencing those decisions. For instance, they include social, demographic, and familial factors as being important to the process by which people make choices, and also include elements of social learning theory in their model. For these theorists, then, the process of making rational choices is different for every person and is conditioned by a "constellation of opportunities, costs, and benefits attaching to particular kinds of crime" (Cornish & Clarke, 1987:993).

It may be true that there is some element of choice inherent in any behavior, and that even serial murderers are making "rational" choices to kill because for them, the perceived psychological, financial, or symbolic benefits outweigh the negative consequences of committing homicide. However, critics have pointed out that rational choice theory assumes that all behaviors can be understood in terms of rational, calculated decisionmaking, which ignores the fact that "impulsivity, moral ambiguity and expressivity" can, and often do, play an important part in criminal events, particularly homicide (De Hann & Vos, 2003). Put differently, human beings do not simply "choose" behavior on the basis of cold, calculated choices. As Hayward and Young (2004:263) point out, rational choice theory ignores factors such as "intensity of motivation, feelings of humiliation, anger, and rage—as well as love and solidarity," and makes:

> every intellectual attempt. . . . to distance crime from structural inequalities and social injustice. Instead, we have pallid, calculative individuals, committing crime where it is possible, coupled with putative victims who, as likely targets, are only understood through their attempts to calculate their optimum security strategies.

Thus, as a theory of homicide (or an explanation of any other type of crime), rational choice perspectives are too narrow in their conceptualization of human action. In particular, because they are posed at the level of individual choice, as a rule they fail to take account of the social settings and broader macrosociological factors (such as economic conditions or cultural norms) that condition and shape behavior. Even Cornish and Clarke's attempt to examine background factors such as one's family dynamics fail to situate those factors adequately in the *broader* social-political climate in which we live. For instance, it is true that homicide rates are higher in poor ghettoized areas of the United States, but it is not enough simply to include poverty as a dimension of rational choice, because the very condition of poverty demands explanation as well.

In summary, then, rational choice perspectives on homicide are important because they tend to drive criminal justice policy decisions in the United States, particularly in relation to the widespread but erroneous idea that the death penalty is the ultimate deterrent of homicide. In fact, states that use the death penalty actually have higher homicide rates. Because the death penalty is still prevalent in the United States, it is important to understand the basic ideas behind the rational choice perspective. A few homicides are indeed the work of individuals who coldly and carefully calculate the pros and cons of their crime.

Yet, as we shall see, there is plenty of evidence suggesting that the majority of homicides involve a constellation of circumstances, emotions, and processes that make it very difficult to use the same kind of logic we might employ to explain buying a refrigerator to explain the killing of a human being. In particular, we need explanations of homicide that take into account factors such as anger, intoxication, culture, and strain. We now turn to theories that attempt to account for the role of some of these factors.

Strain Theories

As outlined in Chapter 2, strain theories focus attention on the ways in which social structure conditions behavior, and thus turn attention away from properties of the individual (such as individual psychopathology or biological factors). Further, we know that modern capitalist societies are structured in fundamentally unequal ways, thus leading to strain for some population groups and individuals. It is the experience of, and reaction to, strain that is of core interest for strain theorists. Not surprisingly, then, the focus of much research on homicide within the strain tradition has been on the role of inequality of opportunity, whether this is determined by race, age, gender, or social class.

One of the most provocative statements about homicide within this field of thought is that of Messner and Rosenfeld (1999:27), who argue that "strain influences" constitute "structural forces that push or pressure persons into violence." Specifically, and following the thought of Merton (1938), they argue that when people are deprived of the resources to achieve the desires or needs they expect, they may resort to violence or other types of crime in which the chances of being victimized by homicide are high. Societies that diminish people's life chances to achieve what they expect to achieve, are in danger of fostering criminal activity, including homicide, because people in such circumstances may experience anger, frustration, or hopelessness at not being able to achieve the "American Dream." Messner and Rosenfeld further argue that while the American Dream creates pressures on people to possibly engage in criminal behavior to achieve their goals, it also creates a society in which the economy dominates in all areas of life. As a result, the family and educational and political institutions are unable to function properly to help people cope with the pressure to commit crimes (Pratt & Godsey, 2003).

A variant of the strain perspective on homicide has been developed by Robert Agnew (1992), who maintains that strain can be experienced not just by experiencing a contradiction between culturally transmitted goals and legitimate means of achieving them, but also through other avenues. For instance, people could undergo strain because of negative relationships with others in which one person creates unpleasant experiences for another, blocks their goals, or endangers something they value. In turn, these experiences may create anxiety, anger, or depression, which may result in criminal, possibly violent, behavior (Tittle, 2000).

As noted in the section above on incidence and prevalence rates, there is very good evidence that some disadvantaged groups in the United States are more likely than others to be both the victims and perpetrators of homicide. Moreover, as the data in that section illustrate, African-American males (who are more likely to be poor) are disproportionately the victims and perpetrators of homicide. Further, in cross-national studies, Messner (1980) and Messner and Rosenfeld (1997) have found that homicide rates are positively associated with income inequality, a finding that has consistently been replicated by a host of scholars. However, other empirical tests of strain approaches to homicide have yielded mixed results, with some showing the expected positive association between homicide and inequality, and others yielding statistically insignificant relationships. Scholars have pointed out that these inconsistencies are probably due to methodological difficulties including problems with the nature of homicide data and issues around the measurement of poverty itself (Pratt &

Lowenkamp, 2002). Despite these obstacles, it appears clear that that there is a significant positive association between economic inequality and homicide rates; that is, countries with higher income inequality levels and weakened mechanisms that might insulate people from the effects of economic inequality exhibit higher homicide rates (Savolainen, 2000). It is also true that homicides and violent assault are more likely to occur among low-income groups (DeKeseredy, Alvi, Schwartz & Tomaszewski, 2003), particularly because such populations also tend to experience a host of other social pathologies, including lack of resources, low educational achievement, and family disruption (Kovandzic, Vieraitis & Yeisley, 1998; Patterson, 1991).

Subcultural Theories

Subcultural theories of homicide proceed from the observation that homicide rates vary according to the characteristics of certain social groups. As pointed out above, one of the most enduring examples of such observations is the greater rate of homicide found in the southern states of the United States (Loftin & Hill, 1974; Nisbett, 1993; Nisbett & Cohen, 1996; Parker & Pruitt, 2000). In contrast to strain explanations of homicide, which would highlight higher rates of social inequality and poverty in the South, subcultural explanations focus on possible differences in culture between northern and southern states. Work of this type generally draws upon a groundbreaking thesis advanced by Wolfgang and Ferracuti (1967), who contended that subcultures of violence (see Chapter 2 for a detailed discussion of subculture) exist when its members share common norms and practices regarding the use of violence, and where there are avenues of socialization enabling these norms to be legitimated and reproduced. Thus, according to some scholars (e.g., Ellison, Burr & McCall, 2003:328-329), higher southern state homicide rates might be attributable to:

- The alleged presence of a code of honor in the South that creates a mentality in which disrespect is legitimately met with violence. Allowing oneself to be insulted is interpreted as a sign of weakness, or

- Heightened frustration, "sensitivity to interpersonal slights," and tolerance toward violence stemming from the South's defeat in the Civil War.

Ellison, Burr, and McCall (2003) found some support for the argument that another important but generally ignored factor might be high levels of religious belief in conservative Protestantism in the South, which is a belief system that tends to emphasize strong punishment and retaliation in the face of transgressions.

Another set of subcultures that has received a great deal of attention are those formed by minority groups, particularly in socially disadvantaged neighborhoods. For example, some ethnographic research (Anderson, 1990, 1999; Bourgois, 1995) asserts that many men living in such circumstances legitimate their existence and bolster their self-esteem by engaging in "tough guy" poses, or "refusing to back down" in the face of conflict. In turn, this "search for respect" is more likely to lead to violent confrontations, some of which result in murder.

However, other academics have warned against generalizing such claims. They point out, for example, that not all African-Americans approve of violence, and that claiming that some minority groups are more prone to violence because their subculture validates "pro-violent attitudes and norms" stereotypes blacks and also ignores the role of broader economic factors, the behavior of the criminal justice system, and the "historical devaluing of black life" (Hawkins, 1987).

Another variation of the subculture-homicide linkage has been developed by Swidler (1986), who advances the idea that culture is a "tool kit" of resources used by individuals to shape their actions. Swidler's argument is that culture—defined as symbols, stories, rituals, and world-views—offers a range of possible "tools" that people use in different ways and combinations to deal with everyday life on an ongoing basis. Moreover, these cultural toolkits will vary from one person to another. Thus, individuals may have different "inventories" of cultural knowledge and different skills that will dictate possible responses and outcomes in given situations. For instance, some people may have a world view that determines (for them) when it is appropriate to engage in a physical fight (e.g., when one feels they have been disrespected, or perhaps the desire not to appear "weak), and may also possess the skills to do so (including how to use a knife, gun, or other weapon). In effect, cultural toolkits help people to determine "what's going on here" and how to respond.

Empirical tests of subcultural theories of homicide have yielded inconsistent results. As with strain theory, one of the reasons is likely related to measurement issues, particularly the measurement of "culture." This is because culture is a very subjective concept (people hold values individually), and therefore it is not easy to measure culture at the aggregate level. One example of this problem, as pointed out by Alvarez and Bachman (2003), is that it is very difficult to take a measure of culture seriously when it is defined simply as a "region," because not all people in a geographical area necessarily share similar beliefs and values. Similarly, as pointed out earlier, lumping all blacks together as if they are a homogenous subculture "entails an implicit pejorative indictment of urban minority residents and communities which is unfair and racist in nature" (Parker, 1989:985). Accordingly, before a reliable assessment of the relationship between subculture and homicide can be made, much more work needs to be done to derive valid measures of culture.

Social Control Theories

As noted earlier in this book, the central question asked by control theorists is not why someone commits a crime, but rather why all of us do not. The answer is that those of us who do not commit homicide possess strong bonds to the norm in our society that we should not kill another human being. Thus, those who do kill do so because these bonds have been broken or weakened. So, what are the implications of this view for understanding homicide? The most influential social control theorist, Travis Hirschi (1969), argued that because people possess a "natural impulse" toward crime, the degree to which they possess strong social bonds plays a crucial role in determining how they will act in a conflict situation (see Chapter 2 for a review of the elements of social bond theory). In later work, Gottfredson and Hirschi (1990) focused attention on the ways that lack of **self-control** interact with other factors, including whether the individuals are intoxicated, the proximity and availability of weapons, and the degree to which participants possess conflict resolution skills. Thus, homicide might be a way for some people lacking in self control to satisfy the impulse to deal with a situation relatively quickly and easily. Moreover, such people will also demonstrate low verbal ability, a tendency toward risky behavior, and insensitivity to others (C. Taylor, 2001).

Control theorists maintain that self-control and strong social bonds originate largely in the family. Thus, children in families that are close and in which discipline is effective are more likely to demonstrate strong social bonds. Because schools are also an important socialization mechanism, control theorists have also emphasized the role of the school in both determining one's life chances and in creating conforming or prosocial attitudes in children.

As noted in Chapter 2, there is some empirical support for control theories of crime, but only in relation to less serious crimes. Moreover, there are numerous problems with this type of perspective. For example, while there is some modest and consistent empirical support for the social bonding variant of social control theory, the self-control viewpoint remains to be adequately tested because it suffers from circular reasoning. As Akers (1991) points out, Gottfredson and Hirschi do not satisfactorily operationalize "low self-control" and do not sufficiently distinguish low self-control from the inclination to commit crime. Thus, low self-control seems to cause low-self control (Akers, 2000), and until such time that this tautology is resolved, we will not fully understand whether this theory adequately explains homicide.

Another criticism of control theories stems from its overemphasis on the individual. As with all theories emphasizing individual traits, control theories fail to properly examine the role of social structural factors in producing violent crime. Another way of thinking about this is to ask *how* social structures and patterns (e.g., racism, poverty, or social exclusion) interact to condition people so that they are impulsive, insensitive, or lacking in verbal skills. Indeed, the fact that most developed countries have much lower homicide rates than the United States points to factors other than lack of self-control in understanding homicide. At the level of individuals, and as suggested in Chapter 2, the fact that males are overwhelmingly more likely to be both the victims and perpetrators of homicide suggests that there are likely to be different mechanisms by which males and females are socialized into strong social bonds or high/low self-control. Yet control theories remain largely silent on this empirical problem.

Finally, it has been alleged that Gottfredson and Hirschi do not pay sufficient attention to the role played by opportunities to commit crime (Grasmick, Tittle, Bursik & Arneklev, 1993), that is, that it may be that homicide rates are higher in countries like the United States (or within certain communities) because of the greater availability of attractive opportunities or targets.

Interactionist Theories

Interactionist perspectives on homicide focus on micro-level interactions between people and the ways in which those individuals "construct" or "frame" the situations in which they find themselves. Thus, the key elements in interactionist approaches involve detailed analysis of victims, offenders, audiences (e.g., bystanders), and the contexts in which these actors interact. A classic example of such an approach is the work of Luckenbill (1977), whose study of homicide as a "**situated transaction**" emphasizes the intense exchanges that occur between victim and offender in what often amounts to a "character contest." Luckenbill posits that there are six stages that make up the dynamics of a homicide event.

- Stage 1. The victim does or says something that the perpetrator interprets as an "affront." Generally, this could by an insult, a threat, or a refusal to cooperate.

- Stage 2. The perpetrator interprets the affront as intentional (rather than an accident or the result of intoxication, for example).

- Stage 3. The offender attempts to reaffirm face by standing his or her ground.

- Stage 4. The victim must make a choice between "standing up" (and thereby saving face) to the offender's attempt to reaffirm face, fleeing, or apologizing. In many cases, bystanders may escalate the situation (for example, urging the two to fight it out), thereby making the latter two choices difficult or impossible.

- Stage 5. The combatants commit to battle.

- Stage 6. The victim falls, and the perpetrator flees, is held by bystanders, or waits for the authorities to arrive.

Luckenbill's analysis is valuable because it breaks down homicide into the set of *interactions* between individuals and emphasizes the critical importance of the ways in which individuals interpret situations that might escalate out of control and cascade into violence. Because interaction is a "two-way street," it stands to reason that understanding homicide requires an appreciation of the roles of *both* the victim and offender. In effect, it is not true that homicides consist of an "innocent victim" who is just minding his or her own business only to be murdered by a stranger. Indeed, Wolfgang (1958) goes so far as to suggest that victims can be the "authors" of their own demise because they are often the ones who initiate the argument or confrontation that begins the process, a situation he terms **victim precipitation**.

Another approach that draws heavily on the insights of symbolic interactionism can be found in the work of Lonnie Athens (1980, 1992). Athens argues that anyone socialized into violence, a process he calls **violentization**, will in all likelihood become a violent criminal. His analysis, which is based on interviews with violent offenders in five prisons, emphasizes the importance of understanding how individuals interpret situations, which then forms the basis for their actions. Like Luckenbill, Athens provides a detailed description of the manner by which the "meaning" of situations is interpreted and may create violentization. According to him, the process has four stages, taking place over a longer time frame than that suggested by Luckenbill:

- **Brutalization**: in which the individual is dominated by violence, witnesses violent victimization (often of an intimate other), and learns which situations seem to "demand" violence and the techniques necessary to enact that violence.

- **Defiance**: in which the individual tries to come to terms with their experiences of brutalization and does so by committing to become violent so that they will never be dominated again.

- **Dominance Engagement**: in which the individual puts their new found resolve (defiance) to the test by engaging in violent acts on numerous occasions.

- **Virulency**: in which the person gains a reputation for violence, people begin to treat him or her as a violent person, and where the person now makes a firm commitment to attack or kill if aggravated.

Athens claims that his theory can be generalized to all forms of violence, and its strength lies not only in the "deconstruction" of the homicide process into discrete parts, but also in its detailed specification regarding the characteristics of each stage.

In summary, interactionist approaches to homicide focus on the quality and nature of interactions between offenders and victims, and emphasize the importance of issues such as attacks on identity, "honor contests," and the ways in which offenders and victims interpret the situations in which they find themselves, and then use these interpretations to guide their actions.

One of the difficulties with interactionist theories of homicide, like interactionist theories in general, is that by definition they focus only on the micro level of human interactions and interpretations. Thus, such theories tend to neglect the role played by macro social factors (such as poverty, unemployment, racism, hypermasculinity, and underprivileged social environments) in *setting the conditions* in which confrontations and their interpretation take place. Put another way, if we are to fully understand homicide we must attempt to account for the ways in which broader social forces *interact* with, shape, and set limits on human behavior.

Interactionist accounts also must contend with measurement problems. Traditionally, empirical studies of homicide utilizing the interactionist paradigm have used imprecise measures of the relationship between offender and victim. For example, Silverman and Kennedy (1993) used a continuum of "relational distance" (defined as close family relationships on one end, and stranger relationships on the other) as a surrogate measure for "relationship." Although such an approach might generate some useful information, it is not a very good indicator of the quality of specific aspects of the relationship between two combatants. Two people could be strangers, but that tells us little about the *nature* of the character contest they might engage in outside a pub after a heavy night of drinking.

Another criticism of the interactionist approach concerns the claim that *all* homicides involve situational transactions. In other words, some people may kill for reasons that have nothing to do with how they interpret a situation or their relationship to the individual they intend to kill. Consider the case of femicide for example, which may often involve cold calculating behavior by the male partner and have nothing to do with arguments that escalate out of control. This kind of variation in the reasons for homicide counters the argument that all homicides follow a neat set of linear steps culminating in violence.

Finally, the emphasis on "situations" and their interpretation in this set of theories does not allow an account of the role played by people's individual characteristics or learned behaviors in homicides (although Athens's work is somewhat of an exception). For example, while it is probably true that homicide can often be the tragic consequence of a series of interactions that escalate out of control, the question still remains: why do some people seem to have the ability to avoid such escalation (choosing perhaps to walk away, ignore the situation, or attempt to resolve it peacefully) while others do not?

Ecological Theories

As noted earlier in this chapter, the fact that homicide rates tend to be higher in particular locations is a clear and persistent finding in criminological research. Ecological perspectives such as social disorganization theories emphasize the ways in which the social structure of urban areas (particularly in communities characterized by high rates of residential turnover, population diversity, and economic deprivation) contribute to a weakening of social control, thereby increasing the possibility of violent crime. The social disorganization perspective is not new, having its roots in the work of Shaw and McKay (1942), who, as you will recall from Chapter 2, had proposed that the organizational features of urban environments made a difference to levels of social disorganization. The central ideas within this perspective are that *strong ties* between people (for example, people who get together with neighbors on a regular basis, join community associations, or participate in neighborhood recreational activities) coupled with high levels of *informal control* (such as neighbors' efforts to reduce disorderly behavior, scolding children who are misbehaving, or questioning suspicious persons who might be "hanging around" in the neighborhood) work to reduce the level of criminal offending within those neighborhoods, because they *mediate* (i.e., act as a kind of "cushion" against) the potentially negative effects of social disorganization.

The first, and now classic, study providing persuasive empirical evidence of this relationship was conducted by Sampson and Groves (1989), who, in their examination of British Crime Survey data from 1982, found that the levels of local friendship networks, organizational participation, and supervision of teenagers did predict levels of both property crime and violent crime.

Later researchers have developed this perspective, arguing that factors such as the prevalence and quality of social networks and friendship ties, trust, and social cohesion might also play an important role in explaining variation in crime rates (Bursik, 1999; Sampson, Raudenbush & Earls, 1997; Wilson, 1987, 1996), More recently, researchers have focused on different dimensions of social disorganization, including family dysfunction, relative poverty, and racial segregation, while others have begun to examine the possibility that some social ties can actually *increase* crime.

Another, quite different variant of the ecological perspective is **routine activities theory**, which, as you will recall from Chapter 3, maintains that criminal offending is more likely to take place where there are motivated offenders, suitable victims, and in the absence of capable guardians (Cohen & Felson, 1979). Thus, homicide rates will be higher where there are greater opportunities for homicide to occur and because people's lifestyles might be conducive to such opportunities (Hindelang, Gottfredson & Garofalo, 1978). Examples of intersecting opportunities and lifestyles would be young, unemployed males congregating together in unsupervised situations in which there is an expectation of aggressive behavior on the part of some individuals, or when elderly people are victimized by theft-related homicide because they are more likely to be perceived as suitable targets and lack capable guardianship (Nelsen & Huff-Corzine, 1998).

According to Cohen and Felson, crimes such as homicide are more likely to occur when all three of the elements discussed above are present. Motivated offenders are individuals with criminal intentions who also possess the ability to carry out these intentions. Suitable victims are individuals the offender perceives to be useful targets because (1) they offer some kind of value (e.g., financial or symbolic gain), (2) are accessible, (3) the crime would have low visibility, and (4) the victim can be defeated. Finally, the lack of capable guardians refers to the absence of individuals (e.g., police or bystanders) who might protect a person from being victimized.

In the past, one of the persistent problems with the social disorganization thesis was that we did not know much regarding the role of variables that may intervene between "social disorganization" on the one hand, and homicide/crime rates on the other (Lowenkamp, Cullen & Pratt, 2003). In the past few decades, however, numerous studies have used the social disorganization framework to study homicide and have attempted to account for the role of intermediate variables (e.g., poverty, ethnic heterogeneity, low levels of supervision, and the like) (Anderson, 1990; Peterson & Krivo, 1993; Sampson, 1987; Sampson & Groves, 1989).

On the whole, these studies have provided fairly strong support for a link between social disorganization and homicide rates. However, there remains controversy over the role played by "**collective efficacy**" (neighborhood social cohesion and informal social control) in possibly preventing or reducing homicide. For example, it is not clear whether high levels of collective efficacy will necessarily prevent men from killing their female partners (DeKeseredy et al., 2003). In addition, some research suggests that different aspects of social disorganization may influence different types of homicide. As Kubrin and Weitzer (2003a:390-391) point out:

> . . . while high homicide rates likely influence residential mobility patterns in general, certain types of homicide may especially influence mobility; street-level homicides between strangers are more likely to affect neighborhood structure than domestic homicides. As domestic killings generally occur in the home and are more private affairs. . . . residents are less likely to be effected by these killings. Residents are more likely to change their behavior in the community or relocate in the presence of frequent killings between strangers that appear to occur more randomly. Reciprocal effects models are ideal for addressing these issues.

Another issue is that while contemporary research within this perspective has "unpacked" the notion of social disorganization, there may still be aspects of communities that have so far remained unexamined. For instance, very little attention has been directed at the role of neighborhood culture, formal social control mechanisms, or the urban political economy in explaining crime (Kubrin & Weitzer, 2003a).

Furthermore, researchers working in this tradition have noted that it may be implausible to assume that "communities" are cozy "urban villages" characterized by strong ties and high levels of interpersonal interaction, or that neighborhoods can be defined in terms of traditional, "neat and tidy" geographical boundaries (Morenoff, Sampson & Raudenbush, 2001).

There are also some problems with routine activities approaches. One major issue with the routine activities perspective is that it has traditionally been gender-blind, ignoring the ways in which women's lifestyles and patterns of social behavior influence victimization (although some, such as Schwartz and Pitts, have begun the process of taking gender seriously within this framework; see Chapter 3). Another serious difficulty with the routine activities perspective is that it does not deal with the problem of where criminal motivation comes from; it assumes motivated offenders, but does not offer an analysis of what motivates offenders. It therefore cannot be considered a theory that *fully* explores the causes of homicide.

Regardless of these issues, the routine activities theory has garnered some empirical support in relation to property and personal crimes. In a study of homicide rates in a New York borough, Messner and Tardiff (1985) found that the characteristics of victims were in line with the assumptions of routine activities theory. In addition, a study of Milwaukee homicides conducted by Caywood (1998) found partial support for the routine activities perspective. However, Caywood cautions that more definitive evidence is needed before we can have full confidence in the usefulness of the perspective for explaining homicide.

Critical Perspectives

As we noted earlier in this book, critical criminology encompasses a range of theories, including postmodernism, left realism, classical Marxism, peacemaking, and feminist approaches. So far in this chapter we have focused on the most widely cited criminological theories of homicide, but as you may have noticed, some of these theories, with modest modifications, could easily fall under the label of critical perspectives. Strain theory, for instance, focuses on the role of social inequality—a key concern of critical criminologists—in explaining homicide, but does not go far enough in addressing the structural *sources* of strain. Similarly, interactionist accounts emphasize homicide as a "transaction" between individuals in which meaning is central to understanding the outcomes of confrontation. However, little is said regarding *how* and *why* such meanings come into play in the first place. Could it be, for instance, that males are more likely to kill one another in a confrontation because they have been socialized into a belief system (which in itself is a consequence of patriarchal social systems) regarding "appropriate male behavior" or the ideals of a "male honor code"?

As many of our criticisms of extant theories of homicide are advanced from a critical perspective, we will not here attempt to rework those theories to fit within the critical paradigm. Rather, in this section, we focus our attention on two critical perspectives on homicide: left realism and masculinities theory.

Left Realism

In Chapter 2, we pointed out that left realism is a critical perspective on crime emphasizing the potentially deadly intersection between relative deprivation, low levels of formal and informal social control, and individualism, which is in turn a consequence of the way market societies operate. One of the outcomes of this interaction is the brutalization of communities and the classes of people who live in them. Building on the empirical realities of homicide, particularly the fact that most homicides are intra-class and occur in deprived communities, a left realist perspective on homicide emphasizes that homicide is an individual's "solution" to a perceived problem in social environments that have become little more than pockets of urban warfare (see Box 4.3). When people's way of life is governed by an "every man for himself" culture, where like-minded people encourage and perpetuate violence, why should we be surprised when they sometimes resort to killing one another (Young, 1997)? In short, what is "left" in the left realist perspective is the recognition that violent, brutalizing societies tend to create violent, antisocial people, and that such societies are the outcome of an economic and political system (late capitalism) that is itself brutally efficient.

The "realist" component of this perspective emphasizes that solutions to the problem of homicide must emphasize progressive attempts to reform the nature of capitalism, by creating programs, institutions, and, more broadly, human relationships that encourage cooperation (rather than competition) and humane, fair economic relationships.

Although we would argue that at least in terms of homicide, it is less of a theory and more of a perspective in search of theoretical development and empirical verification, left realism nevertheless offers a promising synthesis of a perspective critical of prevailing social relations and elements of extant theories that appear to have been partially successful in explaining homicide.

Box 4.3
America's Formidable Enemy Within
When the Underclass Has Had Enough, The Result Will Resemble Civil War

It is just after 10 P.M. in downtown Seattle when the evening is suddenly punctured by a man's scream. Far below the hotel window, in a well-lit alleyway, two young African-Americans are trying to separate a middle-aged white man from his wallet.

The man flails wildly, kicking the shin of one of his assailants, knocking him backwards, but it is his unrelenting, attention-attracting shouting that finally drives them away.

They race down the alleyway and disappear into the drizzling night. But long after they have gone, the man—violated yet relatively unharmed—keeps shouting a torrent of racist invective against his attackers.

"Go back to your cages," he howls. But he doesn't report the attack to the police. "What's the use?" he says. "This is normal now."

The next morning, inside the same hotel, William Julius Wilson, a leading Harvard sociologist and respected African-American academic, looks and sounds frustrated as he talks about "America's disintegrating social fabric." The incident outside the hotel has become normal, routine, and unexceptional in a nation where murder often hardly raises an eyebrow. . . .

Paul Jargowsky, a University of Texas social scientist who specializes in poverty and has written the book *Poverty in Place*, says the population of U.S. high-poverty neighborhoods has risen from four million to eight million over the past 10 years. There are 2.5 million children "growing up in intolerable conditions," he adds.

Jargowsky says riots and even a form of civil war are possible. "It's unthinkable, I know, but the anger and frustration are growing every day. The ghettos are socially and economically isolated from American society. They're breeding grounds for the development of dysfunctional behavior. And there's no escape."

"America doesn't have any external enemies now, but it may have the most powerful internal enemy of all: itself. We're already seeing massive crime spilling out of these areas because of what amounts to racial and economic segregation. Concentrated poverty makes people increasingly hostile. The question is, how long will it take before it erupts". . . .

Ghettos have become a fact of life in America's largest inner-cities, but are also growing in such mid-size cities as Seattle, San Francisco, Atlanta, and New Orleans. They are increasingly isolated from the communities around them.

Haysom, I. (1997). "America's Formidable Enemy Within: When the Underclass Has Had Enough, The Result Will Resemble Civil War." *Ottawa Citizen* (February 23):A4.

Masculinities and Homicide

As discussed earlier in this chapter, homicide is overwhelmingly a male preoccupation (Bowker, 1998b). What is it about "maleness" that so powerfully predicts homicidal behavior and victimization? As Chapter 2 pointed out, masculinities scholars argue that some men believe that the only valid way of expressing and validating their masculinity lies in criminal behavior. Other scholars have taken a less sociological approach, arguing that the roots of male violence lie in biology or evolution. For instance, Wilson and Daly (1998) maintain that males evolved the mechanism of "sexual proprietariness" to ensure their reproductive success, a strategy involving the use of violence to coerce and control female partners (and see Chapter 3). In addition, and like some interactionists, they argue that the nature of confrontational homicide often consists of themes around male "honor" or "escalated showing off contests," which for them are also rooted in evolutionary patterns (Wilson & Daly, 1985).

However useful these ideas may be in alerting us to the *substance* of confrontation, Polk (1998) argues that evolutionary theories are impossible to test directly (because we will never know the psychology of humans in prehistoric environments). Drawing on the insights of Gould (1996), he also reminds us that culture is more likely than genetics to produce human behavior, but that culture does not work in Darwinian fashion. Moreover, in modern societies, men do not *need* to use violence to win over women, but are far more likely to achieve the latter by virtue of their social class, status, or power.

Given the limited explanatory power of evolutionary perspectives, what can we say about the link between masculinities and homicide? One provocative answer to this question comes from the work of Messerschmidt (1993), whose ideas about masculinities and crime were also encountered in Chapter 2. Briefly, Messerschmidt's **structured action theory** puts forward the idea that men's violence is, in a sense, easy to accomplish because it is so "normal." "Boys will be boys" in different ways because they grow up and exist in varying social structures that offer them differential access to power and resources. Consider, for example, the fact that men in some cultures are much less likely to kill than in others. If there is something biological in men that makes them homicidal, why do we not find similar rates of homicide across cultures and societies? Messerschmidt goes on to assert that together with other men in similar structural circumstances, these individuals construct ideals about hegemonic masculinity, the dominant idea of what it means for that particular group of men to "be a man," coupled with the exclusion and demonization of all other views about "being a man." All kinds of institutions, such as schools, relationships with other men, and life on the street, in bars, or elsewhere, "pattern" representations of what it means to be a man. In effect, men's use of violence is a consequence of men "doing" a form of masculinity that, for many men, is considered the only appropriate way to act. Again, when we consider that a disproportionate number of homicides occur between economically marginal males, this perspective helps us to understand that for these men, being tough, using violence, or killing another male might be the only way they are capable of asserting their masculinity.

Clearly, one of the advantages of masculinities approaches is their focus on the cultural and social pathways through which men become and then "do" masculinity. Certainly, peer groups play an important role in providing men with the psychological resources to be violent, as the discussion on male peer support in Chapter 3 suggests. But so do other interactions, including those with media, parents, entertainers, and politicians (Connell, 1995). The relatively young but growing field of masculinities and crime will no doubt continue to inform our understanding of the most important predictor of homicidal behavior and victimization.

Perhaps the most significant contribution of critical perspectives is that they attempt to reconcile features of some existing theories of homicide with the empirical realities of homicide. However, empirical tests of these perspectives are only beginning now. To the best of our knowledge, there are no tests of the left realist model of homicide, and clearly, more work needs to be done to flesh out the perspective and operationalize concepts before testing can occur. There is also much work to be done within the masculinities perspective, although the field has witnessed an explosion of work since the early 1990s. In particular, there is a need for more research on how men differ in terms of masculinities and in terms of sexual orientation (not all men who kill are heterosexual), as well as work on how gender can change over time ("maleness," or "femaleness" for that matter, need not be fixed in stone).

Summary

This chapter has outlined the incidence, prevalence, and contours of homicide in the United States, and has also explored some of the most widely cited theories of homicide. After reading this chapter, you should understand that like other crimes, homicide is multidimensional in nature, and that single-factor explanations cannot adequately explain it. Hopefully, you will have also noted that many of the arguments in the theories outlined above seem to dovetail and overlap with one another, thus providing a good foundation for a multifactorial approach to explaining homicide. For example, although interactionist theories are treated as a separate category in this chapter to simplify explanation, it is clear that the arguments made by some masculinities theorists such as Polk are directly relevant to explaining the contours and nature of character contests that might escalate out of control. In other words, it is not just that people sometimes interact with one another in ways that might end in violence, they may do so *because they are men* who hold hypermasculine ideas about appropriate behavior. In addition to alerting us to micro-level issues of interpretation of the situation, many of these theories point to the importance of the role played by broader social contexts and processes (such as poverty, subculture, and socialization) in explaining homicide.

The next steps in understanding homicide will involve integrating promising theoretical approaches as well as empirical tests of the resulting models. But there is also a need for homicide research on understudied groups such as gays and lesbians, the elderly, female murderers, and ethnic minorities other than African Americans or Hispanics. In addition, there is still no consensus among criminologists as to the reasons for the recent decline in homicide rates in the United States. Such theoretical and methodological issues, not to mention policy implications, will continue to preoccupy homicide researchers for the foreseeable future.

Discussion Questions

1. What would you consider to be the most important factors in explaining homicide? Why?

2. Why are some "places" more likely to have higher homicide rates than others?

3. How might we explain why some people do not kill, even though they live in similar circumstances and have similar backgrounds to those who do?

4. What developments might help us to understand why the homicide rate has fallen in recent decades?

5. Does capitalism generate homicidal behavior?

6. Why is the homicide rate in the United States higher in the South?

Problem-Solving Scenarios

1. How would you design a public space to reduce the possibility of homicide?

2. In a group, identify the similarities and differences between the homicide theories reviewed in this chapter.

3. How would you increase public awareness of the correlates of homicide?

4. How should homicides be classified?

5. What kinds of challenges would need to be overcome before we could change our ideas about what it means to "be a man"?

6. What kinds of things could bystanders do to prevent the escalation of arguments into homicide?

Suggested Readings

Lane, R. (1997). *Murder in America: A History*. Columbus, OH: Ohio State University Press.

> This book provides perhaps the most comprehensive historical perspective on homicide in the United States, and emphasizes the complex interplay of social structural, cultural, and historical forces in explaining homicide.

Smith, D.M & M. Zahn (eds.) (1999). *Homicide: A Sourcebook of Social Research*. Thousand Oaks, CA: Sage.

> This book compiles the work of some of the leading experts in homicide research. The chapters provide comprehensive overviews of theoretical and methodological issues in the study of homicide, and also in-depth analyses of particular issues such as youth and gang homicide and the role of alcohol and other drugs.

Alvarez, A. & R. Bachman. *Murder American Style*. Belmont, CA: Wadsworth.

> A brief but excellent introduction to the incidence, prevalence, and contours of homicide in the United States. The book provides comparisons with other countries, reviews and evaluates theoretical perspectives on homicide, and discusses important related issues such as the impact of homicide on victim's families.

Polk, K. (1994). *When Men Kill: Scenarios of Masculine Violence*. Cambridge, UK: Cambridge University Press.

> This book uses qualitative case studies to focus attention on the ways in which men kill. Polk emphasizes the centrality of masculinity and gender and class issues and also raises policy questions.

Online Resources

1. **Homicide Research Working Group**
    http://www.icpsr.umich.edu/HRWG/
    According to their web site, the Homicide Research Working Group has the following goals:

    - to forge links between research, epidemiology, and practical programs to reduce levels of mortality from violence,

    - to promote improved data quality and the linking of diverse homicide data sources,

    - to foster collaborative, interdisciplinary research on lethal and nonlethal violence,

    - to encourage more efficient sharing of techniques for measuring and analyzing homicide,

    - to create and maintain a communication network among those collecting, maintaining, and analyzing homicide datasets, and

    - to generate a stronger working relationship among homicide researchers.

2. **Bureau of Justice Statistics: Homicide Trends in the United States**
    http://www.ojp.usdoj.gov/bjs/homicide/homtrnd.htm
    This site provides the most up-to-date official data on U.S. homicide trends and patterns. It contains a series of charts that describe homicide patterns and trends in the United States since 1976.

3. **Families of Homicide Victims and Missing Persons Inc.**
    http://www.unresolvedhomicides.org/about.html
    This is the site of a nonprofit organization in Colorado that attempts to "find, support and empower families suffering from a loved one's unresolved murder or long-time disappearance."

4. **Violence and Injury Prevention Program**
    http://www.fmhi.usf.edu/amh/homicide-suicide/
    According to their web site, the Violence and Injury Prevention Program has several goals.

    - To conduct research to improve our ability to detect, intervene, and prevent suicide, homicide-suicide, and homicide in older and younger persons.

- To train professionals in the aging, mental health, public health, forensic, and community networks to detect, intervene, and prevent these situations.

- To provide traumatic grief resources for family survivors.

- To maintain a high media profile to educate the public about depression, suicide, and homicide-suicide.

- To participate in continuing medical education programs to educate the primary care community about depression, suicide, and homicide-suicide.

Think of a crime, any crime. Picture the first "crime" that comes into your mind. What do you see? The odds are you are not imagining a mining company executive sitting at his desk, calculating the costs of proper safety precautions and deciding not to invest in them. Probably what you do see with your mind's eye is one person attacking another physically or robbing something from another via the threat of physical attack (Reiman, 2004:65).

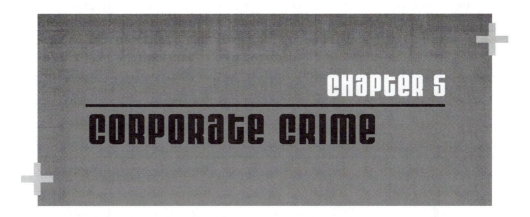

CHAPTER 5

CORPORATE CRIME

We started writing this chapter at the end of October 2004. At the same time, Academy Award–winning filmmaker Michael Moore released his controversial film *Fahrenheit 9/11* on DVD and video to influence U.S. citizens to vote President George W. Bush out of office. If you have seen this film, you probably know that it sharply attacks President Bush and the U.S. corporate elite, which is one of the key reasons why on October 31 President Bush's father made the following statement in a television interview in West Palm Beach, Florida: "Michael Moore is a despicable character. He has smeared my family. He has been gravely unfair about the President and he's part of that Hollywood elite who loves the limelight" (quoted by Harper, 2004:A16). Bush's father and his corporate supporters are also upset with Michael Moore because of statements like this one included in his best selling book, *Dude, Where's My Country?*: "The fear drug works like this: You are repeatedly told that bad, scary people are going to kill you, so place all your trust in *us*, your corporate leaders, and we will protect you" (2003:138; emphasis in original).

Whether or not you like Michael Moore, he is right about the fear instilled by corporate leaders. So is Jeffrey Reiman, who is quoted at the start of this chapter. Most U.S. citizens are very scared of being preyed upon by strangers on the street or by terrorists, yet corporations that routinely harm their workers, consumers, the economy, and the environment "enjoy a relatively high level of trust and respectability" and work hard to ensure that we hold them in high regard (Friedrichs,

2004a:1). Consider crime reporting. Today, 80 percent of U.S. newspapers are owned by corporate chains, which is one of the main reasons why people who read them know a lot about professional boxer Mike Tyson's many conflicts with the law but very little about situations like those listed in Box 5.1 (Hartman, 2002). By overrepresenting acts of interpersonal violence, corporate-owned media divert attention away from crimes of the powerful and reinforce the image that it is the socially and economically disenfranchised who pose the greatest threat to society (Reiman, 2004). Did you hear or read about any of the situations in Box 5.1?

Box 5.1
Examples of Harms Not Typically Considered Criminal

- A major cruise line concedes that it has been illegally dumping waste into Caribbean waters.

- A leading tire corporation recalls a huge number of tires deemed defective and complicit in motorists' deaths.

- Doctors, chiropractors, and lawyers in New Jersey are charged with staging automobile accidents and filing false insurance claims.

- The world's largest software company is charged with illegal, anticompetitive practices.

Source: Friedrichs, D.O. (2004:1). From *Trusted Criminals: White Collar Crime in Contemporary Society*, 2nd ed. Belmont, CA: Wadsworth. © 2004. Reprinted with permission of Wadsworth, a division of Thomson Learning. www.thomsonrights.com Fax 800-730-2215

As stated in Chapter 1, just because most people don't realize that situations such as those in Box 5.1 are serious threats to our social order does not mean that they are not harmful. Referred to here as examples of corporate crime, before we describe the extent, distribution, and theories of key variants of this social problem, it is first necessary to define it.

What is Corporate Crime?

Corporate crime is a type of **white-collar crime** (Friedrichs, 2004a; Simpson, 2002). Recall from reading Chapter 1 the theoretical contribution Edwin Sutherland made to an interactionist account of deviance and crime. He is also widely recognized as the "pioneer" of research on white-collar crime. In 1940, he defined this harm as "crime in the upper or white-collar class, composed of respectable or at least respected business and professional men" (p. 1). In a later publication, Sutherland (1949:9) defined white-collar crime as "crime committed by a person of respectability and high status in the course of his occupation." By now you may be asking, "What is the difference between what Sutherland was talking about and corporate crime?" This is a valid question, giving that both white-collar offenses and corporate crimes occur in the context of occupational roles and are committed by people like Martha Stewart who "wear nice clothes" at work. However, some sociologists like us contend that it is important to make conceptual distinctions within the class of crimes that Sutherland called "crimes of the respectable."

One important attempt to separate what many people join together was made by Clinard and Quinney (1973) (and later Clinard, Quinney & Wildeman, 1994). They accepted Sutherland's concept of white-collar crime as business crime, but they then divided business crime into two major categories: *occupational* and corporate. They defined occupational crimes as "offenses committed by individuals for themselves in the course of their occupations [and] offenses by employers against their employees." Corporate crime they defined as "offenses committed by corporate officials for their corporation and the offenses of the corporation itself" (1973:188). Thus, an executive who steals computer equipment from his office to use at home to view pornographic web sites has committed an occupational or white-collar crime. When the same executive attempts to bribe a foreign buyer to induce him to purchase his company's airplanes, he is engaging in corporate crime. The major difference between the two offenses is in the victims and beneficiaries of the crime. For example, corporate crime benefits both the company and the offender(s), while white-collar crime benefits only the offender. In sum, then, following Braithwaite (1984:6), corporate crime is defined here as the "conduct of employees acting on behalf of a corporation, which is proscribed and punishable by law."

The distinction made here between two types of crimes committed by executives is not always easy to make because many corporate crimes also benefit the individual. For example, executives who save their company money by insisting on maintaining unsafe working conditions for factory workers may be in line for a promotion to a higher salary. In general, though, white-collar crime is committed without the knowledge or permission of the company and is designed to profit only the individual. Corporate crime is, on the other hand, designed to benefit the company and only secondarily will profit the individual, if at all (DeKeseredy & Schwartz, 1996).

There are many different types of corporate crime, and it is beyond the scope of this chapter to examine all of them. Instead, we situate the wide range of corporate misdeeds under two broad categories: **corporate violence** and **economic corporate crimes**. It is also important to note that many of the harms that fall under these headings are dealt with through **civil** or **administrative law**—not criminal law. Heavily influenced by critical criminologists such as Frank and Lynch (1992), we, however, do not base our definition of corporate crime only on legal considerations. For us, and others, harmful corporate criminal conduct is criminal whether or not the behavior is proscribed by criminal law.

Corporate crimes are not typically treated as criminal cases in the United States and elsewhere (e.g., Canada). We are currently witnessing a small shift toward treating some major corporate misdeeds as crimes in the strict sense of the word. Consider what Friedrichs (2004b) refers to as "Enron et al." cases that occurred between 2001 and 2004. They have inspired many criminal investigations, resulting in some guilty pleas, indictments, and pending trials. Friedrichs (2004b:113-114) uses the term "Enron et al." to refer to:

> specific cases involving the Enron Corporation and some of its top personnel, but also to the linked case of the Anderson accounting firm, and a series of cases that surfaced in the wake of the Enron case. Enron, then, becomes a metaphor for a series of other cases, part of a domino effect: these cases in alphabetical order, include Adelphia Communications, Computer Associates, Dynergy, Global Crossing, Qwest, Rite Aid, Tyco International, WorldCom, and Xerox.

However, don't expect radical changes in the government's response to corporate crime, because fundamental legal reforms involving widespread use of punitive measures are not likely under the leadership of any ruling party.[1] After all, the United States is a capitalist country, and many people view the government as dedicated to protecting the interests of big business (Szockyj & Frank, 1996). Further, as Hartman (2002:172) reminds us, "At the moment, the world's largest corporations are able to influence—and, in most cases today, even write—legislation that benefits them because their personhood gives them the constitutionally protected rights of free speech, assembly, and to meet with 'their' elected representatives."

The Extent and Distribution of Corporate Crime

There are enough data gathered from a variety of sources to demonstrate that corporate crime is highly injurious and endemic to North America. Still, it is extremely difficult, if not impossible, to obtain accurate statistics on the extent of "suite crime." Even world-renowned experts on corporate crime offer little more than educated guesses on the "dark figure" of this problem. The amount of corporate crime known to government agencies and to social scientists, and the incidence and prevalence data that are included in many scholarly books on corporate crime, amount to little more than the tip of the iceberg. It is to why we know so little about the extent and distribution of corporate crime that we now turn.

The Limitations of Corporate Crime Statistics[2]

There are some distinct measurement problems with corporate crime that continue to exist no matter how much money, time, and energy criminologists devote (Snider, 1993). For example, what Clinard and Yeager (1980:6) argued 25 years ago still holds true today: "[G]overnment inquiries have shown that corporate violations are exceedingly difficult to discover, to investigate, or to develop successfully as legal cases because of their extreme complexity and intricacy." In addition, in many cases, researchers or government agencies do not record incidents because many, if not most, victims are unaware of the corporate threats to their financial, physical, and psychological well-being. Recall the case described in Box 1.2 (see Chapter 1). DuPont dumped the dangerous chemical C8 into the Ohio River, but thousands of people who lived in the surrounding river valley did not know they were drinking and breathing this chemical everyday (Hawthorne, 2003). Unfortunately, as described in a subsequent section of this chapter, undetected types of "poisoning for profit"[3] are not rare.

In addition, it is difficult to determine the frequency of congenital malformation and childhood development problems caused by daily work conditions because these afflictions remain unnoticed by the victims, their relatives, and medical professionals for months or years. Many people are also unaware that stillbirths, spontaneous abortions, lactation problems, and other reproductive disorders are products of dangerous work conditions. Others may recognize that their reproductive systems have been damaged in or by the workplace, but are reluctant to report their experiences because they are worried about the loss of privacy or employment (DeKeseredy & Ellis, 1996; DeKeseredy & Goff, 1992).

We also know very little about the extent of economic corporate crime in the United States and elsewhere. This problem, too, is difficult to discover and investigate. A widely cited example of the discrete and sophisticated nature of economic corporate crime is found in Gilbert Geis's (1986) "The Heavy Electrical Equipment Antitrust Cases of 1961." Here, several high-ranking corporate executives employed by the two largest U.S. heavy electrical companies—the General Electric Corporation and the Westinghouse Corporation—violated the Sherman Antitrust Act of 1890 by engaging in **price-fixing**. This crime was very serious because, in essence, it represented the theft of an extraordinary amount of money from ordinary citizens like you and us. The theory of the capitalist market is that companies will engage in competition, with the one able to offer the best product at the best price "winning" more business. By engaging in price-fixing, these companies undermined the ideal of the free marketplace and made sure that the government or other industries (and always eventually the consumer or taxpayer) never got the best price.

The high-ranking officials of these companies were well aware that they were engaging in "wrong" behavior. It would be difficult for them to argue that they were just doing business as usual when they were:

- Using plain envelopes to mail information to each other.

- Avoiding being seen together when traveling.

- Hiding behind a "camouflage" of fictitious names and conspiratorial codes.

- Using public telephones to communicate with each other, and meeting at trade conventions where their social exchanges would appear appropriate, or other sites that facilitated anonymity.

- Filing false travel claims to mislead their superiors about the cities they visited (Geis, 1986:142-143).

The relevance of this example in a section on measuring the extent and distribution of corporate crime is that it again shows how difficult it is for anyone who counts crime or uses victimization surveys like those described in Chapter 3 to obtain accurate data on corporate crime. Obviously, many people are not aware that their taxes have just been raised to pay for the criminal acts of criminal entities. On a personal level, this crime might cost you two or three cents. So what? But, of course, a few cents from everyone amounts to large sums of money. For reasons thus far presented here, corporate crimes have often been called "quiet acts" because people not only don't know who to blame, but they may not even know that they have been victimized (DeKeseredy & Schwartz, 1996; Frank & Lynch, 1992).

We do not want to distract you from reading this chapter or "stress you out," but while you are reading it, several corporations are committing crimes against you, your friends, your relatives, coworkers, and, yes, even the co-authors of this book. For example, the playground near your house or even your own backyard may be slowly poisoning you, your significant others (e.g., parents), and your pets if it has been "treated" with widely available pesticides, herbicides, and fertilizers. Similarly, if you are an avid golfer, you are at great risk of being poisoned by pesticides routinely sprayed on golf courses across this continent. Common lawn-care products damage the environment and drinking water in many neighborhoods, causing thousands of major illnesses and life-threatening allergic reactions. These lawn-care products have even killed a large number of people (Community Action Publications, 2004; Frank & Lynch, 1992).

We could provide many more examples of how difficult it is to count corporate crime, but they do not answer an important question: What, then, is the extent of corporate crime in the United States? The most general and valid answer seems to be this: it is much more widespread than most U.S. citizens, government agencies, and sociologists realize. Most of the data used to support this assertion are derived from regulatory agencies, which is problematic because very few corporate crimes ever come to their attention and because these agencies "have considerable discretionary leeway in defining (and responding to) offenses" (Friedrichs, 2004a:44). Moreover, government agencies are ideologically opposed to generating better corporate crime data because they do not want to tarnish the reputations of "respectable" members of the corporate community (Rosoff, Pontell & Tillman, 2001).

Despite the fact that most victims of corporate crime do not know that they have been harmed by this problem, some researchers have conducted victimization surveys. For example, in the United Kingdom, Frank Pearce (1992) conducted one in the London Borough of Islington and focused on three forms of what he defines as **commercial crime**:[4] workplace hazards, unlawful trading practices, and the victimization of housing tenants. His survey data showed that the accident rate per 100,000 workers was 30 times greater than the national average reported in official British statistics. Another relevant victimization survey was conducted in the United States by the National White Collar Crime Center. Data generated from a national survey of 1,169 U.S. households showed that more than one out of every three households were victimized in 1999 by fraud through the following offenses:

- Internet transactions.

- Unauthorized use of their credit cards.

- Use of 800 or 900 telephone numbers.

- Unauthorized use of a personal identification number (PIN).

- A free prize or vacation that turned out not to be free.

- A free product sample that turned out not to be free (Rebovich & Layne, 2000).

Other research methods are used to study corporate crime.[5] However, they do not generate reliable data, so they are rarely used. Until researchers conduct better studies, authors will be forced to rely primarily on official statistics gathered by government agencies because they are the only regularly published data available. Box 5.2 suggests some ways for developing more reliable measures of corporate crime. Hopefully, researchers will try these techniques in the near future.

Box 5.2
Suggestions for Developing More Reliable Measures of Corporate Crime

Simpson, Harris, and Mattson (1993) have suggested that we can more reliably measure corporate crime by developing a model that takes into account such factors as opportunities to commit offenses, interconnections among actors, and numbers of transactions. This is, admittedly, a complex challenge. Zimring (1987) has made an innovative proposal for measuring the incidence of insider trading, one form of white-collar crime that is surely underreported. He has suggested sampling corporations that have made major announcements (e.g., about takeovers), using computers to construct baseline data on the volume of the corporations' stocks traded under normal circumstances, and then scanning for significant deviations from baseline trading figures in the period preceding such public announcements. Such an approach, he believes, could be applied to other forms of white-collar crime, including the performance of unnecessary surgery. The resulting information might not identify individual offenders, but it could hypothetically provide us with reliable indicators about the distribution of white-collar crime.

Source: Friedrichs, D.O. (2004). From *Trusted Criminals: White Collar Crime in Contemporary Society*, 2nd ed., p. 45. Belmont, CA: Wadsworth. © 2004. Reprinted with permission of Wadsworth, a division of Thomson Learning. www.thomsonrights.com Fax 800-730-2215

Having identified major problems associated with measuring the extent and distribution of corporate crime, we can now examine two broad categories of this problem: **corporate violence** and **economic corporate crimes**. Again, these data constitute only the tip of the corporate-crime iceberg.

Corporate Violence

Corporate violence is defined here as:

> any behavior undertaken in the name of the corporation by decision makers, or other persons in authority within the corporation, that endangers the health and safety of employees or other persons who are affected by that behavior. Even acts of omission, in which decision makers, etc., refuse to take action to reduce or eliminate known health and safety risks, must be considered corporate violence. It is the impact the action has on the victim, not the intent of the act, which determines whether or not it is violence (DeKeseredy & Hinch, 1991:100).

There are numerous types of corporate violence. However, a review of the literature shows that sociologists who study this problem focus mainly on three issues: violence against workers, violence against consumers, and corporate pollution.

Violence Against Workers

Corporate violence is most clearly visible in the area of occupational health and safety. Just as taverns in poorer areas of cities represent a significant site for assaults, woundings, manslaughters, murders, and other crimes (Daly & Wilson, 1988; Messner & Blau, 1987; Sherman, Gartin & Buerger, 1989), the workplace is a primary site for corporate violence.

In the spring of 2000, Walter DeKeseredy had a male student in one of his Ohio University classes who was on the brink of failing his course. So, DeKeseredy asked him to come to his office to discuss the situation. When DeKeseredy asked him why he is not doing well in the class, the student sarcastically responded, "Work is not good for my health." Well, for many U.S. workers, this student's statement is not a joke. For example, according to the American Federation of Labor and Congress of Industrial Organizations (AFL-CIO), excluding the deaths caused by the terrorist attacks on September 11, there were 5,900 workplace deaths resulting from traumatic injuries in 2001, and in the United States, 50,000 to 60,000 workers die each year from occupational diseases. Further, in 2001, private-sector workplaces recorded 5.2 million injuries and illnesses, and 639,500 illnesses and injuries occurred among state and local employees in 29 states and territories (2003:2).

Within the last 20 years, the number of Hispanic and immigrant workers has markedly increased in the United States. In fact, 12.5 percent of the U.S. population is Hispanic, and more than 21 million of the 35 million Hispanics currently living in this country are of working age. It is also estimated that between 28 and 30 million immigrants live in the United States, which is a little more than 10 percent of the entire country's population. Approximately 90 percent of immigrants are old enough to work in legitimate jobs. Not surprisingly, then, given the increase in the Hispanic and immigrant population and given that most of these people don't work in luxurious offices, there was an increase in Hispanic and immigrant workplace deaths and injuries (AFL-CIO, 2003).

For example, since 1992, the number of Hispanic workers who died from workplace-related injuries increased by 67 percent (533 fatalities in 1992 and 891 in 2001), and the states with the highest Hispanic populations (Texas, Florida, and New York) recorded the highest number of Hispanic work-related deaths (AFL-CIO, 2003). Hispanic workplace-related injuries also increased by 3 percent between 1992 and 2001. However, the Occupational Safety and Health Act does not require companies or public-sector workplaces to report the race of an injured worker (AFL-CIO, 2003). Workplace fatalities among immigrant workers also increased between 1992 ($n = 635$) and 2000 ($n = 849$).[6] Still, the rate of injuries and illnesses is not known because data on this problem are yet to be collected (AFL-CIO, 2003).

The above data analyzed by the AFL-CIO are Bureau of Labor Statistics (BLS) figures and do not tell the whole story due to problems associated with the OSHA, which was passed in 1970. Consider the AFL-CIO's (2003:4) cautionary notes:

> OSHA's heavy reliance on injury rates in targeting inspections and measuring performance may create an incentive for some employers to under-record and under-report injuries and illnesses. Workplace policies and programs that reward workers for low reported rates of injuries, or alternatively discipline workers for injuries also discourage the full reporting of injuries. With an increasing reliance being placed on work injury and illness statistics by the government, employers and policy makers, it is even more critical that this information be fully evaluated to ensure its validity.

In other words, the above government data understate the problem. There are other reasons for this. For example, many immigrant workers are not counted because they are unaware of their rights and lack training in occupational health and safety. Language and other cultural barriers also come into play, with workers who lack immigration status being especially fearful of reporting corporate violence (AFL-CIO, 2003).

Many conservative politicians, members of the general public, and corporate officials argue that the bulk of accidents and deaths that occur in the workplace are caused by workers' own carelessness (DeKeseredy & Schwartz, 1996). However, as Reiman (2004:79) reminds us, "To say that . . . workers died from accidents due to their own carelessness is about as helpful as saying that some of those who died at the hands of murderers asked for it." Reiman also correctly points out that workers often don't have time to be extra careful because they are under extreme pressure to meet corporate executives' production quotas. Keep in mind, too, that:

> The people who own corporations try to exact as much wealth as they can from the workers. Improvements in working conditions to eliminate health hazards would eat into the profits that could be exacted. . . . In particular, the asbestos industry would rather spend millions of dollars trying to prove that asbestos is safe, than spend the money necessary

to eliminate exposures. In oil refineries many of the exposures to chemicals result from inadequate maintenance of plant equipment. Maintenance costs come to 15 percent of total refinery costs, but these costs are considered controllable. In other words, skipping on maintenance is a good way to cut costs. Only the worker suffers (Swartz cited in Simon, 2002:141).

Of course, workers' carelessness causes some workplace deaths, illnesses, and injuries, but corporate executives may be responsible for the vast majority of injuries and deaths because they have violated occupational health and safety standards or have chosen not to create adequate standards (Michalowski, 1985; Reiman, 2004). This is not to say, however, that criminal corporations intentionally harm their workers. Rather, they set the conditions in which workers are harmed by violating the OSHA regulations. In the same way, a person who commits armed robbery does not intend to murder a store clerk, bank teller, or Brinks guard. Rather, he or she wants to make a "fast buck." Even so, this person has set the conditions for homicide. The key difference between these two situations is the legal outcome: violent corporations are typically fined, while armed robbers go to jail or prison, even though both parties threatened violence for monetary gain. What makes the information presented here even more disturbing is that it is estimated that for every two U.S. citizens killed by predatory street criminals, more than three U.S. workers are killed by reckless, greedy employers and the government's selective inattention to their conduct (Reiman, 2004).

Based on the small amount of data reviewed here, we can draw several conclusions. First, many workplaces are major centers of violent activity. Second, given that the above data and statistics presented elsewhere greatly underestimate the annual rate of corporate violence against workers, we can conclude that workers are safer on the streets than they are on the job (Reiman, 2004). In fact, some scholars estimate that the corporate death rate is more than six times greater than the street crime death rate, and the rate of nonlethal assault in the workplace is more than 30 times greater than the rate of predatory street assault (Ellis & DeKeseredy, 1996).

We consider the act of reading this chapter as work, and we assume that you are currently working at home, at school, or at another place that is not riddled with toxic fumes and other industrial health hazards. So, is it logical to assume that you and the authors of this text are at very low risk of being victimized by corporate violence? Unfortunately, this is not the case, because we are all consumers, and shopping can be very hazardous to your health. Indeed, Sykes and Cullen (1992) are correct in stating that the old adage "let the buyer beware" has special meaning in light of the data described in the next section.

Violence Against Consumers

Some people reading this chapter are pregnant or are planning to have children. Some other readers are currently parents of young children. If you belong to one of these groups, don't buy this toy car manufactured by Mattel Inc.: BATMAN BATMOBILE (Model Number B4944). Hopefully, it is no longer available on store shelves because, according to the U.S. Consumer Product Safety Commission (CPSC) (2004a:10):

> The rear tail wings of the Batmobile are made of rigid plastic and come to a point, which pose a potential puncture or laceration hazard to young children. Mattel has received 14 reports of injuries consisting of scrapes, scratches, lacerations, and punctures. Four of the injuries required medical treatment.

Most of us like to watch television or videos. And, some of us are in need of a TV/VCR cart. If so, don't buy models 2655 and 2755 produced by the Sauder Woodworking Company, especially if you have children. The CPSC found that:

> The carts can tip over and injure or kill young children when the cart and television fall. Sauder Woodworking has received 13 reports of these carts tipping over. The firm received a report of the death of a 19-month-old girl in North Wales, Pa., who suffered a fractured skull when the cart and television fell on her. There were four reports of additional injuries involving children and adults. One report involved a skull fracture to a child who recovered and three reports involved bumps and bruises (2004a:10).

The good news is that the dangerous products identified here were recalled. The bad news is that the harms caused by them constitute just the tip of the iceberg. In fact, it is estimated that consumer products injure 20 million U.S. citizens in their homes (Simon, 2002). It is also estimated that tens of thousands consumers die each year from product-related accidents, and millions more suffer disabling injuries (Friedrichs, 2004a). Further, deaths, injuries, and damage from product-related incidents cost the United States $700 billion each year (U.S. Consumer Product Safety Commission, 2004b). Of course, some products are "intrinsically dangerous" (e.g., lawnmowers, all-terrain vehicles, etc.), but many are dangerous as a result of corporations' blatant disregard for consumer safety (Friedrichs, 2004a). Consider the case of the exploding Ford Pintos in the early 1970s.[7] Twenty-four people were burned to death in rear-end collisions because of the Pinto's faulty gas tank. Ford knew that the gas tank was dangerous, but instead of installing a safer one that would have cost 11 dollars, the company decided that this was not "cost-effective" (Rosoff, Pontell & Tillman, 2001). In fact:

Ford reasoned that 180 burn deaths, 180 serious burn injuries, and 2,100 burned vehicles would cost $49.5 million (each death was figured at $200,000). But doing a recall of all Pintos and making each $11 repair would amount to $137 million (Simon, 2002:123).

So much for the television advertisement that asks, "Have you driven a Ford lately?" You might say, "This is unfair or a cheap shot. What Ford did was wrong, but this company really cleaned up its act." Well, again, "Have you driven a Ford lately?" If so, we hope it was-n't a Ford Bronco II built in the early 1990s, because some of them rolled over and some people in them died (Meier, 1992). Moreover, at the start of this century, dozens of deadly crashes were caused by defective Firestone tires mounted on Ford Explorers (Eisenberg, 2000). Ford put the blame on Firestone for these incidents, but there is substantial evidence showing that both companies were aware of the defective tires and took action only when they were forced to (Bradsher & Wald, 2000; Friedrichs, 2004a).

Ford is not the only automobile company that has jeopardized consumer safety. In fact, the automobile industry in general is one of three major industries that violate government regulations and laws more often than others. The other two are the oil and pharmaceutical industries (Clinard & Yeager, 1980).

At this point in time, many readers may be saying to themselves that we have presented extreme examples of products that can be very dangerous in the first place. Still, many products that most people view as being intrinsically safe are also major threats to your physical health, such as some food additives and other chemicals added to drinking water and hygienic products. For example, tampons can cause toxic shock syndrome, a deadly illness caused by staphylococcus bacteria from the vagina or cervix entering the uterus and then the bloodstream. Some scientists contend that tampons provide an environment for the proliferation of these bacteria and their resultant toxins. Symptoms of toxic shock include a skin rash and peeling of thin layers of skin from women's bodies. Toxic shock also affects the kidneys, liver, intestines, and stomach. In many cases, toxic shock is first detected as flu-like symptoms followed by a rash. Women who have had vaginal, cervical, or uterine surgery or who have given birth are advised not to use tampons until they are completely healed (DeKeseredy & Hinch, 1991). Another problem for women is that some develop allergic reactions to deodorant or scented pads and tampons, which are marketed as something essential for a woman to be "clean and fresh" even though such products have no noticeable advantages over washing with soap and water.

It is beyond the scope of this chapter to provide examples of the myriad of other products that harm consumers,[8] including tobacco, a substance examined in another chapter. The most important points to consider here are that shopping can be hazardous to your health and that what the National Commission on Product Safety (1974:322, 325) said 20 years ago still holds true today:

> Manufacturers have it in their power to design, build, and market products in ways that will reduce if not eliminate most unreasonable and unnecessary hazards. Manufacturers are best able to take the longest strides to safety in the least time. . . .

Corporate Pollution

Hopefully, by the time you read this chapter, Walter DeKeseredy will have stopped smoking. In addition to telling him that he is harming his health, his family, and his friends, tell him that he is polluting the environment with toxic secondhand smoke. Of course, this is true, but when he is a defensive mood, he responds to this claim by stating, "There are other things in the environment that are equally, if not more poisonous. Why don't you complain about them?" Perhaps the main reason why they don't is that they can't see or don't hear about corporate pollution. Indeed, right now, many corporations are dumping toxic waste into oceans, rivers, streams, and other waterways. There are many other environmental or "green crimes" (Frank & Lynch, 1992), but they are generally committed for the sake of profit, and they all cause major harm. Consider the case described in Box 5.3.

Box 5.3
The Corporate Assault on Minamata Bay

Minamata is the name of a small fishing village in Japan. Chisso is the name of a corporation that built a carbide and fertilizer factory in Minamata. This factory used mercury to produce carbide and fertilizer, and the waste, contaminated with deadly mercury, was dumped in Minamata Bay. It was in this bay that local fishermen caught the fish they sold and consumed. In 1956, a young girl who ate the fish was brought in "suffering severe symptoms of brain damage" (Smith & Smith, 1975:28). She was suffering from mercury poisoning, and by the end of 1975, more than 100,000 Minamata residents were afflicted with this ailment to a greater or lesser degree. After members of Chiso's dominant coalition learned of the socially harmful effects of dumping mercury into Minamata Bay, they continued to do so, "covered their actions, intimidated those who had fallen ill and failed to go public with evidence of hazard" (Ermann & Lundman, 1982:13).

Crimes similar to the one in Box 5.3 are still committed today in the United States, as briefly described in Chapter 1. However, despite the fact that it occurred decades ago, the Love Canal case is perhaps the most widely known example of corporate pollution (Friedrichs, 2004a). If you ever get a chance to visit Niagara Falls, New York, while you are enjoying the picturesque scenery, museums, and restaurants, also think about atrocities committed by the Hooker Chemical Company. Between the late 1930s and 1953, this company dumped approximately 40 million tons of toxic waste into the abandoned Love Canal, which is near there. In 1953, a local school board bought this dumpsite for a dollar and later sold it to a private developer. The canal was filled in, and houses were built on top of it. Unfortunately, those who bought the houses got more than they bargained for. Twenty years later, the toxic wastes dumped by Hooker caused miscarriages, birth defects, and other illnesses and forced more than 200 families to leave their homes (Tallmer, 1987).

In 1979, Michael Brown was in the Love Canal. Below is an account of what he witnessed there:

> I saw homes where dogs had lost their fur. I saw children with serious birth defects. I saw entire families in explicably poor health. When I walked in the Love Canal, I gasped for air as my lungs heaved in fits of wheezing. My eyes burned. There was a sour taste in my mouth (1979:xii).

This case and other examples of corporate pollution described in this book are not unique. In fact, it is estimated that, annually, the United States generates between 255 million and 275 million tons of hazardous waste and 90 percent of it is illegally disposed (Seis, 1998). Consider the techniques of illegal disposal uncovered by Hammett and Epstein (1993:5):

> In recent years, hazardous waste violations have increasingly involved forging waste transportation manifests, mislabeling drums and waste shipments, disposing of wastes on the generator's property (for example, pouring it down the drain or burying it), mixing hazardous waste with nonhazardous waste (sometimes called "cocktailing"), and shipping waste to neighboring states or nations with less stringent or effective regulation and enforcement.

Some researchers suggest that the illegal disposal of hazardous waste is the number-one corporate offense, and one of the most common variants of this crime is referred to as **midnight dumping** (Seis, 1998). This involves disposing of wastes "in the nearest isolated area. Agents of generating companies can directly commit these offenses or criminally conspire with waste transporters or treaters who, for a percentage of the legitimate treatment cost, will illegally dump the wastes" (Rebovich, 1992:3-4).

There are also other forms of corporate pollution, such as **thermal pollution**, which is "waste heat from the generation of electric power that (1) raises the temperature of the water (affecting fish and plant life in waters), and (2) increases heat in the atmosphere" (Simon, 2002:146). Unfortunately, most corporate polluters never go to prison, due in large part to their power and influence, as well as to the fact that pollution laws are weak. However, you can be sure that the poor would be severely punished if they polluted the waterways used by the rich. Further, you would never see the following situation described by Henslin and Reynolds (1976:220-221): "Can you . . . imagine the poor polluting the streams used by the rich, and then not only getting away with it and avoiding arrest, but also being paid by the rich through the government to clean up their own pollution."

Economic Corporate Crimes

There are many giant corporations in the United States and because of the vast economic resources they control and the wide range of goods and services they provide (everything from birth control products to coffins), they vitally influence the lives of most U.S. citizens from the cradle to the grave. When very large corporations steal, many people are victimized, and the amounts involved are staggering, just by virtue of the giant scale of their operations. For example, insurance swindles and corporate fraud on health insurance/HMO/hospital billings run between $100 billion and $400 billion a year, which is 100 times higher than all of the burglaries in the United States combined (Hartman, 2002). There are many different types of economic corporate crimes, but only two major ones are briefly described here: price-fixing, which was briefly discussed earlier in the chapter, and **false advertising**.

Price-Fixing[9]

There are two major types of price-fixing: **tacit** and **overt** (Michalowski, 1985:347). Also referred to as **parallel pricing** (Friedrichs, 2004a), the former occurs when a small number of controlling companies in a particular market follow the lead of their competitors in price increases (Currie & Skolnick, 1988). For example, periodically, you will hear, see, or read media reports of a company's decision to increase the cost of its goods and services and its competitors following suit. As Michalowski (1985:347) points out, we frequently hear news like, "GM announced today that it would increase the price of its automobiles by an average of $160 per model. Ford and Chrysler are expected to follow suit." If there are a few competitors within a given industry, as with U.S. automobile manufacturers, non-competitive prices can be kept for similar goods without any blatant, conspiratorial actions. Even on a smaller level, many businesses set their prices to match the competition. Consider that gas station managers frequently drive up and down the "strip" of similar stations to make sure that their prices are in line with the competition.

Overt price-fixing, on the other hand, involves secret meetings and subtle communications between competitors in given industries, such as those who were involved in the heavy electrical equipment conspiracy discussed previously. These executives decided, in advance, to use collusive strategies to increase profits.

Similar strategies were evidenced in a recent price-fixing scandal involving music companies and retailers. In August 2000, it was alleged in a case filed by U.S. state prosecutors that an industry practice called "minimum advertised pricing" (MAP) violated antitrust laws by artificially inflating the prices of music CDs. The MAP practice subsidized advertising for retailers who agreed not to sell CDs below a minimum price determined by the record labels.

Although the companies involved (Vivendi Universal's Universal Music Group, Sony Music, Bertelsmann AG's BMG Music Group, AOL Time Warner Inc.'s Warner Music Group, EMI Group PLC, Musicland Stores Corp., Trans World Entertainment Corp., and Tower Records) refused to admit wrongdoing, the settlement reached required them to pay $67.4 million in cash to the 43 states and commonwealths who brought the action. In addition, as part of the settlement, the record labels and retailers agreed to stop using MAP policies and to distribute $75.7 million worth of CDs to public entities and nonprofit organizations in all 50 states (Reuters News Agency, 2002).

The ramifications of corporate deviance are widespread. Perhaps the illegal activities outlined above contribute to other deviant criminal practices, such as illegally copying music in response to the high costs of music CDs.

Price-fixing is widespread and costly, and for some companies, it is a way of life (Coleman, 2002; Cullen, Maakestad & Cavender, 1987). Almost every industry has engaged in price-fixing, even corporations that produce vitamins, soft drinks, and infant formula (Friedrichs, 2004a; Labaton, 2001). According to some estimates, price-fixing costs consumers about $60 billion a year (Simon, 2002) and, thus, it is probably the most expensive type of corporate theft (Beirne & Messerschmidt, 2000). Each individual consumer may be paying only a few pennies extra for juice, bread, and perhaps canned cranberry sauce because of price-fixing, but the theft eventually adds up to a financial loss as serious as when someone is victimized by burglary or larceny-theft. Further, individuals, as taxpayers, pay higher taxes because of price-fixing in government contracts (Hartman, 2002).

False Advertising

Also referred to as **misleading, deceptive,** or **questionable advertising,** false advertising is another widespread type of corporate crime. It occurs when companies use false advertisements to entice consumers to buy products or services that offer few, if any, of the publicized benefits (Cullen, Maakestad & Cavender, 1987). Simon (2002) identifies two key types of false advertising: **blatantly false advertising** and **puffery.** Below he offers one example of blatantly false advertising (2002:110):

> In 1994, the Unocal oil company agreed to stop advertising claims concerning the performance of its high-octane gasoline. Several studies have found that American motorists waste billions of dollars per year on higher octane fuels, which add nothing to a vehicle's performance.

Such corporate behaviors are not rare. In fact, blatantly false advertising is what Simon (2002:110) contends is a "cardinal principle in U.S. advertising." Consider this retired advertising executive's statement:

> Don't worry whether it's true or not. Will it sell? The American people . . . are now being had from every bewildering direction. All the way from trying to persuade us to put dubious drug products and questionable foods into our stomachs to urging young men to lay down their lives in Indochina, the key will-it-sell principle and the employed techniques are the same. Caveat emptor has never had more profound significance than today, whether someone is trying to sell us war, God, anti-communism or a new improved deodorant. Deceit is the accepted order of the hour (Cohane, 1978:172).

Puffery is a legal and subtler form of false advertising that typically involves making exaggerated claims for a product or service. Although this practice does not violate civil, administrative, or criminal law, it is still designed to mislead consumers: Below, Simon (2002:112) provides some salient examples of puffery:

- "Nestlé makes the very best chocolate."
- "Ford gives you better ideas."

- "Coke is it."

- "Wheaties, Breakfast of Champions."

- "Seagram's, America's Number One Gin."

Another form of puffery occurs when a spokesperson in an advertisement says something that sounds intelligent but that is really meaningless. Listen to television ads carefully sometime and try to count how often you hear people say things like, "No other product on the market quenches your thirst like ours" (translation: All products in this category do the same; ours just costs more) (DeKeseredy & Schwartz, 1996).

The Distribution of Corporate Crime

It is often said that "bigger is not better." This statement is directly relevant to a sociological understanding of corporate crime. Indeed, company size is a major determinant of "crime in the suites." For example, listed in Box 5.4 are the top 10 corporate criminals in the 1990s. Compiled by Russell Mokhiber (2004), this list, which is part of "The Top 100 Corporate Criminals of the Decade," includes big and powerful corporations that have pleaded guilty or no contest to crimes and have been criminally fined. Further, the 100 corporate criminals were identified as committing the following 14 types of crime:

- Environmental (38)

- Antitrust (20)

- Fraud (13)

- Campaign finance (7)

- Food and drug (6)

- Financial crimes (4)

- False statements (3)

- Illegal exports (3)

- Illegal boycott (1)

- Worker death (1)

- Bribery (1)

- Obstruction of justice (1)

- Public corruption (1)

- Tax evasion (1) (Mokhiber, 2004:1)

Box 5.4
The Top 10 Corporate Criminals of the 1990s

---

1) **F. Hoffmann-La Roche Ltd.**
   Type of Crime: Antitrust
   Criminal Fine: $500 million

2) **Daiwa Bank Ltd.**
   Type of Crime: Financial
   Criminal Fine: $340 million

3) **BASF Aktiengesellschaft**
   Type of Crime: Antitrust
   Criminal Fine: $225 million

4) **SGL Carbon Aktiengesellschaft (SGLAG)**
   Type of Crime: Antitrust
   Criminal Fine: $135 million

5) **Exxon Corporation and Exxon Shipping**
   Type of Crime: Environmental
   Criminal Fine: $125 million

6) **UCAR International, Inc.**
   Type of Crime: Antitrust
   Criminal Fine: $110 million

7) **Archer Daniels Midland**
   Type of Crime: Antitrust
   Criminal Fine: $100 million

8) **(tie) Banker's Trust**
   Type of Crime: Financial
   Criminal Fine: $60 million

8) **(tie) Sears Bankruptcy Recovery Management Services**
   Type of Crime: Fraud
   Criminal Fine: $60 million

10) **Haarman & Reimer Corp.**
    Type of Crime: Antitrust
    Criminal fine: $50 million

Source: Mokhiber, R. (2004). "Top 100 Corporate Criminals of the Decade" [Online]. Available at: http://www.corporatepredators.org/top100.html

We cannot emphasize enough that the top 100 corporate criminals identified by Mokhiber (2004) constitute only a small tip of a huge iceberg. Again, most corporate offenders are never or rarely prosecuted. As Mokhiber (2004:2) reminds us, "For every company convicted of health care fraud, there are hundreds of others who get away with ripping off Medicare and Medicaid, or face only mild slap-on-the-wrist fines and civil penalties when caught." Consider, too, that some big companies, such as Royal Caribbean Cruise Lines, routinely commit corporate crimes. This company pleaded guilty to more than one crime during the 1990s, and so did Exxon, Rockwell International, Warner-Lambert, Teledyne, and United Technologies (Mokhiber, 2004).

Theories of Corporate Crime

Steven Box was a path-breaking British critical criminologist and a dear friend of Jock Young, who is also a close friend of ours. In 1978, at the Trent Park underground station near London, he asked Young if he had an explanation for corporate crime:

> He gave me that wild-eyed, glazed stare of a man suddenly possessed by the light of truth (or finally overcome by the magical influence of too much *grand cru* Chablis—two bottles of Les Preuses 1970). After a moment, he yelled 'greed'!, and silenced the noise of the incoming train (1983:ix).

This is not a surprising answer, and as a student in one of Walter DeKeseredy's classes at Carleton University in Ottawa, Ontario, once said, "Why complicate what is the obvious?" This student has a point. Still, as you will discover from reading theories described in this section, there is more to corporate crime than simply greed or the insatiable hunger for profit (Box, 1983, Friedrichs, 2004a). As Frank and Lynch (1992:97) point out, a "full understanding [of corporate crime requires a] more sophisticated approach." In addition to understanding the profit motive, we need to address the role of subcultural dynamics, masculinities, organizational factors, the role of the state, social structure, and other determinants.

There are several theories of corporate crime, and it is beyond the scope of this chapter to discuss all of them.[10] Instead, we review some widely cited, contemporary sociological perspectives that fall under the following categories: strain, social control, interactionist, and critical.

Strain Theories

Strain theories of corporate crime take two general forms. One is derived from Merton's (1938) anomie theory, while the other can be traced back to Sutherland's (1939) differential association theory. It is to a contemporary anomie explanation that we turn to first.

Anomie Theory

Merton's anomie explanation is based on the assumption that criminal or deviant behavior is motivated by the strain experienced by individuals who have learned to value making money but who are denied access to legitimate opportunities (e.g., jobs) for achieving this cultural goal. As stated in Chapter 2, some scholars, such as Snider (1993), contend that Merton's perspective cannot adequately explain corporate crime because it was specifically designed to explain lower-class, individual responses to strain. However, some criminologists, such as Box (1983), Keane (1993), Passas (1990), and Vaughn (1983), offer novel challenges to this criticism and offer anomie theories of corporate crime.

For example, according to Box, Merton's assumption is more likely to be valid for corporate executives in capitalist societies than for lower-class individuals.[11] For this reason, Box believes that Merton's formulation does a good job of explaining corporate crime, but a poor job of explaining lower-class crime. Central to Box's Mertonian analysis is the idea that corporate crime is a response to corporate anomie. Obviously, the primary goal of companies is profit, but they frequently lack legitimate opportunities to achieve this goal because they operate in an "uncertain and unpredictable environment" (Box, 1983). According to Box (1983:35-36), there are a number of factors that potentially preclude corporations from achieving their monetary goals. Some factors, such as employee unions, are internal to companies. Others are external to them and fall into two groups. Consumers (with their complaints) and governments (with their laws) represent one group. Companies' competitors—that is, other organizations producing the same or similar goods and services—form the second group.

Taken together, the presence of unions, consumer groups, governments, and competitors induces uncertainty in the business environment. Corporations are not always certain about the reaction of one or more of these groups to their business decisions. In Box's strain hypothesis, an actual or perceived "increase in these environmental uncertainties will increase the strain towards corporate criminal activity. . . ." (1983:37). The strain referred to by Box is caused by a disjunction between an emphasis on corporate goal achievement and uncertainty regarding the actual achievement of these objectives. Corporate executives are highly motivated toward the achievement of corporate objectives, and the existence of unpredictable hindrances posed by the "problem groups" noted above induces a strain toward evading, avoiding, and transgressing laws designed to protect consumers, the environment, the health and safety of workers, and so on. The result is corporate crime.

In sum, Box and others who have applied anomie theory to corporate crime should be commended for showing how this perspective advances a sociological understanding of suite crime. Perhaps their work will influence others to follow suit. Of course, some improvements could be made in future theoretical work, such as devoting more attention to broader political forces (DeKeseredy & Schwartz, 1996). Individuals and corporations do not operate in a vacuum; rather, their desires for financial success are heavily influenced by the larger capitalist social structure in which they exist. Indeed, capitalist systems are designed to achieve monetary goals regardless of the costs involved (Frank & Lynch, 1992).

Strain-Subcultural Theory

Corporate crime is often encouraged and justified by workplace or corporate subcultures (Croall, 1992; Messerschmidt, 1993, 1997). A corporate subculture consists of definitions of corporate situations and methods of identifying and solving corporate problems. The primary carriers of corporate subcultures are executives. The content of corporate subcultures is transmitted and maintained by word of mouth—nothing is written down. In other words, within a corporate subculture, communication and control are informally organized.

Corporate subcultures are, then, collective, problem-solving, informally organized entities. As such, they owe their origin to the presence of problems requiring solutions that are forbidden by corporate rules, civil and criminal laws, and/or general societal norms such as fairness. Where the subcultural solutions involve the selection of means punishable by the government, the corporate subculture is **criminogenic**. Not all business corporations have criminogenic corporate subcultures, but those that do tend to produce more corporate crime offenders. This is because, as they rise in the corporate hierarchy, executives tend to come into more frequent and intimate contact with other executives holding authoritative definitions favorable to breaking the law (Messerschmidt, 1993)—that is, with members of the criminogenic corporate subculture. In this section, we review one attempt to explain how corporate subcultures contribute to crooked business practices. Referred to by Ellis and DeKeseredy (1996) as a **corporate subculture/differential association theory**, this perspective was heavily influenced by the work of Edwin Sutherland (1939).

Sutherland's differential association theory was one of the earliest theories of corporate crime. He argued that this crime, like any other crime:

> is learned in direct or indirect association with those who already practice the behavior. . . . [Those] who learn the behavior are segregated from frequent and intimate contacts with law-abiding behavior. Whether a person becomes a criminal or not is determined largely by the comparative frequency and intimacy of his contacts with the two types of behavior. This process may be called the process of differential association (1939:5).

Almost 40 years after the publication of Sutherland's original theory, Marshall Clinard and Peter Yeager (1980) returned to it to look more rigorously at corporate crime in the United States. According to these scholars, corporate violations "stem from the corporate way of life" (1980:298). The subculture or corporate way of life of a company consists of norms (rules) and values (conceptions of the desirable). Put another way, the subculture of a corporation refers to its "living code," its "business norms," or its "way of life." A corporation's way of life is influenced by a variety of internal and external factors.[12] Among the most important of the internal influences is the ethical/moral atmosphere created or maintained by the corporation's **dominant coalition** (Clinard, 1983; Clinard & Yeager, 1980). The degree to which top management creates or sustains a corporate culture supportive of or opposed to illegal conduct depends in turn on: (1) the primacy given to the goal of profit, (2) the degree of competition, (3) the stability of the economic and political environment, and (4) how widespread illegal conduct is among firms that constitute the industry.

The more widespread the diffusion of illegal conduct, the greater the pressure for profits—and the more uncertain and competitive the market or the consequences of governmental action, the more likely top management is to create or maintain an atmosphere or way of life conducive to corporate crime.

The culture or way of life of a corporation is learned through the process of socialization and social control. Where the corporation's way of life is criminogenic, the individual executive or manager learns to become a crook as part of his or her occupational role. Socialization refers to this kind of occupational role learning. Should a manager attempt to question some of the more crime-conducive outlooks that are being taught (e.g., the achievement of short-term corporate objectives is more important than the means used to achieve them), then prospects for promotion, if not continued employment, may be jeopardized. Social control refers to the corporation's use of sanctions designed to inhibit deviation from the norms of its culture.

Having described the process in terms of which individuals learn to become corporate crooks, Clinard and Yeager (1980) conclude their theoretical account of corporate crime by identifying the **content** of socialization. Among the things that executives learn is how to deal with the problem of breaking rules they may have believed in or may still believe in outside of the job. Specifically, they learn a number of rules that help neutralize any guilt they may feel. Included among these rules are the following: all legal measures constitute government interference with the free enterprise system; there is little deliberate intent in corporate violations, many of them are errors of omission rather than commission, and many are mistakes; if there is no increase in corporate profits, a violation is not wrong.

Only a few criminologists have applied strain-subcultural theory to corporate crime. Nevertheless, their arguments are valid, and the assertion that corporate crime is learned "can hardly be challenged" (Coleman, 2002). Even so, some proponents of macro-level explanations (for example, Marxists and feminists) contend that subcultural accounts devote little attention to the ways in which corporate subcultural dynamics are influenced by wider economic, cultural, and political forces that exist outside of corporations (Coleman, 2002; Croall, 1992; Friedrichs, 2004a). According to Frank and Lynch (1992:117), key examples of these broader social forces are "the type of economic system, the state of the economy (economic uncertainties), and the degree to which law enforcement is sensitive to particular types of violations of the law."

Social Control Theories

Contemporary social control explanations of corporate crime fall into three major groups: (1) anomie-control theorists influenced by Durkheim's anomie-at-the-top thesis, (2) social bond theorists influenced by Durkheim's social-attachments-equal-social-control equation, and (3) deterrence theorists influenced by Beccaria and his followers.

Anomie-Control Theory

As described in Chapter 2, Emile Durkheim (1897/1951) had a strong and abiding interest in the sources of social order, in the process of social control, and in the vulnerability of people. All three concerns are reflected in his anomie theory, which differs from Merton's (1938) in two important respects. First, whereas Merton drew attention to lower-class crime or "anomie-at-the-bottom," Durkheim emphasizes "anomie-at-the-top," that is, among members of society's most successful and powerful class groupings. Second, for Merton, the major instigator of the strain that led to crime was the disjunction between goals and the availability of legitimate means. By contrast, Durkheim locates the major cause of anomie in the *too successful* achievement of cultural goals.

The anomie that is induced in individuals who achieve great wealth and power facilitates deviant and criminal behavior in two ways. First, their past success leads them to believe that they can achieve any goal. Thus, they set increasingly higher goals for themselves. At the same time, anything less than complete success in achieving these goals is viewed as failure. To such individuals, failure is intolerable, and intolerable strain facilitates such strain-reducing activities as crime or deviance. Second, great success inculcates in individuals the belief that their success is due to their own individual efforts. They do not have to rely on others, and they become individuated. Individuated individuals tend not to have strong group attachments. Rather, they are loners. To be a loner is to be vulnerable, that is, to weaken the restraining effects of the opinions, praise, and blame conferred on one by others. A weakening of such group-based restraints facilitates crime and deviance (Durkheim, 1897/1951).

Durkheim did not apply the anomie-at-the-top thesis to the topic of corporate crime, but Box (1983) and Passas (1990) do. Box (1983:39) argues that the "competitive ambition and moral flexibility" displayed by corporate executives who make their way to the very top of the corporate hierarchy "prepares them to engage in crime should they perceive it as being necessary for the good of the company." The higher they go, the less accountable and constrained they feel. Consequently, the most wealthy and powerful corporate executives tend to be the biggest crooks. This, according to Box, explains why the largest corporations—multinational ones—are more criminogenic than large ones and why large ones are more criminogenic than small ones.[13]

Thus far, hypotheses based on anomie-control theory have not been tested. Hopefully, others will fill this research gap, perhaps starting by conducting interviews with executives. The same can be said about Messerschmidt's (1993) structured action theory of corporate crime, which will be reviewed later in this chapter.

Bond Theory

In applying Durkheim's anomie thesis to corporate crime, Box emphasizes the moral deregulation or normlessness caused by great success. By way of contrast, Hirschi's (1969) social bond theory builds upon Durkheim's (1897/1951) individuation route to crime. Durkheim believed that moral behavior and being attached to others went together. This occurs because those who are motivated to violate social or legal norms are inhibited from doing so by the negative reactions or sanctions they expect from others to whom they are attached. Loners, however, are not attached to others and therefore, they tend to be indifferent to their reactions.

Executives who become members of the dominant coalition in a very large corporation acquire great wealth, power, and prestige. Their achievements tend to individuate them, to make them loners. Following the thinking of Hirschi (1969), corporate loners would tend not to use the anticipated reactions of others as a guide to behavior because the norms of others are not their norms. The norms that help bind others together do not apply to them. Because their bond to others—to society—is weak, successful corporate loners feel "free to deviate," free to do what is effective rather than what is right, legal, or appropriate.

Hirschi's social bond theory can also be integrated with organizational theories of corporate crime. According to Cressey (1972:26), "the phenomenon to worry about" when studying corporate crime is "organization," and Mary McIntosh (1975:8) contends that "the study of organizational crime requires organizational concepts." Which concepts? According to Clinard and Yeager (1980), **hierarchy** and **differentiation** are among the most criminogenic attributes of bureaucratically organized corporations. Hierarchy of authority and differentiation of occupational roles facilitate corporate crime because they enable executives to "pass the buck." Specifically, hierarchy permits executives to say they were ordered to do what they did by their bosses. It's not their fault.

Differentiation means making one of many corporate decisions that together result in criminal conduct. This tends to attenuate the sense of responsibility each executive feels for the final outcome. Thus, Clinard and Yeager found that large business corporations were more criminogenic partly because they contained more levels of authority and specialized work roles and divisions. This finding does not surprise critical criminologist Stuart Henry (1985:73), for he maintains that "the structure of a system of relations which divides responsibility for human lives into authority and hierarchy relations is the most lethal devised by man. It simultaneously commands action and limits responsibility." This means that corporate executives are "free to deviate" because the structure of their corporate bureaucracy frees them from responsibility for their decisions. Their stake in conformity, they believe, will not be jeopardized by the job-related decisions they make. After all, they are not fully responsible for making them.

Stake in conformity is, according to Hirschi, one element of the individual's bond to society. The possibility that criminal or deviant conduct will jeopardize the investments in conformity built up by an individual acts as a major inhibitor of such conduct. Corporate business organizations characterized by hierarchy and differentiation tend to sever or attenuate the association between corporate conduct and stake in conformity. Therefore, they are criminogenic.

Deterrence Theory

Cesare Bonesana Marchese de Beccaria (1738-1794) was an economist, mathematician, and one of the founding fathers of deterrence theory. In 1767, he published his ideas on deterrence in a book titled *On Crimes and Punishment*. In this book, he outlined his plan for a more effective system of justice. Deterrence was one of the basic principles of this system.

The idea of deterrence as a crime control strategy rests on two assumptions. First, human beings are motivated primarily by pain and pleasure. Second, in their efforts to obtain a balance of pleasure over pain in satisfying their wants, they act in a rational or calculating manner. The best or more effective law in the criminal justice system is one that ensures that the costs of criminal conduct outweigh the gains. In such a system, punishment controls criminal conduct by creating realistic fears concerning the consequences of engaging in such conduct.

Contemporary formulations of deterrence theory improve upon the original ones by specifying more precisely the conditions under which and the extent to which the objective of deterrence is achieved. In this regard, present-day contributors such as Wilson (1985) share the view that legal punishments that are swift, certain, and severe are the most likely to deter criminal conduct under the following conditions. First, they must be applied to offenses that are most clearly rational or calculative in nature. Corporate crimes constitute this kind of offense. Second, they must be backed up by **extralegal sanctions**, such as public opinion.

In considering deterrence itself as an objective, contemporary deterrence theorists make an important distinction between **general** and **specific deterrence**. Specific deterrence has to do with the effects of punishments on the individuals to whom they are applied. General deterrence refers to the effects of the punishment of specific individuals on a wider audience. Recall that in 1961, General Electric broke the law by fixing prices. It pleaded guilty and was fined (Geis, 1986). A concern with specific deterrence would lead one to focus on the effect of this punishment on General Electric, while a concern with general deterrence would divert attention to the effects of this punishment on other corporations in the same industry, and/or on business corporations in general.

Deterrence theory was used by Goff and Reasons (1978) to explain corporate crime in Canada. Their overall conclusion is that corporate crime occurs because it pays. For example, law prohibits creating unsafe work conditions. Yet, such behavior is common because the penalties are insufficient deterrents, with the financial rewards far outweighing the possible costs (e.g., fines imposed by the government).

North American governments do not accord corporate crime control a very high priority. For example, in their recent report titled *Death on the Job: The Toll of Neglect*, the AFL-CIO (2003:1) note that the "dollar amounts of both Federal and state OSHA penalties continue to decline." The AFL-CIO also discovered that:

> There continues to be no substantial regulatory activity by the Bush Administration at OSHA or MSHA. Important standards close to completion at the end of the Clinton Administration—including standards on tuberculosis and employer payment for personal protective equipment—have been repeatedly delayed by the Bush Administration. Budget cuts in job safety agency programs proposed by the Administration will, if enacted, reduce the already inadequate resources devoted to workers' safety and health. At a time when challenges and problems are mounting, the nation's commitment to protecting workers from job injuries, illnesses and death is faltering.

This finding and those produced by other researchers support the assertion that:

> [I]t is profitable for firms to violate the law because the risk
> of discovery is low and the benefits of crime outweigh the rel-
> atively modest monetary cost of prosecution and guilty find-
> ings. Low sanction severity coupled with low sanction
> certainty produce a relatively insignificant threat (Simpson,
> 2002:49).

More generally, deterrence theorists contend that a deterrent effect is not achieved because each one of the factors that make deterrence effective has been undermined. The various laws intended to regulate corporate crime have so many loopholes that they are very difficult to enforce. In addition, most corporate crimes remain undiscovered, that is, they are also corporate secrets. The government cannot pun-ish conduct if it doesn't know about it. If government agents do become aware of a corporate crime, corporate lawyers specializing in corporate law can often get the better of government lawyers whose training is not as specialized (Ellis & DeKeseredy, 1996; Mokhiber, 2004). The result is delays in court proceedings and/or failures to convict. When perpetrators are convicted, the penalties are rarely severe (Simpson, 2002). When fines are imposed, they amount to lit-tle more than a "licensing fee" and tend to be regarded as such by cor-porate executives (Braithwaite & Geis, 1981; Fisse, 1986). Finally, corporate executives work in a society that more or less tolerates cor-porate criminal activity. Consequently, they tend not to anticipate community or societal sanctions. In sum, then, neither certainty, nor swiftness, nor severity, nor extralegal sanctions characterize the polic-ing of corporate crime in the United States. This is one of the key rea-sons why it is endemic in our society.

In concluding this review of deterrence theory, one caveat is nec-essary. Like most other deterrence theories of corporate crime, Goff and Reason's perspective concludes that deterrence does not work. This may be a valid conclusion. However, because they relied exclusively on offi-cial statistics on discovered corporate criminals to test their theory, they have no way of knowing how many corporations who might have engaged in criminal conduct did not do so either because of their respect for the law and/or because they wished to avoid experiencing legal punishments of any kind. In other words, Goff and Reasons's con-clusions may apply to specific but not to general deterrence.

Interactionist Theories

To the best of our knowledge, only one variant of interactionist the-ory—the labeling perspective—has been applied to corporate crime. Here, we review this attempt to explain why harmful corporate acts are not officially designated as deviant or criminal.

The Labeling Process

As described in Chapter 1, one problem of central interest to interactionist theorists is how individuals and groups come to be defined as deviant or criminal. For scholars such as Rubington and Weinberg (1973:vii), the definitional or labeling process occurs in the following manner:

> For deviance to become a social fact, somebody must perceive an act or event as a departure from social norms, must categorize that perception, must report that perception to others, must get them to accept this definition. Unless all these requirements are not met, deviance as a social fact does not come into being.

Ermann and Lundman (2001:27) contend that, "A similar view of the deviance-defining process should be taken for organizational actions." From their interactionist perspective, business corporations who pollute, lie, kill, injure, and steal are deviant "only to the extent that they are perceived, reported, accepted, treated, and defined as deviant" (2001:27). A corporation that gets away with committing such offenses is not deviant. Why and how this happens are questions of considerable importance to interactionist theorists.

Dowie and Marshall (1982) provide a good illustration of an interactionist account of successful corporate crime. Following Becker (1973), they describe a sequence of events that constituted a **moral drama** in which the accusers and the accused attempted to impose one of four labels on a drug: "not recommended," "possibly effective," "probably effective," and "effective." The label that emerged out of the interaction among accusers, accused, and government regulative agencies had major consequences for consumers as well as for the pharmaceutical corporation marketing the drug. If the federal Food and Drug Administration (FDA) had labeled the drug "not recommended," it would have had to be taken off the market. The label "effective" meant it could be sold anywhere. The in-between labels meant that the firm had to conduct more vigorous testing. These labels, then, directly affected profits by allowing, prohibiting, or restricting sales. In addition, if further tests were stipulated, it would have increased the costs of producing the drug, which would have also decreased profits.

Bendectin was a drug made by a subsidiary of a large pharmaceutical company, Richardson-Merrell. It was prescribed for pregnant women suffering from nausea and vomiting, and it helped relieve both. Like thalidomide, it caused serious birth defects and was first marketed in 1957. In 1963, after the thalidomide scandal, Bendectin was tested for the presence of chemicals (teratogens) known to cause birth defects. Robert Staples, a doctor who conducted this research, discovered the same kinds of birth defects in rabbits who were given Bendectin as were found in those to whom thalidomide was administered. According to Dowie and Marshall (1982), Richardson-Merrell executives were aware of these results.

In the United States, the FDA must by law approve all drugs before they are sold, and Bendectin was submitted for approval. What Richardson-Merrell wanted was the FDA's "effective" label and, obviously, it wished to avoid the label "harmful." In the latter endeavor, the corporation was successful. Between 1957 (when it was first marketed) and 1980, Bendectin caused birth defects in 140,000 children (Dowie & Marshall, 1982).

U.S. federal law requires drug manufacturers to report all adverse side effects to the FDA, and failure to do so is an offense liable to criminal prosecution. Staples's original report was never shown to the FDA, nor was his experiment repeated. In addition, as time went by, increasing evidence of Bendectin's deadly side effects was presented to both the FDA and Richardson-Merrell executives. In 1966, especially good evidence of the drug's harmful effects was provided by a Canadian doctor, Donald Patterson. Other doctors all over the world read his study and confirmed his conclusions. Yet, as time went by, the label applied by the FDA got better: it went from "possibly effective" to "probably effective" to "effective" (Dowie & Marshall, 1982:273).

From Richardson-Merrell's point of view, the labeling process was quite successful. No executive was prosecuted, and the corporation was not punished. Bendectin continued to be sold, and profits accrued. A number of factors were responsible for the outcome of this moral drama.

First, Richardson-Merrell used its great resources to manipulate doctors who were asked to perform additional tests. Second, the company lied and actually hid files containing information harmful to its case. Third, Marion Finkel, a doctor and former employee of a pharmaceutical company, seemed to believe that she was responsible for the welfare of the pharmaceutical industry while she acted as Associate Director of the FDA's new drug evaluation section. She was ultimately responsible for labeling Bendectin. FDA researchers working under her would routinely be transferred to other jobs or have their reports altered if they found that Bendectin could have harmful side effects (Dowie & Marshall, 1982).

In sum, a large company's resources, the willingness of company executives to use these resources in almost any way to reduce losses and increase profits, and a sympathetic, strategically placed FDA official all combined to overcome efforts by a number of doctor-researchers to label Bendectin harmful. Some of these researchers worked for the FDA, and others were employed by prestigious groups such as the American Medical Association and the National Academy of Sciences.

One of the key limitations of the interactionist account reviewed here is that it does not explicitly address the broader structural and cultural forces that contributed to Richardson-Merrell's ability to avoid stigmatization. Perhaps this shortcoming will be overcome when or if more interactionist theorists develop an interest in corporate crime.

Critical Theories

Critical theorists are clearly interested in the ways in which broader structural and cultural forces shape crime and its control. Further, as stated in Chapter 1, they are deeply concerned about crimes of the powerful, such as those described in this chapter. Here, we review and critique two types of critical theories: Marxist formulations and structured action theory.

Marxist Theories

As Lynch, Michalowski, and Groves (2000:72) point out, "corporate crime represents the most widespread and costly form of crime in America (Michalowski, 1985:325) while the regulatory system designed to control it remains more sensitive to the interests of corporate capital than to the people it is supposed to protect." To explain these problems, Marxist criminologists argue that it is essential to examine the role of the state. Although he did not offer a systematic theory of the state, Marx influenced many contemporary sociologists and criminologists who study it. The **instrumental Marxists** have posited an analysis of corporate crime that is rooted in a classic statement set out by Marx and Engels: "The executive of the modern state is but a committee for managing the common affairs of the whole bourgeoisie" (1848/1975:82). Instrumental Marxists interpret this to mean that the state is but a tool or instrument used by the ruling class to promote its financial interests and maintain its control over the disenfranchised. The law, then, is seen by instrumentalists as a "weapon of class rule' (Comack & Brickey, 1991:24). To support their arguments, instrumentalists cite evidence that members of the government and the bourgeoisie come from similar class backgrounds, attended the same schools, have the same financial goals, and share the same ideology (Miliband, 1969; Quinney, 1974).

Instrumental Marxists are challenged by a number of questions directed at them by their critics. Some of the most challenging of these are: If the state serves as a handmaiden to the corporate community, why do we have laws to regulate corporate conduct? Why are some corporations prosecuted and punished by government agencies? Why do these policing agencies exist in the first place?

Close to 20 years ago, sociologist Frank Pearce identified himself as an instrumental Marxist, and in his 1976 book *Crimes of the Powerful*, he tried to explain the development of laws regulating U.S. business activity, specifically anti-trust laws. According to Pearce, these laws were created because they were useful to the business community and because they helped the state perform its "objective function" of guaranteeing "the reproduction of the economic system" (1976:61). According to Pearce, the state can best ensure the maintenance of capitalism by inculcating in citizens generally a belief in its legitimacy. By passing laws that give the impression that the law is fair, that is, that it applies to the powerful as well as to the powerless, it helps buttress its claim to legitimacy. Occasional punishment of individual corporations works toward the same end. Individual corporations are punished or sacrificed so that capitalists, as a class, can preserve their dominant position. Additionally, laws regulating corporate conduct are written in such a way as to be virtually unenforceable. This means that corporations, or at least the major ones, will not be unduly interfered with by charges, prosecutions, convictions, and punishments.

For their part, business corporations actually cooperated with the state in creating anti-trust legislation because it "provided a means by which monopoly capital could be achieved against dangerous competitors . . . without danger of popular reactions" (Pearce, 1976:87). Pearce contends that the attitude of big business toward the law is essentially pragmatic. They will support laws that help increase the ratio of profits to losses and oppose those that increase the ratio of losses to profits. From this, it follows that all extant laws intended to regulate business conduct exist because they serve the interests of business, especially big business.

But, why are citizens generally not aware of what is going on so they can do something about more effective legislation and enforcement? The answer is "mystification." The state and big business, by virtue of their control of educational, religious, and the mass media, help create and maintain an "imaginary social order" (Pearce, 1976:94). We are all led to believe that this imaginary social order is real and, believing in this order, we also tend to accept the claims for legitimacy made by the state: a belief in the sanctity of the market as a regulator of business activity, that bigness is due to efficiency, that democracy prevails in business because numerous small shareholders really control things, that a free-enterprise system exists, and so on.

For Pearce, then, theorizing about corporate crime means "demystifying" it. This is done by contrasting an imaginary social order with the real social order. Important clues to the nature of the real social order in capitalist society are provided for Pearce by Karl Marx.

In response to criticisms of instrumental Marxist theories such as Pearce's (e.g., they are seen by some scholars as conspiracy theories), several critical criminologists developed alternative Marxist explanations of corporate crime—**structural Marxist** perspectives. Their starting point is that a capitalist state has not just one function, capital accumulation, but three: capital accumulation, legitimation, and coercion. These three functions stand in a contradictory relation to each other, and devoting too many resources to one may jeopardize the others. Thus, catering to capital accumulation by completely ignoring corporate crime may jeopardize the legitimacy of the state itself, and the state is vitally interested in creating or maintaining its legitimacy. The central ideas here are that the state has **relative autonomy** to pursue its own objectives and that the pursuit of these entails not only catering to but also regulating corporate conduct.[14]

Canadian criminologist Russell Smandych (1985) provides one example of a structural Marxist theory of corporate crime. He argues that the Canadian anti-combines legislation originated during a period (1890-1910) of labor-capitalist conflict and represented an attempt by the state to secure industrial peace, which would, in turn, facilitate capital accumulation, an outcome dear to the hearts of both the state and the business community. This structural Marxist account of corporate crime is designed to capture the complexity of the relationship between the state and the corporate community—complexity that appeared not to have been fully appreciated in instrumental Marxist theories. The notions of the relative autonomy of the state and of multiple, contradictory state functions constitute an attempt to provide a more complex and therefore better theoretical conception of the state. However, the linkage problem, that is, the problem of identifying the relation between specific kinds of corporate crime or crime control in given historical circumstances is not well attended to.[15]

Instrumental and structural Marxist theorists make important contributions to a sociological understanding of corporate crime. However, they are criticized by both mainstream and critical scholars.[16] For example, some critics contend that instrumental Marxists incorrectly assume that the capitalist class always acts as a "united whole" (Comack & Brickey, 1991), while others assert that corporate elites and politicians are not sufficiently organized to behave in a consistent conspiratorial manner (DeKeseredy & Schwartz, 1996). Below are some shortcomings of structural Marxist theories:

- Although structural Marxists use the concept of the relative autonomy of the state from the ruling class to explain many things, they have not really explained how this is determined or what factors create it (Comack & Brickey, 1991).

- Structuralists often treat the state as if it were a real thing with a life of its own, rather than a collection of relationships (Sheley, 1985).

Structured Action Theory[17]

Some individuals are more likely to engage in crooked business practices than others. For example, women rarely commit corporate crime (Daly, 1989; Friedrichs, 2004a), while white men commit the vast majority of corporate crimes (DeKeseredy, 2000a). Why is this so? Messerschmidt's (1993) structured action theory answers this question, and he asserts that to understand why men monopolize these crimes of the powerful, we must examine the gender and racial division of labor within corporations. Men, especially white males, have the major decision-making power in corporations. Although women occupy about 40 percent of all corporate management, executive, and administrative positions in the United States, they are generally restricted to lower-level positions in these areas, such as personnel and affirmative action (Mooney, Knox & Schacht, 2005; Renzetti & Curran, 2000). Because these management positions generally do not lead to more powerful positions within corporations, women have relatively few opportunities to commit criminal acts that further the goals of the corporation (Braithwaite, 1993).

Messerschmidt (1993) further argues that the "old boy" network plays a key role in both maintaining the gender division of labor and perpetuating corporate crime. For example, senior executives selectively recruit junior male employees who share their norms, attitudes, values, and standards of conduct. If these young executives meet their senior counterparts' expectations, they are rewarded with money, authority, corporate control, and power over men and women. Senior executives also teach their recruits to act according to "executive conceptions of masculinity." One of the most important practices that exemplifies these conceptions is the sacrifice of personal principles to meet corporate goals, one of which is the accumulation of profits through illegitimate means.

If young executives have "nondemanding moral codes," they are more likely to be promoted to senior positions that free them to, if necessary, commit corporate crimes. Such behavior benefits them and the corporation. According to Messerschmidt:

> Corporate crime simply assists the corporation and young upwardly mobile men reach their goals. In other words, corporate crime is a practice with which men gain corporate power through maintaining profit margins. Moreover, as corporate executives do corporate crime, they simultaneously do masculinity—construct a masculinity specific to their position in the gender, race, and occupational divisions of labor and power (1993:135).

Corporate masculinity is distinct from masculinities found on the street, on assembly lines, in the family, and elsewhere. For example, being a corporate "real man" entails "calculation, rationality as well as struggle for success, reward, and corporate recognition" (1993:136). Male executives compete with each other and measure masculinity according to their success in the business community. Corporate crime, then, is one technique of advancing this "gendered strategy of action."

As stated earlier in this chapter, uncertain and competitive markets, fluctuating sales, government regulations, and relations with unions all obstruct corporate attempts to increase profits legitimately. Messerschmidt asserts that these obstacles also threaten white corporate-executive masculinity. Thus, corporate crime is a solution to both of these problems. That is, illegal and unethical practices are techniques of reestablishing or maintaining a particular type of masculinity as well as profit margins.

Although Messerschmidt's account is about men, it is a feminist perspective. However, unlike many feminist accounts of crime, his theory is based on research specifically designed to gain knowledge about the factors that influence men to engage in criminal behavior. Indeed, it is difficult to understand the ways in which broader patriarchal forces influence men by interviewing only women, a method that was used in many criminological studies. Messerschmidt's work supports those who contend that it is equally important to study the subcultural "rituals of bonding" that help create, support, and maintain patriarchal male identities (Morra & Smith, 1993). His theory is also one of the first accounts of corporate crime to explain the relationship between three important sociological variables: gender, class, and race/ethnicity.

Thus far, hypotheses based on Messerschmidt's structured action theory have not been tested. Hopefully, others will do so by conducting interviews with junior and senior corporate executives.

Summary

This chapter shows that many people we assume to have what Toby (1957) refers to as a strong "stake in conformity" engage in behaviors that actually do more harm, cost more money, and destroy more lives than predatory street crimes such as mugging, theft, and so on. In fact, as Snider (1993:1) discovered, "Corporate crime is a major killer, causing more deaths in a month than all the mass murderers combined do in a decade." If what you read here surprised you, you are not alone. On any given day, pick up your local newspaper, and you will be hard-pressed to find much journalistic attention devoted to the harms described in this chapter. Note, too, as Reiman (2004:65) asks, "How often do you see the cops on *NYPD Blue* investigate consumer fraud or failure to remove occupational hazards?" Thus, a key objective of this chapter was to introduce you to the sociological study of major harms that receive "selective inattention" from politicians, the criminal justice system, the media, and most social scientists (Dexter, 1958).

Although corporate crime is widespread in advanced capitalist societies such as the United States, some corporations are more criminogenic than others. For example, big, powerful companies are more likely to commit corporate crime than are smaller ones. Further, male rather than female corporate executives commit most of the illegal and unethical acts because they have more opportunities to do so by virtue of their powerful decision-making positions within corporations.

Why do corporations engage in "bad business" (Snider, 1993)? Here we reviewed and evaluated several sociological answers to this question, all of which have strengths and limitations. Still, as noted by Friedrichs (2004b:128), who is one of the world's leading experts on corporate crime, "much further work is called for, especially in terms of the application of sophisticated forms of critical theories of the political economy to an understanding of this type of crime."

What is to be done about corporate crime? Well, our answer is: much more than is being done now. In Chapter 8 we describe some progressive proposals suggested by critical criminologists that could make a difference. Nevertheless, these solutions are not likely to be implemented in the near future because most U.S. citizens strongly adhere to the ideology of competitive individualism (Currie, 1985). Further, many powerful people are not likely to give up the rewards accumulated under the current social order (Barak, 1986). Moreover, Friedrichs (2004b:129) may well be correct in assuming that "if major new terrorist attacks along the lines of 9/11 occur, or the occupation of Iraq becomes increasingly costly and chaotic, governmental and public attention (and resources) are proportionately less likely to focus on corporate crime cases."

Notes

[1]   Friedrichs (2004b), however, argues that tougher laws would be put into place if a liberal democratic government were to be elected in the United States.

[2]   This section includes modified sections of work published previously by DeKeseredy and Ellis (1996) and DeKeseredy and Schwartz (1996).

[3]   This is the title of Block and Scarpitti's (1985) book on how the Mafia profits from illegally dumping toxic waste in the United States.

[4]   Pearce used Snider's (1988:232) definition of commercial crime. She states that this concept refers to "a violation of law committed by a person or group of persons of an otherwise respected and legitimate occupation or financial activity."

⁵   See Friedrichs (2004a) for a comprehensive review of research methods used to study white-collar and corporate crimes.

⁶   Data for 2001 are not yet available (AFL-CIO, 2003).

⁷   See Cullen, Maakestad, and Cavender (1987) for one of the most thorough criminological analyses of this widely known case.

⁸   See Friedrichs (2004a) and Simon (2002) for recent in-depth overviews of the extant literature on violence against consumers.

⁹   This section includes modified sections of work published previously by DeKeseredy and Schwartz (1996).

¹⁰   See DeKeseredy and Schwartz (1996), Friedrichs (2004a), and Snider (1993) for in-depth reviews of various theories of corporate crime.

¹¹   This is because lower-class individuals are not as exclusively committed to the cultural goals of success as Merton assumes. They have a variety of goals, and so far as occupational achievement goes, their goals are realistic and limited. Hence, the disjunction is not as great as Merton supposes (Box, 1983).

¹²   When the primary emphasis is placed not on profit but on the pursuit of other kinds of organizational objectives, other kinds of corporate crime will likely occur more frequently. For example, when the goal of a corporation is to create a stable market environment, corporations attempt to influence the government in a number of legal and illegal ways.

¹³   One of Clinard and Yeager's (1980) major findings is that large corporations are more criminogenic than small ones.

¹⁴   For some scholars, the growth of the state is criminogenic because it tries to run everything, including business corporations, by creating and applying hundreds of rules or laws. The end result is that most businesses, in the normal course of business, violate one rule or another. Corporate crime becomes normal not only because of the presence of so many rules but also because conformity with one rule means breaking another (Young, 1981). In sum, the state helps cause corporate crime in the process of achieving an objective—growth of state bureaucracies—made possible by taxes generated by the very corporations whose conduct becomes increasingly subject to state regulation.

¹⁵   Visano (1985) attempted to do this.

¹⁶   See DeKeseredy and Schwartz (1996) for a more in-depth review of the major criticisms of instrumental and structural Marxist theories of the state and law.

¹⁷   This section includes revised sections of work published previously by DeKeseredy (2000a) and DeKeseredy and Schwartz (1996).

Discussion Questions

1. What, in your opinion, are effective ways of raising public awareness about corporate crime?

2. In a group, identify major forms of corporate crime that were not examined in this chapter.

3. What are the major problems with government corporate crime data?

4. What is the difference between white-collar and corporate crime?

5. In a group, discuss examples of corporate crimes that were committed in your community.

6. Which one of the theories reviewed in this chapter do you think best explains corporate crime?

Problem-Solving Scenarios

1. Contact a local politician and ask him or her what he or she is doing to curb corporate crime.

2. Clip five articles on corporate crime from newspapers and magazines. Identify theories of corporate crime reflected in these articles.

3. Get together with a few people and discuss ways in which you can influence the media to devote more attention to corporate crime.

4. Divide up into small groups of six people. Devise a plan of action that you can undertake as a small group to help prevent corporate crime in your community.

5. Try to imagine what the United States would look like without corporate crime. How would it affect the way people treat each other? How would it affect the legal system, the economy, the social service system, and other elements of the society?

6. In a group, identify the similarities and differences between instrumental and structural Marxist theories of corporate crime.

Suggested Readings

Clinard, M.B. & P.C. Yeager (1980). *Corporate Crime: The First Compre-hensive Account of Illegal Practices among America's Top Corporations.* New York: Free Press.

> To the best of our knowledge, still to this date, no one else has con-ducted such a rigorous, in-depth study of corporate crime in the United States. Included in this important book are: an analysis of crim-inal, civil, and administrative actions either initiated or completed dur-ing 1975 and 1976 by 25 federal agencies against the 477 largest publicly owned corporations; data derived from additional sources (such as newspapers, business journals, magazines, and a sample of the 105 largest wholesale, retail, and service corporations); and an overview of several important theoretical and policy issues.

Cullen, F.T., W.J. Maakestad, and G. Cavender (1987). *Corporate Crime Under Attack: The Ford Pinto Case and Beyond.* Cincinnati: Anderson.

> This book offers a thorough analysis of the Ford Pinto trial. The authors' main purpose is to explain why businesses such as Ford are becoming more vulnerable to criminal prosecution. Their main the-sis is that social and legal changes have combined to generate an attack on corporate wrongdoing and to make powerful members of the corporate community vulnerable to criminal prosecution. An updated version of this book is expected in 2006.

Friedrichs, D.O. (2004a). *Trusted Criminals: White Collar Crime in Con-temporary Society,* 2nd ed. Belmont, CA: Wadsworth.

> Written by one of the world's leading experts on crimes of the pow-erful, this widely read and cited book is essential reading for students and faculty alike seeking an in-depth review of the extant empirical and theoretical literature on crimes such as those covered in this chapter.

Hills, S.L. (ed.) (1987). *Corporate Violence: Injury and Death for Profit.* Totowa, NJ: Rowman & Littlefield.

> This book provides an excellent collection of articles on the prevalence and types of violent corporate acts inflicted on workers and consumers. Informative articles on the ways in which corporate violence destroys communities and the environment are included, as well as essays describing the personal experiences of corporate employees, whistle-blowers, and middle managers. Readers may also find Hills's intro-duction and epilogue enlightening.

Messerschmidt, J.W. (1993). *Masculinities and Crime: Critique and Reconceptualization of Theory*. Lanham, MD: Roman & Littlefield.

> This book will be of special interest to those seeking a rich sociological understanding of the ways in which gender is related to corporate crime and other harms.

Simpson, S.S. (2002). *Corporate Crime, Law, and Social Control*. New York: Cambridge University Press.

> This is a unique book, given that very few studies have been done on corporate deterrence. Simpson assesses several theoretical assumptions about why criminalization should work and explains why it often does not. Further, she argues that cooperative models work best with most corporate offenders.

Online Resources

1. **National White Collar Crime Center**
   http://www.nw3c.org/mission.html
   This is a federally funded, nonprofit corporation. Its site provides rich information on some key issues examined in this chapter. The questionnaire used in the National Public Survey on White Collar Crime is also available at this site, as well as the final report on this study.

2. **National White Collar Crime Centre of Canada**
   http://www.recol.ca/nw4c.aspx
   NW4C is a private not-for-profit organization established to provide an effective response to combating and preventing economic crime by establishing a nationwide and internationally linked support network for organizations involved in the prevention, investigation, and prosecution of economic crime. Its vision, as stated on the web site, is "to provide an effective response, through partnership with the private, public, and law enforcement sectors, to combat and prevent economic crime."

3. **Top 100 Corporate Criminals of the Decade**
   http://www.corporatepredators.org/top100.html
   This site includes Russell Mokhiber's report on the top 100 corporate criminals of the 1990s. You may want to think twice about buying products made by some of the companies included in Mokhiber's list.

4. **Paul's Crime and Justice Page on Corporate Deviance**
   http://www.paulsjusticepage.com/elite-deviance.htm
   As stated at the end of Chapter 1, various links on crimes of the powerful are included in this widely used web site.

. . . . is it possible to conceive of a happy, healthy, golden community, surrounded by a sea of drug use prevalence amongst the rest of the population, but remaining immune to it? Of course it is not (Khan, 1999).

CHAPTER 6
DRUG USE AND ABUSE

In the wide range of human behaviors that might be considered deviant or criminal, perhaps none has generated such widespread fear, anger, or misunderstanding than drug use and abuse. Why has this been the case, and why have perceptions of drugs historically been so inconsistent in the United States? How much of a "problem" are drugs in American society? Why do we use drugs? What are the connections between drugs and other social problems? Who's winning America's "war on drugs"? These are a few of the questions we will attempt to shed light on in this chapter. The literature on drug use and abuse as well as related themes around drug control is voluminous. Here, we will concentrate on drug issues that are both widely debated and contemporary. Before we begin this discussion, though, we want to provide a bit of context around drugs and drug-related issues.

It is often assumed that drug "problems" in America are a manifestation of a society gone morally wrong, or that those who take drugs are simply "weak." It is true that some addictions are harder to break than others, but it is equally true, and extremely important, to understand that drug "problems," so-called "solutions" to supposed drug epidemics, the definition of drugs, and many of the harms they purportedly cause are all social constructions. We make this point because the tendency to argue that drug abuse is a problem faced by "other" (morally bankrupt) people such as "hippies," "druggies," or "misfits," seems to be a pervasive feature of America's view of drugs, a position that is highly problematic. It is difficult to imagine, for example, that people believe heroin, marijuana, and crack cocaine to be "dangerous" drugs, taken primarily by "dangerous people," when, as you will note below, over-the-counter medicines and alcohol (taken by "normal" and "respectable" people) are responsible for far more deaths than all of these drugs combined.

Another example of misplaced policies is the contemporary "war on drugs" in America, a war that most criminologists would argue cannot be won. As the experience with alcohol prohibition between 1920 and 1933 showed us, making drugs completely illegal will only result in the creation of black markets and associated criminal activities. Even in supposedly more "peaceable kingdoms" such as Canada, recent events highlight the continued failure of prohibitionist strategies to control the alleged "drug problem" (see Box 6.1). In short, it would appear that understanding the basic human desire for drugs must be the backdrop for any coherent analysis of drug issues. Indeed, Lyman and Potter (2003:34-35) point out that human beings have been taking drugs for one reason or another since the beginning of recorded history. Chinese emperors made tea from cannabis as long ago as 2000 BCE, the Incas chewed coca leaves (from which cocaine is made), and drugs were used for religious purposes in ancient Aztec society, in India, and other early cultures. Some have even suggested that the pervasive use of drugs throughout human history is a result of a basic human need to alter consciousness (Weil, 1986). In short, some kind of drug use has always been part of the human experience. In the next section, we provide a discussion exploring debates over a fundamental question: what, precisely, is a drug?

Box 6.1
Stricter Drug Laws Called More Risky: Prohibition Causes Grow Ops, Many Say

The slaying of four young RCMP officers in rural Alberta is being cited by some as evidence of the dangers marijuana grow ops pose to the public and police and has brought renewed calls for tougher laws and sentences.

But what makes grow ops dangerous are Canada's marijuana laws, say many legal and narcotics experts who argue further "criminalization" would only lead to more bloodshed. Public Safety Minister Anne McLellan has said she's prepared to consider tougher penalties and noted legislation before Parliament will require a judge to provide written reasons if he or she decides not to hand out jail time to anyone convicted of running a grow op.

Federal legislation, reintroduced in November, recommends reducing penalties for possession of small amounts of pot while providing harsher sentences for marijuana growers. Anyone convicted of having more than 50 plants could be imprisoned up to 14 years.

Debate on Canada's marijuana laws has been renewed following the shooting deaths of the RCMP officers near Rochfort Bridge, Alta., Thursday during an investigation into stolen property and a marijuana grow op.

Box 6.1, *continued*

Lawyer Eugene Oscapella, former chairman of the Law Reform Commission of Canada's drug policy group, calls Ottawa's "get tough stance" in the wake of the Alberta tragedy "absurd." "The whole reason grow ops exist is because of prohibition," Oscapella said yesterday.

"This is very simple economics and it's really appalling that the governments, not just this but the past governments, profess to have such a sophisticated understanding of economics but can't seem to grasp the fact that they've created this incredibly powerful, lucrative and violent black market in Canada."

Tougher drug laws "actually are going to make it far more dangerous for the beat cop," he said, because it is going to drive the trade "more and more out of the hands of non-violent, ma-and-pa producers and into the hands of organized crime," he said from Ottawa.

Oscapella and others caution that this week's violence is also an anomaly, with the vast majority of indoor grow ops continuing to be run by small operators for personal use.

A senior officer with the OPP's drug squad says that police rarely encounter violence during grow-op busts, facing significant resistance at only about two in every 800 search warrants they carry out.

But Det. Staff Sgt. Rick Barnum says that is due almost entirely to the training of drug squad officers, who often storm the operations without any warning to the growers.

But Barnum says that of more than 1,800 grow operation raids in Ontario since 2002, some 1,975 weapons have been found.

"That's more than one per search warrant, and those weapons aren't there for decorations," he says.

Barnum, however, says that relaxing marijuana laws will not help get rid of the grow op plague, as much of the marijuana grown in them is destined for lucrative, but illicit markets in the U.S. Jack Cole, a former undercover narcotics agent from New Jersey, who now heads the pro-legalization Law Enforcement Against Prohibition (LEAP), agrees the Alberta tragedy is likely a direct result of laws that make marijuana's growth and use illegal.

"And creating rigid laws with stiffer penalties because of this situation is a knee-jerk thing that policy makers (will likely) do because they don't seem to know anything else," says Cole, "But when they do that it will only make things worse . . . the harsher the penalties, the more likely it is that (more) officers will be killed."

Cole, who worked 14 years undercover with the New Jersey State Police, says his country's 35-year-old war on drugs and its 1920s alcohol prohibition experience show restrictive policies make the use of banned substances more pervasive and their distribution more lethal.

"What does prohibition of anything get us?

"Prohibiting drugs does not cause less people to use them; we know that," he says.

Indeed, Cole says, the U.S. war on drugs, declared by President Richard Nixon in 1970, has coincided with an exponential increase in the number of illegal drug users in America.

Box 6.1, *continued*

Federal U.S. data shows the number of people using illegal drugs grew from about 4 million in the late 1960s to more than 37 million in 1999.

"As soon as we prohibit a drug we create an underground market for that drug," Cole says. "And that underground market is instantly filled with criminals."

With the "obscene" profits available to those selling the drugs, motivation to protect their trade by any means possible becomes overwhelming, says Cole. "I'll guarantee you that whole armies of police cannot arrest our way out of this when there's such profits to be made," he says.

Prominent Toronto criminal lawyer Paul Copeland says current laws against marijuana growers are "incredibly stupid" and that even more violence would likely occur if they were actually toughened.

Source: Powell, B. & J. Hall (2005). "Stricter Drug Laws Called More Risky." *Toronto Star*, March 5. Reprinted with permission.

What Are Drugs?

The simplest answer to the question of how to define a drug is one focusing on the chemical properties of drugs themselves, and the impact these substances have on human beings. According to Goode (1989), an **objectivist** definition of drugs draws attention to specific chemical characteristics or properties of substances that alter human consciousness or physical being. The idea here is that there is something about a drug (it possesses an objective quality) that exists independently of human definition. By this definition, *any* substance that alters human physiology or consciousness, including sugar, bread, caffeine, and water, could be considered a drug. However, Goode points out that all substances that might be considered drugs do not share a common characteristic that would allow us to include or exclude them from a category called "drugs." Moreover, the substances we commonly call "drugs" can have different effects and purposes. Some drugs can kill you, others can cure disease, and the effects of some drugs depend upon the qualities of the user and the dosage one takes.

These kinds of issues alert us to the importance of the role of human beings, their sociocultural values, historical circumstances, and power relations in defining drugs and social problems such as drug addiction. For example, though it is a controlled substance today, at one time heroin was a common ingredient in cough syrup. In addition at one point in history, the soft drink Coca-Cola actually contained cocaine, as did many other medicines one could buy over the counter (Allen, 1994).

In other words, the definition of drugs and associated concepts such as drug addiction, are social constructions, and the only quality that "drugs" share is that they have been labeled as such. This latter **subjective** definition is the one that we shall use throughout this chapter. We believe that such a definition is superior to objectivist ones because they allow us to understand not only the effects of drugs on people and society, but also the process by which some drugs become defined as "legal or illegal," "harmful or safe," as well as the societal response to these labels. It is important to note that we are not claiming that all drugs are harmless. On the contrary, drug use can cause a multitude of social, health, and economic problems. Rather, we wish to underscore the point that there is nothing inherent in the term "drugs" that makes them dangerous, and that we should use caution in interpreting the meaning of terms like "drug abuse," given that some illegal drugs such as marijuana are no more dangerous than some foods, and that alcohol kills, maims, and is associated with far more problems than many illegal substances (Kappeler, Blumberg & Potter, 1996).

Having dealt with sociological questions around the definition of drugs, we now turn to a specification of the four different types of drugs and their effects. Table 6.1 provides an overview of the main categories of illicit drugs and some examples within those categories that have been developed by the U.S. Substance Abuse and Mental Health Services Administration (SAMHSA).

Many in the social scientific world use similar categories. For example, Lyman and Potter (2003) divide drugs into narcotics, stimulants, hallucinogens, depressants, cannabis, inhalants, steroids, mood drugs, and diet drugs. In the SAMHSA classification below, inhalants such as butyl nitrate are included in the category of stimulants, and alcohol and steroids are in separate categories. Regardless of the way in which drugs are categorized, the effects of these drugs, as suggested earlier, depends greatly on the dosage, the purity of the drug, the social setting in which they are consumed, and many other factors. As a rule, however, effects of drugs are usually discussed within four main categories described below (SAMHSA, 2005a):

- **Narcotics:** Drugs used medicinally to relieve pain; have high potential for abuse, cause relaxation with an immediate "rush," and include initial unpleasant effects, such as restlessness and nausea.

- **Depressants:** Drugs used medicinally to relieve anxiety, irritability, tension; have high potential for abuse, tend to develop tolerance in the user, produce a state of intoxication similar to that of alcohol, and combined with alcohol, increase effects and multiply risks.

- **Stimulants:** Drugs used to increase alertness, relieve fatigue, feel stronger and more decisive. They are also used for euphoric effects or to counteract the "down" feeling of tranquilizers or alcohol.

- **Hallucinogens:** Drugs that produce behavioral changes that are often multiple and dramatic. They have no known medical use, but some block sensation to pain and use may result in self-inflicted injuries. Within this category, "designer drugs," made to imitate certain illegal drugs, are often many times stronger than the drugs they imitate.

Table 6.1
Drug Categories for Substances of Abuse

Narcotics	Alfentanil	Stimulants	Amphetamine
	Cocaine		Benzedrine
	Codeine		Benzphetamine
	Crack Cocaine		Butyl Nitrite
	Fentanyl		Dextroamphetamine
	Heroin		Methamphetamine
	Hydromorphone		Methylphenidate
	Ice		Phenmetrazine
	Meperidine		
	Methadone	Hallucinogens	Bufotenine
	Morphine		LSD
	Nalorphine		MDA
	Opium		MDEA
	Oxycodone		MDMA
	Propoxyphene		Mescaline
			MMDA
Depressants	Benzodiazepine		Phencyclidine
	Chloral Hydrate		Psilocybin
	Chlordiazepoxide		
	Diazepam	Cannabis	Lorazepam
	Glutethimide		Marijuana
	Meprobamate		Tetrahydrocannabinol
	Methaqualone		
	Nitrous Oxide	Alcohol	Ethyl Alcohol
	Pentobarbital	Steroids	Dianabol
	Secobarbital		Nandrolone

Source: SAMHSA (2005). *National Survey on Drug Use and Health, 2002 and 2003* [Online]. Washington, DC: U.S. Department of Health and Human Services Available at: http://oas.samhsa.gov/nhsda/2k3tabs/toc.htm

The Extent and Distribution of Drug Use

Prior to 2002, the Substance Abuse and Mental Health Services Administration of the U.S. Department of Health and Human Services conducted an annual survey entitled the National Household Survey on Drug Abuse (NHSDA). As of 2003, this survey's name was changed to the National Survey on Drug Use and Health (NSDUH). Like its predecessor, it is an annual survey of the civilian, noninstitutionalized population of the United States ages 12 or older. It provides one of the most comprehensive set of measures regarding the incidence, prevalence, and distribution of drug use in the United States. We begin this section with some data on the overall use of drugs in the United States, and then we will provide more detailed summaries and discussions around issues of sex, age, socioeconomic position, and race/ethnicity.

In Table 6.2, we see that nearly one-half of Americans over the age of 12 report that they have used an illicit drug in their lifetime. Moreover, marijuana and hashish seem to be the illicit drugs of choice. Looking further down the table however, we can see that tobacco and alcohol use far outweighs that of illicit drugs, with nearly three-quarters of Americans over 12 stating that they have used some form of tobacco in their lifetime, and more than 80 percent stating they have used alcohol. Notably, binge and heavy drinking (respectively defined as drinking five or more drinks on the same occasion—i.e., at the same time or within a couple of hours of each other—on at least one day in the past 30 days and drinking five or more drinks on the same occasion on each of five or more days in the past 30 days) is also something done by many Americans. Indeed, nearly one-quarter reported binge drinking in the past month.

The next most popular illegal drug category is hallucinogens. This category includes LSD (or "acid"), PCP, and Ecstasy. Cocaine ranks as a close third in the rankings, having been tried by nearly one in seven Americans. It is also interesting to note that nearly one in five people have used psychotherapeutic drugs to get "high" (as opposed to the functions for which they are supposed to be used). This brief overview not only provides us with a sense of the most popular drugs and their levels of use, it also suggests that a substantial proportion of Americans have tried these drugs at least once in their lifetime, and that by far, the most popular drugs are tobacco and alcohol. Moreover, if we read across the table, in the columns titled "past year" and "past month," we can see that the rates of what might be considered current usage are markedly lower than those in the "lifetime" use column. This suggests that while many people may have used such drugs in the past, fewer say that they continue to do so.

Table 6.2
Illicit Drug Use and Tobacco and Alcohol Use in Lifetime, Past Year, and Past Month among Persons Aged 12 or Older: Percentages, 2002 and 2003

| | Time Period | | | | | |
| | Lifetime | | Past Year | | Past Month | |
Drug	2002	2003	2002	2003	2002	2003
ANY ILLICIT DRUG	46.0	46.4	14.9	14.7	8.3	8.2
Marijuana and Hashish	40.4	40.6	11.0	10.6	6.2	6.2
Cocaine	14.4	14.7	2.5	2.5	0.9	1.0
Crack	3.6	3.3	0.7	0.6	0.2	0.3
Heroin	1.6	1.6	0.2	0.1	0.1	0.1
Hallucinogens	14.6	14.5	2.0	1.7	0.5	0.4
LSD	10.4	10.3	0.4	0.2	0.0	0.1
PCP	3.2	3.0	0.1	0.1	0.0	0.0
Ecstasy	4.3	4.6	1.3	0.9	0.3	0.2
Inhalants	9.7	9.7	0.9	0.9	0.3	0.2
Nonmedical Use of Any						
Psychotherapeutic	19.8	20.1	6.2	6.3	2.6	2.7
Pain Relievers	12.6	13.1	4.7	4.9	1.9	2.0
Tranquilizers	8.2	8.5	2.1	2.1	0.8	0.8
Stimulants	9.0	8.8	1.4	1.2	0.5	0.5
Methamphetamine	5.3	5.2	0.7	0.6	0.3	0.3
Sedatives	4.2	4.0	0.4	0.3	0.2	0.1
Any Illicit Drug Other than Marijuana	29.9	29.9	8.7	8.5	3.7	3.7
Any Tobacco	73.1	72.7	36.0	35.1	30.4	29.8
Cigarettes	69.1	68.7	30.3	29.4	26.0	25.4
Smokeless Tobacco	19.9	19.4	4.5	4.4	3.3	3.3
Cigars	37.4	37.1	11.0	10.7	5.4	5.4
Pipe Tobacco	17.0	16.9	—	—	0.8	0.7
Alcohol	83.1	83.1	66.1	65.0	51.0	50.1
Binge Alcohol Use	—	—	—	—	22.9	22.6
Heavy Alcohol Use	—	—	—	—	6.7	6.8

Source: Adapted from SAMHSA (2005). *National Survey on Drug Use and Health, 2002 and 2003* [Online]. Washington, DC: U.S. Department of Health and Human Services. Available at: http://oas.samhsa.gov/nhsda/2k3tabs/toc.htm

With these data in mind, a brief scan of Table 6.3 should begin to alert you to one of the contradictions of American drug policy. In this table we can clearly see that tobacco and alcohol, both of which are legal but controlled substances, rank first and third respectively in terms of causes of death over the past decade, compared to illicit drug use, which ranks ninth. Thus, despite a "war" on illicit drug use that has cost billions of dollars and ruined the lives of thousands, tobacco and alcohol use are 20 and five times, respectively, more likely to cause death than all illicit drugs combined.

Table 6.3
Actual Causes of Death in the United States in 2000

Actual Cause	No. (%) in 2000
Tobacco	435,000 (18.1)
Poor diet and physical inactivity	400,000 (16.6)
Alcohol consumption	85,000 (3.5)
Microbial agents	75,000 (3.1)
Toxic agents	55,000 (2.3)
Motor vehicle	43,000 (1.8)
Firearms	29,000 (1.2)
Sexual behavior	20,000 (0.8)
Illicit drug use	17,000 (0.7)
Total	**1,159,000 (48.2)**

Source: Adapted from Mokdad, A.H., J.S. Marks, D.F. Stroup & J.L. Gerberding (2004). "Actual Causes of Death in the United States, 2000." *Journal of the American Medical Association*, 291, 1238-1245.

Table 6.4 breaks down illicit drug use by age category. From these data we can see that people between the ages of 18 and 25 are the most likely to report that they are currently using illegal drugs and to report ever having used them. Overall, then, illicit drug use appears to be more of a youthful phenomenon, with use declining as one ages.

Table 6.4
Past Illicit Drug Use by Age, 2001

Respondent age	Ever used	Past year	Past month
12–17	28.4%	20.8%	10.8%
18–25	55.6	31.9	18.8
26–34	53.3	16.1	8.8
35 or older	38.4	6.3	3.5

Source: Office of National Drug Control Policy (2003). *Drug Data Summary*. Washington, DC: National Drug Control Policy Information Clearinghouse.

In Table 6.5, we can see that men are more likely to use illicit substances than women, and that despite the fact that illegal drug use is sometimes portrayed as a crime committed by people of color, with the exception of indigenous peoples, white people are slightly *more* likely than blacks, Asians, Hispanics, or Latinos to have used drugs in their lifetime. However, if we look at which ethnic/racial groups use specific drugs, a different picture emerges.

Table 6.5

Any Illicit Drug Use in Lifetime, Past Year, and Past Month among Persons Age 12 or Older, by Demographic Characteristics: Percentages, 2002 and 2003

| | Time Period | | | | | |
Demographic Characteristic	Lifetime 2002	2003	Past Year 2002	2003	Past Month 2002	2003
Gender						
Male	50.7	51.2	17.6	17.2	10.3	10.0
Female	41.7	41.9	12.5	12.4	6.4	6.5
Hispanic Origin And Race						
Not Hispanic or Latino	47.0	47.7	14.9	14.7	8.5	8.2
White	48.5	49.2	14.9	14.9	8.5	8.3
Black or African-American	43.8	44.6	16.8	15.4	9.7	8.7
American Indian or Alaska Native	58.4	62.4	19.4	18.9	10.1	12.1
Native Hawaiian or Other Pacific Islander	*	51.0	17.0	18.5	7.9	11.1
Asian	25.6	25.6	7.6	7.1	3.5	3.8
Two or More Races	54.0	60.1	20.9	20.1	11.4	12.0
Hispanic or Latino	38.9	37.0	15.0	14.7	7.2	8.0

*Low precision; no estimate reported.

Source: Adapted from SAMHSA (2005). *National Survey on Drug Use and Health, 2002 and 2003* [Online]. Washington, DC: U.S. Department of Health and Human Services. Available at: http://oas.samhsa.gov/nhsda/2k3tabs/toc.htm

Table 6.6 shows that in terms of drug use in the past month (in 1998), whites were less likely to report that they were using marijuana than blacks and American Indians/Alaskan Natives, while Asian/Pacific Islanders and Hispanics reported lower levels than whites. A similar pattern exists for cocaine use, with the exception of Hispanics, who reported using cocaine at the same rate as blacks. Whites, on the other hand, were most likely to use alcohol in the past month, and were the third most likely to engage in heavy drinking, after American Indians/Alaskan Natives, and Hispanics.

Drug use in America also appears to be prevalent in every geographical location and in both rural and urban communities. As Figure 6.1 shows, as one moves from completely rural to more urbanized and then metropolitan areas in the United States, rates of drug use rise gradually, so that when we compare completely rural to large metropolitan areas with more than 1 million inhabitants, the difference is approximately 10 percent.

Table 6.6
Estimated Prevalence of Past-Month Drug Use in the United States, by Race/Ethnicity and Type of Drug (percent): 1998

Drug	Percent Using in Past Month
Any illicit drug	
White, non-Hispanic	6.1
Black, non-Hispanic	8.2
American Indian/Alaska Native	9.3
Asian/Pacific Islander	2.8
Hispanic	6.1
Marijuana	
White, non-Hispanic	5.0
Black, non-Hispanic	6.6
American Indian/Alaska Native	8.0
Asian/Pacific Islander	2.6
Hispanic	4.5
Cocaine	
White, non-Hispanic	0.7
Black, non-Hispanic	1.3
American Indian/Alaska Native	1.4
Asian/Pacific Islander	0.0
Hispanic	1.3
Alcohol	
White, non-Hispanic	55.3
Black, non-Hispanic	39.8
American Indian/Alaska Native	43.3
Asian/Pacific Islander	34.5
Hispanic	45.4
Heavy alcohol*	
White, non-Hispanic	6.0
Black, non-Hispanic	4.9
American Indian/Alaska Native	13.7
Asian/Pacific Islander	2.9
Hispanic	6.5
Tobacco cigarettes	
White, non-Hispanic	27.9
Black, non-Hispanic	29.4
American Indian/Alaska Native	31.2
Asian/Pacific Islander	22.5
Hispanic	25.8

*Heavy alcohol use has been defined as "5 or more drinks on the same occasion on at least 5 or more days in the month prior to assessment."

Source: Adapted from National Institute on Drug Abuse (2003). *Drug Use Among Racial/Ethnic Minorities: Revised.* (Rep. No. 03-3888). Bethesda, MD: Author.

Figure 6.1
**Any Illicit Drug Use in Lifetime Among Persons Age 12 or Older,
by Geographic Characteristics: Percentages, 2003**

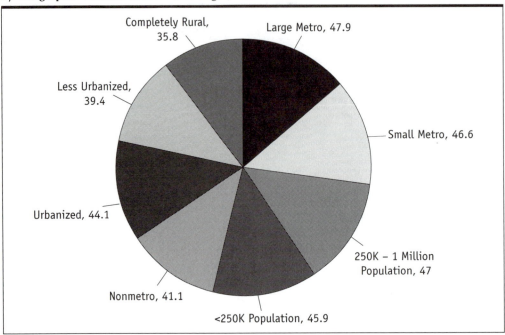

Completely Rural, 35.8

Large Metro, 47.9

Less Urbanized, 39.4

Small Metro, 46.6

Urbanized, 44.1

250K – 1 Million Population, 47

Nonmetro, 41.1

<250K Population, 45.9

Source: Adapted from SAMHSA (2005). *National Survey on Drug Use and Health, 2002 and 2003* [Online]. Washington, DC: U.S. Department of Health and Human Services. Available at: http://oas.samhsa.gov/nhsda/2k3tabs/toc.htm

Table 6.7 shows that illicit drug use appears to be more prevalent in western parts of the United States. Moreover, in terms of family income, there does not seem to be much difference between those living on less than $20,000 per year compared to those who earn between $20,000 and $40,000. However, there are marked differences in illegal drug use when we compare those who possess health insurance or receive welfare benefits with those who do not. Thus, we can conclude that illegal drug use tends to be more prevalent among those who are very poor, and, as many criminologists have observed, there is a strong link between economic inequality and illicit drug use (Currie, 1993).

A more micro-level question that is illuminating is "where do people get these drugs?" The answer to this can be seen in Table 6.8, which shows that for marijuana (the most commonly used illicit drug), the vast majority of users obtained the drug from a friend, and most of these transactions appear to occur in private social settings such as homes or dorms. Only 16 percent stated they obtained marijuana from "someone they just met or did not know well," thereby debunking the myth of the "dope pusher" waiting in school playgrounds to sell marijuana to unsuspecting teens or juveniles. Moreover, according to official U.S. government data, the vast majority of marijuana users either bought the drug (40%) or received it "free or shared it" (56%) (SAMHSA, 2005b).

Table 6.7
Percentage Using Illicit Drugs in Past Year by Race/Ethnicity and Selected Sociodemographic Characteristics, 1991-1993, Respondents Age 12 and Older

	Total	Asian/ Pacific Islander	Hispanic	Hispanic Mexico	Hispanic Puerto Rico	Hispanic Other	Non Hispanic Black	Non Hispanic White
Region:								
Northeast	11.0	8.7	5.9	*	12.3	6.9	14.0	10.8
North Central	10.4	3.9	*	11.2	10.3	6.6	15.8	9.9
South	10.9	3.4	8.6	9.7	14.6	9.4	10.8	11.2
West	15.8	7.5	7.9	14.4	23.3	9.7	19.2	17.0
Family Income								
<$20,000	13.7	9.5	7.3	11.4	14.1	8.7	13.9	14.2
$20-40,000	12.3	4.4	7.0	13.2	13.9	7.7	13.6	12.4
Health Insured:								
Yes	10.5	6.6	6.6	13.0	12.7	8.3	12.0	10.4
No	19.6	6.4	13.7	12.1	15.8	9.8	18.3	22.9
Welfare:								
Receives	21.7	4.3	*	17.1	15.6	12.8	22.0	24.5
Does not	11.3	6.7	8.1	12.3	12.8	8.4	11.7	11.4

* signifies low precision

Source: Adapted from SAMHSA (1993). *National Household Survey on Drug Abuse.* Washington, DC: U.S. Department of Health and Human Services.

Table 6.8
Source and Location Where Marijuana Was Obtained among Past Year Marijuana Users Who Bought Their Most Recently Used Marijuana; Percentages, 2003

Source and Location of Bought Marijuana

Source
Friend	77.8
Relative or Family Member	3.7
Someone Just Met or Did Not Know Well	15.8
Source Unspecified	2.7

Location
Inside Public Building[1]	5.9
Outside in Public Area[2]	15.8
Inside School Building	1.4
Outside on School Property	1.3
Inside Home, Apartment, or Dorm	54.3
Some Other Place	18.3
Location Unspecified	3.1

[1] For example, a store, restaurant, sports arena, bar, or club.
[2] For example, a parking lot, street, or park.

Source: Adapted from SAMHSA (2005). *National Survey on Drug Use and Health, 2002 and 2003* [Online]. Washington, DC: U.S. Department of Health and Human Services. Available at: http://oas.samhsa.gov/nhsda/2k3tabs/toc.htm

Data on the use of other drugs such as heroin, crack cocaine, LSD, and other hallucinogens (presented in Table 6.9) challenge the picture of drug use often presented by popular media. For instance, Ecstasy (popularly known as "X" or "E") is a drug that has been catapulted to public attention because of its association with feelings of well-being, "rave" dance parties (designed to enhance hallucinogenic experiences through light and music), and other aspects of youth culture. Fueled by the mass media, in Europe, and more recently the United States, Ecstasy use has been constructed as a "dangerous drug" that could result in individuals starting on the "slippery slope" to using harder drugs (Jenkins, 1999). Thus, as with crack cocaine in the 1990s, marijuana in the 1960s, and other drugs throughout modern history, a **moral panic** has been created around Ecstasy use, despite the fact that rates of use of LSD and psilocybin ("magic") mushrooms are higher for all users over the age of 12, and about the same for young people ages 12 to 25 (SAMHSA, 2005b).

To be sure, science still has no definitive answer regarding the harmfulness of Ecstasy (and studies continue to be done to determine if ecstasy can have some beneficial uses in certain circumstances), but the issue here, as a subjective definitional framework would suggest, is that the risks and harms associated with this drug (and many others) are probably overstated. Moreover, while it may be true that the use of Ecstasy is increasing worldwide, the real question to be answered is why this is so. It is to this question, framed as a broader inquiry into why people use drugs, that we turn next.

Theories of Drug Use and Abuse

In this section, we offer various sociological perspectives aimed at answering a central question; why do people "do" drugs? Given the harsh nature of current drug policies in the United States, why do so many people risk their freedom to buy, sell, and consume illicit substances? And why, given the fact that drug abuse can result in injury, pain, suffering, and even death, do people insist on using them? As you will see, sociological theories of drug abuse, use, and addiction provide different answers to these questions. Before we begin to survey these theories, however, it is necessary to outline some basic information regarding types of drug users. As we suggested earlier, people take drugs for a host of reasons, including (but not limited to) peer pressure, stress relief, to cope with social or economic distress, to increase energy or to relax, to alleviate boredom, for pain relief, to escape reality and alter consciousness, to feel more self-esteem or elevate status, or to enhance their bodies (as in the case of anabolic steroids, for example). It is

Table 6.9
Specific Hallucinogen, Inhalant, Needle, and Heroin Use in Lifetime, Percentages, 2003

Drug or Method of Administration	Percent
Hallucinogens	14.5
PCP (Angel Dust, Phencyclidine)	3.0
LSD (Acid)	10.3
Peyote	2.4
Mescaline	4.0
Psilocybin (Mushrooms)	8.2
"Ecstasy" (MDMA)	4.6
Inhalants	9.7
Amyl Nitrite, "Poppers," Locker Room Odorizers, or "Rush"	3.8
Correction Fluid, Degreaser, or Cleaning Fluid	1.0
Gasoline or Lighter Fluid	1.6
Glue, Shoe Polish, or Toluene	1.8
Halothane, Ether, or Other Anesthetics	0.6
Lacquer Thinner or Other Paint Solvents	0.8
Lighter Gases (Butane, Propane)	0.4
Nitrous Oxide or "Whippets"	4.9
Spray Paints	0.9
Other Aerosol Sprays	0.9
Any Needle Use[1]	1.5
Heroin Needle Use[1]	0.7
Cocaine Needle Use[1]	0.9
Stimulant Needle Use[1]	0.7
Methamphetamine Needle Use[1]	0.5
Heroin	1.6
Smoke Heroin	0.5
Sniff or Snort Heroin	1.1

[1] Refers to lifetime use of a needle to inject a drug that was not prescribed, or that was taken only for the experience or feeling it caused.

Source: Adapted from SAMHSA (2005). *National Survey on Drug Use and Health, 2002 and 2003* [Online]. Washington, DC: U.S. Department of Health and Human Services. Available at: http://oas.samhsa.gov/nhsda/2k3tabs/toc.htm

important to understand that regardless of the theory used to explain drug use, there are basically four kinds of drug users as outlined by Inciardi and McElrath (1998:2-3):

- **Experimenters** are those who try drugs infrequently in social settings, generally out of curiosity piqued by friends or acquaintances who may claim that the drug is pleasurable. The drug use does not play a major role in their lives.

- **Social-Recreational** users are similar to experimenters, except that their drug use will be more frequent and will continue longer than mere experimentation.

- **Involved** users are those who actively seek to possess and consume drugs. Unlike experimenters and social-recreational users, those who are involved in drug use do not necessarily find themselves in situations where the drugs have essentially "come to them." Rather, they pursue drugs because those drugs do something more for them than just make them feel good (i.e., they may use the drugs to enhance self-esteem, or to cope with stress). As they increase the frequency and duration of consumption, they may begin to lose their ability to perform adequately in their everyday roles in intimate relationships, as workers, or in other walks of everyday life.

- **Dysfunctional** users fit the traditional notion of the "alcoholic" or "drug addict." In this category, finding and using drugs becomes the dominant activity in the user's life. They cannot control their drug use and have become significantly dysfunctional in terms of personal and social relations.

We now turn to the most commonly invoked sociological explanations of drug use and abuse, beginning with strain theory.

Strain Theories

If you have been reading the chapters in this book in sequence, by now you should understand that strain theories focus on the role of inequality in explaining social problems. Strain perspectives eschew the notion that people who take drugs are maladjusted individuals who are also wicked, weak, or immoral. Instead the strain perspective, as a macro-oriented theory, draws attention to the ways in which blocked opportunities to realize socialized and culturally transmitted goals might propel people to use drugs.

A classical statement of the strain perspective on drug use comes from the work of Robert Merton (1938), whose typology of adaptation suggests that people whose opportunities are blocked may engage in **retreatism**, wherein individuals reject culturally transmitted goals (such as the "American Dream"), as well as legitimate means of achieving them (getting a good education, working hard at a job, etc.), and instead resort to using drugs. According to this theory, then, to meet the everyday challenges of living in society, retreatists use drugs and participate in drug subcultures to reward themselves in a context in which socially legitimate rewards are unavailable to them. As we saw in the previous section of this chapter (take another look at Table 6.7), on the face of things, there is some good evidence that drug use tends to be more prevalent among those who cannot meet their aspirations because of lack of access to legitimate opportunities to achieve them. Other theorists have modified strain theory by including the notion of access to illegitimate opportunity structures. Cloward and Ohlin (1960), for instance, argue that it is not enough to show that people lack access to legitimate opportunities to achieve culturally defined goals, but that many people who get involved with drugs do so because they also do not have access to *illegitimate* opportunities such as becoming involved in drug dealing or other criminal activities that might exist in disadvantaged neighborhoods. Thus, individuals who cannot access either legitimate or illegitimate opportunities to pursue status or "success" are in a sense "double failures" and may form **retreatist subcultures** in which drugs become the vehicle by which solutions to problems might be found.

A recent variation of strain theory has been articulated by Agnew (1992), whose General Strain Theory proposes that there are different experiences of strain (not just in terms of frustration with access to goals) and that we should conceptualize strain in terms of negative relationships with others. Strain may be experienced as a result of (1) the failure to achieve valued goals, (2) the removal of stimuli that are valued positively (e.g., a loved one, the opportunity to play a sport or engage in a recreational activity), or (3) the presence of stimuli that are viewed negatively (e.g., abuse, violence in the family, bullying, etc.). The first idea is consistent with Merton's basic idea of strain, while Agnew presents the second and third forms of strain as potentially important in understanding why people engage in particular behaviors. Given that some people experience these types of strain, he argues that we should study how such experiences give rise to negative feelings such as hopelessness, inadequacy, anger, or disappointment. Experiencing these negative emotions may result in people using drugs to escape from them, or people may use drugs as a way of retaliating against the forces they perceive to have caused the strain in the first place. Agnew also seeks to remind us that drug use or criminal activity is only one possible adaptation to strain, and that there are many other factors that may come into play in this regard. For instance, a person may or may not choose to use drugs, depending not only on their experience of strain and decisions on how to deal with it, but also according to the kinds of relationships they have with their peers, the amount of control they perceive to have over their life, the kinds of social support available to them, the degree to which they feel morally inhibited from committing deviant acts, and their degree of self-control (Baron & Hartnagel, 2002).

One of the problems with strain perspectives is that while they may help to explain drug use and abuse in particular subcultures, particularly the disadvantaged, they do not help to explain why so many people who are not in these circumstances also turn to drugs. Again, as the data above suggest, although illicit drug use is disproportionally higher among the poor compared to those who are more well off, drug use is clearly not the prerogative of the poor alone. In effect, the question that strain theory does not answer very well is: why do people who *do* have access to legitimate means to attain culturally defined goals successfully still use illegal drugs such as cocaine or marijuana?

There are also measurement difficulties associated with testing strain theory. Specifically, there is some disagreement as to how strain should be measured. Should it be operationalized as a desire to receive high incomes, education, or occupational success, coupled with low perceptions of the chances of achieving these goals, as suggested by Liska (1971)? Or are some of these indicators better predictors of strain than others (Farnworth & Leiber, 1989)?

Another problem with strain theory is that it does not help us to understand why some people choose retreatism over other modes of adaptation, such as conformity or ritualism. As we have seen in other chapters, another common criticism of strain theory is that while it highlights the importance of unequal access to opportunities, it does not attempt to explain the sources of strain within the broader structural and economic relations of society. In short, it is not critical enough of the roots of inequality, and can therefore only be considered a kind of "reluctant radicalism." Furthermore, research on the lives of drug addicts tends to discredit the idea of retreatism, for as Lukoff (1980:203) points out, far from retreating into a hermit-like existence: "Life is almost frenetic for addicts. In order to survive they must keep out of the way of the police, raise the considerable funds they require, and keep abreast of where drugs might be obtained."

Last, empirical tests of the link between strain and drug use have yielded mixed results, probably because strain has been narrowly defined in most of these studies. Although Agnew's work has introduced more variables via his general strain perspective, in general, the theory tends to ignore major variables that might help to explain illicit drug use, such as quality of family relationships, age, and gender.

Social Control Explanations

The extent to which people bond to the "conventional social order" is at the heart of social control perspectives on drug use. As you will recall from Chapter 2, control theorists maintain that when people have weakened bonds to conventional ideas, such as "don't do drugs" or "keep your nose clean," their chances of using drugs increases. An application of Hirschi's (1969) four elements of the social bond to drug use might look something like this:

> **Attachment:** If people have strong attachments to conventional others who do not take illegal drugs, they will be less likely to use them. Those lacking in such attachments will be more likely to use such drugs.
>
> **Commitment:** Those who have a strong "stake in conformity" are less likely to use illegal drugs or engage in drug abuse, because, as the term suggests, they have too much to lose if they do. Getting caught with cocaine might seriously jeopardize their relationships, work circumstances, or other things they hold to be important.
>
> **Involvement:** People who spend a lot of time engaging in legitimate pursuits are less likely to use illegal drugs or abuse drugs. Conversely, those who do not have the time or access to such pursuits may be more likely to engage in illegitimate ones, including drug use.
>
> **Belief:** The extent to which people believe in the rules or laws of society determines the likelihood of them violating those rules. Thus, people who see marijuana laws as unfair or inappropriate might be more likely to justify to themselves that marijuana use is acceptable.

As pointed out in Chapter 2, Hirschi's original formulation focuses on the nature and quality of people's bonds to *society*. Later in his career, along with Michael Gottfredson, Hirschi formulated a theory of **self-control** that focuses on people's capacity to control their impulses. Thus, within this framework, one may succumb to temptation if one finds oneself in a situation where drugs are readily available. Moreover, according to Gottfredson and Hirschi (1990), succumbing to such temptation is a consequence of inadequate socialization early in life.

There have been numerous empirical studies of the relationship between the quality and strength of self-control/social bonds and crime, delinquency, and drug use, and most of these studies have demonstrated some type of link between controls and these kinds of outcomes. One of the problems with such research, however, is that drug use is usually "bundled" with a range of other dependent variables (such as petty theft, larceny, or serious crime) to create a general variable representing "deviance" or "criminal behavior." Moreover, the strength and nature of the relationships vary, with some research finding that the link is stronger for minor delinquent acts and some research finding the opposite. Moreover, very little research has focused on adult samples, and few have explored the possibility of integrating social bond theory with low self-control theory (Longshore, Chang, Hsieh & Messina, 2004).

Other common criticisms of control theory have been covered elsewhere in this book and will therefore not be repeated here. However, it is worth focusing on one important criticism as it relates directly to the problem of drug abuse. One of the problems with control theory is that it does not speak to the problem of motivation. In the context of drug use, then, control theory has nothing to say about why people might be motivated to try marijuana or cocaine. As Elliott, Ageton, and Canter (1979) remind us, weak bonds are not enough to explain deviant behavior; we also need to understand the sources of the motivation toward continued involvement in deviant behavior. Control theory's most important weakness, then, lies in the assumption that everyone is equally likely to be motivated toward using drugs.

Interactionist Theories

Interactionists have had much to say about drugs. As you know, this micro-oriented perspective focuses on the ways in which people go about using symbols (such as language) and rituals to construct and define meaningful experiences. Thus, much of the work around drug issues from an interactionist point of view has focused on the ways in which people come to define drug-taking activities as "normal," the characteristics of "addiction," or the ways in which drug use is demonized as deviant behavior. In this section, we will explore some of these perspectives.

Perhaps one of the most important analyses of drug use from an interactionist perspective is that of the late Alfred Lindesmith. Lindesmith was a key figure during the time when drugs such as marijuana and opiates were becoming politicized as "highly dangerous" substances warranting strong prohibitive legal responses. Between 1930 and 1962, Harry Anslinger, a long-serving federal bureaucrat, led the Federal Bureau of Narcotics in a crusade to enforce drug-control laws. He is widely credited as being the mind behind what many scholars consider to be fundamentally irrational drug control policies in the United States. According to Keys and Galliher (2000:131), Lindesmith waged an essentially single-handed battle against the arguments advanced by Anslinger, who believed that "ethnic minorities and foreign nationals were at the heart of American drug problems," and blamed addiction on what he considered to be the moral shortcomings of addicts. The crux of Lindesmith's position, which was derived from in-depth interviews with addicts themselves, was that the nature of drug addiction had more to do with how addicts see themselves, rather than moral weakness or the addictive properties of drugs. His research showed that the alleged pleasure derived by addicts from drugs like cocaine or heroin is greatly overstated, and that "people become addicted after experiencing physical withdrawal and learning what it is and how to interpret it from their cultural environment" (Keys & Galliher, 2000:93). Thus, Lindesmith drew attention to the role of social processes (such as the consequences of hanging around in addict subcultures or the controlling influences of harsh drug laws) and how addicts interpret these situations in constructing self-images of themselves as addicted people. In turn, this perspective on drug addiction would mean that treatment and harm reduction, not harsh punishment, should form the core of drug policy—a position fundamentally at odds with the growing "lock 'em up and throw away the key" policy environment.

Lindesmith's work is important not only because it challenged prevailing views of drug use and addiction, but also because it is considered by some scholars to be the only sociological theory of addiction (Keys & Galliher, 2000). Still debated today, the theory continues to generate controversy, as U.S. policy persists in demonizing drugs and drug users.

Another approach within the interactionist tradition has been offered by Howard Becker (1973), who, in a study of marijuana users, maintained that "getting high" properly requires that users learn the experiences or meanings of using marijuana. They do so by constructing, in concert with other users, a set of shared meanings in relation to what getting and being "high" are all about. Like Lindesmith, Becker downplays the pharmacological effects of drugs, arguing instead that it is the social context and the meanings people share that determine their attitudes and experiences with and toward drugs. Thus, deviance is conceived of as "collective action," a kind of "cooperation" that takes place between deviants, supporters, bystanders, and those who might accuse the deviant of doing "bad" things. By extension, deviant behavior like drug use is, for Becker, not inherently wrong, but is a product of the labels that people attach to this behavior. Obviously, the more power particular individuals or groups possess, the more likely that their definitions of what constitutes labels like "drug abuse" or "drug addict" will become the dominant societal "yardstick" by which such labels are taken for granted (Becker, 1967, 1973).

More recent formulations of interactionist applications to drug use and abuse have continued the tradition of examining how people construct their "identity" as drug users. For example, Anderson (1993) has examined the role of identity transformation among former drug addicts, and other work has begun to examine the links between identity formation and drug subcultures (Anderson & Mott, 1998)

Although it has generated a great deal of policy interest, there has been some debate as to whether labeling theory constitutes an oversimplified model of drug use (Shoemaker, 2000). Overall, however, labeling theory has been useful because it reminds us of the centrality of power relations in defining drug use as good or bad. On the other hand, another accusation is that labeling theorists do not attempt to uncover and locate the nature of power relations in broader structures of power, thereby failing to link micro-level insights with macro-level ones. For example, it is one thing to argue that drugs and "drug addicts" are labels, but this realization requires an analysis of whose interests might be served by the labeling process. Another objection, common to many other criminological theories, is that interactionist theories have not adequately theorized gender. Certainly, Lindesmith's sample was based on the experiences of mostly male drug addicts, and the bulk of other, more recent studies have tended to use male samples as well (Sterk-Elifson, 2005). Clearly, more work is required to answer these objections, particularly in relation to linking micro-level with macro-level concerns.

Ecological Perspectives

Unlike theories that attempt to explain drug use by reference to individual traits, ecological theories emphasize the role of social, demographic, and geographic factors in creating conditions in which drug use and abuse might occur. Rather than treating the individual, the focus of these theories is in understanding the ways in which social institutions shape behavior, and in transforming those social institutions to effect change.

As Chapter 2 pointed out, social disorganization theories, a variant of the ecological perspective, argue that factors such as levels of community social control, social cohesion, and trust, in the context of disadvantaged neighborhoods and communities, influence criminal and deviant behavior. For instance, people who live in disadvantaged conditions with very little social support or opportunities to engage in legitimate activities may be more likely to turn to using or selling drugs to cope with their situation. The following passage from Maher's (2000:21) ethnographic study of "Bushwick" provides an acute sense of the kinds of conditions that prevail in such neighborhoods:

> In summer, Bushwick is a pastiche of sensory awareness. When the mercury rises, the neighborhood is cloaked in the sweet and unmistakable stench of ripe garbage. A steady stream of salsa pulses from the bodegas, ruptured by the occasional burst of rap from a passing car. Drug dealers adorn the stoops and children compete with their customers for space on congested sidewalks. Dealers' lookouts and watchful parents keep an eye on proceedings from wooden

frame windows. The banter of childhood is punctuated by dealers calling out brand names that reek of death—*Fatal Attraction, Body Bag, Homicide,* and *DOA.* Mothers and fathers, aunts and uncles, sisters and brothers pound the sweltering pavements, threading their way through a milieu of drug users, criminals, and assorted street people. Bushwick is a vibrant oxymoron—a neighborhood where drugs are both a way of life and a way of death.

As you can see, in such neighborhoods, exposure to drugs and those who use drugs on a regular basis is near pervasive, a situation that is not surprising given that drug transactions and dealers are everywhere (Ensminger, Anthony & McCord, 1997). Though he is best regarded as a scholar whose work fits within the critical paradigm, Elliott Currie's (1993) argument about the four ways that drug use may be explained in communities that are "severely distressed" (Kasarda, 1992) is germane here:

- The **Status** model maintains that when the poor are denied legitimate opportunities to obtain status, they may turn to drug use as a way of attaining self-esteem, a sense of respect, or a sense of community. There is good evidence to suggest that for some people, drug use in the context of social disorganization is a way to gain respect from peers. For example, in one study, the status peers give to drug using was found to be related to alcohol and other drug use among youths in an inner-city community (Dembo, Farrow, Schmiedler & Burgos, 1979). In addition, there appears to be some association between the quality of a drug and the status it gives the user. Heroin, for instance, is seen as a "bad" or "dangerous" drug, thereby bestowing the status of "bad" or "dangerous" on the user (DeKeseredy & Schwartz, 1996)

- In the **Coping** model, drugs are seen as a way of coping with the intense stresses of everyday life in inner-city ghettos. Coupled with lack of social support, positive role models, family disruption, lack of economic resources, and a host of other ills, inner-city residents also have to face potential victimization, and, if they do work, they face boring, repetitive, and low-wage jobs. In such circumstances, then, it is not surprising that inner-city residents use drugs to "escape" from the drudgery of everyday life.

- The **Structure** model maintains that precisely because disorganized neighborhoods are disorganized, many residents use the rituals of procuring, preparing, using, or selling drugs to structure their day, in the absence of legitimate everyday rituals, such as getting up, going to work, and then spending time with one's family. In short, in the absence of "something to do," some people will use the rituals of drug use to organize their lives.

- Finally, the **Saturation** model contends that in isolated communities suffering from the kinds of social pathologies already described, drugs become part and parcel of the fabric of everyday life. Drugs are so pervasive, that many people simply drift into "what everyone else is doing" (Goode, 1989; Wilson, 1996). Research conducted by DeKeseredy and his colleagues provides further support for the saturation model. In their study of Canadian public housing neighborhoods, they found that many respondents reported that it was easy or very easy to buy illicit drugs, particularly marijuana and hashish, and that local drug dealers were known to almost all of the neighborhoods (Dekeseredy, Schwartz, Alvi & Tomaszewski, 2003).

It is important to note that these models are not mutually exclusive. It is possible—and indeed, even likely—that many people in such communities use drugs for two or more of the reasons specified in these models. Moreover, they may drift from one reason to the next, depending on their stage of life, the structure of opportunities, and their shifting relationship to the subcultures of drug life existing at any given time. Currie argues that the status model best explains initial stages of drug use, but that as users get older, they derive less pleasure from the drug, and sink into persistent drug use for one or more of the other reasons specified above.

It is also worth mentioning that drug use is not necessarily the only "end point" resulting from life in impoverished neighborhoods. Increasingly, scholars are pointing to the links between drug use and other social problems such as assault, domestic violence, or homicide, and particularly to the ways in which these social problems can and often do contribute to increased use of alcohol or other drugs (Kilpatrick, Acierno, Resuick, Saunders & Best, 1997; Sampson & Lauritsen, 1990).

Beginning with the path-breaking research of Shaw and McKay (discussed in Chapter 2) and through to the present day, research in the ecological tradition continues to find alarmingly high rates of social problems in severely distressed neighborhoods. Nevertheless, there remain important challenges within this tradition that warrant brief exploration here. Conceptualization and measurement issues continue to present major problems for ecological researchers. Concepts such as "social disorganization" are often not carefully measured, and, as Bursik and Grasmick (1993b) point out, some research suffers from circular reasoning—communities that have high levels of crime are seen to be socially disorganized, and vice versa. In addition, it is clear that not *all* people living in socially disorganized neighborhoods are addicted to or even use drugs, which raises the question of what factors (personal or otherwise) might help to "insulate" them from the effects of these neighborhoods.

Traditionally, the research literature on social disorganization has attempted to show that some of these mediating, or insulating factors might be things like levels of informal social control, social ties, collective efficacy, or social capital (see Chapter 2 for a review of these). Recently, some have suggested that other mechanisms should be considered, including variables such as neighborhood culture, levels of *formal* social control, and urban political economy (Kubrin & Weitzer, 2003a). In addition, many studies in this tradition rely on official statistics to measure the extent of drug use and social disorganization. However, micro-level ethnographic work is also necessary to add texture to these accounts, and to unpack important variations that might exist in neighborhoods along ethnic, gender, cultural, or other lines. As research continues to include these and other related concepts, and to develop better measures of existing ones, the future utility of ecological models for explaining drug use and other social problems will likely grow.

Critical Theories

Because the problem of inequality is so central to much critical criminology, many working in this tradition draw upon some of the arguments presented in the theoretical sections above. As pointed out earlier, for example, critical criminologist Elliott Currie's work makes sense within the context of elements of social disorganization theory. But critical theories have also taken different aspects of drugs as the subject of inquiry. For instance, Musto (1988) offers a historical analysis of the "drug war" in the United States, while others, such as Wacquant (2000), argue that contemporary responses to drugs in America cannot be understood without taking racial politics and racism into account. Still others have focused attention on the drug industry, the link between drugs and crime, court responses to drug use, or drug use as a gendered social phenomenon (Campbell, 2000; Maher, 2000).

We cannot here provide in-depth coverage of all these issues, and the reader is encouraged to examine some of the suggested readings at the end of this chapter. In this section, we will focus attention on the work of criminologists who have critically examined the "war on drugs," and look at feminist perspectives on drugs.

The War on Drugs

There have actually been a series of drug wars in the United States. As we noted at the beginning of this chapter, Harry Anslinger can rightly be credited with beginning the war through his persistent and often vicious campaign targeting minorities—demonizing them and the drugs they allegedly used (of course, little mention was made of the fact that whites were also using drugs and always have) and creating a legal edifice of consequences that ensued. There is a large and useful historical literature on the drug war, and here we focus on contemporary versions of the "battle" to eliminate illegal drugs.

The most important statement that can be made about drug wars, including recent ones, is that they have been a failure. Over the course of many years, increasingly larger allocations of taxpayers' money have been appropriated to combat the "drug problem." In 2000, the federal government of the United States spent $18 billion (Lock, Timberlake & Rasinski, 2002), and in 2002, $18.8 billion (Jensen, Gerber & Mosher, 2004). The arrest level for drug offenses in the United States is astonishing. In 1996, there were more than 1.5 million arrests, and for cities with populations greater than 250,000, arrests for drugs were higher than any other crime category of offense (Mosher, 2001). Data from the Bureau of Justice Statistics, cited by Jensen and his colleagues, show that between 1980 and 2001, the number of persons in state and federal prisons for drug offenses increased by approximately 1,300 percent (Jensen, Gerber & Mosher, 2004). More prisons have been built to accommodate the problem, criminal courts are overloaded, and increasingly more people are being criminalized.

This uncompromising war has also produced numerous serious social problems. Many drug users return to their communities after being incarcerated, creating problems of reintegration. The imprisonment of breadwinners has resulted in the impoverishment of families, many of which were barely self-sufficient in the first place, and when offenders return to ghettoized communities, many face harsh surveillance and suspicion rather than social support (Hagan & Coleman, 2001). Prisons are also expensive to run, and their construction and management have become industries:

> As the size of the prison system has increased so too has its costs. Between 1984 and 1996, the U.S. Department of Justice reported that amount of money required to operate just the nation's prisons (excluding the massive jail system) grew from $6.8 billion to $24.5 billion. In the same year, a total of more than $120 billion was spent on civil and criminal justice functions with most of those costs associated with police (over $50 billion) and corrections (over $40 billion).

The other major cost is prison construction. As of 1998, there were approximately 83,500 new prison beds under construction with another 86,500 being planned to be constructed or total of 170,000 new prison beds. Assuming an average construction cost of $50,000, the nation will be spending $8.5 billion to build new prisons in an effort to keep pace with the growing prison population. Even with all of these costs, over thirty state prison systems were operating above their rated bed capacities (Austin, Bruce, Carroll, McCall & Richards, 2000:7).

We should remember that these costs have to placed in the context of estimates that for every dollar spent on treatment the nation would save between $7 and $18 (Males, Macallair & Jamison, 2002).

These facts compel us to ask a fundamental question: What is the reasoning behind the war on drugs, particularly when the evidence so clearly shows that it has failed to reduce—and has probably even increased—illegal drug use?

According to Lyman and Potter (2003), modern drug policy in the United States is composed of several strategies, including reducing demand, reducing supply, eradication, education, treatment, and, of course, incarceration. All of these strategies, however, have failed to reduce illegal drug use. Critical perspectives draw attention to the root causes of social problems. As critical criminologists we would agree with those who highlight experiences of poverty, family disruption, and social exclusion as important reasons for why people use or sell drugs. As for those who do not live in such conditions, Currie points out that drug use among the affluent is both manageable and decreasing. Yet drug use continues to plague America's deteriorating inner cities. As one character in the popular television depiction of prison life "Oz" puts it: "If you want to stop drug use, stop pain." As you might imagine, however, the kinds of social, economic, and political changes that would be required to stop, or even alleviate, pain are unlikely to occur in a society that continues to create low-wage jobs, slash welfare benefits, and limit access to higher education, and fails to provide health care to more than 45 million of its citizens.

In addition to the reluctance of powerful groups to change social and economic conditions to benefit more people, there is, in our view, also a powerful component of social exclusion to the war on drugs. For instance, blacks, Hispanics, and Latinos are disproportionately incarcerated for drug crimes relative to both their population and their use of drugs. So clearly, racism and racial exclusion are part of the war on drugs. In addition, if more people are going to prison for drug crimes, and prison is a way to control the socially disenfranchised (Wacquant, 2000), then the war on drugs may also be seen as part of an arsenal of legal tools to control populations deemed to be "social junk or social dynamite"—those who have fallen between the cracks of the socioeconomic system and must rely on others to subsist, and those whose conditions make them potentially dangerous to the system (Spitzer, 1975). Additionally, the drug war has, in some states, meant incarceration of prisoners who are unable to vote, but whose participation in elections would likely have resulted in dramatic changes in electoral results, even a reversal of the 2000 presidential election (Uggen & Manza, 2002).

Thus, the drug war is not only bankrupt when it comes to its objectives of reducing the sale and use of drugs, it has and will continue to have major social consequences. Jensen and his colleagues (2004117) caution criminologists that ignoring these consequences will:

> . . . . make us "enablers." Limiting our studies to the making and breaking of law, and its societal responses, will reify the "drug problem" (or more broadly, "the crime problem") as nothing more than that. If we expand our inquiry, however, to the study of the societal consequences of public policies, we begin the process of challenging the assumptions underlying our (society's) proposed solutions.

Feminist Perspectives on Drugs

As we saw in Table 6.5, women are less likely than men to use drugs. Most drug research has focused on men, but early research examining women's use and experiences with drugs found that many women use hard drugs for the same reasons as men. For instance, because women who live in inner-city ghettos experience many of the same deprivations as men would in these areas, to a great extent, they use drugs to cope or escape in the same way as men do (Barkan, 1997). However, some research also suggests that men are more likely to use drugs for excitement while women are more likely to use them to cope with depression or other psychological problems (Chesney-Lind, 1995; Inciardi, Lockwood & Pottieger, 1993). Moreover, initial research on women's use of drugs focused on their legal use of prescribed pharmaceuticals, particularly in relation to their reproductive capacity, as well as the use of prescription drugs such as tranquilizers to help them cope with their subordinate roles relative to men (Lexchin, 1984).

It is now recognized that female drug users need to be studied in their own right, rather than as comparison groups in studies of males. As Sterk-Elifson (2005) points out, women's reproductive capacity, societal expectations of women in modern societies, their smaller numbers and subordinate position in most drug subcultures, and the fact that they are more "hidden" than men all make women a group whose experiences are likely to be very different in some regards than those of their male counterparts.

Gender socialization plays an important conceptual role in feminist explanations of differences between male and female drug use. Essentially, this approach attempts to explore the ways in which expectations around feminine and masculine roles are related to drug use. For instance, being a "real man," particularly for adolescents, is often associated with risk-taking behavior, such as drinking large amounts of alcohol or trying hard drugs. Similarly, pressures associated with being a "real woman" may create a "resistance effect," in which some women use drugs as a way of rejecting narrow conceptions of their "appropriate" feminine roles (Anderson, 1998).

A substantial body of research also indicates that women's pathways to drug use differ from those of men. Many women begin using drugs because of their relationship to men. For instance, there is abundant empirical evidence that many women began using and continue to use drugs as a consequence of experiencing sexual, physical, psychological, and other forms of abuse at the hands of their male partners or in childhood.

Nancy Campbell's (2000) work provides a good example of a feminist analysis of women's illicit drug use. One of her central arguments is that despite the rhetoric of women's equality, the reality is quite different. For example, in her analysis of the social construction of women's use of methamphetamines and crack cocaine during the 1990s, Campbell shows that government officials portrayed both drugs as being particularly attractive for women. In addition to having the power to "shatter a mother's love for her children," these drugs were depicted as:

> . . . . overcom[ing] women's intuition, their "natural instincts," and the redemptive power of maternal love. Women's turn to these drugs thus signified that the scope and impact of illicit drug use in the late twentieth century had exceeded a natural limit (2000:1)

Campbell also draws attention to the racialized nature of these official views. Methamphetamines were seen as drugs used primarily by white women to "remain functional, orderly and clean," to help them meet their multiple obligations of juggling service jobs, caring for children, and cleaning their houses. On the other hand, African-American women crack users were seen as "nonproductive inhabitants of chaos, decay and squalor" who were not willing to care for their children, and as "sexual compulsives, bad mothers, and willing prostitutes who lack even the capacity for remorse that might redeem them" (2000:3). In effect, female drug users are seen as "doubly deviant," in that they are perceived to be acting out of their "proper" or "natural" character, and are also seen as "social failures."

The portrayal of women who use drugs as "fallen women" who demonstrate a range of deviant behaviors (not just drug use but prostitution, illegal drug selling, etc.), and who are "passive" (drug use happens to them) rather than active choice-makers, has also been successfully challenged by ethnographic work. Morgan and Joe (1997) show that most women who use illegal drugs do not come from socially disadvantaged neighborhoods, nor are they engaged in other kinds of illegal activities (Maher, 1995, 2000; Taylor, 1993).

In sum, feminist studies on women's use of drugs have built a persuasive body of evidence indicating that their pathways, experiences, and exit strategies are different than those of men, and that these processes are deeply rooted in broader problems of sexism and patriarchy in modern societies, as well as class and race issues. As this evidence builds, it is critically important for policymakers, healthcare workers, and other practitioners to take women's different experiences seriously.

Summary

In this chapter we have examined empirical and theoretical aspects of drug use and abuse. After reading it, you should understand why it is important to use subjectivist definitions of "drugs." In addition, we presented an overview of the levels of drug use in the United States, the kinds of drugs people use, and the characteristics of drugs and the people who use them. As we have noted in other chapters in this book, none of the theoretical explanations offered in this chapter are by themselves capable of explaining the multiple realities of drug use and abuse. Indeed, because this book focuses on the *sociology* of deviant and criminal behavior, we have not explored emerging research emphasizing the biological and psychological correlates of addiction, and how these are related to social settings and relationships.

The theories explored here, however, do point to the centrality of social conditions such as poverty, deprivation, and gender relations in explaining drug use and abuse. Moreover, the chapter has attempted to show that the current drug war in America has not worked, and that the time to consider alternative strategies—perhaps one of "reducing the harm" caused by drug abuse—is long overdue.

Discussion Questions

1. What are the policy implications of using a subjective definition of drugs?

2. Why are people living in disadvantaged social conditions more likely to use hard drugs?

3. Speculate on the political and social consequences of labeling certain drugs as more dangerous than others.

4. What aspects of personal identity might be important in understanding drug use?

5. What kinds of alternatives can you think of for dealing with drug issues in America?

6. Should certain drugs be decriminalized? Which ones, and why?

Problem-Solving Scenarios

1. Divide into groups and come up with different strategies for curbing the high rates of illegal drug use in disenfranchised communities.

2. In a group, identify the similarities and differences between the drug use theories reviewed in this chapter.

3. Create your own theory of drug abuse, drawing upon insights of the theories discussed in this chapter.

4. How would you test the effectiveness of a drug awareness program such as DARE (Drug Abuse Resistance Education)?

5. Devise a research strategy to help illuminate the contours of illegal drug use among middle- and upper-class people.

6. Discuss some of the broader societal expectations of women and men that might influence their use of legal and illegal drugs.

Suggested Readings

Inciardi, J. & K. McElrath (1998). *The American Drug Scene: An Anthology.* Los Angeles: Roxbury.

> This book provides a collection of classic and contemporary essays on patterns, problems, perspectives, and policies on legal and illegal drug use. It includes historical perspectives as well as contemporary essays that are both theoretical and empirical in nature.

Keys, D. P. & J.F. Galliher (2000). *Confronting the Drug Control Establishment: Alfred Lindesmith as a Public Intellectual.* Albany: State University of New York Press.

> A fascinating historical analysis and biography of Alfred Lindesmith, who, from an interactionist perspective, formulated the only sociological theory of addiction. The book is also useful for understanding the historical foundations of the drug war, and the role of important sociologists in a rapidly changing America.

Currie, E. (1993). *Reckoning: Drugs, the Cities and the American Future.* New York: Hill and Wang.

> An excellent account of the roots of contemporary drug problems in the United States. Currie also analyzes the drug war, and points to progressive strategies for reform.

Palacios, W.R. (2005). *Cocktails and Dreams: Perspectives on Drug and Alcohol Use.* Upper Saddle River, NJ: Prentice Hall.

> Provides an introduction to the world of drug subcultures from an interactionist perspective. The book gathers research from scholars employing qualitative methodologies, to identify, describe, and analyze the personal experiences of drug users.

Maher, L. (2000). *Sexed Work: Gender, Race, and Resistance in a Brooklyn Drug Market.* New York: Oxford University Press.

> A detailed account of the lives of female drug users in a socially disadvantaged neighborhood. Maher reveals the details of women's lives and their drug use in the context of their multiple victimization by AIDS, poverty, racism, and violence.

Gaines, L.K. & P.B. Kraska (1997). *Drugs, Crime, and Justice: Contemporary Perspectives.* Prospect Heights, IL: Waveland.

> A reader emphasizing the societal and legal response to drug use, and the consequences of these responses. The book points to the multifaceted nature of drug issues, and is especially significant for students of the criminal justice system.

Online Resources

1. **National Institute of Drug Abuse (NIDA)**
   http://www.nida.nih.gov/OtherResources.html
   Established in 1974, NIDA supports more than 85 percent of the world's research on the health aspects of drug abuse and addiction.

2. **Substance Abuse and Mental Health Services Administration (SAMHSA)**
   http://www.samhsa.gov/index.aspx
   This is the web site to go to for the best official data on patterns of drug use and the characteristics of users.

3. **Drug Policy Alliance**
   http://www.drugpolicy.org/homepage.cfm
   This is the site of the leading organization working to end the war on drugs. It has many important links to other progressive organizations and numerous publications on drug issues.

"Now we'll start this band of robbers and call it Tom Sawyer's Gang. Everybody that wants to join has got to take an oath, and write his name in blood." Everybody was willing (Mark Twain, *Huckleberry Finn*, 1884:7).

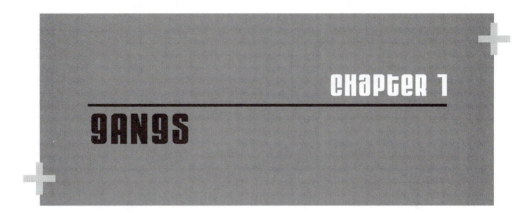

CHAPTER 7

GANGS

In this chapter we examine the problem of youth gangs in America. The literature on gangs is voluminous, and so rather than including adult, motorcycle, or prison gangs in our discussion, we have chosen to focus on youth gangs. The main reason for doing so, other than space limitations, is that youth gangs in America have been the focus of a great deal of public and media attention. If you were to ask the average person what they are most afraid of, many would probably respond that they are scared of being victimized or that they are worried about youth gangs. In fact, fear of criminal victimization and gangs were two of the strongest motivators behind criminal justice policy in the United States during the 1990s. The problem of gang proliferation and gang violence was so salient in the public mind that President Clinton even declared a "war" on gangs in 1997 (Lane & Meeker, 2000). Historically, there has been a certain romance attached to youth gangs, but today, popular perceptions have it that youth gangs are associated with a range of criminal activities, especially drug trafficking (Spergel, 1995), and the media seem to focus on "gang-related" stories of all kinds (Jankowski, 1991; Peronne & Chesney-Lind, 1997). Indeed, it would not be an exaggeration to suggest that like so many of the other issues covered in this book, there is a "moral panic" around the problem of gangs (McCorkle & Miethe, 2002).

In what follows, we attempt to answer questions such as: Are youth gangs a problem? What do they look like, and where are they? What do they do? And why do young people join, stay, or leave gangs? We cannot begin to answer these questions, however, until we examine a perennial problem in gang research, namely, defining what, exactly, a gang is.

What is a Gang?

Although sociologists such as Shaw and McKay had written about juvenile delinquency and youth friendship groups, formal research on gangs in the United States really began with the work of Frederic Thrasher (1927), who analyzed more than 1,300 "gangs" in Chicago. Like others working in the early Chicago school tradition (see Chapter 2), Thrasher was fundamentally interested in social reform. Believing that youth gangs were essentially the predictable outcome of young people's attempts to adapt to their poor social conditions, he referred to them as "street urchins," rather than criminals, and felt that these misguided youths required the intervention of youth courts and social service agencies in their lives. Thus, Thrasher defined gangs as follows:

> The gang is an interstitial group originally formed spontaneously, and then integrated through conflict. It is characterized by the following types of behavior: meeting face to face, milling, movement through space as a unit, conflict, and planning. The result of this collective behavior is the development of tradition, unreflective internal structure, esprit de corps, solidarity, morale, group awareness, and attachment to a local territory (1927:57)

As you can see, Thrasher does not mention criminality as a defining feature of gangs. His broad approach to defining gangs dominated thinking around gang research for many years. By the 1980s, though, researchers had begun to criminalize the definition of youth gangs. For instance, Miller's (1980:121) definition is:

> . . . . a self forming association of peers, bound together by mutual interests, with identifiable leadership, well-developed lines of authority, and other organizational features, who act in concert to achieve a specific purpose or purposes which generally include the conduct of illegal activity and control over a particular territory, facility, or type of enterprise.

And another luminary of gang research, Malcolm Klein (Klein & Maxson, 1989:205), defines gangs similarly as:

> any denotable group of youngsters who: (a) are generally per-
> ceived as a distinct aggregation by others in their neighbor-
> hood; (b) recognize themselves as a denotable group (almost
> invariably with a group name) and (c) have been involved in
> a sufficient number of delinquent incidents to call forth a con-
> sistent negative response from neighborhood residents and /or
> law enforcement agencies.

In our view, the changing definition of gangs belies a shift in attitudes toward youths generally, from "normal" children in need of protection, supervision, and guidance, toward a model that sees young
people as responsible for their actions in a society that increasingly, and
erroneously, perceives an epidemic of dangerous youth crime (Alvi,
2002). It is also clear, however, that public and law enforcement perceptions of youth gangs as criminal were, and continue to be, motivated
by fears around gang involvement with drugs (particularly the crack
cocaine epidemic of the 1990s), the recognition that gangs were prominent in declining inner-city communities, and policy responses to
gangs that were oriented toward highly developed law enforcement
strategies (Katz, Webb & Armstrong, 2003). In effect, because gangs
were defined as engaging in criminal activity, criminality became part
of the definition of gangs. Because criminality is the variable that we
criminologists try to explain, and given the fact that gangs engage in
criminal behaviors to varying degrees, we prefer definitions rooted in
the tradition started by Thrasher. Thus, following Short (Short,
1997:81), we define youth gangs as:

> groups, whose members meet together with some regularity,
> over time, on the basis of group-defined criteria of member-
> ship and group-defined organizational characteristics; that is,
> gangs are non-adult-supervised, self-determining groups that
> demonstrate continuity over time.

While we do not want to suggest that gangs are simply groups of
unsupervised youths who happen to "hang around" with one another,
we contend that this definition permits us to understand the *wide
variety* of activities in which youth gangs may engage. In other words,
gangs *may* demonstrate various levels of organization around criminal activities, but they are also likely to spend a lot of time engaging
in conformist ones, and their members may commit offenses that
have nothing to do with the gang per se (DeKeseredy, 2000a).

In the next section, we will look into the prevalence and characteristics of gangs by examining data from both official sources (which
define gangs as criminal groups) as well as studies employing broader
definitions.

The Extent and Distribution of Gangs

The National Youth Gang Survey has been conducted annually since 1996 by the National Youth Gang Center (NYGC), which is funded by the Office of Juvenile Justice and Delinquency Prevention (OJJDP). Consisting of a nationally representative sample of 3,018 urban and rural law enforcement agencies, the survey asks these agencies to define gangs as "a group of youths or young adults in your jurisdiction that you or other responsible persons in your agency or community is willing to identify or classify as a 'gang.'" In the context of the previous discussion of definitions, you should immediately realize that this definition is problematic because the survey allows officials to define gangs according to their own, variable standards. However, the survey does allow respondents to clarify which elements of a youth gang they consider to be most important, and includes a category regarding whether the group "commits crimes together." New data from the 2002 National Survey of Youth Gangs has been produced. At the time of writing this book, these data are currently available in summary form only. For that reason, much of the data below come from the last complete report from the National Survey of 1998, which was published in complete form in 2000.

Prevalence

Table 7.1 shows that while gangs are primarily an urban phenomenon, they have a significant presence in smaller cities and rural areas as well. We can also see that between 1996 and 1998 there was a decrease in the number of jurisdictions reporting active youth gangs, a trend that seems to be continuing. Longitudinal data covering the years between 1996 and 2000 suggest that gang activity has declined quite markedly in this time frame. Fifty-three percent of respondents reported youth gangs in their jurisdiction in 1996, but by 2000 this had declined to 40 percent (Egley, 2002).

Table 7.1
Percentage of Jurisdictions Reporting Active Youth Gangs, by Area Type, 1996, 1997, and 1998

Area Type	1996	1997	1998
Large city	74%	72%	70%
Small city	34	33	32
Suburban county	57	56	50
Rural county	25	24	21
Overall	53	51	48

Source: Office of Juvenile Justice and Delinquency Prevention (2000). *1998 National Youth Gang Survey*. Washington, DC: Office of Justice Programs, U.S. Department of Justice, p. 7.

In terms of how many gang members and gangs there are in the United States, Table 7.2 shows that there were estimated to be more than three-quarters of a million youth gang members active in more than 28,000 gangs in 1998. In addition, the table illustrates that while large cities have relatively fewer gangs than small ones, they have more members per gang. You will note that the number of gangs and gang members reported by respondents is smaller (in some cases, very much smaller) than the estimated numbers. This is because the survey relies on a sample of agencies within each jurisdiction. Thus, to obtain the most accurate picture of gangs, the authors of the report extrapolate by multiplying the percentage of agencies reporting gangs by the total number of jurisdictions from which the sample was derived.

Table 7.2
Reported and Estimated Number of Youth Gangs and Gang Members, by Area Type, 1998

Area Type	Reported		Estimated	
	Gangs	Gang Members	Gangs	Gang Members
Large city	11,196	440,298	12,538	482,380
Small city	354	3,994	8,413	94,875
Suburban county	4,152	116,533	6,040	176,610
Rural county	472	7,250	1,716	26,368
Total	16,174	568,075	28,707	780,233

Source: Office of Juvenile Justice and Delinquency Prevention (2000). *1998 National Youth Gang Survey.* Washington, DC: Office of Justice Programs, U.S. Department of Justice, p. 13.

Gangs exist in all 50 states. Figure 7.1 shows the top states by number of gangs reported and as you can see, the highest concentration is in the western part of the United States, particularly California, and there are correspondingly fewer gangs in the northeastern states. In addition to California, the areas with the largest concentrations are Texas and Illinois, reflecting high gang membership in very large cities like Los Angeles, Houston, and Chicago.

Age and Gender

The age structure within these groups ranges between those younger than 15 to those over 24. Figure 7.2 shows that youth gangs are primarily made up of youths 18 to 24 years old, and that youth gangs are aging. This is significant because it is well known that most young people desist from crime as they move into adulthood, and also because it may mean that fewer young people are joining gangs.

Figure 7.1
Top Ten States by Number of Gangs Reported

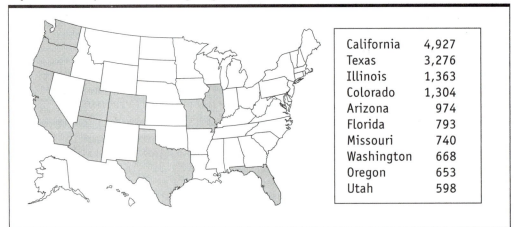

California	4,927
Texas	3,276
Illinois	1,363
Colorado	1,304
Arizona	974
Florida	793
Missouri	740
Washington	668
Oregon	653
Utah	598

Source: Office of Juvenile Justice and Delinquency Prevention (1997). *1995 National Youth Gang Survey.* Washington, DC: Office of Justice Programs, U.S. Department of Justice.

Figure 7.2
Age of Youth Gang Members, 1996 and 1998

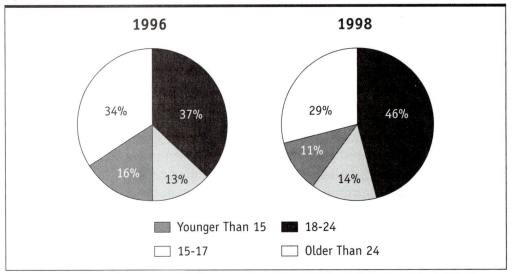

Source: Office of Juvenile Justice and Delinquency Prevention (2000). *1998 National Youth Gang Survey.* Washington, DC: Office of Justice Programs, U.S. Department of Justice, p. 15.

In terms of gender, it is widely agreed that youth gangs are over-whelmingly controlled by males. In fact, according to the OJJDP, in 1998 less than 2 percent of all gangs in the United States were domi-nated by females. Females do represent approximately one-tenth (8%) of all gang members (Office of Juvenile Justice and Delinquency Pre-vention, 2000). However, it should be noted that estimates of female participation in gangs are complicated by the fact that law enforcement agencies may tend to underreport their involvement because they believe that females engage in fewer criminal activities than males (Curry, 1998; Curry & Decker, 1998). Indeed, as we shall see later in this chapter, the notion that female gang members are appendages or merely "satellites" of male gangs has been a constant and lamentable feature of much early gang research.

There are some studies that do not use law enforcement statistics to garner estimates of female involvement in gangs. In this regard, Moore and Hagedorn (2001:2) point out that in self-report surveys of youths in a range of cities in the United States, estimates of female membership in gangs range from 8 to 38 percent. Moreover, although early female gangs tended to be auxiliaries affiliated with male gangs, some researchers have contended that the number of independent female gangs has increased, while others, such as Chesney-Lind (1993), have cautioned that there is little evidence that there is a "new breed of violent female gangsters breaking into this historically male-dominated phenomenon" (Howell, 1998:3).

Ethnicity

In Figure 7.3 we can see that Hispanics constitute the largest ethnic group among all gang members in the United States, and that the ethnic composition of these groups did not change significantly between 1996 and 1998. The ethnic composition of gangs largely reflects the demographics of the communities in which they live. Most gangs are "monoracial," that is, their members are of the same ethnic background. However, a significant proportion of gangs (about 36%) are "mixed," composed of two or more ethnic/racial groups. In addition, so-called "hybrid" gangs have flourished in the past decade. While these gangs are often mixed in terms of ethnic/racial background, they are also diverse in a number of other ways, making it difficult to study these groups and raising challenges for law enforcement (see Box 7.1). For example, they may consist of individuals participating in a number of gangs, or, there may be ambiguous rules of conduct, cooperative relationships, symbolic associations, or mergers with other gangs (Starbuck, Howell & Lindquist, 2001).

According to Howell (1998:3), there is a relationship between type of ethnic/racial gang and particular crimes. African-American gangs tend to be more involved in drug offenses, Hispanic gangs in "turf-related" violence, and Asian and white gangs in property offenses.

Figure 7.3
Race/Ethnicity of Youth Gang Members, 1996 and 1998

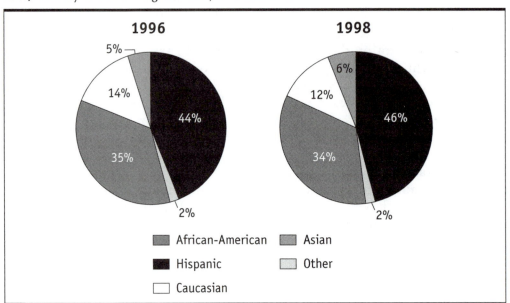

Source: Office of Juvenile Justice and Delinquency Prevention (2000). *1998 National Youth Gang Survey.* Washington, DC: Office of Justice Programs, U.S. Department of Justice, p. 21.

Gangs and Crime

As we noted earlier, youth gangs have frequently been associated with criminal activities. In a longitudinal study comparing delinquent and nondelinquent youths, Battin (1998) and her colleagues found that there were significant differences between gang members and non–gang members on levels of self-reported criminal activity. Being in a gang increased an individual's chances of engaging in delinquent or criminal behavior. Furthermore, although gang members were only 15 percent of the sample, of all the crimes committed by the entire sample, they reported committing (Howell, 1998:8):

- 58 percent of general delinquent acts
- 51 percent of minor assaults
- 54 percent of felony thefts
- 53 percent of minor thefts
- 62 of drug-trafficking offenses
- More than 59 percent of property offenses

Box 7.1
Practitioner's View: The Challenges of Hybrid Gangs

Law enforcement officers from communities unaffected by gangs until the 1980s or early 1990s often find themselves scrambling to obtain training relevant to hybrid gangs. When gang-related training first became widely available in the early 1990s, it often emphasized historical information, such as the formation of the Los Angeles Crips and Bloods in the late 1960s or the legacy of Chicago-based gangs (the Black Gangster Disciples, Latin Kings, and Vice Lords). As law enforcement officers learned about the origins of these influential gangs, they sometimes attempted to apply this outdated information in their efforts to deal with hybrid gangs in their jurisdictions. The assumption that new gangs share the character-istics of older gangs can impede law enforcement's attempts to identify and effectively counter local street gangs, and actions based on this assumption often elicit inappropriate responses from the community as a whole. Citizens may react negatively to law enforcement efforts when they sense that gang suppres-sion actions are geared to a more serious gang problem than local gangs appear to present.

Because of uncertainty in reporting on problem groups such as "cliques," "crews," "posses," and other nontraditional collectives that may be hybrid gangs, some police department staff spend an inordinate amount of time trying to pre-cisely categorize local groups according to definitions of traditional gangs. When training law enforcement groups on investigative issues surrounding drug trafficking or street gangs, instructors must resist the tendency to connect gangs in differ-ent cities just because the gangs share a common name. If the groups engage in ongoing criminal activity and alarm community members, law enforcement offi-cers should focus on the criminal activity, regardless of the ideological beliefs or identifiers (i.e., name, symbols, and group colors) of the suspects. This practical approach would circumvent the frustration that results from trying to pigeonhole hybrid gangs into narrow categories and would avoid giving undue attention to gangs that want to be recognized as nationwide crime syndicates.

Source: Starbuck, D. J.C. Howell & D.J. Lindquist (2001). *Hybrid and Other Modern Gangs.* Washington, DC: Office of Juvenile Justice and Delinquency Prevention, p. 3.

Thus, it appears that youth gangs are responsible for more than their fair share of criminal offenses. Table 7.3 sheds more light on this issue, showing that a fair proportion of youth gang members engage in violent, property, and drug crimes, particularly if the "most/all" and "some" categories are combined. In addition, while criminal activities appear to be more prevalent in urban and suburban areas, youth gang crime is no longer an inner-city problem, having moved to suburban areas (which actually reported more problems with certain crimes than large cities) and rural counties as well. Note also that, at least in 1998, drug sales constituted the offense in which gangs were most likely to engage.

Table 7.3
Jurisdictions Reporting Youth Gang Member Involvement in Criminal Activity, by Area Type, 1998

Type of Offense/ Proportion of Gang Members Involved	All Area Types		Large City		Small City		Suburban County		Rural County	
	No.	Pct.	No.	Pct.	No.	Pct.	No.	Pct.	No.	Pct.
Aggravated assault										
Most/all	147	12%	100	14%	6	5%	29	12%	12	9%
Some	515	43	334	47	33	28	109	44	39	29
Few	473	40	252	36	63	54	93	38	65	48
None	69	6	20	3	14	12	16	7	19	14
Robbery										
Most/all	39	3	22	3	3	3	10	4	4	3
Some	362	30	252	36	13	11	80	33	17	13
Few	580	49	349	50	52	45	117	48	62	46
None	215	18	77	11	48	41	39	16	51	38
Burglary/Breaking and Entering										
Most/all	157	13	79	11	12	10	38	15	28	21
Some	539	45	314	45	43	37	120	49	62	46
Few	426	36	266	38	52	45	75	31	33	25
None	69	6	37	5	8	7	13	5	11	8
Motor Vehicle Theft										
Most/all	136	11	95	14	6	5	27	11	8	6
Some	491	41	308	44	29	25	117	48	37	27
Few	442	37	250	36	52	45	75	31	65	48
None	126	11	47	7	28	24	26	11	25	19
Larceny/Theft										
Most/all	209	17	124	18	15	13	45	18	25	19
Some	591	49	358	51	53	46	130	53	50	37
Few	347	29	198	28	41	35	59	24	49	37
None	51	4	22	3	7	6	12	5	10	8
Drug Sales										
Most/all	329	27	196	28	23	20	75	30	35	26
Some	540	45	311	44	52	44	114	46	63	46
Few	299	25	179	26	39	33	52	21	29	21
None	34	3	15	2	3	3	7	3	9	7

Note: The percentages within each offense category may not total 100 percent because of rounding.

Source: Office of Juvenile Justice and Delinquency Prevention (2000). *1998 National Youth Gang Survey.* Washington, DC: Office of Justice Programs, U.S. Department of Justice.

Gang homicide is one of the most important issues in the public consciousness, in political arenas, and among criminal justice officials. There are, however, some limitations associated with gang homicide data. Homicide records maintained by law enforcement agencies are limited because they reflect only what is known to those agencies. In addition, there are distinct problems with missing information, and often information on the characteristics, circumstances, settings, and participants are missing from police surveys. In addition, measures of gang homicides depend not only on how a gang is defined (see above), but also on how definitions attributing homicide to gangs are assigned. Some law enforcement agencies only count "gang-motivated" homicides, in which killings result out of gang functions such as territorial disputes or rivalries, while other agencies employ the notions of "gang-related" or "gang-involved" homicides, in which a murder is counted as a gang homicide if there is *any* involvement of a gang member (Maxson, Curry & Howell, 2002).

Keeping these issues in mind, Table 7.4 shows that the gang homicide rate is positively related to city population size; that is, the larger the city, the higher the gang homicide rate. The vast majority of cities under 200,000 reported no gang homicides. In their study of youth gang homicide in the 1990s, Maxson and her colleagues report that:

> . . . . although the numbers fell, they varied from city to city and in the early and later parts of the decade. From 1991 to 1996, when 408 cities were studied, the total number of gang homicides declined nearly 15 percent from 1,748 to 1,492. Of the 237 cities that reported having both a gang problem and a gang homicide in all 3 years of the period 1996 to 1998, the total number of gang homicides fell 18 percent from 1,293 to 1,061. Although these decreases are heartening and relatively few cities reported large numbers of gang homicides, they conceal the fact that one city—Los Angeles—accounted for 30 percent of the decrease in the early part of the decade. Along with Chicago, Los Angeles stands out as having the highest gang homicide rate. Moreover, the percentage of cities reporting an increase in that period (29 percent) was about the same as the percentage reporting a decrease (32 percent); 39 percent reported no change. The second part of the decade brought news that was more encouraging, as more cities reported a decrease (49 percent) than an increase (36 percent) (Maxson, Curry & Howell, 2002:109)

For the most part, gang homicides are also qualitatively different from typical homicides (see Chapter 4). Fluctuations in gang homicide rates tend not to follow the same patterns as overall homicide rates (Block, 1993), and in many cases, such killings involve more than two participants, are less likely to involve people who know each other, are more likely to occur in public settings (e.g., the street), and are more likely to involve guns (Howell, 2004).

Table 7.4
Largest Number of Gang Homicides Reported for 1996, 1997, or 1998, by City Size Population

Number of Gang Homicides Reported	25,000-49,999 Cities Reporting This Many Homicides	50,000-99,999 Cities Reporting This Many Homicides	100,000-199,999 Cities Reporting This Many Homicides	200,000 and above Cities Reporting This Many Homicides	Total Cities Reporting
0	340	163	24	5	532
1-10	140	135	78	30	383
11-50	2	3	10	30	45
51-100	0	1	2	3	6
100+	0	0	0	2	2
Total	482	302	114	70	968

Source: Maxson, C.L., G.D. Curry & J.C. Howell (2002). "Youth Gang Homicides in the United States in the 1990s." In W.L. Reed & S. Decker (eds.), *Responding to Gangs: Evaluation and Research* (pp. 107-137). Washington, DC: National Institute of Justice.

In summary, although it is impossible to provide a definitive portrait of gangs, the data presented in this section portray a *general* picture of youth gangs as follows:

- They tend to be young, male, or male-dominated.
- They exist in almost all jurisdictions, are territorial, and are no longer confined to the inner city.
- They vary greatly in terms of criminal activity, but are more likely to be involved in criminal activities than non-gang youth.
- Most gangs are monoracial, but there are also mixed-ethnicity gangs, and, increasingly, "hybrid" gangs.

In the next section, we will examine some of the most widely cited sociological theories of gangs.

Theories of Gangs

Theories purporting to explain the existence of gangs or the dynamics of gang behavior have occupied sociological criminologists for many decades. However, it is important to note that the nature of these explanations has varied according to shifting social and economic conditions in the United States. The most important of these shifts has probably been the deindustrialization of urban America. Thus, as McCorkle and Miethe (2002:99) remind us:

> . . . . most criminologists now believe gangs have become institutionalized in impoverished communities, representing alternative opportunity structures and agents of socialization that aggressively compete with families and schools for the hearts and minds of urban youth.

The importance of broader economic shifts, their role in shaping the perceptions and realities of inequality in inner-city communities, and the impact these factors have had on the formation, reproduction, and dynamics of gangs naturally leads us to first examine strain-subcultural theories of gangs.

Strain-Subcultural Theories

Strain and subcultural theories of gangs are related in that different models of strain focus on macro social pressures leading to different modes of adaptation to those pressures. Among these potential modes of adaptation is the impetus for young people to form subcultures of deviant behavior—that is, gangs. In Chapter 2, we presented a detailed discussion of classic strain theories of delinquent youths, highlighting the work of Albert Cohen and Cloward and Ohlin. As you will recall, Cohen argued that gangs developed as a reaction to the failure of underclass youths to measure up to middle-class values, while Cloward and Ohlin's differential opportunity theory emphasized the idea that young people joined gangs for economic opportunity. Because both legitimate and illegitimate opportunities are limited at any given time, competition for criminal jobs led to the development of criminal gangs (focusing on profit and money), conflict gangs (focusing on toughness and violence), and retreatist gangs (focusing on using drugs, drinking, or sex).

Another classic theory of gang delinquency was advanced by Walter Miller (1958), who argued that lower-class gangs formed because they were functional means to achieving desired ends. Unlike Merton and Cloward and Ohlin, however, Miller contended that the desired ends were not necessarily material ones. Rather, lower-class youths formed gangs because the gangs provided them with a means of successfully conforming to the norms and values associated with lower-class culture. Miller suggested that lower-class culture was composed of a different set of values—which he called **focal concerns**—than those of the middle or upper classes. These focal concerns were:

- **Trouble:** The ability to get away with breaking the law and be seen as a troublemaker, which in turn, confers status.

- **Toughness:** Being tough and fearless.

- **Smartness:** Referring to the ability to con or outsmart others.

- **Excitement:** The desire to take risks or seek thrills in an ultimately boring environment.

- **Fatalism:** The idea that luck or fate determines one's destiny, rather than staying in school, staying out of trouble, or earning good grades.

- **Autonomy:** The notion that one should be independent and free from the domination of authoritative figures.

For Miller, if young people could demonstrate that they possessed these qualities they could achieve status. The "lower-class culture" they were attempting to conform to had, in his view, developed out of the realities of slum life, and gangs were the mechanism by which lower-class values could be reproduced and amplified. In effect, then, Miller felt that far from being deviants, youth gang members were actually conforming to the environment of cultural values that characterized poor, lower-class neighborhoods.

Edwin Sutherland's (1947) approach to explaining deviant behavior is also germane to the study of gangs. For Sutherland, the formation of subcultures is absolutely critical to explaining gangs, because the theory emphasizes the ways in which deviant values and "skills" are learned in interaction with others (see Chapter 2 for a detailed explanation). Thus, if there are gangs that already exist in a social setting, one of their functions is to socialize members into the "correct" set of motivations that exist around the purpose of the gang, as well as the techniques that might be associated with being in a particular gang (e.g., learning how to "tag," how to sell drugs, or how to steal cars).

A more contemporary attempt to construct explanations of gang behavior based on the insights of strain theory can be found in the work of Agnew (2002) and his associates. As we saw in Chapter 2, Agnew modified strain theory into what he calls General Strain Theory (GST), which advances the idea that young people are forced into delinquency as a response to noxious states or emotions that themselves emanate from negative experiences and relationships.

Joanne Moore (1990) has also conceptualized strain in terms of barriers to economic and social opportunities. In her study of intra-gang variations in violence in East Los Angeles, she points to the logical effects of lack of legitimate opportunities:

> If a community's economy is not based solidly on wages and salaries, other economies will begin to develop. Welfare, bartering, informal economic arrangements, and illegal economies become substitutes—simply because people must find a way to live. Young people growing up in these communities have little to look forward to (Moore, 1990:172).

John Hagedorn's (1998) ethnography of gang members in the Midwest also found that a declining manufacturing economy, coupled with deteriorating inner-city social supports and resources, removed the "ladders" of opportunity for many youths, who then found ways to cope with these conditions by joining gangs, which then become permanent features of inner-city life.

Given the lack of legitimate opportunities experienced by these youths, it is not surprising that many contemporary strain-influenced studies of youth gangs focus on the connections between youth gangs and drug dealing or other illicit activities. For instance, Jankowski (1991) found that gangs engage in illicit opportunities almost as a matter of rational business decisionmaking—if such opportunities present themselves, they will take advantage of them. However, other studies have not been as supportive of the conclusions implied by strain theory, and the consensus now seems to be that drug trafficking may only be conducted by a small proportion of all gangs, and that this activity is subordinate to other functions, including identity formation, protection of neighborhood turf, and recreational activities (Coughlin & Venkatesh, 2003).

A further development within the strain tradition has been advanced by John Hagan (1993), whose discussion of "social embeddedness" reverses the direction of causality between unemployment and crime. Traditionally, we might expect that unemployment and its various associated deprivations might lead to criminal behavior, particularly for youths who have few skills and fewer prospects. Hagan reverses this notion, arguing that some youths may be unemployed or otherwise "out" of the legitimate opportunity structure because they have become embedded in illegitimate activities and socialization processes. For example, a youth may be born into a disrupted family, with no exposure to people who can model mainstream behaviors, go to a school where he or she associates with delinquent peers, and live in a community where drug use saturates the neighborhood (see Chapter 6). Thus, as Hagan notes in reference to Anderson's (1990) ethnographic work, the social networks in which people find themselves may actually act like an "employment agency" for illegal activities and the gangs that support them.

Gangs are not only formed as a way to solve problems resulting from material deprivation. Subcultural theories draw attention to the fact that people often form groups that provide alternative and often deviant ways of dealing with strain, but also provide ways of integrating with the mainstream culture. For example, in addition to the perception that joining a gang is a way of making money, Jankowski (1991) points to other reasons such as recreation, finding refuge in group identity, physical protection from danger, resistance to the likely possibility that they may be forced into the kinds of jobs their parents have had to endure, and as a way of demonstrating commitment to their communities. Moreover, gang members tend to solidify their bonds to one another through the use of symbols such as shared specialized language, specialized graffiti, and clothing style (Moore, 1990). Thus, as one might predict from strain theory, the gang acts as a substitute mechanism by which mostly disenfranchised youths can achieve the kinds of things—identity, independence, status, respect, and so on—that most American youths desire (see Box 7.2)

Box 7.2
Flaunting Wealth on the Street is a Must

At the time Elbert "Pierre" Mahone was gunned down last year, the leader of one of the city's most notorious street gangs drove a Rolls-Royce, wore full-length fur coats and had built up a reputation as a Robin Hood for spreading money around his impoverished Lawndale community.

While it would seem people living on the wrong side of the law would want to draw as little attention to themselves as possible, many gang members are attracted to the designer clothing, luxury autos, large glitzy jewelry and other "flash" paid for by their illicit activities.

In their world, a person's "rep" for being a ruthless and savvy businessman can protect him.

"My notoriety do demand a certain amount of respect in the community. I can walk around and I'm going to be respected because of my past experience and my involvement in the gangs," said Willie Lloyd, who claims he is a retired gang leader. "There is a notoriety about Willie Lloyd."

When Lloyd left Logan Correctional Center in 1992 after serving time for a gun conviction, he wore a black-and-white leather outfit under a mink coat.

His subordinates—who themselves were dressed in leather, fur, gold, diamonds with alligator shoes—picked him up from the jail in five limousines.

Wearing the latest styles, driving the flashiest must-have vehicles and using their cash to parlay good faith in the neighborhoods can add to the gangs' allure on the street.

For future gang members, it's seen as a lucrative alternative to working a minimum-wage job flipping burgers.

"Once the money starts comin' in, you got to figure out what to do with it," said Ranell Rogers, a 23-year-old Mafia Insane Vice Lords gang member. "Nine times outta 10, it might be a young guy who doesn't know what to do with it. It might go to drugs, women, guns, cars. Those are necessary; everybody wants 'em. If you don't have 'em, you ain't cool."

The most obvious gang status symbol is the right car.

Box 7.2, *continued*

Gang members, especially mid-level gang members who are in charge of a local crew of "slingers" who actually sell the drugs, will sometimes own a small fleet of vehicles that they have put in the names of family members and friends to keep officials from establishing a paper trail against them.

The "must-have" cars these days are the fully decked out Cadillac Escalade SUV truck, which runs more than $45,000; the GMC Envoy SUV, which averages $30,000, and Jaguars, which run about $46,000. The colors of choice are black or white.

"They are trend-setters, they'll always go with the biggest trend," Chicago police Sgt. John Lucki said.

When Satan Disciples gang member Santos Garcia was arrested in 1998, police recovered $44,644 in cash, thousands of dollars in jewelry and several vehicles, including a Lincoln Continental, a Chrysler Intrepid, a Ford Mustang, a Lincoln Navigator SUV—and two Chevy Astro vans used to cart dope from the Mexican border.

Garcia was sentenced to 15 years in prison in March after being convicted of drug dealing, but fled before he saw a day in prison. Two men who worked with him pleaded guilty in December to drug charges and received three years probation, Cook County State's Attorney Anthony Kyriakopoulos said.

While Garcia, a 28-year-old native of Mexico, allegedly held down a $19,000-a-year job as a machine operator, he owned a $71,644 28-foot power boat and a Jet Ski worth $10,000. He also owned a $200,000 five-bedroom home in Marquette Park, which prosecutors are trying to seize because they say it was bought with his drug profits.

Like any good business person, a gang leader often showers underlings with gifts and clothing as a way to keep employees in their good graces and to keep them from "flipping" to a rival gang, Lucki said.

"You'll hear how the guy who is supplying them will throw a picnic for them or buy them all gym shoes or different types of uniforms, whether it's current trendy jackets or hats, pants or clothes," Lucki said. "Essentially he becomes an employer for the community."

Along with the cars, gang members seek out "hip-hop" designer clothing such as Pelle Pelle, which has leather jackets selling for $500 and velour warmup suits going for $200; FUBU clothing, especially a $135 denim jacket called the "Gang In Boxes Jacket." And anything with the name Sean Jean, a line launched by rap star Sean "P. Diddy" Combs, is also hot among gang members, Chicago police Sgt. Marc Moore said.

"You see 19-year-olds driving down the street in a 2001 Cadillac Escalade, and when you ask them who it belongs to, they'll say my aunt, my cousin, my—," Moore said.

"One guy said he was driving his mama's car, and he had about $10,000 in speakers in the back. I said your mama must be really deaf."

The gangs have bought into the pop culture—especially the black gangs, who see their enterprise more as a business than do the Latin gangs, which usually set up family members in their gang, said Andrew Papachristos, director of field research for the National Gang Crime Research Center.

"They employ the business jargon, 'The Godfather' mentality that they see in pop culture," said Papachristos. "The day you can identify a gang member by a baseball hat is pretty much over because people are getting smarter, and it's a business."

Source: Sadovi, C. & F. Main (2005). "Flaunting Wealth on the Street Is a Must." As published in the *Chicago Sun-Times*. Copyright 2005. Chicago Sun-Times, Inc. Reprinted with permission. Available at: http://www.sun times.com/special_sections/crime/cst-nws-gangbflash08.html

Ethnographic studies such as those undertaken by Anderson (1999) provide invaluable information on the realities and pressures of street life in urban ghettos. Anderson argues that there is a "code" of the streets, at the heart of which lies a longing for status and respect. Within inner-city communities, two kinds of families—"decent" and "street"— promulgate and live by different sets of values. Decent families tend to accept mainstream "normal" values and attempt to inculcate these in their children, whereas street families tend to experience many problems, including alcohol and other drug abuse, interpersonal violence, an inability to discipline children effectively, depression, anger, and bitterness. As a result, they have developed values that are in opposition to mainstream culture (such as toughness, the importance of "watching your back," and not "backing down" to challenges), which they then transmit to their children. As in the work of earlier subcultural/strain theorists, Anderson's work illustrates why we should not be surprised when these values, in the context of deteriorating social conditions and the desire for status and respect, compel young people to create associations that provide them with shared solutions to perceived problems.

The basic premises of strain theories suggest that gang activity is concentrated among disadvantaged youths with limited access to legitimate opportunities. While it is true that most research points to the greater presence and illegal activities of gangs in poor neighborhoods, self-report studies of delinquency, as well as new data showing that gangs are migrating or forming in middle-class areas, suggest that the link between disadvantaged status and gang formation may be overstated. Using official police statistics, others have argued that while gangs cut across social classes and neighborhoods, gangs in underclass communities are more likely to engage in serious forms of delinquent or criminal behavior (Thornberry & Farnworth, 1982). However, this finding may be a consequence of the fact that more serious crimes are more likely to come to the attention of police.

The general criticisms of strain theory that have been advanced in other chapters of this book apply to strain perspectives on gangs as well. To review, there is no question that youth gangs are more prevalent and more likely to commit crimes in disadvantaged communities compared to advantaged ones. Yet, as we have seen in other applications of strain theory, the evidence for the relationship between forms of strain and the formation, persistence, and delinquency of youth gangs is inconclusive. Again, methodological difficulties with operationalization of concepts like deprivation, or how we might measure young people's aspirations and expectations, the process by which strain operates at the psychological level, the definition of gangs, and the limitations inherent in different sources of data, continue to challenge criminologists working in the strain-subcultural tradition.

Social Control Theories

You may have surmised that the basic question asked by control theories in relation to gangs is: Why don't all young people, particularly those living in similar social conditions, join gangs? Travis Hirschi's work, which has already been covered in other chapters of this book, proposes that youths join gangs because they lack attachment to conventional institutions and individuals, have low commitment to conformity, have low involvement in conventional activities, and do not have strong beliefs in the validity of law (see Chapter 2).

Hirschi's work owes much to the earlier work of Walter Reckless (Reckless, 1961; Reckless, Dinitz & Kay, 1957). Reckless conducted a study of juvenile delinquency in Columbus, Ohio, which over the course of a decade and a half eventually led him to develop his **containment theory** of delinquency. Reckless was interested in the factors that might insulate young people from delinquent behavior despite the fact that such individuals might live in high-delinquency areas. In his comparison of "good boys" (those who did not have contact with the criminal justice system) and "bad boys" (those who were likely to have such contact), Reckless suggested that parental supervision and interest in children's welfare, family stability, and parent's capacity to indoctrinate children into prosocial norms explained why good boys did not engage in deviant behavior. In contrast, bad boys had parents who were relatively disinterested in what their children were doing, their whereabouts, and the kinds of friends they had. Moreover, the families of these children were characterized by conflict, and parental participation in family activities was minimal (see Box 7.3 for a contemporary example).

In addition to focusing on the role of parents, Reckless proposed that two forms of control, or containments as he called them—**internal** and **external**—interacted to produce youth deviance. Briefly, his argument was that society both "pushes and pulls" young people into delinquent behavior. Examples of "pushes" include factors common to young people's lives such as feelings of restlessness, discontent, hostility, rebellion, or other negative emotions, whereas "pulls" might include factors such as associations with deviant others, pressures to join gangs, or adverse social conditions.

For Reckless, internal containment referred to inner resilience or strength, as demonstrated in personality traits such as a strong self-concept, high levels of tolerance for frustration, or a sense of responsibility to society and others. External containments referred to positive associations with others in one's environment, such as belonging to and identifying with prosocial groups, being properly supervised and disciplined, experiencing positive reinforcement, and having decent opportunities for achievement. Emphasizing inner containment as being more important than outer containment, Reckless argued that such controls insulated and buffered young people from the pushes and pulls of delinquent behavior (Nye, 1958; Reiss, 1951).

Box 7.3
Reckless Youths: Control Our Kids, You Say? We Can Only Do So Much

It's easy to agree that 13-year-old Devin Brown should not have been riding around South-Central Los Angeles in a stolen car at 4 a.m. on the Sunday morning he was shot to death by police.

It's easy to blame his family, and that's exactly what people are doing in letters to editors, calls to talk shows and conversations over vanilla lattes. "What kind of mother lets her kid run the streets in the middle of the night?" goes the radio talk show refrain. As if a 13-year-old asks Mom for permission before he slips out to steal a car. We might feel better if it were that simple, if we could hold that neglectful mother to account for her young son's tragedy. That would let "good" parents off the hook, allow us to look in the mirror and say, "Not me."

But how much control, really, does any parent have over a reckless, willful, impetuous teen?

Ask former LAPD Chief Daryl Gates, whose son has spent his adult life cycling in and out of jail for drug-related crimes that began when he was a teenager. Or former Orange County Assistant Sheriff Don Haidl, whose son is now on trial for participating in an alleged gang rape when he was 16.

The truth is that teenagers are intrinsically unruly, often unpredictable and uncharacteristically devious when they need to be. Even the best occasionally veer off course. Most ultimately right themselves without tragedy.

And rebellious, destructive behavior isn't only the province of broken families and inner-city teens. The graffiti that recently appeared on bus benches and trash bins near my home in Northridge was not the handiwork of gang members motoring up from Compton but bored, belligerent teenage boys from a nearby gated community. Where were the parents? Probably in bed. The only way to control some kids is for Mom and Dad to go without sleep.

Ask Bernard Melekian, the Pasadena police chief. He has three sons, now adults. "As a dad, I was very involved," he says. "Went everywhere with them, did everything, talked to them about values. They did everything a parent would want . . . went to college, turned out great." But listening to them reminisce about high school, he learned things he still finds hard to believe.

As teens, they'd sneak out after Dad went to sleep, go party-hopping, run the streets with friends, congregate in a nearby canyon and drink. "The things I didn't know," he says now, "are mind-boggling to me."

Their misbehavior was no more or less the full measure of their character than young Devin's tragic escapade provides his full rendering. That night was merely one snapshot of his young life—proof of a boy's dumb choice and its dangerous risk. If the night had ended differently, if he'd never attracted the attention of police as he drove that stolen car, who knows what might have happened to him? Perhaps, like many of us, he would have changed course in time, gained wisdom with maturity. That

Box 7.3, *continued*

night would have become a vivid, regrettable, cautionary tale, resurrected to shock his mom or warn his own wayward offspring. Instead, we pull back on the lens and see only the sad scenes and ex post facto plot line that accrues to a tragedy—a confused boy whose dad had recently died; an exhausted mom, now working two jobs; a neighborhood full of rudderless kids.

Maybe Devin had the makings of a heartless gangbanger, or maybe he was just a mischievous boy who would have grown up to be a responsible man. Either way, do not make the mistake of assuming it was solely his parent's fault. Devin's neighborhood, where violence is part of the background noise, is not as forgiving as mine or Chief Melekian's. And even the most diligent parents make mistakes, misjudge their kids, lose children to delinquent friends or dangerous streets.

Control your kids. It's a nice sound bite, aimed in radio talk show lectures at Devin's grieving mom and neighbors: "You're not going to get sympathy from the rest of this city until you learn to control your kids," one show's host said.

Too bad, because Devin's tragic end reflects not so much the failure of one mother as the limitations of parental influence. Who among us can say with certainty our kids don't lie, don't steal, don't cheat? A teen is a work in progress, struggling clumsily to weigh parental expectations against peer group credibility. So we guide them, lecture them, listen to them, watch them. We need help from our neighbors, pastors, teachers, coaches and even the police. And, ultimately, we hope our kids learn to control themselves.

Source: Banks, S. (2005). "Reckless Youths: Control Our Kids, You Say? We Can Only Do So Much." *Los Angeles Times*, February 20, 2005. Reprinted with permission. Available at: http://www.latimes.com/news/opinions/sunday/commentary/la-op-control20,1,5077694.story?ctrack=1&cset=true

Sykes and Matza (1957) proposed a slightly modified version of classical control theory, arguing that although youths may be socialized into prosocial norms and values, they may neutralize or "rationalize" their deviant behavior, and thereby "drift" into delinquency and crime. They proposed a series of "**techniques of neutralization**" by which this drift might occur:

- **Denial of the victim:** The view that a victim "had it coming to them" or that "they deserved it."

- **Denial of responsibility:** The individual essentially claims that "it wasn't my fault."

- **Denial of injury:** The delinquent argues that there was really no harm caused by his or her actions.

- **Condemnation of the condemners:** Those who are condemning the delinquent (such as authority figures) are seen as being as bad as anyone else and consequently hypocritical.

- **Appeal to higher loyalties:** The delinquent views loyalty to friends or peer groups (such as gangs) as more important than the rules of society.

Contemporary control theories of gangs have built upon such claims to advance more nuanced perspectives and to test the explanatory power of control theory. Some have argued, along the lines of Reckless, that gangs are attractive to young people when particular forces, such as the opportunity to make money, meet the opposite sex, have fun, or protect one from other gangs, pushes or pulls them toward joining the group (Decker & Van Winkle, 1996). Still others have tentatively confirmed the importance of parental monitoring in preventing delinquency (Hay, 2001), while other scholars have shown that attachment and commitment to school (combined with poor school achievement and having a learning disability) are also important predictors of joining a gang, (although parental bonding was not a significant predictor) (Hill, Howell, Hawkins & Battin-Pearson, 1999). We cannot here review the myriad control theories of delinquency that have proliferated in the past few decades. Indeed, as one set of scholars put it, "much like the character of Bubba in *Forrest Gump*, who recounted virtually every way to serve shrimp, criminologists today serve us a seemingly endless variety of control theories (Cullen, Wright & Chamlin, 1999:189). Suffice it to say by way of summary that control theorists maintain that explanations for the existence of gangs cannot rely solely on environmental factors such as poverty, inequality, or blocked opportunities, but must also account for factors that help to explain personal choices to join a gang. They locate these choices within the realm of "bonds" to society—social controls emanating from parents, families, peers, and schools, as well as personal controls consisting of self-concept, the need for identity, or one's commitment to conventional values.

There appears to be considerable evidence to support these claims. However, as we saw in several other chapters, there are limitations to control theory explanations. Some that should be raised here in reference to gangs include:

- The lack of control theory models of gang membership that take gender differences seriously. Some research suggests that girls' bonds to family (Canter, 1982) and school (Cernkovich & Giordano, 1992) are different than those of boys, but more work is required to test whether the various dimensions of control theory apply equally for boys and girls. On another gender front, many control theorists problematically either implicitly or explicitly blame mothers for their alleged lack of ability to control their children.

- Control theory's attempt to explain all criminality and deviance by reference to "lack of control" is far too narrow. Increasingly, the evidence suggests that while lack of controls are related to youth gang membership, there are numerous other factors, that in *conjunction* with low control, predict whether someone will join a gang (Howell, 1998).

- Control theories tend to diminish the importance of race and class differences. As noted above, modern gangs are extremely diverse, and hybrid gangs are becoming increasingly common. These differences need to be factored into control theories of juvenile delinquency and gangs.

Interactionist Theories

The study of gangs has long been characterized by macro-level attempts to explain their existence, or by studies attempting to map out their prevalence, composition, and distribution; the nature of their relationships with communities; or the social and legal responses to gangs. However, comparatively little attention has been paid to micro-level issues around how gang members interact with one another, particularly in conflict situations (Hughes & Short, 2005). In this section we will explore the theoretical contributions of scholars who try to unpack the content of interpersonal interaction within gangs, as well as the contribution of labeling theorists.

Labeling theory can be considered as an offshoot of the symbolic interactionist perspective, the essence of which is discussed in some depth in Chapter 2. Here we will focus on the specific application of the labeling perspective to gangs. As you will recall, the labeling, or societal reaction, approach focuses on the processes by which some behaviors come to be defined as deviant or criminal, the ways in which official agents of social control respond to such behaviors, and the consequences of these responses for those who are labeled as deviant. As discussed in Chapter 1, Lemert distinguishes between primary and secondary types of deviance. The former refers to violations of societal norms that are "symptomatic and situational." Lemert (1951:75) argues that for those who are engaged in primary deviance, "normal and pathological behaviors remain strange and somewhat tensional bedfellows in the same person." By this definition, most people have engaged in primary deviance at one time or another. However, according to Lemert, when people begin to *see themselves* as deviants, they can be said to experience *secondary deviance*—they are *identifying* themselves as "deviants" per se, and the label becomes a self-fulfilling prophecy. In addition, the remainder of society may have difficulty seeing the individual in terms other than "deviant," even after such an individual has paid his or her dues. It may be difficult to find and keep a job, for instance, or the person might be shunned by the community or their peers, thus perpetuating and intensifying the tendency to engage in the same behaviors that "got them in trouble" in the first place (Alvi, 2000).

How does this perspective illuminate the phenomenon of gangs? One important contribution of the labeling perspective is that it problematizes the very definition of phenomena like "gangs," an issue we discussed at length earlier in this chapter. Moreover, by shining the spotlight on the sometimes capricious nature of definitions of deviance, including gang behavior, labeling theorists draw attention to the ways in which social control is exercised by those who have the power to define and enforce rules. If someone with authority decides that a group hanging around on a corner is a "gang," then they become a gang, with many or all the attendant labels and stereotypes that accompany that label. In effect, having the capacity to label a group of youths a gang may be a cause of them being a gang because young people who are labeled as such, may, in this perspective, come to see themselves as such.

Similarly, as many scholars have pointed out, low school achievement is one of the strongest among a range of factors predicting gang membership, and it is well known that in addition to low aspirations and commitment to school, teachers' negative labeling of youths is related to some young people's inability to do well in school (Howell, 2003; Thornberry, Krohn & Lizotte, 2003). Further, within gangs, negative labeling of members is linked to increased levels of offending, suggesting that when young people are "named" as "hoods," delinquents, or criminals, they may in fact try to live up to that label (Esbensen & Huizinga, 1993). Finally, the implications of the labeling perspective would suggest that rather than locking up gang members and throwing away the key, or engaging in other draconian methods of social control such as prohibiting "gangs" from congregating in public, the best way to deal with gangs is to focus on the environmental factors that generate gangs. (See Box 7.4 for a good example of what labeling theorists would *not* recommend.)

Another important strand of work within the interactionist tradition examines the nature of interaction between gang members. As we saw in the discussion of Luckenbill's work on homicide (Chapter 4), this perspective is useful because it helps us to understand micro-level interactions as "situated practices." Put another way, our understanding of gangs can be greatly enhanced by describing the ways in which gang members relate to one another, their community, and other institutions (Venkatesh, 1998). As you will recall, the interactionist approach draws attention to the ways in which particular outcomes— for instance, gang violence—are structured and determined by character contests that escalate out of control. Decker (1996), for example, has shown that most gang violence is retaliatory, aimed at members of other gangs who have been perceived as violating elaborate street codes, intruding on territory, or showing affront or disrespect to their rivals.

Box 7.4
Mayor Vows to Pursue a Citywide Gang Injunction

Mayor James K. Hahn said Monday that he would pursue a far-reaching injunction to prevent street gang members from gathering and causing trouble throughout the city of Los Angeles—though he offered few details of a proposal that would likely face both logistical and legal hurdles.

Hahn's announcement came in the midst of his mayoral campaign against City Councilman Antonio Villaraigosa, who lost to Hahn in the last mayoral runoff in 2001. In that campaign, Hahn argued that he was the tougher anti-crime candidate and contrasted his vigorous support for gang injunctions with Villaraigosa's more cautious endorsement.

The city currently has 22 injunctions that restrict gang members from such activities as congregating in public, carrying cell phones and entering private property without permission. They typically cover a few defined blocks. If gang members violate the rules, they may face sentences of a few months in jail.

Critics, including the American Civil Liberties Union, have long maintained that the injunctions violate the constitutional right to associate, although the state Supreme Court and the U.S. Supreme Court have upheld them.

Hahn unveiled the citywide plan in front of a group of young children at the Challengers Boys and Girls Club in South Los Angeles. He portrayed it as an extension of his work as city attorney, when he was among the first to sue gangs in civil court on grounds that they are a nuisance.

"When I was city attorney, I pioneered the use of gang injunctions, a controversial subject at that time . . . but it has worked," Hahn said. "A citywide gang injunction will stop every gang member in every neighborhood from working with other gang members to take away the quality of life of the law-abiding residents of the city of Los Angeles."

Critics and observers immediately questioned the plan. On Monday, Ricardo Garcia, criminal justice director for the ACLU of Southern California, called the plan a "non-solution to a very serious and real problem" and said it would violate the rights of innocent residents.

"A gang injunction of this broad of a nature permits the targeting of those youths who are not engaged in criminal conduct," he said.

Jeffrey Grogger, a University of Chicago public policy professor who has studied Los Angeles County gang ordinances, said he wondered how the city could file an injunction that would have to name thousands of known gang members. "It would require a herculean effort," he said.

Los Angeles is home to 39,565 known gang members, according to Los Angeles Police Department statistics.

Hahn said that would not deter him. "We are actually going to name specific individuals. And if it takes us, you know, thousands of pages to list all the gang members, we'll do that," he said.

"I realize this is going to be difficult for some people to comprehend. It's going to take some time, it's going to take some work, but we're committed here. . . ."

Source: Fausset, R. (2005). "Mayor Vows to Puruse a Citywide Gang Injunction." *The Los Angeles Times*, March 29, 2005. Reprinted with permission. Available at: http://www.latimes.com/news/local/la-me-gangs 29mar29,1,1413015.story

Hughes and Short (2005:49) offer another good example of the insights that can be gained via interactionism. Their analysis of the micro-level contexts of gang member confrontations highlighted 16 kinds of disputes, which they boil down to three major categories:

- *Normative or order violations,* which include all behaviors that are inappropriate or likely to be perceived as such, thereby subsuming incidents initiated by a norm violation, noncompliance with an order, actions that suggest a need to defend others, money/debts, and unfair/rough play.

- *Identity attacks,* which include all behaviors that represent or are likely to be perceived as an attack on another's personal or gang identity, thus accounting for incidents that occur as a result of direct identity attacks as well as concerns regarding opposite-sex relations, territory/neighborhood honor, racial concerns, and fun/recreation.

- *Retaliation,* which includes all behaviors undertaken to exact revenge for a wrongdoing committed or perceived as such on the basis of rumors. A residual category, *other,* includes all described behaviors for which no commonality could be discerned. Although these categories are to some extent arbitrary, examination suggested that gang *norms* included defense of others, payment of debts, and fairness in sports activities; and relations with girlfriends, race, gang turf, and such recreational activities as body punching were viewed in terms of boys' personal or gang identities.

Hughes and Short argue that macro-level processes like the ones discussed in previous sections of this chapter "structure" or create the micro-contextual conditions in which gang members play out disputes. They also point to the importance of understanding the extent to which disputants know each other, the ways in which they interact, and the role of peers and the audience in understanding the consequences of gang disputes. Their work therefore adds much "texture" to our understanding of the process by which gang disagreements can escalate (or not) into violence.

Ecological Theories

We saw earlier that the seminal work of Shaw and McKay can be considered to be part of the strain theory tradition. However, it is also true that their work can be understood as laying the foundation for modern ecological perspectives on gangs. Rather than repeat the tenets of classical ecological theories, in this section we will concentrate on contemporary examples of ecological perspectives on gangs.

As you are aware, Shaw and McKay used Chicago as their natural social "laboratory" to develop the ecological perspective. Today, there has been a resurgence of interest in applying the insights of the ecological perspective to large urban centers such as Chicago, New York, and Los Angeles. As such, these ecological theories stress the ways in which gangs interact with their broader social context and surrounding spaces. For example, Sudhir Venkatesh (1997) studied the social organization of gangs in an urban ghetto. Similar to the arguments offered by William Julius Wilson, Venkatesh argues that deindustrialization, the simultaneous rise of a low-wage service sector, the flight of successful blacks to suburban and non-ghetto areas, and the decline of welfare state policies brought many negative consequences to black ghettos. In his study, Venkatesh observed how a gang in one such community attempted to establish itself not necessarily always as a criminal enterprise, but in ways that provided important "services" to the community such as protection, defense against perceived threats, policing, building empathy from community residents, participating in nondelinquent social activities, and punishment for transgressions. Thus, his ecological approach sheds light on the multifaceted nature of gangs and on the importance of studying gangs in local contexts and communities.

In a similar vein, Pattillo (1998) examined social networks in black middle-class neighborhoods that, she notes, have higher poverty rates and are closer to high-poverty/high-crime areas than white middle-class neighborhoods. She found that while some social networks worked to supervise neighborhood youths and facilitate the activities of legitimate institutions, the fact that these networks included gang members (including the leader of a major gang) acted to limit the chances that criminal activity would be curtailed.

Another study of gang homicide in St. Louis found that retaliatory killings were almost always found to occur in the poorest areas of the city, and that these homicides tended to lead to other murders in adjacent (and also very poor) neighborhoods (Kubrin & Weitzer, 2003b). These, and other studies utilizing a social disorganization/ecological viewpoint, provide valuable information on the relationships between gangs, their surrounding spaces, and the networks of social relations to which they belong.

Along with some other criticisms of ecological theory advanced in earlier chapters, it is important to remember that care must be taken about generalizing from observations of gang behavior to all communities that have gangs. In addition, it is essential to note that aggregate-level data (e.g., data at the level of neighborhoods or "communities), as well as data emanating from official sources, can be highly problematic in that they do not tell us about the "nitty gritty" of everyday life in disadvantaged neighborhoods. With the exception of the studies cited above, very few studies using aggregate data can make sense of the "complex of interpersonal networks and mutual obligations that exist in high crime neighborhoods" (Almgren, 2005:221). Moreover, and as we saw in the work of Pattillo, while it is true that socially disorganized neighborhoods are more prone to problems with gangs, ecological theory's focus on such neighborhoods tends to shift attention from gang problems that might exist in middle- and upper-class neighborhoods, an issue that deserves attention given that gangs are now migrating to such vicinities.

Critical Approaches

Perhaps the most exciting critical research on gangs to emerge in recent decades comes from the work of feminist scholars who are "taking gender seriously." Because we have already discussed the role played by masculinities in male gang formation (Chapter 2), in this section we will concentrate on the work of feminist theorists who are radically altering previous conceptions of gangs as all-male groups in which women play a peripheral role, and challenging media myths of "violent girls out of control." As we have seen, it is true that girls are joining gangs in greater numbers than in previous decades, but it is equally true that their experiences of gang life are different than those of males, and although early efforts to include females in studies of gangs tended see these women as "ladies auxiliaries" to all male groups, this is no longer the case.

One of the first scholars to direct attention to the role of women in gangs was Anne Campbell (1984), whose work on "girls in the gang" disputes stereotypes of female gang members as mere "tomboys," "sluts," or appendages to male gangs. Campbell argued that there were several reasons for these stereotypes and, in particular, singled out the "gendered habits" of researchers. By this she means that most research on gangs has been conducted by male researchers, from a male perspective. Moreover, as a rule in studies of deviance and crime, women have historically been seen as less vulnerable to the kinds of problems shaping men's lives, or to be acting in subordinate roles to men. Thus, more often than not, women's gang activity was perceived only in *relation* to men's activities and roles (think about the idea, for example, that female gang members exist only to provide sexual services or to compete for attention of male gang members), not as independent from them and worthy of study in their own right. In addition, Campbell reminds us that female gang activity has usually been colored by assumptions of "good" and "bad" girls, the former who conform to traditional stereotypes of women and their supposedly "appropriate" roles, the latter conforming to masculine (and therefore "out of character") roles (see Esbensen & Winfree, 1998; Joe & Chesney-Lind, 1995). In these ways, then, girls in gangs have been "present but invisible" (McRobbie & Garber, 1975).

Recent research has rightly turned these misconceptions on their head, by unpacking the experiences of females in gangs and pointing to girls' unique reasons for joining them. As Chesney-Lind and Hagedorn remind us (1999:9):

> Gangs are shaped by class, age, gender, and ethnicity. Gangs, girls' gangs included, are chiefly about economic and political marginality. . . . gangs are also a violent by-product of neighborhoods that are, themselves, the products of that lethal mix of poverty, neglect, and racism that has long haunted America. And this "other America" has haunted our country even during its best times.

In this context, what does recent research tell us about females in gangs? One significant answer to this question comes from the work of Moore and Hagedorn (2004), who state that girls in gangs are subject to an array of forces that condition their experiences in different ways. In short, there are no such things as "typical" experiences for female gang members, and their lives are affected by time, place, ethnicity, local culture, and economic opportunities, all of which vary.

Having said this, Hagedorn and Moore maintain that there are some characteristic factors that shape girls' lives in gangs. For instance, girls in gangs are more likely to come from families with problems, and therefore, when they join gangs "they are not leaving the Brady Bunch for the Hell's angels" (2004:44). In addition, most women in gangs have children, and it is a cultural constant in modern societies that the presence of children affects women differently than men, particularly because females may mature "out" of the gang faster than men due to the demands and obligations of child rearing. Moreover, because different ethnic groups often have varying concepts of appropriate male and female roles, belonging to an "ethnic" gang can have different consequences for women. For example, Moore and Hagedorn argue that in Latino communities women are subject to very traditional expectations compared to their African-American counterparts, who historically have been forced to be independent within the family and the paid economy.

Some other research suggests that whereas boys tend to join gangs to provide vehicles for exercising masculine/aggressive behavior that is in many ways expected of them, girls join gangs because the gang is their symbolic family (Giordano, 1978; Joe & Chesney-Lind, 1995). Interestingly, there is a body of research that reports that even though gang friendships among girls are seen as important, many girls have strong ties to women in their "real" families and rely on them for social, economic, and emotional support (Decker & Van Winkle, 1996; Hunt, Mackenzie & Joe-Laidler, 2000). These studies, like many others that take gender seriously, again challenge traditional ideas about girls in gangs, such as the notion that kinship ties for such women have become unimportant (which is linked to the erroneous broader claim that we are witnessing the "decline" of the "traditional" family) or that women are necessarily always dependent on men. More generally:

> It appears that the gang girls do differ from gang boys in terms of their perceived social isolation, their self-esteem and the emotional fulfillment that they receive from their gangs. Although the girls experience the same structural aspects of the gangs, there appear to be qualitative differences between the gang boys and girls. As is the case in other contexts (e.g., educational institutions, workplace, and family), males and females may well describe the organizational context in the same manner, but their reaction and experiences in these settings are different (Esbensen, Deschenes & Winfree, 1999:48).

It is important to realize that such studies are useful not only because they point to girls' different experiences, but also because they direct attention to the role played in their lives of broader social forces, particularly patriarchy (see Chapter 2 for a discussion), which highlights, among other things, the effects of socialized gender roles, structural oppression, vulnerability to abuse from males, and women's responses to male domination (Holsinger & Holsinger, 2005: 213). However, as Jody Miller (2001) has argued, criminologists need to go beyond approaches emphasizing simple "differences" or "similarities" between boys and girls because such perspectives tend to pigeonhole women and men into particular "male and female" roles, ignore similarities between them, and overlook racial, class, and age differences *between* women. Moreover, she contends that we need to see girls in gangs as more than just "hapless victims," as was common in early studies, or as women who are "resisting" their victimization. She goes on to say that while it is true that many women are victimized and do join gangs as a way of resisting patriarchy and other oppressive social forces, it is also true that they join gangs for reasons similar, if not identical, to men, including the allure and financial rewards of crime.

Like males, females' reasons for joining gangs center around broader structural conditions such as the disappearance of meaningful, remunerative work; the restructuring of the welfare state; and the rise of illegal drug markets (indeed, drug offenses are the most common crimes committed by female gang members). But women's experiences with gangs are also different from those of men because women's roles in society are circumscribed by forces of patriarchy. For instance, compared to men, the decline of welfare support has different implications for poor women with children, who traditionally have relied on welfare to provide food and shelter for their families (Moore & Hagedorn, 2001). We have also seen that the demands faced by women of different ethnicities also shapes their experiences with gang life, and future research should take these ethnic variations into account, particularly as the United States is currently undergoing the largest growth in immigration since the turn of the twentieth century (Coughlin & Venkatesh, 2003).

Having once been ignored or marginalized in scholarly work on gangs, female gangs are now being examined vigorously and through the lenses of alternative theories. Though many of the findings from such studies have thus far been inconsistent with one another, this work will continue to challenge stereotypical and exaggerated portrayals of girls in gangs.

Summary

In this chapter we have explored a range of issues having to do with gangs, beginning with the thorny issue of how to define exactly what a gang is. In that section we showed that this is a critical problem in gang research because there are important and obvious differences between groups of youths who are "hanging around" one another, gangs organized around criminal activity, and gangs who band together to engage in recreational activities or minor offenses.

We examined empirical data from official and unofficial sources that provided us with some insight into what gangs look like, where they exist, and some of their basic characteristics. In doing so, we emphasized both the wide geographical distribution and the great diversity of contemporary gangs in the United States. We also draw attention to the age, gender, and ethnic makeup of gangs, and showed that most gangs are made up of young people between 18 and 24, are mostly male (although female gangs do exist), and are generally ethnically homogenous (although new, mixed-ethnicity gangs have appeared). There is considerable evidence that gangs are not homogeneous entities, with some engaging in multiple kinds of criminal and noncriminal behavior, and others sharing rules and symbols with other gangs.

For those who study gangs, it is clear that the insights of critical perspectives, especially feminist ones, have laid the groundwork for much important work yet to be done, particularly in relation to issues around masculinities and femininities and the emergence of female gangs. Among other issues that still need to be explored are the precise ways in which youths enter gangs, the internal dynamics of gang life, the phenomenon of gang migration, the characteristics and behavior of gangs in middle-class communities, the ways in which schools can intervene in gang members' lives, and many others.

Our discussion of theoretical explanations of gangs focused on a number of issues, including why young people join gangs, and their experiences of gang life. While these theories offer different perspectives and focus on different aspects of gangs, one thing is clear: gangs are generally a collective response to terrible social conditions characterized by poverty, frustration, low educational attainment, family disruption, and violence. Until policymakers undertake strategies addressing these issues, it is likely that gangs and gang problems will persist into the distant future.

Discussion Questions

1. What are the implications for strain-subcultural theories of the rise of gangs in middle-class communities?

2. Why is the definition of gangs so crucial to the study of gangs?

3. What kinds of gender stereotypes might shape public perceptions of female gangs?

4. Speculate on the ways in which increased immigration from non-European countries might shape the gang landscape in America.

5. What are some policy implications of control theories of gangs?

6. Discuss the idea that it is impossible to eliminate gangs.

Problem-Solving Scenarios

1. In groups, hold a debate on the issue of whether joining a gang is a personal choice.

2. You have been given the chance to study gangs in an inner-city community. Come up with a methodological strategy to conduct your study, and justify your choices.

3. Find examples of gang graffiti on the Internet, and create a presentation discussing the symbolic functions of gang graffiti.

4. Research some attempts to curb the problem of youth gangs in the United States. What did these strategies consist of, and what sociological theories of gangs could be said to have influenced these strategies?

5. Evaluate a fictional film on gangs in light of what you know about gang life and behavior from this chapter.

6. You have been given the job of creating gang policy in your community. What would this policy consist of, and why?

Suggested Readings

Petersen, R. (2004). *Understanding Contemporary Gangs in America: An Interdisciplinary Approach*. Upper Saddle River, NJ: Pearson.

> This book is a collection of important contemporary readings on gangs in the United States. It covers a number of topics, including definitions of gangs, gender, race and ethnicity, violence, and criminal activities of gangs.

Miller, J. (2004). *One of the Guys: Girls, Gangs, and Gender*. New York: Oxford University Press.

> An important book using original data and drawing upon new directions in feminist theory to focus on the trajectories by which girls join gangs, their experiences, and their personal stories. The lives of girls in the gangs studied are compared with non-gang members.

Hagedorn, J. (1998). *People and Folks: Gangs, Crime and the Underclass in a Rustbelt City*, 2nd ed. Chicago: Lake View Press.

> This book reconceptualizes the study of gangs by linking their formation to deindustrialization in America. Hagedorn's study pays particular attention to race, class, gender, and age, and focuses on the ways in which gangs have become institutionalized within communities. His analysis is also sharply critical of dominant "law and order" approaches to gangs.

McCorkle, R.C. & T.D. Miethe (2002). *Panic: The Social Construction of the Street Gang Problem*. Upper Saddle River, NJ: Prentice Hall.

> In this work, McCorkle and Miethe discuss the rise of the "gang problem" in America in the late 1980s and early 1990s, and analyze the notion of a generalized "moral panic" around gangs and gang violence. Of particular interest is the discussion of the role of law enforcement agencies and the media in constructing panics around gangs, and the benefits that accrued to these institutions as a result.

Kontos, L., D.C. Brotherton & L. Barrios (eds.) (2003). *Gangs and Society: Alternative Perspectives*. New York: Columbia University Press.

> This volume contains a series of articles highlighting the complex functions of gangs in modern communities, and challenges the idea that all gangs are superpredators. There are also articles focusing on theoretical and methodological issues, women and gangs, gangs and politics, youths and gang life, and control of gangs.

Curry, G.D. & S. Decker (1998). *Confronting Gangs*. Los Angeles: Roxbury.

> This book emphasizes the links between gangs and communities and neighborhoods. In addition to theoretical, methodological, and empirical insights, the book offers perspectives from the point of view of gang members themselves.

Online Resources

1. **National Youth Gang Center (NYGC)**
   http://www.iir.com/nygc/maininfo.htm
   This site contains a great deal of information for those interested in researching gangs. The NYGC helps policymakers, practitioners, and researchers to "understand and reduce youth gang involvement and crime by contributing information, resources, practical tools, and expertise towards the development and implementation of effective gang prevention, intervention, and suppression strategies."

2. **Gang Research.net**
   http://www.gangresearch.net
   This web site is organized by John Hagedorn, one of the world's top gang researchers. It includes information on specific gangs, hip-hop and gangs, Chicago's ghetto, and a collection of Hagedorn's writings.

3. **Office of Juvenile Justice and Delinquency Prevention**
   http://ojjdp.ncjrs.org
   A search on this site for gangs will reveal a wealth of statistical and other information on gangs in the United States. The OJJDP is a government organization that is committed to preventing juvenile delinquency and to creating effective intervention programs.

AP Photo/Khue Bui

Theoretical perspectives provide us with an image of what something is and how we might best act toward it. They name something this type of thing and not that. They provide us with the sense of being in a world of relatively fixed forms and content. Theoretical perspectives transform a mass of raw sensory data into understanding, explanations, and recipes for action (Pfohl, 1985:9-10).

THEORY AND SOCIAL POLICY

It is fair to assume that many, if not most, members of the general public view social scientific theories such as those presented throughout this book as simply academic products of "impractical mental gymnastics" or "fanciful ideas that have little to do with what truly motivates people" (Akers, 1997:1). For example, in the late 1990s, Walter DeKeseredy was interviewed about women's use of violence in dating relationships by a neoconservative radio talk show host in Ottawa, Ontario, Canada. DeKeseredy offered what he considered to be a highly intelligible, theoretically informed account for this behavior,[1] but the radio host deemed his explanation to be little more than "psychobabble." Like one of the detectives in the once famous fictional television show *Dragnet*,[2] he wanted DeKeseredy to give him "just the facts." Well, "facts" or data do not speak for themselves; they must be interpreted (Curran & Renzetti, 2001). As stated in Chapter 2, theories help us achieve this goal. Theories are, then, "things we think with" (Smith, 1996). Again, they are conceptual tools that help us make sense of data and assist us in our attempts to understand the ways in which the social world functions (MacLean & Milovanovic, 1997).

Theories also "have consequences" (Szasz, 1987). As Lilly, Cullen, and Ball (2002:5) correctly point out:

> The search for the sources of crime, then, is not done within a vacuum. Even if a theorist wishes only to ruminate about the causes of theft or violence, others will be ready to use these

269

insights to direct efforts to do something about the crime problem. Understanding why crime occurs, then, is a prelude to developing strategies to control the behavior.

Note, too, that the different theories reviewed throughout this text suggest ways of reducing deviance and crime (Lilly, Cullen & Ball, 2002). In fact, theorizing these two problems and the advancement of political views go together (Ellis, 1987). The main objective of this chapter, then, is to describe and evaluate some of the social and legal policy implications of the theoretical perspectives reviewed in Chapter 2. It is to examples of policies derived from strain theories that we turn to first.

Strain Policies[3]

In what is still one of the most widely read and cited social scientific articles in the world, Howard Becker (1967) asks sociologists, "Whose side are we on?" Not surprisingly, strain theorists are on the side of the socially and economically disadvantaged. Further, some strain theorists received considerable recognition from policymakers. Consider Cloward and Ohlin (1960). They were extremely important in the history of criminological and deviance theory, in that perhaps no other theory was responsible for generating so much government funding. The logic was simple: money was better spent on the prevention than on the cure, and if the problem was a lack of legitimate opportunity structures for youths, then the solution was to increase these opportunities. Under President Kennedy, and especially President Johnson with his "War on Poverty" in the 1960s, a wide variety of programs were instituted to deal with educational deficiencies and job training. Box 8.1 provides some examples of these initiatives.

Box 8.1
Policy Development: The Influence of Cloward and Ohlin

> When the Kennedy Administration took office, Lloyd Ohlin became a consultant for the development of federal policy to prevent delinquency. Many of his ideas were incorporated into Lyndon Johnson's War on Poverty campaign. On a national scale, the Johnson administration initiated a variety of social and economic programs in high-crime, high-poverty areas that were very similar to those of Mobilization for Youth: in education, Foster Parents, Head Start, Upward Bound, and numerous other programs under the Elementary and Secondary Education Act; in employment, Volunteers in Service to America (VISTA), Job Corps, and later the Comprehensive Employment and Training Act (CETA); and still other projects, such as Legal Aid, Model Cities, and Supplementary Security Income (SSI).

Source: Curran, D.J. & C.M. Renzetti (2001:129). *Theories of Crime*, 2nd ed. Boston: Allyn & Bacon.

Unfortunately, under what Curran and Renzetti (2001) call President Reagan's "War on the Poor" in the 1980s, those programs not earlier killed off by President Nixon were eliminated, and today, there is still considerable political resistance in the United States to implementing policies informed by the work of Cloward and Ohlin and other progressive strain theorists. Such resistance is heavily fueled by highly questionable "scientific data" generated by conservative researchers. For example, in their 1994 book *The Bell Curve: Intelligence and Class Structure in American Life,* the late Richard Herrnstein and Charles Murray contended that broader social forces, such as class and gender inequality, do not cause poverty. Rather, based on their analysis of data generated by the Armed Forces Qualifications Test (AFQT), Herrnstein and Murray asserted that low intelligence or "cognitive ability" is the main cause of social problems such as crime, poverty, and so on. They also opposed early intervention programs (e.g., Head Start) for economically disenfranchised children, because, in their opinion, such programs do not deal with the problem of low intelligence.

It is true that the test scores of children who participate in Head Start programs are not much different from the scores of those who do not attend. Referred to as "fade-out," this problem does not surprise William Julius Wilson, one of the world's leading sociological experts on the plight of inner-city ghetto residents. However, his interpretation of the convergence of the above test scores is fundamentally distinct from Herrnstein and Murray's. According to Wilson (1996:xv-xvi):

> Anyone familiar with the harsh environment of the inner-city ghetto should not be surprised by the research findings on the Head Start fade-out. It would be extraordinary if the gains from Head Start Programs were sustained in some of these environments. The children of the inner-city ghetto have to contend with public schools plagued by unimaginative curricula, overcrowded classrooms, inadequate plan facilities, and only a small proportion of teachers who have confidence in their students and expect them to learn. Inner-city ghetto children also grow up in neighborhoods with devastating rates of joblessness, which trigger a whole series of other problems that are not conducive to healthy child development or intellectual growth. Included among these are broken families, antisocial behavior, social networks that do not extend beyond the formal confines of the ghetto environment, and a lack of informal social control over the behavior and activities of children and adults in the neighborhood.

How can we expect poor children to do well in school if they have to deal with these problems? Moreover, most geneticists do not draw a line separating biological influences from environmental factors. Thus, it is "intellectually irresponsible" to blame poor children's scholastic abilities on low intelligence (Wilson, 1996). Such an approach is tantamount to **victim blaming,** a discourse that claims that those harmed by crime, poverty, and many other social problems contribute to their own downfall (Karmen, 2003).

Obviously, forces outside the school need to be addressed, but strain theorists such as Albert Cohen (1955) are right to point out that schools are equally important sites for crime prevention interventions. Heavily informed by Cohen's theory of delinquent boys reviewed in Chapter 2, Alvi and DeKeseredy (1997) and DeKeseredy, Alvi, Schwartz, and Tomaszewski (2003) contend that if chronic economic deprivation is a root cause of crime and delinquency, and school failure is an important mechanism of delinquent associations and conduct, then in addition to offering pre-school programs, entrepreneurial skills should be introduced into the classroom. Their rationale is as follows. First, staying in school prevents youths from breaking the law. Still, staying in school is not enough anymore, and many students know that they will eventually face great difficulties finding decent jobs unless they can demonstrate outstanding expertise using computers or in software development. Note, too, that approximately two-thirds of all new jobs require the use of computers (DeKeseredy, Alvi, Schwartz & Tomaszewski, 2003; Wilson, 1996).

A few high school "dropouts" achieve something similar to the "American Dream." However, the official unemployment rate for U.S. youths with a high school degree is approximately three times higher than that for young people with a bachelor's degree or higher (Mooney, Knox & Schacht, 2005). Obviously, it is advantageous for young people to stay in school, which helps them find a "good job" and prevents them from coming into conflict with the law (Alvi, 2000). Nevertheless, the question for sociologists like Alvi and DeKeseredy (1997) and DeKeseredy and his colleagues (2003) still arises: How can they balance the realities of today's labor market with the importance of achieving high levels of educational achievement? These sociologists' answer is to provide youths with entrepreneurial and work-related skills.

Except in community colleges or technical schools, the role of the teacher was never formally designed to facilitate the acquisition of a job or building a lucrative business. These functions, however, are certainly part of what social scientists refer to as the **hidden curriculum,** in that schools have implicitly (and sometimes explicitly) trained students for particular roles in the labor market (Wotherspoon, 1998). DeKeseredy and his colleagues (2003:137) ask: "Why not be honest and make teaching entrepreneurial and job-related skills core parts of the curriculum?" Indeed, emphasizing only reading, writing, and mathematics, and including a few hours of career counseling, are no longer enough to ensure a person's economic viability. Alvi and DeKeseredy (1997) assert that if we continue down these heavily worn paths, we will repeat past mistakes.

Alvi and DeKeseredy further argue that one way to enhance educational experience is to give students a background in math, history, languages, and the social sciences, and to make the linkage between these subjects and the labor market part of the raison d'etre of schooling. As Devine and Wright (1993:209) discovered, except for a few North American schools, most urban high schools have not tried to help students who do want to go to college or university master "a single useful skill that would assist them in the transition from school to work. It seems . . . that next to the basic skills, some sort of marketable skill, craft or trade is the minimum "payoff' any student should expect to receive from his or her high school education."

Students should also be exposed to the realities associated with both the school-to-work transition (e.g., deadlines, punctuality, etc.) and starting their own business. In addition, public and high schools, universities, and other centers of higher learning should invite prominent, successful entrepreneurs, small business owners, and corporate executives to provide seminars and workshops on how students can apply their academic skills in the "business world" and public sector. Ignoring this approach has serious consequences. For example, according to William Julius Wilson (1996:217):

> [I]t removes our best corporations and their important learning systems from involvement in the process of molding young workers; it eliminates a natural communication network for feeding employer information to schools about the changing skills required in the work place, and most important, it disconnects achievements in school from rewards in the workplace, thereby undermining the incentive for academic success.

Youths who are not university/college bound and who are not given rich employment advice, career counseling, and job placement assistance are typically left to "sink or swim" (Wilson, 1996). Moreover, hopelessness and anger generated by joblessness often results in violence, drug use, and/or drug dealing (Blau & Blau, 1982; Currie, 1993; DeKeseredy, Alvi, Schwartz & Tomaszewski, 2003; Young, 1999).

The strategies described here, according to Alvi and DeKeseredy, should not involve only one or two "quick and dirty" presentations and group discussions. Students and teachers alike generally trivialize one-shot seminars or workshops, which only provide a superficial understanding of the issues, hassles, and efforts associated with finding employment and being an entrepreneur. Instead, weekly or biweekly events are necessary and should be mandatory if they are integrated with curricula in meaningful ways.

In addition to teaching students entrepreneurial and work skills, however, presenters and workshop coordinators should emphasize how academic and entrepreneurial skills go hand in hand. They are equally important. In other words, students should not be given the impression (as they often are) that what they learn in the classroom has no bearing on what they do in the workplace or how they go about developing a business (Devine & Wright, 1993). Creating a successful business or finding an upper-tier job generally requires the development of sharp analytical writing and reading proficiency. Unfortunately, and understandably, many students find the process of acquiring these skills uncomfortable and boring. However, Alvi and DeKeseredy and DeKeseredy, Alvi, Schwartz, and Tomaszewski (2003) assert that if entrepreneurial and job-related seminars, workshops, and other related events stress the importance of a broad-based education, students might become more motivated to pursue their traditional studies if they feel that their academic work will eventually lead to financial success or a stable job.

Finally, Alvi and DeKeseredy and DeKeseredy and colleagues state that we need to understand that creating successful business opportunities and skill sets for youths requires an integrated and cooperative approach similar to the School-to-Work Opportunities Act (SWOA) passed by the U.S. Congress in the Spring of 1994. As in Germany and Japan, the SWOA emphasizes government, business, and education partnerships in local communities and stresses the private-sector investment in education (Wilson, 1996). Nevertheless, this strategy should proceed upon the recognition that it is not just the individual who needs to be "motivated" and "provided with skills," but that structural barriers, such as the racial/ethnic, gender, regional, language, and economic disparities need to be overcome as well (Wotherspoon, 1998).

Many teachers agree with Alvi and DeKeseredy's assertion that there is much more to teaching students entrepreneurial and occupational skills than having them sit in a classroom. Hands-on strategies are also necessary. Most teachers already know that the best way to learn something is to actually do it. Thus, educational institutions, government agencies, and private business should work together to help students get summer and/or part-time jobs where they can learn and apply their entrepreneurial skills and gain some job experience. This is not an easy task, as many companies are downsizing and a substantial number of inner-city jobs are being eliminated due to global reorganization. Nevertheless, it is the long-term gain that concerns researchers like Alvi and DeKeseredy. They and other progressive sociologists (e.g., Currie, 1985, 1993) argue that a few dollars spent now have the potential to make a growing number of North American youths avoid committing crime, and helping them to become productive members of society. DeKeseredy and his colleagues (2003:139) argue:

It is either pay now or pay much more later. If the problems of youth unemployment and underemployment become more acute in North America, there will be a substantial increase in illicit drug consumption and dealing, predatory street crime, family violence, homelessness, teen pregnancy, and the like.

Other policies influenced by strain theories include a higher minimum wage and stable, legitimate jobs that pay fairly well. At the heart of these suggestions is the conviction that full and decent employment reduces the motivation to steal, deal drugs, and commit other crimes. Moreover, meaningful and adequately remunerative employment alters people's routine activities by drawing them away from places like bars, street corners, and sidewalks, where they are most likely to experience violence, either as perpetrators or victims (Currie, 1998). Lowering the unemployment rate would also reduce the rate of woman abuse in poor communities. For example, there is a high concentration of unemployed men living in public housing (DeKeseredy & Schwartz, 2002; Raphael, 2001a), who often more strongly adhere to the ideology of familial patriarchy than their employed counterparts (Smith, 1990b). If they cannot financially support their spouses and/or children and live up to their culturally defined role as "breadwinner," jobless men might be more motivated to beat their intimate partners because the more legitimate routes to personal power and prestige have been removed (DeKeseredy, Alvi, Schwartz & Tomaszewski, 2003; Raphael, 2001a; Schwartz, 1990; Walby, 1990).

How, though, are stable meaningful jobs to be created? This is hardly a trivial question, given that traditional working-class jobs are rapidly disappearing in the United States and Canada (DeKeseredy et al., 2003; Wilson, 1996). Informed by both strain and critical theories, some sociologists contend that we need to generate the political will to motivate governments and industry to develop new social and economic policies that essentially involve rethinking the nature and purpose of work. Several of the following possibilities could occur in this scenario:[4]

- Government, industry workers, and their representatives could cooperate to shorten the work week, thereby increasing employment opportunities for those currently experiencing unemployment or underemployment.

- Jobs could be rationed.

- Earlier retirement could be made a condition of employment.

- A value-added tax (already in place in many Western countries) could be created, thus increasing the tax revenue base to create or sustain social programs that act as a buffer for those who fall through the employment cracks.

- Because technology is replacing jobs, there may be some positive social outcomes available in taxing industries employing such labor-saving technologies, again to increase the tax base.

- The United States and other industrialized nations may have reached a stage in their development at which it is imperative to rethink what it means to work. In other words, it may no longer be possible to think of work only as something we do to contribute to the communities in which we live. In this regard, some progressive policy analysts suggest that we need to create a social economy consisting of volunteer community service, for which governments pay a "shadow wage."

In sum, then, a safer tomorrow for all—perpetrators and victims alike—begins with policies that reduce the absolute and relative levels of economic deprivation experienced by people at the bottom of the socioeconomic ladder. These policies guided by strain theories should be national in scope and coordinated with the adequate provision of opportunities for quality education. Still, those people caught up in "deficit mania" (McQuaig, 1987) would probably ask, "What would all this cost" (Devine & Wright, 1993). This is a fair question. These and other strategies aimed at improving schools and at alleviating poverty and unemployment would probably cost billions of dollars. Note, however, that money has not been too tight to build new prisons in the United States. For example, according to Irwin (2005:58), "In the 20-year period from 1980 to 2000, hundreds of new prisons were built, more than had been built in the entire history of prisons in the United States. California added 22 prisons to its 11 that existed in 1975." Irwin also points out that this "imprisonment binge" cost U.S. taxpayers at least $35 billion a year, money that, in our opinion, could be better spent on policies aimed at preventing people from committing crime.

If money has not been too tight to build new prisons, then money can be found for solutions proposed by strain theorists and critical theorists—if that is what people want. Note, too, that it is estimated that the direct and indirect cost of poverty in the United States is half a trillion dollars a year (DeKeseredy, 2000a; Devine & Wright, 1993). In light of this, spending billions of dollars to solve poverty, crime, and other social problems is a solid investment. As pointed out in the large literature on poverty in the United States, "the urban underclass is a time bomb ticking. It would be prudent . . . to defuse the bomb while there is still something to save" (Devine & Wright, 1993:217).

Social Control Policies[5]

As Lilly, Cullen, and Ball (2002:2002) point out, social control theories have "tended to reinforce the sorts of prevention and intervention efforts that have been around for decades and that to many have become a matter of 'common sense'" (Empey, 1982). One major example is the criminalization of incivilities such as public drunkenness, an approach that is "very appealing to the general public" (Kraska, 2004:20). It is also a policy recommendation made by proponents of the "broken windows" thesis reviewed in Chapter 2. Does this approach reduce serious crime? Former New York City Police Commissioner William Bratton claims it does and, "working hand-in-hand" with George Kelling (Nifong, 1999), he put it into practice in 1993. To support his decision, he points to statistics showing that the New York City homicide rate dramatically declined in the period between 1993 and 1996. In fact, it decreased by 49.5 percent during this period, which is the lowest since 1968 (Young, 1999). Further, the rate of gunshot victims treated by the New York City Health and Hospital Corporation decreased by 56.3 percent during the same time period (Jacobson, 1997).

Do the facts speak for themselves? At first glance they do, but note that during the period 1993-1996, the crime rate dropped in U.S. cities that did not use more punitive means to deal with incivilities (e.g., San Diego), jurisdictions that reduced the number of police officers, and in cities where there had been no change in policing (Currie, 1997; Pollard, 1997; Young, 1999). Moreover, crime decreased in industrialized cities around the world long before "zero-tolerance" policing was implemented in New York City and elsewhere (Miller, 2001; Young, 1999). In fact, non-gun homicides were decreasing steadily since 1985, and gun-related homicides began to decrease in 1991 (Fagan, Zimring & Kim, 1998).

It is exceptionally difficult to parcel out what reduces crime rates when so many things are happening simultaneously, including increased prison rates, a better economy with many more jobs available, the decline of the popularity of crack (which meant fewer armed drug dealers), police crackdowns on gun possession, and so on (Blumstein & Wallman, 2000). The most complete survey of the data comes from Eck and Maguire (2000:228), who report that there have been no competent evaluations showing that zero-tolerance policing works, "although serious questions have been raised about their effects on police-community relations."

If the "broken windows" approach did not lower the homicide rate and decrease the extent of other crimes in major North American cities, what did (Shapiro, 1999)? One key factor is the major decline in the number of young males in the "crime-prone years" (e.g., 18-24) (Miller, 2001). Another correlate is the decrease in the number of outdoor illegal drug deals. For example, in New York City, many drug dealers now conduct their "business" indoors to avoid "street-corner shoot-'em-ups" (Shapiro, 1999). Further, some authors (e.g., Johnson, Golub & Dunlap, 2000) believe that rather than the efforts of the police, the biggest reason for the "crime drop" is that potential users themselves turned away from hard drugs and the attendant lifestyle.

Other factors also contributed to the crime drop (e.g., aggressive efforts to get illegal handguns off the streets) (Blumstein & Wallman, 2000; Karmen, 2000). Nevertheless, the most important point to consider here is that, as stated in Chapter 2, there is no empirical support for the assertion that disorder left unchecked directly causes crime (Miller, 2001; Sampson & Raudenbush, 2000). Recall, too, as stated earlier in the book, that James Q. Wilson, cofounder of the "broken windows" thesis (see Wilson & Kelling, 1982), admitted that, "It's only a theory," and shortly after that, told *The New York Times*, "God knows what the truth is" (cited in Miller, 2001:7).

Despite problems with policies derived from the "broken windows" thesis, DeKeseredy and his colleagues (2003) are among a group of sociologists who do not suggest that policymakers, theorists, and researchers ignore physical and social disorders.[6] They feel that they can, over time, *indirectly* lead to more crime and other social problems. For example, buildings that fall into disrepair through aging, neglect, and vandalism influence people and businesses to leave communities if they have the economic means to do so (Sampson & Raudenbush, 2001; Skogan, 1990). The "outmigration of the nonpoor" and "commercial abandonment" increases residential instability and contributes to a rise in concentrated urban poverty "because those with the fewest resources are . . . left behind" (Morenoff, 1994:14; also see Jargowsky, 1997; Jargowsky & Bane, 1991; Sampson & Raudenbush, 2001; Wilson, 1996). Consequently, according to ecological theorists Sampson and Raudenbush (2001:5), "[s]ince residential instability and concentrated poverty are associated with lower collective efficacy and higher crime and disorder, over the course of time this process would lead to more crime and disorder"

According to Alvi, Schwartz, DeKeseredy, and Maume (2001), what neoconservative North American politicians do not recognize is that social and physical disorders do not always have to be dealt with by a massive police presence. In fact, many disenfranchised inner-city residents view police "crackdowns" on public drinking, panhandling, and other minor offenses in their communities as grossly unfair with regard to the level of seriousness of these offenses and the degree to which the police closely monitor some sections of the city instead of others (Sampson & Raudenbush, 2001; Young, 1999). "Hard" police tactics, such as stopping and searching people who are publicly drunk, often serve only to alienate socially, economically, and politically excluded communities (Getlin, 2002). These tactics also influence many people to withhold support and information the police need to solve more serious crimes (DeKeseredy, Alvi, Schwartz & Tomaszewski, 2003; Kinsey, Lea & Young, 1986).

DeKeseredy et al. (2003) contend that if socially and economically marginalized urban dwellers cannot count on the police to cooperate with them and to respond to their well-founded fears and concerns, they should band together to clean up their community and to informally sanction people who make excessive noise, who consume drugs and alcohol in public places, and so on (Alvi, Schwartz, DeKeseredy & Maume, 2001). There are several advantages to this approach, but one of the most significant is that it contributes to a higher level of collective efficacy, which would eventually lower the rate of crime and substance abuse (Sampson & Raudenbush, 2001).

Participating in a neighborhood cleanup also prevents an increase in the concentration of neighborhood poverty, which is a key correlate of crime and illicit substance use. For example, many middle-class people do not want to live in areas characterized by social and physical disorder and thus eventually leave for the suburbs. Even fewer want to move to neighborhoods caught in "the spiral of decay" (Skogan, 1990). However, if houses, apartments, parks, stores, and so on are maintained, and if neighbors demonstrate a solid commitment to act on behalf of the common good by informally dealing with public drunkenness and other minor offenses, there are likely to be less "movers" and more "stayers,"[7] which in turn could prevent a socioeconomically diverse community from becoming a slum (DeKeseredy, Alvi, Schwartz & Tomaszewski, 2003).[8]

Interactionist Policies

Howard Becker's (1973) answer to the question "Whose side are we on?" is this: "outsiders." Other interactionist theorists such as Edwin Schur give the same answer. Outsiders are groups of relatively powerless people who have been stigmatized by insiders with relatively greater power, authority, or resources. Examples of outsiders are the mentally ill, people with weight problems, gays, lesbians, members of youth subcultures, single mothers, HIV carriers, the homeless, and street criminals. Some outsiders are stigmatized because they violate body norms (e.g., hunchbacks), while others are labeled deviant or criminal because they violate conduct norms (e.g., stealing cars) or because they violate both body norms and conduct norms. Still, all outsiders have one thing in common: their identities and their behaviors were changed, sometimes for the better but often for the worse, because of society's reaction to them. Recall from reading Lemert's (1951) theory of primary and secondary deviance in Chapter 1 that social control can lead to further deviance or crime.

What, then, from an interactionist standpoint, is to be done about crime and deviance? Hopefully, you are not too young to have heard of the British rock band, Pink Floyd. There is a line in their famous song "Another Brick in the Wall" that says, "Teacher, leave us kids alone." This makes perfect sense to Edwin Schur (1973) when it comes to dealing with many youths who come into conflict with the law or who break rules in schools. To keep them from becoming secondary deviants, his policy recommendation is **radical nonintervention**. In other words, many behaviors officially designated as delinquent should be decriminalized, and even serious offenders should not be sent to correctional institutions. For Schur (1973:155), the main principle that should guide agents of social control responsible for dealing with youths is "leave kids alone wherever possible."

Indeed, this is a radical proposal—one that clearly makes many people uncomfortable, given the extreme punitiveness of the United States. However, there is some empirical support for Schur's approach. For example, Crespo's (1987) study of skipping school suggests that school authorities would be more successful in preventing continued skipping and in reducing dropout rates, if stigmatizing, segregative measures such as suspension were replaced by reintegrative ones. These could include positive recognition and acceptance of skippers when they do attend classes, pairing regular and conscientious attenders with skippers on school projects, supporting and rewarding the participation of skippers in school activities they do enjoy (e.g., sports or music), and making the curriculum more relevant to the interests and capacities of skippers.

School authorities, from an interactionist perspective, should also be encouraged to accept the fact that not all school skippers and dropouts are **folk devils**, which are "socially constructed, stereotypical carriers or sources of significant social harm" (Ellis, 1987:199) In fact, some skippers may be folk angels. For example, Jarjoura (1993) found that skipping and dropping out are not in themselves predictors of troublemaking. Rather, the *reasons* for doing these things are more reliable predictors of delinquency. Thus, students who skip or drop out of school to help their parents or because of problems at home are as conformist as students who graduate from high school. On the other hand, students who are expelled or who drop out for personal reasons having to do with marriage or pregnancy, or who leave school because of failing grades, are more likely to be delinquent than high school graduates. Reasons, then, mediate the relationship between skipping or dropping out and delinquency. If authorities base their reactions to these forms of deviance on an understanding of the causes, they may help **de-amplify**, or at least not amplify, crime and deviance.

Ecological Policies[9]

Again, what is to be done about crime and deviance? One timely and appealing answer to this question provided by some ecological theorists is to improve the territorial control people have over their buildings and public space. Also referred to as **crime prevention through environmental design (CPTED)**, this strategy assumes that people rationally choose locations to commit crimes that offer high rewards and the lowest risk of being apprehended (Newman, 1972).[10] What is more, they apparently decide to commit a crime in a particular location based on answers to the following questions (Taylor & Harrell, 1996:2; Wright & Decker, 1997):

- How easy will it be to enter the area?

- How visible, attractive, or vulnerable do targets appear?

- What are the chances of being seen?

- If seen, will the people in the area do something about it?

- Is there a quick, direct route for leaving the location after the crime is committed?

Thus, to prevent and/or deter crime, spaces should convey to potential offenders that they are likely to be observed, identified as intruders, and are unlikely to escape if they enter (Cisneros, 1995). In the early part of the 1990s, several U.S. public housing communities tried to express this message to would-be offenders through redevelopment projects. For example, the Outhwaite Homes Project in Cleveland, Ohio:

- Constructed terraces and stoops outside apartments to make it easier for tenants to sit outdoors where they can both see and be seen.

- Delineated areas within the development with iron fencing, providing paved pathways, gates, and landscaping to make interior courtyard areas more attractive (and in so doing, eliminating visual barriers that have made it hard for tenants and police to see what is going on).

- Established proprietary spaces further away from the buildings, including plots for gardening.

- Converted many existing, single-occupant units to multi-bedroom family apartments to encourage working families to move in (Cisneros, 1995:12).

Newman and Franck's (1982) study of 63 public housing communities suggest that strategies like these work. These researchers found that sites with more defensible space features had residents who exercised more control over outdoor spaces and who were less fearful and victimized by crime. On the other hand, while he served under former President Clinton as Secretary of Housing and Urban Development (HUD), Henry G. Cisneros, one of the strongest advocates of building defensible space, admitted that the odds of achieving success in many public housing communities are slim:

> There are many public housing developments where apartments and public spaces have been literally trashed by gang activity and the drug trade. It makes very little sense to spend substantial sums on physical repair and renovation in such housing if it is likely to be vandalized again within a few months. The problems related to criminal behavior must be fixed first, and they must be fixed permanently (1995:25).

Cisneros is correct. For example, in Melbourne, Australia, high-tech security devices did not reduce crime in public housing and merely provided one more expensive item to vandalize. There are other major problems with CPTED, including those presented in Box 8.2. Another shortcoming is the fact that simplistic strategies such as moving people from large public housing complexes into smaller ones[11] do little, if anything, on their own to build high levels of collective efficacy (DeKeseredy, Alvi, Renzetti & Schwartz, 2004; Saville & Cleveland, 1997), a concept examined in Chapter 2. This is not a minor concern, given that rates of some types of interpersonal violence committed on the streets are lower in communities where there is "social cohesion among neighbors combined with their willingness to act on behalf of the common good. . . ." (Sampson, Raudenbush & Earls, 1997:918).

Box 8.2
Major Limitations of CPTED

1. It overemphasizes property crimes in public places.

2. It addresses symptoms and not causes.

3. It is only temporary.

4. It may encourage a (blind) faith in technology that may be unwarranted.

5. Surveillance can be highly intrusive.

6. It is socially divisive.

7. It may increase the social concentration of crime through displacement.

8. It has adverse cultural implications.

Source: Adapted from Crawford, A. (1998). *Crime Prevention and Community Safety: Politics, Policies and Practices.* London: Longman; and Lab, S.P. (2000). *Crime Prevention: Approaches, Practices, and Evaluations*, 4th ed. Cincinnati: Anderson.

Saville and Cleveland (1997) are the founders of **Second Generation CPTED,** which directly addresses the need to build high levels of collective efficacy, but it focuses primarily on reducing public crimes through **community capacity building.** Hence, in its current form, Second Generation CPTED can hardly be considered a "holistic approach" to improving neighborhood safety because, like the above strategies driven by First Generation CPTED, it ignores one of the most pressing social problems facing people today: woman abuse behind closed doors (DeKeseredy & Renzetti, 2004).

This is not to say, though, that Second Generation CPTED has no part to play in efforts to curb wife-beating, date rape, and other variants of woman abuse. In fact, DeKeseredy, Alvi, Renzetti, and Schwartz (2004) contend that it can be modified to deal with these and other forms of male-to-female victimization in public housing communities. The approaches they call for are: community culture, connectivity, community threshold, and social cohesion (Brassard, 2003; Cleveland & Saville, 2003). Still, before any of these suggestions can be implemented, DeKeseredy and his colleagues assert that public housing communities, those who manage them, politicians, social service providers, and criminal justice officials must first publicly announce that "private violence" against women is a major problem and that a holistic integrated community approach is needed to curb it. This requires political will and public education, as well as "the shedding of self-serving professional prejudices that currently separate system groups" (Bowker, 1998a:14). Once this goal is achieved, then the following initiatives are necessary to promote the creation of "domestic violence–free homes" similar to those found in some subsidized housing projects located in Ontario, Canada (Ellis & DeKeseredy, 1996).

Community Culture

For DeKeseredy, Alvi, Renzetti, and Schwartz (2004:30), this approach is essential for the development of a "gender-sensitive Second Generation CPTED," and it entails creating a "shared history in a neighborhood" through the use of festivals, sporting events, music, and art (Cleveland & Saville, 2003). Sometimes referred to as "place-making" (Adams & Goldbard, 2001), this initiative should also involve the use of plays, concerts, and paintings that send out powerful messages to public housing residents about the pain and suffering caused by woman abuse. Such cultural work, including designing tee shirts to memorialize women's victimization, could be done in local parks or community centers with the assistance of a diverse range of public housing residents. Plays, art displays, and other elements of placemaking should also be situated in nearby shopping centers.

Not all types of graffiti are offensive. In fact, some forms contribute to placemaking. For example, Ohio University in Athens, Ohio, maintains a concrete wall near the sociology department where students are allowed to paint pictures and murals and write political messages aimed at promoting social justice. While Walter DeKeseredy taught there from December 2000 to July 2004, he often saw statements such as "Stop Rape" and "Let's Take Back the Night." Also referred to as "signpainting," DeKeseredy and colleagues (2004) recommend that such art work be done on a wall deemed fit by public- housing residents and authorities. It would increase the visibility and legitimacy of young and old artistic members of the community.[12] Perhaps, too, artists could be paid for their work with cash or in the provision of spray paint because many of them are in desperate need of money (Ferrell, 1993).

Connectivity

Like other people, public-housing residents need to socialize with members of other neighborhoods, as well as groups within their communities (Cleveland & Saville, 2003). However, many abused women suffer from social and geographic isolation (Renzetti & Maier, 2002). Obviously, this problem is not restricted to public housing tenants. Indeed, many abused women in rural and more affluent communities are unable to socialize with people in and outside their neighborhoods. Thus, DeKeseredy and colleagues call for constructing easily accessible women's centers in public housing communities or near them. Further, these centers do not have to focus only on problems associated with abuse. For example, women's centers could offer educational programs aimed at training unemployed women for jobs contributing to their economic independence. Artistic events and other social activities should also be organized there, as well as the provision of daycare, which gives women time to seek jobs or to get a brief rest from the pressures of child rearing.

Survey data presented in Chapter 3 and elsewhere show that most men do not abuse female intimates, and a growing number of men want to end woman abuse. Still, regardless of where they live, most anti-sexist men do not routinely socialize with other males who are concerned about women's safety (DeKeseredy, Schwartz & Alvi, 2000). Thus, formal profeminist men's organizations,[13] such as the National Organization of Men Against Sexism (NOMAS), should be invited to hold town hall meetings in community centers where profeminist men can interact and develop individual and collective strategies to reduce woman abuse such as the following:

- protesting and boycotting strip clubs, bars with live sex shows, and "adult" stores that rent or sell pornography;

- confronting men who make sexist jokes and who abuse their female partners;

- supporting and participating in woman abuse awareness programs; and

- actively listening to women and reading literature on their issues, problems, and concerns (Funk, 1993; Johnson, 1997; Thorne-Finch, 1992).

Men's groups can also discuss how and where male members can apply for jobs, effective job interview strategies, and ideas for opening or running a small local business. DeKeseredy, Alvi, Renzetti, and Schwartz (2004) argue that initiatives such as these bring public housing residents together "in common purpose" (Cleveland & Saville, 2003) and connect them with outside groups that can help them acquire financial and other forms of support for their peacemaking efforts. Outside groups also help public housing residents avoid reinventing the wheel. For example, established women's groups and male anti-sexist collectives located in other communities can offer public housing residents existing sets of best practices that can be tailored to meet their needs and quickly implemented at little or no financial cost.

Community Threshold

Fear of crime in public places influences many women to stay indoors, which precludes them from obtaining knowledge about services available to abused women and developing social ties with neighbors who might be willing to informally confront the men who assault them inside their homes. Neighborhood disorder (e.g., vandalism) is a powerful determinant of women's fear of crime in public housing and, as stated in the section on social control policies, does not always need to be dealt with by a massive police presence or architectural tinkering (Alvi, Schwartz, DeKeseredy & Maume, 2001). In fact, a key finding of Sampson, Raudenbush, and Earls's (1997) studies of collective efficacy is that community threshold can be enhanced and violent crimes can be reduced in poor urban communities when neighborhoods band together for informal social control and to pool their collective power to extract such resources as garbage collection and housing code enforcement.

Social Cohesion

Second Generation CPTED studies show that teaching positive communication skills and conflict resolution enhances neighborhood cohesiveness (Gilligan, 2001; Saville & Clear, 2000). To reduce woman abuse behind closed doors, then, DeKeseredy and colleagues recommend that schools located near public housing estates should build empathy into the curriculum through constant attention to the intersections of race, gender, and class, and require students to take on the role or point of view of the "other" (Connell, 1995; DeKeseredy, Schwartz & Alvi, 2000; Messerschmidt, 2000). DeKeseredy and colleagues further recommend that workshops could be given in local schools or public housing community centers specifically designed to train people what to do when confronted with woman abuse on the street and behind closed doors. Participants should also be taught how to support victims, to seek help in appropriate ways, and to work to help abusive men become peaceful (Hazler, 1996). For example, prisons across the United States are now using violent offenders to train guard dogs, under the theory that providing a dependent animal that gives love and attention will help offenders empathize with others. DeKeseredy and colleagues suggest that public housing communities should consider such imaginative ideas.

In sum, then, DeKeseredy and his associates argue that architectural design and location play a role in reducing woman abuse, but only if they are combined with the type of gender-sensitive Second Generation CPTED policies reviewed here. Note, too, that DeKeseredy and colleagues also strongly emphasize that informal crime prevention strategies guided by Second Generation CPTED should not be viewed as substitutes for economic strategies and public spending. As these critical criminologists and others point out, to nourish public-housing communities and to develop those rich in collective efficacy (a community's capacity to sustain itself), stable, quality jobs and effective social programs are necessary (Currie, 1985; Wilson, 1996).

Critical Policies[14]

If you have read Chapter 2 and reviewed critical theories presented in other parts of this text, you have already figured out that critical criminologists are on the side of the socially, politically, and economically disenfranchised. Eliminating inequality in all realms of society is this group of scholars' central goal. To do so, they promote many policies reviewed in previous sections of this chapter; especially those guided by strain theories and interactionist perspectives. Of course, too, although critical criminologists would like to see truly fundamental changes in our society, such as a transition from a capitalist patriarchal social order to one that is socialist and feminist, they do not dismiss criminal justice reforms. After all, every advanced industrial society requires a combination of both formal and informal processes of social control. Still, the types of criminal justice reforms called for by critical criminologists do not include harsher punishment or draconian means of psychological treatment (e.g., shock therapy).

Consider left realists' responses to problems related to "broken windows" policing. As stated in the section on social control policies, "hard" police tactics can alienate people in socially and economically excluded neighborhoods. These tactics also influence many people to withhold support and information the police need to solve more serious crimes (Kinsey, Lea & Young, 1986). In turn, the police respond with more "military tactics," which in turn lead to further community alienation from the police (Ismaili, 2001). This process is depicted in Figure 8.1, which is a slightly modified rendition of a model developed by Kinsey and colleagues (1986:42) to explain the "vicious circle of the collapse of consensus policing" in the United Kingdom during Margaret Thatcher's tenure as Prime Minister. Using the words of left realists Kinsey and colleagues (1986:39), consensus policing is defined here as "police working to control crime with the bulk of the community supporting, or at least tolerating, their activities."

Figure 8.1
The Vicious Circle of Broken Windows Policing in Socially and Economically Marginalized Communities

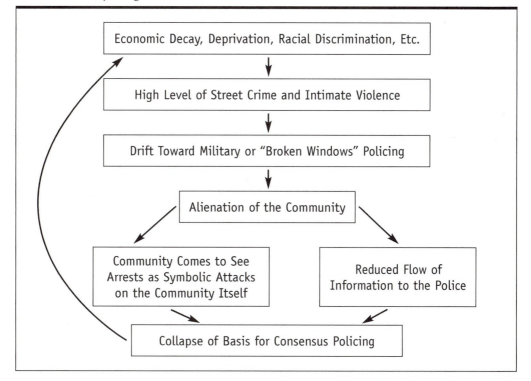

Minimal policing is one alternative to "broken windows" policing offered by left realists. It is designed to foster democratic accountability of police to local communities and local authorities. Minimal policing involves strict limits on police powers and is heavily guided by the notion that the police should cooperate and respond to the demands and concerns of the community, rather than vice versa. The principles of minimal policing are: maximum public initiation of police action, minimum necessary coercion by the police, minimal police intervention, and maximum public access to the police (Kinsey, Lea & Young, 1986). Achieving these left realist goals would denote a major change in policing in the United States and other advanced Western industrial societies. Even so, in view of the hegemony of the "law and order" campaign fostered by President George W. Bush and other neoconservatives, it is unlikely that we will see these four developments in the near future. Consider the U.S. Supreme Court decision described in Box 8.3. This ruling, made on January 24, 2005, hardly reflects a move toward minimal policing and will probably only serve to alienate even more people.

Box 8.3
Supreme Court Rules That Drug-Sniffing Dogs Can Be Used at Traffic Stops

Illinois v. Caballes

PROCEDURAL POSTURE: A state trooper stopped respondent for speeding. A second trooper drove to the scene with his dog and walked the dog around respondent's car while the first trooper wrote a warning ticket. When the dog alerted at respondent's trunk, the officers searched the trunk and found marijuana. Respondent's motion to suppress was denied at his drug trial. The Illinois Supreme Court reversed. Petitioner State's petition for a writ of certiorari was granted.

OVERVIEW: The U.S. Supreme Court granted certiorari on the question of whether the Fourth Amendment required reasonable, articulable suspicion to justify using a drug-detection dog to sniff a vehicle during a legitimate traffic stop. The state trial court concluded that the duration of the stop was entirely justified by the traffic offense and the ordinary inquiries incident to such a stop. The state supreme court concluded that because the canine sniff was performed without any specific and articulable facts to suggest drug activity, the use of the dog unjustifiably enlarged the scope of a routine traffic stop into a drug investigation. The U.S. Supreme Court held that the use of a well-trained narcotics-detection dog—one that did not expose noncontraband items that otherwise would have remained hidden from public view—during a lawful traffic stop, generally did not implicate legitimate privacy interests. The dog sniff was performed on the exterior of respondent's car while he was lawfully seized for a traffic violation. Any intrusion on respondent's privacy expectations did not rise to the level of a constitutionally cognizable infringement.

Source: LexisNexis Total Research System. Available at: http://www.lexis.com

Other criminal justice reforms called for by critical criminologists include prosecuting corporate crimes "as vigorously as crime in the streets" (Reiman, 2004:190) and the strategies listed below:

- Decriminalization of "victimless crimes, such as gambling and prostitution, "as long as these acts involve only persons who have freely chosen to participate" and as long as they do not cause anyone harm (Reiman, 2004:191).

- Prosecuting wife beaters and perpetrators of other forms of woman abuse as vigorously as street crimes.

- Sending fewer people to prison, and those in prison should serve less time (Irwin, 2005).

In addition to proposing criminal justice reforms, critical criminologists call for what William Julius Wilson (1996) refers to as a "broader vision." This involves developing policies that target the key social, cultural, and economic forces that propel people into crime, such as family violence, poverty, and unemployment. Of course, critical criminologists are not the only ones who call for such strategies. Recall that some initiatives informed by strain theories are also designed to minimize inequality and to maximize people's educational and job opportunities. Note, too, that thousands of alternative proposals informed by critical criminologists could be provided here. However, only a few will be discussed. It is to means of reducing child abuse that we turn to first.

Reducing Violence in the Family

As Currie (1998:82) reminds us, "The first priority is to invest serious resources in the prevention of child abuse and neglect." Data generated by numerous studies show that many male and female offenders have a history of child physical and sexual abuse, as well as child neglect (DeKeseredy, 2000a). For example, data gleaned from Widom's (1989) U.S. study show that abused or neglected girls were twice as likely as other girls in her study to have an adult criminal record. Thus, it appears that if we can prevent child abuse and neglect, we can reduce adult crime (Currie, 1998). How do we achieve this goal? Informed by some of the world's leading experts on child abuse, DeKeseredy (2005) contends that the following steps should be taken immediately:

- Eliminate norms that encourage and legitimate violence in our society and families. For example, spanking any child, regardless of his or her age, should be outlawed, as it is in Sweden. Media violence (e.g., computer games), which glorifies and legitimates violence, also should be eliminated (Barnett, Miller-Perrin & Perrin, 2005; Gelles & Cornell, 1990).

- Develop and implement ways of reducing violence-pro-voking stress created by society, such as poverty, gender inequality, and unemployment. Some strategies that help achieve this goal are also advanced by strain theorists, including adequate housing, quality education, and job-creation initiatives.

- Integrate families into a network of kin and community. The reduction of isolation can help alleviate stress and other problems that lead to child abuse (Barnett, Miller-Perrin & Perrin, 2005; Russell, 1984). The Prenatal-Early Infancy Program (PEIP), created in the late 1970s in Elmira, New York, is an excellent example of home visitation; it is described in Box 8.4.

- End the cycle of violence in the family. Physical punishment of children is perhaps the most effective way of teaching violence. Eliminating it would also be an important step in crime prevention (DeKeseredy, 2000a).

- Eliminate the patriarchal nature of society. The adherence to the ideology of familial and societal patriarchy is one of the most powerful determinants of child abuse and other types of violence in the family.

There are, of course, many more initiatives that could be listed here and have been by others, many of whom do not identify themselves as critical criminologists but offer solutions consistent with critical perspectives on crime. The key is for people from all walks of life to work closely together to promote the health and well-being of all children. It is also essential to reduce male-to-female victimization in intimate relationships. The next section posits several solutions informed by feminist theories of crime, deviance, and social control.

Reducing Woman Abuse

Feminist academics have made many major contributions to ending woman abuse. For example, together with feminist "grass roots" organizations, they promoted the creation of **rape shield laws**, and every state now has some variant of rape shield law. Rape shield laws "grew out of the need to protect the rape victim from being raped twice: once by the accused and then again symbolically by the accused's defense attorney probing the victim's past sexual behavior" (Lilly, Cullen & Ball, 2002:180). Feminist scholars also played a major role in the creation of the Violence Against Women Act (VAWA) of 1994. In addition to contributing to major legislative changes aimed at reducing woman abuse, feminists have influenced men to become members

Box 8.4
The Elmira Prenatal–Early Infancy Program (PEIP)

The Elmira Prenatal/Early Infancy Program served mostly white, poor, young, and unmarried women in a semi-rural community with very high levels of child abuse and neglect. The project's goals included: to ensure more healthy pregnancies and births, improve the quality of parental care, and enhance the women's own development—in school, at work, and in family life.

The program was based on the premise that many of the most pervasive, intractable, and costly health problems faced by high-risk women and young children are a consequence of poor maternal health, dysfunctional infant caregiving, and stressful environmental conditions that interfere with individual and family functioning.

A scientific evaluation was undertaken based on a random sample of 400 mothers, some of whom received home visits from nurses on an average of once every two weeks for approximately one hour (during pregnancy and for the first two years of the child's life) and some of whom received no visits. The control group consisted of families who were offered more help during and after pregnancy than most low-income families routinely get.

The differences in outcomes between the two groups were extreme. According to Currie, "Mothers in the treatment group were much less likely to have another pregnancy and much more likely to enter the labor force. Their children were growing up in less hazardous and more stimulating homes, were less often punished, and were much less likely to need emergency-room treatment than the control group's children. Most encouragingly, there was an impressive reduction in official reports to child-protective agencies of abuse or neglect of children in the experimental group."

Source: Adapted from Currie, E. (1998). *Crime and Punishment in America: Why the Solutions to America's Most Stubborn Social Crisis Have Not Worked—And What Will.* New York: Metropolitan Books, pp. 84-85; and "The Elmira Prenatal/Early Infancy Project" [Online]. Available at: http://www.aic.gov.au/publications/rpp/01/rpp01-15.pdf

of the profeminist men's movement and to create strategies like some of those described in the ecological policies section of this chapter. Below are more examples of the type of work profeminist men are doing individually and collectively:

- Ensuring that survivor or victim services have funds to stay open.

- Participating equally in household chores.

- Respecting women's space.

- Exposing the connections between sexism, racism, heterosexism, and other expressions of oppressions in the ways they all support a culture of woman abuse.

- Providing anti-woman abuse education (Funk, 1993:105-128).

Getting men to help prevent woman abuse is not an easy task because many of them do not want to give up their patriarchal power and privilege (DeKeseredy & Schwartz, 1998a). In addition, a critical mass of men is attracted to anti-feminist backlash arguments about "political correctness" (DeKeseredy & Schwartz, 2003; Hornosty, 1996). Some men, however, are opposed to sexism and woman abuse but don't do anything to prevent or stop these problems because they do not know what to do, they do not know other men who are trying to curb male-to-female victimization, or for a host of other reasons (Funk, 1993). Nevertheless, research shows that profeminist men's efforts can make a difference (Klein, Campbell, Sloer & Ghez, 1997).

There are many other strategies advanced by profeminist men and feminist women that help curb woman abuse, some of which were reviewed in the strain policies section (e.g., jobs). Still, it is important to note that female victimization, female crime, and sexist criminal justice practices are all symptoms of a much larger problem: gender inequality (Boritch, 1997). Thus, in addition to implementing the policies reviewed here, feminists contend that it is also necessary to eliminate sexism in all aspects of women's lives.

Eliminating Gender Inequality

Heavily informed by feminist theories, Lynch, Michalowski, and Groves (2000:221) are among many sociologists who argue that there should be gender equality in the workplace, family, schools, athletics, and so on, in order to "make the U.S. a safer place." Many U.S. citizens (including a large number of women), however, sharply disagree with this assertion, contending that U.S. women have achieved equality and that the call for equity is simply "radical feminist rhetoric" that is divorced from reality. As described by Faludi (1991:ix), below are some recent examples of neoconservative responses to calls for gender equity in the United States:

> To be a woman in America at the close of the 20th century— what good fortune. That's what we keep hearing, anyway. The barricades have fallen, politicians assure us. Women have "made it," Madison Avenue cheers. Women's fight for equality has "largely been won," *Time Magazine* announces. Enroll

at any university, join any law firm, apply for credit at any
bank. Women have so many opportunities now, corporate
leaders say, that we don't really need equal opportunity policies. Women are so equal now, lawmakers say, that we no
longer need an Equal Rights Amendment. Women have "so
much," former President Ronald Reagan says, that the White
House no longer needs to appoint them to higher office.
Even American Express ads are saluting a woman's freedom
to charge it. At last, women have received their full citizenship papers.

And yet—if, as some people contend that the "battle has been
won," then why are an alarming number of U.S. girls and women sexually and physically abused by men and boys? Why are married and
cohabiting women still mainly responsible for household chores? Further, if women "have made it," why are so few women running major
corporations, and why are women still making less money for doing
the same jobs as men? Indeed, we could easily provide more evidence
showing that the United States is a country still characterized by gender inequality. Moreover, crimes committed by women are "glaring
examples of gender inequality" in our society (Boritch, 1997:14;
DeKeseredy, 2000a). Nevertheless, there are reasons to be optimistic.
Although the United States is a patriarchal country, every major social
institution, such as the family, the workplace, the military, and so on,
has been affected by laws and other means of eliminating sexism.
Further, public opinion polls reveal that most U.S. citizens support gender equality in most parts of social life (Renzetti & Curran, 2002).

Eliminating Racism and Homophobia

Unfortunately, in the United States and elsewhere, "the end of
the twentieth century was much like its beginning—steeped in racism,
bigotry, and violence" (Perry, 2001:225). Consider the unjust treatment
of ethnic minorities, gays, and lesbians described in Chapter 1. How
do we eliminate hate crimes and racial/ethnic discrimination in the U.S.
criminal justice system? Here, we provide a few answers informed by
critical criminological theories.

To curb hate, Barbara Perry offers many solutions and one of
them "mimics" Connell's (1990, 1992) model for eliminating gender
inequality. Referred to as parts of a "different" bill of rights and free-
doms, the initiatives listed below are designed to weaken "the foundations that support hate violence" (2001:238):

- *In the context of labor:* Equity of wages across race and gender categories; freedom from workplace harassment; elimination of job segregation patters; democratic decisionmaking in the workplace; equitable distribution of household labor; affordable and available childcare.

- *In the context of power:* Democratic and equitable representation and participation in state, workplace, and household politics; freedom to voice dissent; autonomy of thought and action; freedom from public and private forms of violence; freedom to live in the place and conditions of one's choice.

- *In the context of sexuality:* Control over one's sexuality and reproductive capacity; freedom to choose sexual partners and activities; freedom from sexual violence.

- *In the context of culture:* Freedom from stereotypical imagery and expectations; ability to respond to and overturn negative imagery; freedom to define one's own individual and collective identity (2001:237-238).

As Bell (1998:viii) reminds us, "We might wish it otherwise, but the daily reality will not permit us to deny that racism is alive and flourishing. . . ." Indeed, racism is clearly evident in the criminal justice system and other parts of society. To curb racist criminal justice practices, Perry (2001) and other critical criminologists contend that agencies of social control need to recruit more members of ethnic minority groups. Still, just because a criminal justice agency has a critical mass of black or Latino people does not mean an end to discriminatory practices or an increase in sensitivity to cultural diversity. For example, "There are gay men who are racist, women who are sexist, Latinos who are classist. Ignorance and prejudice cut across difference" (Perry, 2001: 234). This is why cultural training is also necessary, as well as progressive efforts to stop the media from exaggerating or distorting racial characteristics and actions, including criminal acts, because they reinforce the belief that people of color and other minority groups are the major threats to our social order. Politicians, too, must be confronted and challenged when they use racist images to show us that they are tough on crime (Mann & Zatz, 1998).

To challenge racial stereotypes presented by the media and politicians, some critical criminologists call for the use of **newsmaking criminology**, which is defined as the "conscious efforts of criminologists and other to participate in the presentation of 'newsworthy' items about crime and justice" (Barak, 1988:565). Newsmaking criminology involves developing relationships with progressive reporters who are most likely to offer readers alternative interpretations of the linkage between race/ethnicity and crime, as well as realistic accounts of what "justice" looks like for minority groups who are constantly and unjustly singled out by agents of social control.

These are, again, just a few examples of strategies aimed at curbing racist criminal behaviors and racist criminal justice practices.[15] More approaches need to, and will be, developed by critical criminologists and other scholars in the near future. Similarly, more effective strategies are necessary to reduce corporate crime.

Reducing Corporate Crime

One strategy that has been suggested by some critical criminologists has been to promote the practice of workplace democracy. One of the prime measures would be to include on the board of directors of a corporation workers and community members who come from different ethnic and gender backgrounds (Messerschmidt, 1986). Presumably, workers could help democratize the workplace and improve the psychological, physical, and material well-being of laborers who, as pointed out in Chapter 5, are a great risk of being either killed or injured in the workplace. Further, community members could ensure that corporate decisions addressed broader social issues, such as environmental hazards, plant locations, exploitation of natural resources, prices, and product safety (Simon, 2002).

If workplaces are democratized, there is a good chance that management and labor will develop union-dominated committees on health and safety, such as those found in Sweden (Messerschmidt, 1986). Some examples of the tasks preformed by these committees are: (1) vetoing dangerous machinery, work processes, and construction; (2) selecting and directing the work of medical personnel, safety engineers, and industrial hygienists; (3) interviewing candidates for health and safety jobs; (4) making sure that proposed budgets include funds for health and safety; and (5) shutting down hazardous projects until they have been rectified (DeKeseredy & Goff, 1992; Engler, 1986; Messerschmidt, 1986).

Michalowski (1983) proposes another community-based solution to curb corporate crime. He suggests that citizen patrols based on democratic principles and representative of all members of the community should be organized to prevent suite crime. Michalowski asserts that these patrols could be used to gather information and to study complaints of business crimes. Such local citizen groups could use their data to pressure companies to stop harming workers, the environment, and the general public, or to initiate legal action. After all, notes Cohen (1986:131), "It still makes sense to say that mutual aid, good neighborliness and real community are preferable to the solutions of bureaucracies, professionals and the centralized state."

Summary

As stated previously, ideas have consequences (Szasz, 1987), and the main objective of this chapter was to review some widely read and cited policies derived from five major sociological perspectives on deviance and crime. Of course, none of the theories reviewed in this text have a monopoly on any particular solution. For example, because strain theorists and critical theorists are deeply concerned about the criminogenic consequences of inequality, it is not surprising that both groups propose policies aimed at reducing this problem. Moreover, just because critical theorists call for a transition to a socialist feminist society does not mean that they disregard criminal justice reform, an issue that is also of central concern to conservative scholars. The difference between these two groups is that critical scholars would like to see a much less punitive and intrusive criminal justice system, while conservative theorists call more severe methods of handling deviance and crime. Note, too, that conservative perspectives pay little, if any, attention to the ways in which gender, class, and race/ethnicity influence the creation and implementation of policies.

It is important to emphasize that the policy implications of each theoretical perspective examined here constitute just the tip of the iceberg. Consistent with one of the main goals of this text, our primary concern here is to replace the "cafeteria concept"—a little bit of many policies—with the concept of *table d'hôte*—a few selected policies. The solutions reviewed in this chapter are limited in number so that each policy can be covered in some depth, which is necessary for the acquisition of more than superficial knowledge of them. Consider, too, that the different approaches to the prevention and control of deviance and crime highlighted in this chapter underscore the ongoing nature of social change and the constant questioning that fuels it.

We will leave the final word for you. Now that you have read this book, what do you make of deviance, crime, and social control? What is missing for you? What did you struggle with? Which empirical and/or theoretical contributions excited you? Did this book influence you to rethink your own position on the causes of crime and means of controlling it? Whose side are *you* on?

Notes

1   Based on data analyzed by him, Daniel Saunders, Martin Schwartz, and Shahid Alvi, DeKeseredy told the radio host that a substantial amount of women's violence in dating was in self-defense or "fighting back." For more information on this research, see DeKeseredy, Saunders, Schwartz, and Alvi's (1997) article.

2   Reruns of this show are televised in the United States on stations such as *Nick at Nite's TV Land*.

3   This section includes slightly revised sections of work published previously by Alvi and DeKeseredy (1997), Alvi, DeKeseredy, and Ellis (2000), DeKeseredy and Schwartz (1996), and DeKeseredy, Alvi, Schwartz, and Tomaszewski (2003).

4   This list is informed by work done by Alvi, DeKeseredy, and Ellis (2000), DeKeseredy and Schwartz (1991), DeKeseredy et al. (2003), Currie (1985, 1993), Michalowski (1983), and Messerschmidt (1986).

5   This section includes slightly revised sections of work published previously by DeKeseredy, Alvi, Schwartz, and Tomaszewski (2003).

6   Following Skogan (1990:4), physical disorder "involves visual signs of negligence and decay," such as abandoned buildings, rat-infested garbage on the streets, broken streetlights, and so on. Also following Skogan, social disorder is defined here as behavior, such as prostitution, vandalism, sexual harassment on the street, and so on.

7   "Movers" and "stayers" are terms used by Skogan (1990) in his analysis of crime and disorder in Chicago. Movers are those who leave the central city; they are typically middle-class, affluent, white, well educated, and have intact families. Stayers, on the other hand, are primarily black and less affluent.

8   See DeKeseredy, Alvi, Schwartz, and Tomaszewski (2003) for several other advantages to using community-based means of eliminating social and physical disorder.

9   This section includes revised sections of work published previously by DeKeseredy, Alvi, Schwartz, and Tomaszewski (2003) and DeKeseredy, Alvi, Renzetti, and Schwartz (2004).

10   Neoclassical criminologists (e.g., Wilson, 1985) and rational choice theorists (e.g., Clarke, 1983, 1992; Clarke & Cornish, 1985) also contend that criminals rationally chose to commit crime.

11   Ireland, Thornberry, and Loeber (2003) contend that this strategy would reduce violent crimes committed by adolescents living in public housing.

12   In Denver, Ferrell (1993) found that some local business people, homeowners, and others often hire signpainters, which fosters their "stake in conformity" (Toby, 1957), enhances their self-esteem, and contributes to their economic well-being.

[13]   As DeKeseredy, Schwartz, and Alvi (2000) point out, although there are variations in the profeminist men's movement, a general point of agreement is that men must take an active role in stopping woman abuse and eliminating other forms of patriarchal and social domination throughout society. Furthermore, profeminist men place the responsibility for woman abuse squarely on abusive men. A widely cited assertion is that "since it is men who are the offenders, it should be men—not women—who change their behavior" (Thorne-Finch, 1992:236).

[14]   This section includes revised sections of work published previously by DeKeseredy (2000a, 2005) and DeKeseredy, Alvi, Schwartz, and Tomaszewski (2003).

[15]   Another policy often mentioned is the use of translators at every level of the criminal justice system for people who cannot speak English (Mann, 1989).

Discussion Questions

1. Based on your reading of this chapter, what do you think are the most effective ways to prevent youths from joining gangs?

2. What are the similarities and differences between the policy implications of strain and critical theories?

3. Are policies stemming from Second Generation CPTED inconsistent with feminist thought?

4. What are the major weaknesses of policies advanced by the "broken windows" thesis?

5. Why are so many people uncomfortable with taking a radical nonintervention approach to dealing with young offenders?

6. Which policy proposal do you find to be the most appealing, and why does it appeal to you?

Problem-Solving Scenarios

1. Divide up into small groups of six people. Devise a plan of action informed by strain theories that you can undertake as a small group to help prevent criminal youth gang activity in your neighborhood.

2. Contact your local police department and ask some officers to express their opinions on policies derived from the "broken windows" thesis.

3. Over the next month, keep track of statements you hear in conversations or in the media that reinforce the belief that people of color are major criminal threats to our social order. Who makes these statements? Are they more or less common than you would have expected? Were you surprised by some of the people who made these statements?

4. Suppose you were asked to help some critical criminologists to engage in newsmaking criminology. What would you do to assist them?

5. Get together with a few students and discuss ways in which you can help curb violence in families living in your neighborhood.

6. In a group, develop a set of strategies designed to enhance collective efficacy in your neighborhood. Identify the strengths and limitations of your proposals.

Suggested Readings

Chesney-Lind, M. & L. Pasko (2004). *The Female Offender: Girls, Women, and Crime*, 2nd ed. Thousand Oaks, CA: Sage.

> This book provides students and faculty with excellent examples of policies informed by feminist thought.

Irwin, J. (2005). *The Warehouse Prison: Disposal of the New Dangerous Class*. Los Angeles: Roxbury.

> Based heavily on data generated by his study of Solano State Prison, John Irwin provides an in-depth critique of the nature and consequences of the massive "imprisonment binge" in the United States.

Lilly, R.J., F.T. Cullen & R.A. Ball (2002). *Criminological Theory: Context and Consequences*, 3rd ed. Thousand Oaks, CA: Sage.

> "Ideas have consequences" is one of the authors' main arguments, and this book is an excellent resource for those seeking more information on the policy consequences of a wide range of social scientific perspectives on crime, deviance, and social control.

Perry, B. (2001). *In the Name of Hate: Understanding Hate Crimes*. New York: Routledge.

> What is to be done about hate crimes? Barbara Perry answers this important question by offering solutions informed by critical theories.

Wilson, W.J. (1996). *When Work Disappears: The World of the New Urban Poor*. New York: Knopf.

> This book is essential reading for anyone seeking a rich sociological understanding of inner-city poverty in the United States. Some of the policy proposals discussed in this chapter are informed by those suggested in Chapter 6 of Wilson's book.

Online Resources

1. **International CPTED Association**
   http://www.cpted.net
   This is the site to go for current information on CPTED research, policies, and activities.

2. **Southern Poverty Law Center**
   http://www.splcenter.org/center/about.jsp
   This site is an excellent resource for timely articles and links about hate crimes.

3. **National Clearinghouse on Child Abuse and Neglect Information**
   http://nccanch.acf.hhs.gov/
   This site is administered by the U.S. Department of Health and Human Services: Administration for Children and Families. Statistics, state laws, publications, and so on are included in this site.

References

Adams, D. & A. Goldbard (2001). *Creative Community: The Art of Cultural Development*. New York: Rockefeller Foundation.

Adler, F. (1975). *Sisters in Crime: The Rise of the New Female Criminal*. New York: McGraw-Hill.

Adler, P.A. & P. Adler (1997). "General Introduction." In P.A. Adler & P. Adler (eds.), *Constructions of Deviance: Social Power, Context and Interaction* (pp. 1-10). Belmont, CA: Wadsworth.

Ageton, S. (1983). *Sexual Assault Among Adolescents*. Lexington, MA: Lexington Books.

Agnew, R. (1992). "Foundation for a General Strain Theory of Crime and Delinquency." *Criminology*, 30, 47-87.

Agnew, R. (2000). "Strain Theory and School Crime." In S. Simpson (ed.), *Of Crime and Criminality* (pp. 105-120). Thousand Oaks, CA: Sage.

Agnew, R., T. Brezina, J.P. Wright & F.T. Cullen (2002). "Strain, Personality Traits, and Delinquency: Extending General Strain Theory." *Criminology*, 40, 43-71.

Akers, R.L. (1968). "Problems in the Sociology of Deviance: Social Definitions and Behavior." *Social Forces*, 46, 455-465.

Akers, R.L. (1973). *Deviant Behavior: A Social Learning Approach*. Belmont, CA: Wadsworth.

Akers, R. (1991). "Self-control as a General Theory of Crime." *Journal of Quantitative Criminology*, 7, 201-211.

Akers, R.L. (1997). *Criminological Theories: Introduction and Evaluation*, 2nd ed. Los Angeles: Roxbury.

Akers, R.L. (1998). *Social Learning and Social Structure: A General Theory of Crime and Deviance*. Boston: Northeastern University Press.

Akers, R. (2000). *Criminological Theories: Introduction, Evaluation and Application*, 3rd ed. Los Angeles: Roxbury.

Allen, F. (1994). *Secret Formula*. New York: Harper Collins.

Almgren, G. (2005). "The Ecological Context of Interpersonal Violence: From Culture to Collective Efficacy." *Journal of Interpersonal Violence, 20,* 218-224.

Alvi, S. (2000). *Youth and the Canadian Criminal Justice System*. Cincinnati: Anderson.

Alvi, S. (2002). "The History of Children and Youth in Canada: A Criminal Justice History." In B. Schissel & C. Brooks (eds.), *Critical Criminology in Canada: Breaking the Links Between Marginality and Condemnation* (pp. 193-209). Toronto: Fernwood.

Alvi, S. (2003). "Teaching about Race in the Deviance Course." In M.D. Schwartz & M.O. Maume (eds.), *Teaching the Sociology of Deviance,* 5th ed. (pp. 54-58). Washington, DC: American Sociological Association.

Alvi, S. & W.S. DeKeseredy (1997). "Youth Unemployment and Entrepreneurial Culture: Improving the Odds?" *Teach*, March/April, 38-40.

Alvi, S., W.S. DeKeseredy & D. Ellis (2000). *Contemporary Social Problems in North American Society*. Toronto: Addison Wesley Longman.

Alvi, S., M.D. Schwartz, W.S. DeKeseredy & J. Bachaus (2005). "Victimization and Attitudes towards Woman Abuse of Impoverished Minority Women." *Western Criminology Review*, 6, 1-11.

Alvi, S., M.D. Schwartz, W.S. DeKeseredy & M.O. Maume (2001). "Women's Fear of Crime in Canadian Public Housing." *Violence Against Women*, 7, 638-661.

Alvarez, A. & R. Bachman (2003). *Murder American Style*. Belmont, CA: Wadsworth.

American Civil Liberties Union. (2002). "Police Practices: Racial Profiling" [Online]. Available at: http://www.aclu.org/PolicePractices/PolicePractices.cfm?ID=9968

American Federation of Labor and Congress of Organizations (2003). *Death on the Job: The Toll of Neglect*. Washington, DC: Author.

Anderson, E. (1990). *Streetwise: Race, Class and Change in an Urban Community*. Chicago: University of Chicago Press.

Anderson, E. (1999). *Code of the Street: Decency, Violence, and the Moral Life of the Inner City*. New York: Norton.

Anderson, T. (1993). "Types of Identity Transformation in Drug Using and Recovery Careers." *Sociological Focus*, 26, 133-145.

Anderson, T. (1998). "Drug Identity Change Processes, Race, and Gender: Part 1. Explanations of Drug Misuse and a New Identity-Based Model." *Substance Use & Misuse, 33*, 2263-2279.

Anderson, T. & J. Mott (1998). "Drug-related Identity Change: Theoretical Development and Empirical Assessment." *Journal of Drug Issues*, 28, 299-329.

Anti-Defamation League (2002). "Racist Groups Using Computer Gaming to Promote Violence Against Blacks, Latinos and Jews" [Online]. Available at: http://www.adl.org/videogames/default.asp

Athens, L. (1980). *Violent Criminal Acts and Actors: A Symbolic Interactionist Study*. London: Routledge and Kegan Paul.

Athens, L. (1992). *The Creation of Violent Dangerous Criminals*. Urbana: University of Illinois Press.

Austin, J., M. Bruce, L. Carroll, P.L. McCall & S.C. Richards (2001). "The Use of Incarceration in the United States." *Critical Criminology, 10*, 1, 17-41.

Bachar, K. & M.P. Koss (2001). "From Prevalence to Prevention: Closing the Gap Between What We Know about Rape and What We Do." In C.M. Renzetti, J.L. Edleson & R.K. Bergen (eds.), *Sourcebook on Violence Against Women* (pp. 117-142). Thousand Oaks, CA: Sage.

Bachman, R. & L.E. Saltzman (1995). *Violence Against Women: Estimates from the Redesigned National Crime Victimization Survey.* Washington, DC: U.S. Department of Justice.

Banfield, E.C. (1974). *The Unheavenly City Revisited.* Boston: Little, Brown.

Barak, G. (1986). "Is America Really Ready for the Currie Challenge?" *Crime and Social Justice,* 25, 200-208.

Barak, G. (1988). "Newsmaking Criminology: Reflections on the Media, Intellectuals, and Crime." *Justice Quarterly,* 5, 565-588.

Barak, G. (1998). *Integrating Criminologies.* Boston: Allyn & Bacon.

Barkan, S. E. (1997). *Criminology: A Sociological Understanding.* Upper Saddle River, NJ: Prentice Hall.

Barnett, O.W., C.L. Miller-Perrin & R.D. Perrin (2005). *Family Violence Across the Lifespan: An Introduction,* 2nd ed. Thousand Oaks, CA: Sage.

Baron, S. W. & T.F. Hartnagel (2002). "Street Youth and Labor Market Strain." *Journal of Criminal Justice,* 30, 519-533.

Barrett, M. & M. McIntosh (1982). *The Anti-social Family.* London: Verso.

Baskin, D., L. Sommers, I. & J. Fagan (1993). "The Political Economy of Female Violent Street Crime." *Fordham Urban Law Journal,* 20, 401-417.

Battin, S.R., K.G. Hill, R.D. Abbott, R.F. Catalano & J.D. Hawkins (1998). "The Contribution of Gang Membership to Delinquency Beyond Delinquent Friends." *Criminology,* 36, 93-115.

Beccaria, C. (1963). *On Crimes and Punishment.* Indianapolis: Bobbs-Merrill.

Becker, G. (1968). "Crime and Punishment: An Economic Approach." *Journal of Political Economy,* 76, 169-217.

Becker, H.S. (1967). "Whose Side Are We On?" *Social Problems,* 14, 239-247.

Becker, H.S. (1973). *Outsiders: Studies in the Sociology of Deviance,* 2nd ed. New York: Free Press.

Belknap, J. (2001). *The Invisible Woman: Gender, Crime and Justice.* Belmont, CA: Wadsworth.

Beirne, P. & J.W. Messerschmidt (1991). *Criminology.* New York: Harcourt Brace.

Beirne, P. & J.W. Messerschmidt (1995). *Criminology,* 2nd ed. New York: Harcourt Brace.

Beirne, P. & J.W. Messerschmidt (2000). *Criminology,* 3rd ed. Boulder, CO: Westview.

Bell, B.J. (1979). *A Time of Terror: How Democratic Societies Respond to Evolutionary Violence.* New York: Basic Books.

Bell, C.C. & J. Mattis, J. (2000). "The Importance of Cultural Competence in Ministering to African American Victims of Domestic Violence." *Violence Against Women,* 6, 515-532.

Bell, D. (1998). "The Perils of Racial Prophecy." In C.R. Mann & M.S. Zatz (eds.), *Images of Color, Images of Crime* (pp. vii-viii). Los Angeles: Roxbury.

Bergen, R.K. (1996). *Wife Rape: Understanding the Response of Survivors and Service Providers*. Thousand Oaks, CA: Sage.

Berjarano, D. (2001). *Vehicle Stop Study Year End Report: 2000*. San Diego: San Diego Police Department.

Best, J. (2004). *Deviance: Career of a Concept*. Belmont, CA: Wadsworth.

Blau, J. & P. Blau (1982). "The Cost of Inequality: Metropolitan Structure and Violent Crime." *American Sociological Review*, 47, 114-129.

Block, A.A. & F. Scarpitti (1985). *Poisoning for Profit: The Mafia and Toxic Waste in America*. New York: William Morrow.

Block, C.R. (1993). "Lethal Violence in the Chicago Latino Community." In A.V. Wilson (ed.), *Homicide: The Victim/Offender Connection* (pp. 267-342). Cincinnati: Anderson.

Blumstein, A., F.P. Rivara & R. Rosenfeld (2000). "The Rise and Decline of Homicide—and Why." *Annual Review of Public Health*, 21, 505-541.

Blumstein, A. & J. Wallman. (2000). "The Recent Rise and Fall of American Violence." In A. Blumstein & J. Wallman (eds.), *The Crime Drop in America* (pp. 1-12). New York: Cambridge University Press.

Boeringer, S.B., C.L. Shehan & R.L. Akers (1991). "Social Contexts and Social Learning in Sexual Coercion and Aggression: Assessing the Contribution of Fraternity Membership." *Family Relations*, 40, 58-64.

Bohm, R. (1982). "Radical Criminology: An Explication." *Criminology*, 19, 565-589.

Bohmer, C. & A. Parrot (1993). *Sexual Assault on Campus: The Problem and the Solution*. New York: Lexington.

Boritch, H. (1997). *Fallen Women: Female Crime and Criminal Justice in Canada*. Toronto: Nelson.

Bourgois, P. (1995). *In Search of Respect: Selling Crack in El Barrio*. New York: Cambridge University Press.

Bowker, L.H. (1998a). "On the Difficulty of Eradicating Masculine Violence: Multisystem Overdetermination." In L.H. Bowker (ed.), *Masculinities and Violence* (pp. 1-14). Thousand Oaks, CA: Sage.

Bowker, L. (1998b). *Masculinities and Violence*. Thousand Oaks: Sage.

Box, S. (1983). *Power, Crime and Mystification*. London: Tavistock.

Bradsher, K. & M. Wald (2000, September 7). "More Indications Hazards of Tires Were Long Known." *New York Times*, A1.

Braithwaite, J. (1984). *Corporate Crime in the Pharmaceutical Industry*. London: Routledge & Kegan Paul.

Braithwaite, J. (1989). *Crime, Shame and Reintegration*. New York: Cambridge University Press.

Braithwaite, J. & G. Geis (1981). "Increasing Community Control over Corporate Crime: A Problem in the Law of Sanctions." *Yale Law Review*, 71, 60-72.

Brassard, A. (2003). "Integrating the Planning Process and Second-generation CPTED." *The CPTED Journal*, 2, 46-53.

Brinkerhoff, M. & E. Lupri (1988). "Interspousal Violence." *The Canadian Journal of Sociology*, 13, 407-434.

Brown, M. (1979). *Laying Waste: The Poisoning of America by Toxic Chemicals*. New York: Pantheon.

Browne, A. & K.R. Williams (1993). "Gender, Intimacy, and Lethal Violent Trends from 1976 through 1987." *Gender and Society*, 7, 75-94.

Brownmiller, S. (1975). *Against Our Will: Men, Women and Rape*. New York: Simon and Schuster.

Brownridge, D.A. & S.S. Halli (2001). *Explaining Violence Against Women in Canada*. Lanham, MD: Lexington Books.

Burgess, E.W. (1925/1967). "The Growth of the City: An Introduction to a Research Project." In R.E. Park, E.W. Burgess & R.D. McKenzie (eds.), *The City* (pp. 47-62). Chicago: University of Chicago Press.

Burgess, R.L. & R.L. Akers (1966). "A Differential Association-Reinforcement Theory of Criminal Behavior." *Social Problems*, 14, 128-147.

Bursik, R.J. (1999). "The Informal Control of Crime through Neighborhood Networks." *Sociological Focus*, 32, 85.

Bursik, R.J., Jr. & H.G. Grasmick (1993a). *Neighborhoods and Crime: The Dimensions of Effective Community Control*. New York: Lexington

Bursik, R.J. & H.G. Grasmick (1993b). "Economic Deprivation and Neighborhood Crime Rates." *Law and Society Review*, 27, 270.

Campbell, A. (1984). *The Girls in the Gang*. New York: Blackwell.

Campbell, N.D. (2000). *Using Women: Gender, Drug Policy, and Social Justice*. New York: Routledge.

Canter, R.J. (1982). "Family Correlates of Male and Female Delinquency." *Criminology*, 20, 149-166.

Carlen, P. (1992). "Women, Crime, Feminism, and Realism." In J. Lowman & B.D. MacLean (eds.), *Realist Criminology: Crime Control and Policing in the 1990s* (pp. 203-220). Toronto: University of Toronto Press.

Caywood, T. (1998). "Routine Activities and Urban Homicides." *Homicide Studies*, 2, 64-82.

Cernkovich, S. & P. Giordano (1992). "School Bonding, Race, and Delinquency." *Criminology*, 30, 261-291.

Chambliss, W.J. (1973). "The Saints and the Roughnecks." *Society*, 11, 22-31.

Chambliss, W.J. (1975). "Toward a Political Economy of Crime." *Theory and Society* (Summer), 167-180.

Chambliss, W.J. (2001). *Power, Politics & Crime*. Boulder, CO: Westview.

Chesney-Lind, M. (1989). "Girls, Crime and Women's Place: Toward a Feminist Model of Female Delinquency." *Crime & Delinquency*, 35, 5-29.

Chesney-Lind, M. (1993). "Girls, Gangs and Violence: Anatomy of a Backlash." *Humanity and Society,* 17, 344.

Chesney-Lind, M. (1995). "Girls, Delinquency, and Juvenile Justice: Toward a Feminist Theory of Young Women's Crime." In B.R. Price (ed.), *The Criminal Justice System and Women: Offenders, Victims and Workers* (pp. 71-88). New York: McGraw-Hill.

Chesney-Lind, M. (1997). *The Female Offender: Girls, Women, and Crime.* Thousand Oaks, CA: Sage.

Chesney-Lind, M. & J. Belknap (2002). "Gender, Delinquency, and Juvenile Justice: What About the Girls?" Paper presented at Aggression, Antisocial Behavior and Violence Among Girls: A Development Perspective: A Conference, Duke University, Durham, North Carolina, May.

Chesney-Lind, M. & J. Hagedorn (1999). *Female Gangs in America: Essays on Girls, Gangs and Gender.* Chicago: Lakeview Press.

Chesney-Lind, M. & L. Pasko (2004). *The Female Offender: Girls, Women, and Crime,* 2nd ed. Thousand Oaks, CA: Sage.

Chesney-Lind, M. & R. Shelden (1992). *Girls: Delinquency and Juvenile Justice.* Pacific Grove, CA: Brooks/Cole.

Cisneros, H.G. (1995). *Defensible Space: Deterring Crime and Building Community.* Washington, DC: U.S. Department of Housing and Urban Development.

Clarke, R.V. (1983). "Situational Crime Prevention: Its Theoretical Basis and Practical Scope." In M. Tonry & N. Morris (eds.), *Crime and Justice: An Annual Review of Research* (pp. 225-256). Chicago: University of Chicago Press.

Clarke, R.V. (ed.) (1992). *Situational Crime Prevention.* Albany: Harrow and Heston.

Clarke, R.V. & D. Cornish (1985). "Modeling Offenders' Decisions: A Framework for Research and Policy." In R.V. Clarke & M. Felson (eds.), *Routine Activity and Rational Choice* (pp. 1-14). New Brunswick, NJ: Transaction.

Cleveland, G. & G. Saville (2003). "An Introduction to Second-Generation CPTED—Part 2" [Online]. Available at: http://www.cpted.net

Clinard, M.B. (1983). *Corporate Ethics and Crime: The Role of Middle Management.* Beverly Hills, CA: Sage.

Clinard, M.B. & R. Quinney (1973). *Criminal Behavior Systems.* New York: Holt, Rinehart and Winston.

Clinard, M.B., R. Quinney & J. Wildeman (1994). *Criminal Behavior Systems: A Typology,* 3rd ed. Cincinnati: Anderson.

Clinard, M.B. & P. Yeager (1980). *Corporate Crime.* New York: Free Press.

Cloward, R.A. & L.E. Ohlin (1960). *Delinquency and Opportunity: A Theory of Delinquent Gangs.* New York: Free Press of Glencoe.

CNN.Com (2005, January 24). "Drug Sniffing Dogs Can Be Used at Traffic Stops, High Court Rules" [Online]. Available at: http://www.cnn.com/2005/LAW/01/24/scotus.drugs.dogs.ap/index.html

Cohane, J.P. (1978). "The American Predicament: Truth No Longer Counts." In M.R. Haskell & L. Yablonsky (eds.), *Criminology: Crime and Criminality* (pp. 172). Chicago: Rand McNally.

Cohen, A. (1955). *Delinquent Boys: The Culture of the Gang*. New York: Free Press.

Cohen, D. (1998). "Culture, Social Organization, and Patterns of Violence." *Journal of Personality and Social Psychology, 75*, 408-419.

Cohen, L. & M. Felson (1979). "Social Change and Crime Rate Trends: A Routine Activities Approach." *American Sociological Review*, 44, 588-608.

Cohen, S. (1986). "Community Control." In H. Bianchi and R. van Swanningen (eds.), *Abolitionism* (pp. 127-132). Amsterdam: Free University Press.

Coleman, J.S. (1990). *Foundations of Social Theory*. Cambridge, MA: Harvard University Press.

Coleman, J.W. (2002). *The Criminal Elite: Understanding White-collar Crime*, 5th ed. New York: St. Martin's Press.

Collins, P.H. (2000). *Black Feminist Thought: Knowledge, Consciousness, and the Politics of Empowerment*, 2nd ed. New York: Routledge.

Colvin, M. (2000). *Crime and Coercion: An Integrated Theory of Chronic Criminality*. New York: St. Martin's Press.

Comack, E. & S. Brickey (1991). Theoretical Approaches in the Sociology of Law. In E. Comack & S. Brickey (eds.), *The Social Basis of Law*, 2nd ed. (pp. 15-32). Halifax: Garamond.

Community Action Publications (2004). "The True Costs of Pesticides: To Our Pocketbook, Our Health, and Our World" [Online]. Available at: http://www.monitor.net/~pestic_costs.html

Conklin, J. (2003). *Why Crime Rates Fell*. Boston: Pearson Education.

Connell, R.W. (1987). *Gender and Power*. Stanford, CA: Stanford University Press.

Connell, R.W. (1990). "The State, Gender and Sexual Politics: Theory and Appraisal." *Theory and Society*, 19, 507-544.

Connell, R.W. (1992). "Drumming Up the Wrong Tree." *Tikkun*, 7, 31-36.

Connell, R.W. (1995). *Masculinities*. Berkeley: University of California Press.

Consumer Product Safety Commission. (2004, Fall). *MECAP News*, pp. 8-11.

Corry, J. (1801). *A Satirical View of London at the Commencement of the Nineteenth Century*. London: G. Kearsley.

Cornish, D. & R. Clarke (1986). *The Reasoning Criminal: Rational Choice Perspectives on Offending*. New York: Springer-Verlag.

Cornish, D. & R. Clarke (1987). "Understanding Crime Displacement: An Application of Rational Choice Theory." *Criminology*, 25, 947.

Cote, S. (2002). "Introduction." In S. Cote (ed.), *Criminological Theories: Bridging the Past to the Future* (pp. xiii-xxiv). Thousand Oaks, CA: Sage.

Coughlin, B.C. & S.A. Venkatesh (2003). "The Urban Street Gang after 1970." *Annual Review of Sociology, 29*, 41-64.

Crawford, A. (1998). *Crime Prevention and Community Safety: Politics, Policies and Practices*. London: Longman.

Crespo, M. (1987). "The School Skipper." In E. Rubington & M.S. Weinberg (eds.), *Deviance: The Interactionist Perspective* (pp. 307-314). New York: Macmillan.

Cressey, D. (1972). *Criminal Organization*. New York: Harper and Row.

Croall, H. (1992). *White Collar Crime*. Philadelphia: Open University Press.

Cullen, F.T., W.J. Maakestad & G. Cavender (1987). *Corporate Crime Under Attack: The Ford Pinto Case and Beyond*. Cincinnati: Anderson.

Cullen, F.T., J.P. Wright & M.B. Chamlin (1999). "Social Support and Social Reform: A Progressive Crime Control Agenda." *Crime & Delinquency*, 45, 188-207.

Curran, D.J. & C.M. Renzetti (2001). *Theories of Crime,* 2nd ed. Boston: Allyn & Bacon.

Currie, E. (1985). *Confronting Crime: An American Challenge*. New York: Pantheon.

Currie, E. (1993). *Reckoning: Drugs, the Cities and the American Future*. New York: Hill and Wang.

Currie, E. (1997). "Market, Crime and Community." *Theoretical Criminology*, 1, 147-172.

Currie, E. (1998). *Crime and Punishment in America*. New York: Metropolitan Books.

Currie, E. & J. Skolnick (1988). *America's Problems*, 2nd ed. Glenview, IL: Scott, Foresman.

Curry, G.D. (1998). "Female Gang Involvement." *Journal of Research in Crime and Delinquency,* 35, 100-118.

Curry, G.D. & S. Decker (1998). *Confronting Gangs*. Los Angeles: Roxbury.

Daly, K. (1989). "Gender and Varieties of White-collar Crime." *Criminology*, 27, 769-793.

Daly, K. & M. Chesney-Lind (1988). "Feminism and Criminology." *Justice Quarterly*, 5, 497-538.

Daly, M. & M. Wilson (1988). *Homicide*. Hawthorne, NY: Aldine de Gruyter.

Davis, N., & C. Stasz (1990). *Social Control of Deviance: A Critical Perspective*. New York: McGraw-Hill.

Decker, S. (1996). "Collective and Normative Features of Gang Violence." *Justice Quarterly*, 13, 243-264.

Decker, S. & B. Van Winkle (1996). *Life in the Gang: Family, Friends, and Violence*. New York: Cambridge University Press.

De Hann, W. & J. Vos (2003). "A Crying Shame: The Over-Rationalized Conception of Man in the Rational Choice Perspective." *Theoretical Criminology*, 7, 29-54.

DeKeseredy, W.S. (1988a). "Woman Abuse in Dating Relationships: The Relevance of Social Support Theory." *Journal of Family Violence*, 3, 1-13.

DeKeseredy, W.S. (1988b). *Woman Abuse in Dating Relationships: The Role of Male Peer Support*. Toronto: Canadian Scholars' Press.

DeKeseredy, W.S. (1990). "Male Peer Support and Woman Abuse: The Current State of Knowledge." *Sociological Focus*, 23, 129-139.

DeKeseredy, W.S. (1995). "Enhancing the Quality of Survey Data on Woman Abuse: Examples from a Canadian Study." *Violence Against Women*, 1, 158-173.

DeKeseredy, W.S. (1996a). "The Left Realist Perspective on Race, Class, and Gender." In M.D. Schwartz & D. Milovanovic (eds.), *Race, Gender, and Class in Criminology: The Intersection* (pp. 49-72). New York: Garland.

DeKeseredy, W.S. (1996b). "The Canadian National Survey on Woman Abuse in University/College Dating Relationships: Biofeminist Panic Transmission or Critical Inquiry?" *Canadian Journal of Criminology*, 38, 81-104.

DeKeseredy, W.S. (2000a). *Women, Crime and the Canadian Criminal Justice System.* Cincinnati: Anderson.

DeKeseredy, W.S. (2000b). "Current Controversies in Defining Nonlethal Violence Against Women in Intimate Heterosexual Relationships: Empirical Implications." *Violence Against Women*, 6, 728-746.

DeKeseredy, W.S. (2003). "Left Realism on Inner-city Violence." In M.D. Schwartz & S.E. Hatty (eds.), *Controversies in Critical Criminology* (pp. 29-42). Cincinnati: Anderson.

DeKeseredy, W.S. (2005). "Patterns of Family Violence." In M. Baker (ed.), *Families: Changing Trends in Canada*, 5th ed. (pp. 229-257). Toronto: McGraw-Hill Ryerson.

DeKeseredy, W.S., S. Alvi, C.M. Renzetti & M.D. Schwartz (2004). "Reducing Private Violence Against Women in Public Housing: Can Second-Generation CPTED Make a Difference?" *The CPTED Journal*, 3, 27-36.

DeKeseredy, W.S., S. Alvi, M.D. Schwartz & B. Perry (1999). "Violence Against and the Harassment of Women in Canadian Public Housing." *Canadian Review of Sociology and Anthropology*, 36, 499-516.

DeKeseredy, W.S., S. Alvi, M.D. Schwartz & E.A. Tomaszewski (2003). *Under Siege: Poverty and Crime in a Public Housing Community.* Lanham, MD: Lexington Books.

DeKeseredy, W.S. & C. Goff (1992). "Corporate Violence Against Canadian Women: Assessing Left-Realist Research and Policy." *Journal of Human Justice*, 4, 55-70.

DeKeseredy, W.S. & R. Hinch (1991). *Woman Abuse: Sociological Perspectives.* Toronto: Thomson Educational.

DeKeseredy, W.S. & C. Joseph (in press). "Separation/Divorce Sexual Assault in Rural Ohio: Preliminary Results of an Exploratory Study." *Violence Against Women.*

DeKeseredy, W.S. & K. Kelly (1993). "Woman Abuse in University and College Dating Relationships: The Contribution of the Ideology of Familial Patriarchy." *Journal of Human Justice*, 4, 25-52.

DeKeseredy, W.S. & K. Kelly (1995). "Sexual Abuse in Canadian University and College Dating Relationships: The Contribution of Male Peer Support." *Journal of Family Violence*, 10, 41-53.

DeKeseredy, W.S. & L. MacLeod (1997). *Woman Abuse: A Sociological Story.* Toronto: Harcourt Brace.

DeKeseredy, W.S. & C.M. Renzetti (2004). "What About the Women? A Feminist Commentary on Crime Inside Public Housing Units." *The Critical Criminologist*, 14, 7-11.

DeKeseredy, W.S., M. Rogness & M.D. Schwartz (2004). "Separation/Divorce Sexual Assault: The Current State of Social Scientific Knowledge." *Aggression and Violent Behavior: A Review Journal, 9*, 675-691.

DeKeseredy, W., D. Saunders, M. Schwartz & S. Alvi (1997). "The Meanings and Motives for Women's Use of Violence in Canadian College Dating Relationships: Results from a National Survey." *Sociological Spectrum*, 17, 199-222.

DeKeseredy, W.S. & M.D. Schwartz (1991). "British Left Realism on the Abuse of Women: A Critical Appraisal." In R. Quinney & H. Pepinsky (eds.), *Criminology as Peacemaking* (pp. 154-171). Bloomington: Indiana University Press.

DeKeseredy, W.S. & M.D. Schwartz (1993). "Male Peer Support and Woman Abuse: An Expansion of DeKeseredy's Model." *Sociological Spectrum*, 13, 394-414.

DeKeseredy, W.S. & M.D. Schwartz (1996). *Contemporary Criminology*. Belmont, CA: Wadsworth.

DeKeseredy, W.S. & M.D. Schwartz (1998a). *Woman Abuse on Campus: Results from the Canadian National Survey*. Thousand Oaks, CA: Sage.

DeKeseredy, W.S. & M.D. Schwartz (1998b). "Measuring the Extent of Woman Abuse in Intimate Heterosexual Relationships: A Critique of the Conflict Tactics Scales." *U.S. Department of Justice Violence Against Women Grants Office Electronic Resources* [Online]. Available at: http://www.vaw.umn.edu/research.asp

DeKeseredy, W.S. & M.D. Schwartz (1998c). "Male Peer Support and Woman Abuse in Postsecondary School Courtship: Suggestions for New Directions in Sociological Research." In R.K. Bergen (ed.), *Issues in Intimate Violence* (pp. 83-96). Thousand Oaks, CA: Sage.

DeKeseredy, W.S. & M.D. Schwartz (2002). "Theorizing Public Housing Woman Abuse as a Function of Economic Exclusion and Male Peer Support." *Women's Health and Urban Life*, 1, 26-45.

DeKeseredy, W.S. & M.D. Schwartz (2003). "Backlash and Whiplash: A Critique of Statistics Canada's 1999 General Social Survey on Victimization." *Online Journal of Justice Studies* (2003). Available at: http://ojjs.icaap.org/

DeKeseredy, W.S. & M.D. Schwartz (2005). "Masculinities and Interpersonal Violence." In M.S. Kimmel, J. Hearn & R.W. Connell (eds.), *Handbook of Studies on Men & Masculinities* (pp. 353-366). Thousand Oaks, CA: Sage.

DeKeseredy, W.S., M.D. Schwartz & S. Alvi (2000). "The Role of Profeminist Men in Dealing with Woman Abuse on the Canadian College Campus." *Violence Against Women*, 6, 918-935.

DeKeseredy, W.S., M.D. Schwartz, S. Alvi & A. Tomaszewski (2003). "Perceived Collective Efficacy and Women's Victimization in Public Housing." *Criminal Justice: The International Journal of Policy and Practice*, 3, 5-27.

Dembo, R., D. Farrow, J. Schmiedler & W. Burgos (1979). "Testing a Causal Model of Environmental Influences on the Early Drug Involvement of Inner-city Junior High School Youths." *American Journal of Drug Abuse*, 6, 313-336.

Devine, J.A. & J.D. Wright (1993). *The Greatest of Evils: Urban Poverty and the American Underclass*. New York: Aldine de Gruyter.

Dexter, L. (1958). "A Note on the Selective Inattention in Social Science." *Social Problems*, 6, 176-182.

Dobash, R.E. & R. Dobash (1979). *Violence Against Wives: A Case Against the Patriarchy*. New York: Free Press.

Donziger, S. (ed.). (1996). *The Real War on Crime*. New York: Harper Perennial.

Dowie, M. & C. Marshall (1982). "The Bendectin Cover-up." In M.D. Ermann & R.J. Lundman (eds.), *Corporate and Governmental Deviance*, 2nd ed. New York: Oxford University Press.

Downes, D. & P. Rock (2003). *Understanding Deviance*, 4th ed. New York: Oxford University Press.

Duffy, A. & J. Momirov (1997). *Family Violence: A Canadian Introduction*. Toronto: James Lorimer.

Dugan, L., D.S. Nagin & R. Rosenfeld (1999). "Explaining the Decline in Intimate Partner Homicide: The Effects of Changing Domesticity, Women's Status, and Domestic Violence Resources." *Homicide Studies*, 5, 187-214.

Dumas, R.G. (1980). "Dilemmas of Black Females in Leadership." In L. Rodgers-Rose (ed.), *The Black Woman* (pp. 203-215). Beverly Hills, CA: Sage.

Durkheim, E. (1950/1895). *Rules of Sociological Method*. New York: Free Press.

Durkheim, E. (1951/1897). *Suicide*. New York: Free Press.

Durkheim, E. (1952/1893). *The Division of Labor in Society*. New York: Free Press.

Dutton, D.G. (1994). "Patriarchy and Wife Assault: The Ecological Fallacy." *Violence and Victims*, 9, 167-182.

Eck, J. & E. Maguire (2000). "Have Changes in Policing Reduced Crime?" In A. Blumstein & J. Wallman (eds.), *The Crime Drop in America* (pp. 207-265). New York: Cambridge University Press.

Edin, K. (2000). "What Do Low-income Single Mothers Say about Marriage?" *Social Problems*, 47, 112-133.

Edwards, S. (1989). *Policing 'Domestic' Violence: Women, the Law and the State*. London: Sage.

Egley, Jr., A. (2002). *National Youth Gang Survey Trends from 1996 to 2000* (Rep. No. 3). Washington, DC: Office of Juvenile Justice and Delinquency Prevention.

Ehrenreich, B. (2001). *Nickel and Dimed: On (Not) Getting by in America*. New York: Metropolitan Books.

Ehrensaft, M.K., P. Cohen, J. Brown, E.M. Smailes, H. Chen & J.G. Johnson (2003). "Intergenerational Transmission of Partner Violence: A 20-year Prospective Study." *Journal of Consulting and Clinical Psychology*, 71, 741-753.

Eisenberg, D. (2000, September 11). "Anatomy of a Recall." *Time*, 29-31.

Ellis, D. (1987). *The Wrong Stuff: An Introduction to the Sociological Study of Deviance*. Toronto: Macmillan.

Elliot, D., S. Ageton & R. Canter (1979). "An Integrated Theoretical Perspective on Delinquent Behavior." *Journal of Research in Crime and Delinquency*, 16, 3-27.

Ellis, D. & W.S. DeKeseredy (1996). *The Wrong Stuff: An Introduction to the Sociological Study of Deviance*, 2nd ed. Toronto: Allyn & Bacon.

Ellis, D. & W.S. DeKeseredy (1997). "Rethinking Estrangement, Interventions and Intimate Femicide." *Violence Against Women*, 3, 590-609.

Ellison, C.G., J.A. Burr & P.L. McCall (2003). "The Enduring Puzzle of Southern Homicide: Is Regional Religious Culture the Missing Piece?" *Homicide Studies*, 7, 326-352.

Empey, L.T. (1982). *American Delinquency: Its Meaning and Construction*. Homewood, IL: Dorsey.

Engels, F. (1963). "Eulogy." In E. Fromm (ed.), *Marx's Concept of Man* (pp. 258-260). New York: Frederick Ungur.

Engler, R. (1986). "Political Power Aids Health and Safety." *In These Times*, January, 15-21.

Ensminger, M., J. Anthony & J. McCord (1997). "The Inner City and Drug Use: Initial Findings from an Epidemiological Study." *Drug and Alcohol Dependence*, 48, 175-184.

Ermann, M.D. & R.J. Lundman (1982). "Overview." In M.D. Ermann & R.J. Lundman (eds.), *Corporate and Governmental Deviance*, 2nd ed. (pp. 1-25). New York: Oxford University Press.

Ermann, M.D. & R.J. Lundman (2001). "Overview." In M.D. Ermann & R.J. Lundman (eds.), *Corporate and Governmental Deviance*, 6th ed. (pp. 1-36). New York: Oxford University Press.

Esbensen, F.-A., E.P. Deschenes & L.T. Winfree (1999). "Differences Between Gang Girls and Gang Boys: Results from a Multisite Survey." *Youth & Society*, 31, 27-53.

Esbensen, F. & D. Huizinga (1993). "Gangs, Drugs, and Delinquency in a Survey of Urban Youth." *Criminology*, 31, 565-589.

Esbensen, F. & L.T. Winfree (1998). "Race and Gender Differences Between Gang and Nongang Youths: Results from a Multisite Survey." *Justice Quarterly*, 15, 505-525.

Fagan, J., F.E. Zimring & J. Kim (1998). "Declining Homicide in New York City." *National Institute of Justice Journal*, 237, 12-13.

Faith, K. (1993). *Unruly Women: The Politics of Confinement and Resistance*. Vancouver: Press Gang.

Faludi, S. (1991). *Backlash: The Undeclared War Against American Women*. New York: Crown.

Farley, M. & H. Barkan (1998). "Prostitution, Violence Against Women, and Post-traumatic Stress Disorder." *Women & Health*, 27, 37-49.

Farley, M. & V. Kelly (2000). "Prostitution: A Critical Review of the Medical and Social Sciences Literature." *Women and Criminal Justice*, 11, 29-63.

Farnworth, M. & M. Leiber (1989). "Strain Theory Revisited." *American Sociological Review*, 54, 263-274.

Fekete, J. (1994). *Moral Panic: Biopolitics Rising*. Montreal: Robert Davies.

Fenstermaker, S. (1989). "Acquaintance Rape on Campus: Responsibility and Attributions of Crime." In M. Pirog-Good & J. Stets (eds.), *Violence in Dating Relationships: Emerging Social Issues* (pp. 257-271). New York: Praeger.

Ferenchik, M. (2003, June 26). "White Drivers Less Likely to be Stopped by Police Here." *The Columbus Dispatch*, C1-C2.

Ferrell, J. (1993). *Crimes of Style: Urban Graffiti and the Politics of Criminality*. New York: Garland.

Figlio, R.M., S. Hakim & G.F. Rengert (1986). "Introduction." In R.M. Figlio, S. Hakim & G.F. Rengert (eds.), *Metropolitan Crime Patterns* (pp. xi-xvii). Monsey, NY: Criminal Justice Press.

Figueira-McDonough, J. (1985). "Are Girls Different? Gender Discrepancies Between Delinquent Behavior and Control." *Child Welfare*, 64, 273-289.

Finkelhor, D. & K. Yllo (1985). *License to Rape: Sexual Abuse of Wives*. New York: Holt, Rinehart and Winston.

Fisher, B.S., F.T. Cullen & M.G. Turner (2000). *The Sexual Victimization of Women*. Washington, DC: U.S. Department of Justice.

Fisse, B. (1986). "Sanctions Against Corporations: Economic Efficiency or Legal Efficacy." In W.B. Groves & G. Newman (eds.), *Punishment and Privilege* (pp. 23-54). Albany, NY: Harrow and Heston.

Fitzpatrick, D. & C. Halliday (1992). *Not the Way to Love: Violence Against Young Women in Dating Relationships*. Amherst, Nova Scotia: Cumberland County Transition House Association.

Flavin, J. (2004). "Feminism for the Mainstream Criminologist: An Invitation." In B. Raffel Price & N.J. Sokoloff (eds.), *The Criminal Justice System and Women: Offenders, Prisoners, Victims and Workers* (pp. 31-50). New York: McGraw-Hill.

Fleury, R.E., C.M. Sullivan & D.I. Bybee (2000). "When Ending the Relationship Does Not End the Violence: Women's Experiences of Violence by Former Partners." *Violence Against Women*, 6, 1363-1383.

Fox, J.A., J. Levin & K. Quinet (2005). *The Will to Kill*, 2nd ed. Boston: Allyn & Bacon.

Fox, J.A. & A.R. Piquero (2003). "Deadly Demographics: Population Characteristics and Forecasting Homicide Trends." *Crime & Delinquency*, 49, 339-359.

Fox, J.A. & M.W. Zawitz (2004). "Homicide Trends in the United States" [Online]. Available at: http://www.ojp.usdoj.gov/bjs/homicide/homtrnd.htm#contents

Frank, N. & M. Lynch (1992). *Corporate Crime, Corporate Violence: A Primer*. New York: Harrow and Heston.

Friedrichs, D.O. (2003). "Corporate Crime and the Sociology of Deviance." In M.D. Schwartz & M.O. Maume (eds.), *Teaching the Sociology of Deviance*, 5th ed. (pp. 31-32). Washington, DC: American Sociological Association.

Friedrichs, D.O. (2004a). *Trusted Criminals: White Collar Crime in Contemporary Society*, 2nd ed. Belmont, CA: Wadsworth.

Friedrichs, D.O. (2004b). "Enron et al.: Paradigmatic White Collar Crime Cases for the New Century." *Critical Criminology*, 12, 113-132.

Funk, R.E. (1993). *Stopping Rape: A Challenge for Men*. Philadelphia: New Society.

Furstenberg, F.F., T.D. Cook, J. Eccles & G.H. Elder (1999). *Managing to Make It: Urban Families and Adolescent Success*. Chicago: University of Chicago Press.

Gabor, T. (1994). *Everybody Does It! Crime by the Public.* Toronto: University of Toronto Press.

Gardiner, J.K. (2005). "Men, Masculinities, and Feminist Theory." In M.S. Kimmel, J. Hearn & R.W. Connell (eds.), *Handbook of Studies on Men and Masculinities* (pp. 35-50). Thousand Oaks, CA: Sage.

Gartner, R. (1995). "Homicide in Canada." In J. Ross (ed.), *Violence in Canada: Sociopolitical Perspectives* (pp. 186-222). Toronto: Oxford University Press.

Gartner, R., M. Dawson & M. Crawford (2001). "Women Killing: Intimate Femicide in Ontario, 1974-1994." In D.E.H. Russell & R.A. Harmes (eds.), *Femicide in Global Perspective* (pp. 147-165). New York: Teachers College Press.

Geis, G. (1986). "The Heavy Electrical Equipment Antitrust Cases of 1961." In M. Ermann & R. Lundman (eds.), *Corporate and Governmental Deviance* (pp. 124-144). New York: Oxford University Press.

Gelles, R.J. (1980). "Violence in the Family: A Review of Research in the Seventies." *Journal of Marriage and the Family,* 42, 873-885.

Gelles, R.J. & C.P. Cornell (1985). *Intimate Violence in Families.* Beverly Hills, CA: Sage.

Gelles, R.J. & C.P. Cornell (1990). *Intimate Violence in Families,* 2nd ed. Newbury Park, CA: Sage.

Gelles, R.J. & M.A. Straus (1988). *Intimate Violence: The Causes and Consequences of Abuse in the American Family.* New York: Simon & Schuster.

Gelsthorpe, L. & A. Morris (1988). "Feminism and Criminology in Britain." *British Journal of Criminology,* 28, 93-110.

Getlin, J. (2002, November 30). "N.Y. Officer Suspended for Refusing to Arrest Homeless." *The Columbus Dispatch,* A3.

Gibbs, J.P. (1981). "The Sociology of Deviance and Social Control." In M. Rosenberg & R.H. Turner (eds.), *Social Psychology: Sociological Perspectives* (pp. 483-524). New York: Basic Books.

Gilbert, N. (1994). "Miscounting Social Ills." *Society,* 31, 18-26.

Gilkes, C.T. (1983). "From Slavery to Social Welfare: Racism and the Control of Black Women." In A. Swerdlow & H. Lessinger (eds.), *Class, Race, and Sex: The Dynamics of Control* (pp. 288-300). Boston: G.K. Hall.

Gilligan, J. (2001). *Preventing Violence.* New York: Thames and Hudson.

Giordano, P. (1978). "Research Note: Girls, Guys and Gangs: Then Changing Social Context of Female Delinquency." *Journal of Criminal Law & Criminology,* 69, 126-132.

Glaser, D. (1956). "Criminality Theory and Behavioral Images." *American Journal of Sociology,* 61, 433-444.

Godenzi, A., M.D. Schwartz & W.S. DeKeseredy (2001). "Toward a Gendered Social Bond/Male Peer Support Theory of University Woman Abuse." *Critical Criminology,* 10, 1-16.

Goff, C. & C. Reasons (1978). *Corporate Crime in Canada.* Scarborough, ON: Prentice Hall.

Goldstein, M. (1977, September 18). "When Did You Stop Beating Your Wife?" *Long Island Magazine*, 9ff.

Goode, E. (1989). *Drugs in American Society,* 3rd ed. New York: Knopf.

Gordon, D. (1971). "Class and the Economics of Crime." *Review of Radical Political Economics*, 3, 51-75.

Gottfredson, M.R. & T. Hirschi (1990). *A General Theory of Crime.* Stanford, CA: Stanford University Press.

Gould, S. J. (1996). *The Mismeasure of Man.* New York: W.W. Norton and Company.

Grasmick, H.G., C. Tittle, R.J. Bursik & B.J. Arneklev (1993). "Testing the Core Empirical Implications of Gottfredson and Hirschi's General Theory of Crime." *Journal of Research in Crime and Delinquency,* 30, 5-29.

Greenberg, D. (ed.) (1983). *Crime and Capitalism: Readings in Marxist Criminology.* Palo Alto: Mayfield.

Hackler, J. (1994). *Crime and Canadian Public Policy.* Scarborough, ON: Prentice Hall.

Hagan, F. (1993). *Research Methods in Criminal Justice and Criminology,* 3rd ed. New York: Macmillan.

Hagan, J. (1989). *Structural Criminology.* New Brunswick, NJ: Rutgers University Press.

Hagan, J. (1993). "The Social Embeddedness of Crime and Unemployment." *Criminology*, 31, 465-491.

Hagan, J. (1994). *Crime and Disrepute.* Thousand Oaks, CA: Pine Forge Press.

Hagan, J. & J.P. Coleman (2001). "Returning Captives of the American War on Drugs: Issues of Community and Family Reentry." *Crime & Delinquency*, 47, 352-367.

Hagan, J., A. Gillis & J. Simpson (1987). "Class in the Household: A Power-Control Theory of Gender and Delinquency." *American Journal of Sociology*, 92, 788-816.

Hagedorn, J.M. (1988). *People and Folks: Gangs, Crime and the Underclass in a Rustbelt City.* Chicago: Lakeview Press.

Hammett, T.M. & J. Epstein (1993). *Local Prosecution of Environmental Crime.* Washington, DC: U.S. Department of Justice.

Harcourt, B.E. (1998). "Reflecting on the Subject: A Critique of the Social Influence Conception of Deterrence, the Broken-Windows Theory, and Order Maintenance Policing New York Style." *Michigan Law Review*, 97, 291-389.

Hardesty, J.L. (2002). "Separation Assault in the Context of Postdivorce Parenting: An Integrative Review of the Literature." *Violence Against Women*, 8, 597-621.

Harding, S. (1987). "Is There a Feminist Method?" In S. Harding (ed.), *Feminism and Methodology* (pp. 1-14). Bloomington, IN: Indiana University Press.

Harney, P.A. & C.L. Muehlenhard (1991). "Rape." In E. Grauerholz & M.A. Koralewski (eds.), *Sexual Coercion: A Sourcebook on its Nature, Causes, and Prevention* (pp. 3-16). Lexington, MA: Lexington Books.

Harper, T. (2004, November 1). "Dad Gives Thumbs-down to Filmmaker Moore." *Toronto Star*, A16.

Harris, A.R., S.H. Thomas, G.A. Fisher & D.J. Hirsch (2002). "Murder and Medicine: The Lethality of Criminal Assault 1960-1999." *Homicide Studies,* 6, 128-166.

Harris, T. (1982). *From Mammies to Militants: Domestics in Black American Literature.* Philadelphia: Temple University Press.

Hartman, T. (2002). *Unequal Protection: The Rise of Corporate Dominance and the Theft of Human Rights.* New York: Rodale.

Hassel, W. (1992). "Survivor's Story." In G. Herek & K. Berrill (eds.), *Hate Crimes: Confronting Violence Against Lesbians and Gay Men* (pp. 144-148). Newbury Park, CA: Sage.

Hatty, S.E. (2000). *Masculinities, Violence, and Culture.* Thousand Oaks, CA: Sage.

Hawkins, D.F. (1987). "Devalued Lives and Racial Stereotypes: Ideological Barriers to the Prevention of Family Violence Among Blacks." In R.L. Hampton (ed.), *Violence in the Black Family: Correlates and Consequences* (pp. 189-205). Lexington, MA: Lexington Books.

Hawthorne, M. (2003, February 16). "Internal Warnings: Industry Memos Show DuPont Knew for Decades that a Chemical Used to Make Teflon is Polluting Workers and Neighbors." *The Columbus Dispatch,* A1, A8-A9.

Hay, C. (2001). "Parenting, Self-control, and Delinquency: A Test of Self-control Theory." *Criminology,* 39, 707-736.

Haysom, I. (1997). "America's Formidable Enemy Within: When the Underclass has had Enough, The Result will Resemble Civil War." *Ottawa Citizen* (February 23):A4.

Hayward, K. & J. Young (2004). "Cultural Criminology: Some Notes on the Script." *Theoretical Criminology,* 8, 259-273.

Hazler, R. (1996). *Breaking the Cycle of Violence: Interventions for Bullying and Victimization.* Washington, DC: Accelerated Development.

Henry, S. (1985). "Review of M.B. Clinard's Corporate Ethics and Crime." *British Journal of Criminology,* 35, 70-73.

Henry, S. (1999). "Is Left Realism a Useful Theory for Addressing the Problems of Crime? No." In J.R. Fuller & E.W. Hickey (eds.), *Controversial Issues in Criminology* (pp. 137-144). Boston: Allyn & Bacon.

Henry, S. & M.M. Lanier (eds.) (2001). *What is Crime? Controversies Over the Nature of Crime and What to Do About It.* Lanham, MD: Rowman & Littlefield.

Henslin, J.M. & L.T. Reynolds (1976). *Social Problems in American Society,* 2nd ed. Boston: Holbrook.

Herrnstein, R.J. & C. Murray (1994). *The Bell Curve: Intelligence and Class Structure in American Life.* New York: Free Press.

Hey, V. (1986). *Patriarchy and Pub Culture.* London: Tavistock.

Hill, K.G., J.C. Howell, D.J. Hawkins & S.R. Battin-Pearson (1999). "Childhood Risk Factors for Adolescent Gang Membership: Results from the Seattle Social Development Project." *Journal of Research in Crime and Delinquency,* 36, 300-322.

Hills, S.L. (ed.) (1987). *Corporate Violence: Injury and Death for Profit.* Totowa, NJ: Rowman & Littlefield.

Hindelang, M.J., M.R. Gottfredson & J. Garofalo (1978). *Victims of Personal Crime.* Cambridge, MA: Ballinger.

Hirschi, T. (1969). *Causes of Delinquency.* Berkeley, CA: University of California Press.

Hobsbawm, E. (1994). *The Age of Extremes.* London: Michael Joseph.

Hodgson, J.F. (1997). *Games Pimps Play: Pimps, Players and Wives-in-law.* Toronto: Canadian Scholars' Press.

Holsinger, K. & A.M. Holsinger (2005). "Differential Pathways to Violence and Self-injurious Behavior: African-American and White Girls in the Juvenile Justice System." *Journal of Research in Crime and Delinquency,* 42, 211-242.

Hornosty, J.M. (1996). "A Look at Faculty Fears and Needed University Policies Against Violence and Harassment." In C. Stark-Adamec (ed.), *Violence: A Collective Responsibility* (pp. 31-56). Ottawa: Social Science Federation of Canada.

Hotaling, G. & D. Sugarman (1986). "An Analysis of Risk Markers and Husband to Wife Violence: The Current State of Knowledge." *Violence and Victims,* 1, 102-124.

Howell, J.C. (1998). *Youth Gangs: An Overview* Washington, DC: Office of Juvenile Justice and Delinquency Prevention.

Howell, J.C. (2003). *Preventing and Reducing Juvenile Delinquency: A Comprehensive Framework.* Thousand Oaks, CA: Sage.

Howell, J.C. (2004). "Youth Gang Homicides: A Literature Review." In R. Petersen (ed.), *Understanding Contemporary Gangs in America: An Interdisciplinary Approach* (pp. 205-232). Upper Saddle River, NJ: Prentice Hall.

Hughes, L.A. & J.F. Short (2005). "Disputes Involving Youth Street Gang Members: Microsocial Contexts." *Criminology,* 43, 43-76.

Hull, J. & C. Bond (1986). "Social and Behavioral Consequences of Alcohol Consumption and Expectance: A Meta-analysis." *Psychological Bulletin,* 99, 347-360.

Hunt, G., K. Mackenzie & K. Joe-Laidler (2000). "'I'm Calling my Mom': The Meaning of Family and Kinship Among Homegirls." *Justice Quarterly,* 17, 1-31.

Hunter, A. (1974). *Symbolic Communities.* Chicago: University of Chicago Press.

Hunter, A. (1985). "Private, Parochial and Public School Orders: The Problem of Crime and Incivility in Urban Communities." In G.D. Suttles & M.N. Zald (eds.), *The Challenge of Social Control, Citizenship and Institution Building in Modern Society* (pp. 230-242). Norwood, NJ: Ablex.

Inciardi, J.A., D. Lockwood & A.E. Pottieger (1993). *Women and Crack-Cocaine.* New York: Macmillan.

Inciardi, J.A. & K. McElrath (1998). *The American Drug Scene.* Los Angeles: Roxbury.

Iovanni, L. & S.L. Miller (2001). "Criminal Justice System Responses to Domestic Violence: Law Enforcement and the Courts." In C.M Renzetti, J.L. Edleson & R.K. Bergen (eds.), *Sourcebook on Violence Against Women* (pp. 303-328). Thousand Oaks, CA: Sage.

Iraq Body Count Project. (2003). "Reported Civilian Deaths" [Online]. Available at: http://www.iraqbodycount.net/background.htm#methods

Ireland, T.O., T.P. Thornberry & R. Loeber (2003). "Violence Among Adolescents Living in Public Housing: A Two Site Analysis." *Criminology & Public Policy*, 3, 3-38.

Irwin, J. (2005). *The Warehouse Prison: Disposal of the New Dangerous Class*. Los Angeles: Roxbury.

Ismaili, K. (2001). "The Social Costs of Urban Crime Reduction Initiatives: Some Lessons from New York City." Paper presented at the annual meeting of the Academy of Criminal Justice Sciences, Washington, DC, April.

Jacobson, M. (1997). "New York City: An Overview of Corrections, Probation and Other Criminal Justice Trends." Paper presented at the Symposium on Crime and Prisons in the City, London, Middlesex University Centre for Criminology, September.

Jankowski, M. (1991). *Islands in the Street*. Berkeley: University of California Press.

Jargowsky, P.A. (1997). *Poverty and Place: Ghettos, Barrios, and the American City*. New York: Russell Sage Foundation.

Jargowsky, P.A. (2003). *Stunning Progress, Hidden Problems: The Dramatic Decline of Concentrated Urban Poverty in the 1990s*. Washington, DC: The Brookings Institution.

Jargowsky, P.A. & M.J. Bane (1991). "Ghetto Poverty in the United States, 1970-1980." In C. Jencks & P.E. Peterson (eds.), *The Urban Underclass* (pp. 235-273). Washington, DC: The Brookings Institution.

Jarjoura, G.R. (1993). "Does Dropping Out of School Enhance Delinquent Involvement? Results from a Large-scale National Probability Sample." *Criminology*, 31, 149-170.

Jasinski, J.L. (2001). "Theoretical Explanations for Violence Against Women." In C.M Renzetti, J.L. Edleson & R.K. Bergen (eds.), *Sourcebook on Violence Against Women* (pp. 5-22). Thousand Oaks, CA: Sage.

Jenkins, P. (1999). *Synthetic Panics*. New York: New York University Press.

Jensen, E., J. Gerber & C. Mosher (2004). "Social Consequences of the War on Drugs: The Legacy of Failed Policy." *Criminal Justice Policy Review*, 15, 100-121.

Jensen, G.F. (1990). "Power-Control vs. Social Control Theories of Delinquency: A Comparative Analysis." Paper presented at the annual meeting of the American Society of Criminology, Baltimore, MD, November.

Jiwani, J. (2000). "The 1999 General Social Survey on Spousal Violence: An Analysis." [Online]. Available at: http://www.casac.ca/survey99.htm

Joe, K. A. & M. Chesney-Lind (1995). "Just Every Mother's Angel: An Analysis of Gender and Ethnic Variations in Youth Gang Membership." *Gender & Society*, 9, 408-430.

Johnson, A.G. (1997). *The Gender Knot: Unraveling Our Patriarchal Legacy*. Philadelphia: Temple University Press.

Johnson, B.D., A. Golub & E. Dunlap (2000). "The Rise and Decline of Hard Drugs, Drug Markets, and Violence in Inner-city New York." In A. Blumstein & J. Wallman (eds.), *The Crime Drop in America* (pp. 164-206). New York: Cambridge University Press.

Johnson, M.P. (1995). "Patriarchal Violence and Common Couple Violence: Two Forms of Violence Against Women." *Journal of Marriage and the Family*, 57, 283-294.

Jones, T., B.D. MacLean & J. Young (1986). *The Islington Crime Survey*. London: Gower.

Kanin, E.J. (1967). "Male Aggression in Dating-Courtship Relations." *American Journal of Sociology*, 63, 197-204.

Kantor, G.K & J.L. Jasinski (1998). "Dynamics and Risk Factors in Partner Violence." In J.L. Jasinski & L.M. Williams (eds.), *Partner Violence: A Comprehensive Review of 20 years of Research* (pp. 1-43). Thousand Oaks, CA: Sage.

Kappeler, V.E., M. Blumberg & G.W. Potter (1996). *The Mythology of Crime and Criminal Justice*, 2nd ed. Prospect Heights, IL: Waveland.

Karmen, A. (2000). *New York Murder Mystery: The True Story Behind the Crime Crash of the 1990s*. New York: New York University Press.

Karmen, A. (2003). *Crime Victims: An Introduction to Victimology*, 5th ed. Belmont, CA: Wadsworth.

Kasarda, J. (1992). "The Severely Distressed in Economically Transforming Cities." In A. Harrell & G. Peterson (eds.), *Drugs, Crime, and Social Isolation: Barriers to Urban Opportunity* (pp. 45-98). Washington, DC: Urban Institute Press.

Katz, C.M., V.J. Webb & T.A. Armstrong (2003). "Fear of Gangs: A Test of Alternative Theoretical Models." *Justice Quarterly*, 20, 95-130.

Katz, P.A. (1979). "The Development of Female Identity." In C.B. Koop (ed.), *Becoming Female: Perspectives on Development* (pp. 3-27). New York: Plenum.

Kayser, K. (1993). *When Love Dies: The Power of Marital Disaffection*. Boston: Beacon.

Kazemipur, A. & S.S. Halli (2000). *The New Poverty in Canada: Ethnic Groups and Ghetto Neighbourhoods*. Toronto: Thomson Educational.

Keane, C. (1993). "The Impact of Financial Performance on Frequency of Corporate Crime: A Latent Variable Test of Strain Theory." *Canadian Journal of Criminology*, July, 293-308.

Kelling, G. & C. Coles (1997). *Fixing Broken Windows*. New York: Free Press.

Kelly, L. (1987). "The Continuum of Sexual Violence." In J. Hanmer & M. Maynard (eds.), *Women, Violence and Social Control* (pp. 46-60). Atlantic Highlands, NJ: Humanities Press International.

Kennedy, L.W. & D.G. Dutton (1989). "The Incidence of Wife Assault in Alberta." *Canadian Journal of Behavioural Science*, 21, 40-54.

Keys, D.P. & J.F. Galliher (2000). *Confronting the Drug Control Establishment: Alfred Lindesmith as a Public Intellectual*. Albany: State University of New York Press.

Khan, K. (1999). "Commentary: Race, Drugs and Prevalence." *International Journal of Drug Policy*, 10, 83-88.

Kilpatrick, D.G., R. Acierno, H. Resuick, B. Saunders & C.L. Best (1997). "A 2-Year Longitudinal Analysis of the Relationships Between Violent Assault and Substance Use in Women." *Journal of Consulting and Clinical Psychology*, 65, 835-847.

Kimmel, M.S. (2000). *The Gendered Society*. New York: Oxford University Press.

Kinsey, R., J. Lea & J. Young (1986). *Losing the Fight Against Crime.* Oxford, UK: Blackwell.

Kirkwood, C. (1993). *Leaving Abusive Partners.* Newbury Park, CA: Sage.

Klein, E., J. Campbell, E. Soler & M. Ghez (1997). *Ending Domestic Violence: Changing Public Perceptions/Halting the Epidemic.* Thousand Oaks, CA: Sage.

Klein, M. & C.L. Maxson (1989). "Street Gang Violence." In M. E. Wolfgang & N. A. Weiner (eds.), *Violent Crime, Violent Criminals* (pp. 198-234). Newbury Park, CA: Sage.

Klein, M.W. (2002). "Street Gangs: A Cross-National Perspective." In C.R. Huff (ed.), *Gangs in America III* (pp. 237-256). Thousand Oaks, CA: Sage.

Koss, M. (1996). "The Measurement of Rape Victimization in Crime Surveys." *Criminal Justice and Behavior,* 23, 55-69.

Koss, M.P., C.A. Gidycz & W. Wisniewski (1987). "The Scope of Rape: Incidence and Prevalence of Sexual Aggression and Victimization in a National Sample of Higher Education Students." *Journal of Consulting and Clinical Psychology,* 50, 455-457.

Kovandzic, T.V., L.M. Vieraitis & M.R. Yeisley (1998). "The Structural Covariates of Urban Homicide: Reassessing the Impact of Income Inequality and Poverty in the Post-Reagan Era." *Criminology,* 36, 569-599.

Kposowa, A.J. (1999). "The Effects of Occupation and Industry on the Risk of Homicide Victimization in the United States." *Homicide Studies,* 3, 47-77.

Kraska, P. (2004). "Criminal Justice as Rational/Legalism." In P. Kraska (ed.), *Theorizing Criminal Justice: Eight Essential Orientations* (pp. 19-22). Long Grove, IL: Waveland.

Krohn, M.D. & J.L. Massey (1980). "Social Control and Delinquency Behavior: An Examination of the Elements of the Social Bond." *Sociological Quarterly,* 21, 529-543.

Kubrin, C.E. & R. Weitzer (2003a). "New Directions in Social Disorganization Theory." *Journal of Research in Crime and Delinquency,* 40, 374-402.

Kubrin, C.E. & R. Weitzer (2003b). "Retaliatory Homicide: Concentrated Disadvantage and Neighborhood Culture." *Social Problems,* 50, 157-180.

Kurz, D. (1995). *For Richer or Poorer: Mothers Confront Divorce.* New York: Routledge.

Lab, S.P. (2000). *Crime Prevention: Approaches, Practices and Evaluations,* 4th ed. Cincinnati: Anderson.

Labaton, S. (2001, June 3). "The World Gets Tough on Price Fixers." *New York Times,* 3/1.

Lane, R. (1999). "Murder in America: A Historian's Perspective." In M. Tonry (ed.), *Crime and Justice: An Annual Review of Research* (pp. 191-224). Chicago: University of Chicago Press.

Lane, J. & J. Meeker (2000). "Subcultural Diversity and the Fear of Crime and Gangs." *Crime & Delinquency,* 46, 497-521.

Langan, P.A., L.A. Greenfield, S.K. Smith, M.R. Durose & D.J. Levin (2001). *Contacts Between Police and the Public: Findings from the 1999 National Survey.* Washington, DC: Bureau of Justice Statistics.

Lawson, J. (2004, September 29). "Woman Slain in Front of Police Had Court Order on Ex-husband." *Las Vegas Sun* [Online]. Available at: http://archives.listbox.com/cavent

Lea, J. & J. Young (1984). *What Is to Be Done About Law and Order?* New York: Penguin.

Lefkowitz, B. (1997). *Our Guys.* New York: Vintage.

Lemert, E.M. (1951). *Social Pathology.* New York: McGraw-Hill.

Lemert, E.M. (2000). "Societal Reaction, Differentiation, and Individuation." In C.M. Lemert & M.F. Winter (eds.), *Crime and Deviance: Essays and Innovations of Edwin M. Lemert* (pp. 26-40). Lanham, MD: Rowman & Littlefield.

Levant, R. (1994). "Male Violence Against Female Partners: Roots in Male Socialization and Development." Paper presented at the annual meeting of the American Psychological Association, Los Angeles.

Levinson, D. (1989). *Family Violence in Cross-cultural Perspective.* Newbury Park, CA: Sage.

Lewis, N. (1992, December 23). "Delinquent Girls Achieving a Violent Equality in DC." *The Washington Post*, A1, A14.

Lewis, O. (1966). "The Culture of Poverty." *Scientific American*, October, 19-25.

Lexchin, J. (1984). *The Real Pushers: A Critical Analysis of the Canadian Drug Industry.* Vancouver: New Star.

Liazos, A. (1972). "The Poverty of the Sociology of Deviance: Nuts, Sluts, and Perverts." *Social Problems*, 20, 109.

Lilly, J.R., F.T. Cullen & R.A. Ball (2002). *Criminological Theory: Context and Consequences*, 3rd ed. Thousand Oaks, CA: Sage.

Liska, A.E. (1971). "Aspirations and Expectations." *Sociological Quarterly*, 12, 99-107.

Lloyd, S. (1991). "The Dark Side of Courtship: Violence and Sexual Exploitation." *Family Relations*, 40, 14-20.

Lock, E.D., J.M. Timberlake & K.A. Rasinski (2002). "Battle Fatigue: Is Public Support Waning for 'War'-Centered Drug Control Strategies?" *Crime & Delinquency*, 48, 380-398.

Loftin, C. & R.H. Hill (1974). "Regional Subculture and Homicide: An Examination of the Gastil-Hackney Thesis." *American Sociological Review*, 39, 714-724.

Longshore, D., E. Chang, S. Hsieh & N. Messina (2004). "Self-Control and Social Bonds: A Combined Control Perspective on Deviance." *Crime & Delinquency*, 50, 542-564.

Lowenkamp, C.T., F.T. Cullen & T.C. Pratt (2003). "Replicating Sampson and Groves's Test of Social Disorganization Theory: Revisiting a Criminological Classic." *Journal of Research in Crime and Delinquency*, 40, 351-373.

Luckenbill, D.F. (1977). "Criminal Homicide as a Situated Transaction." *Social Problems*, 25, 176-186.

Lukoff, I. (1980). "Toward a Sociology of Drug Use." In D.J. Lettieri, M. Sayers & H. Wallenstein Pearson (eds.), *Theories on Drug Abuse: Selected Contemporary Perspectives* (pp. 201-211). Rockville, MD: National Institute on Drug Abuse.

Lundman, R.J. & R.L. Kaufman, R.L. (2003). "Driving While Black: Effects of Race, Ethnicity, and Gender on Citizen Self-reports of Traffic Stops and Police Actions." *Criminology*, 41, 195-219.

Lupri, E. (1990). "Male Violence in the Home." *Canadian Social Trends*, 14, 19-21.

Lyman, M.D. & G.W. Potter (2003). *Drugs in Society: Causes, Concepts and Control,* 4th ed. Cincinnati: Anderson.

Lynch, M.J., R. Michalowski & W.B. Groves (2000). *The New Primer in Radical Criminology: Critical Perspectives on Crime, Power and Identity*, 3rd ed. Monsey, NY: Criminal Justice Press.

MacLean, B.D. & D. Milovanovic (1997). "Thinking Critically About Criminology." In B.D. MacLean & D. Milovanovic (eds.), *Thinking Critically About Crime* (pp. 11-16). Vancouver: Collective Press.

MacLeod, L. (1987). *Battered But Not Beaten: Preventing Wife Battering in Canada.* Ottawa: Advisory Council on the Status of Women.

Maher, L. (1995). "In the Name of Love: Women and Initiation into Illicit Drugs." In R.E. Dobash (ed.), *Gender and Crime* (pp. 132-166). Cardiff: University of Wales Press.

Maher, L. (2000). *Sexed Work: Gender Race and Resistance in a Brooklyn Drug Market.* New York: Oxford University Press.

Mahoney, M.R. (1991). "Legal Issues of Battered Women: Redefining the Issue of Separation." *Michigan Law Review*, 90, 1-94.

Mahoney, P. & L.M. Williams (1998). "Sexual Assault in Marriage: Prevalence, Consequences, and Treatment of Wife Rape." In J.L. Jasinski & L.M. Williams (eds.), *Partner Violence: A Comprehensive Review of 20 years of Research* (pp. 113-162). Thousand Oaks, CA: Sage.

Mahoney, P., L.M. Williams & C. West (2001). "Violence Against Women by Intimate Relationship Partners." In C.M. Renzetti, J.L. Edleson & R.K. Bergen (eds.), *Sourcebook on Violence Against Women* (pp. 143-178). Thousand Oaks, CA: Sage.

Males, M., D. Macallair & R. Jamison (2002). *Drug Use and Justice 2002: An Examination of California Drug Policy Enforcement.* San Francisco: Center on Juvenile and Criminal Justice.

Mann, C.R. (1989). "Minority and Female: A Criminal Justice Double Bind." *Social Justice*, 16, 93-114.

Mann, C.R. (1993). *Unequal Justice: A Question of Color.* Bloomington: Indiana University Press.

Mann, C.R. & M.S. Zatz (1998). "Before and Beyond the Millennium: Possible Solutions." In C.R. Mann & M.S. Zatz (eds.), *Images of Color, Images of Crime* (pp. 257-270). Los Angeles: Roxbury.

Martin, P.Y. & R.A. Hummer (1989). "Fraternities and Rape on Campus." *Gender & Society*, 3, 457-473.

Marx, K. (1844/1963). *The Economic and Philosophical Manuscripts*. New York: Frederick Ungar.

Marx, K. (1872/1959). *Manifesto of the Communist Party*. Moscow: Foreign Languages Publishing House.

Marx, K. & F. Engels (1846/1939). *German Ideology*. New York: International.

Marx, K. & F. Engels (1848/1975). *The Communist Manifesto*. Great Britain: C. Nickolls.

Matthews, R.A. (2003a). "Teaching Elite Deviance and Crony Capitalism: Enron and Arthur Andersen." In M.D. Schwartz & M.O. Maume (eds.), *Teaching the Sociology of Deviance*, 5th ed. (pp. 35-38). Washington, DC: American Sociological Association.

Matthews, R.A. (2003b). "Marxist Criminology." In M.D. Schwartz & S.E. Hatty (eds.), *Controversies in Critical Criminology* (pp. 1-14). Cincinnati: Anderson.

Matthews, R.A. & D. Kauzlarich (2000). "The Crash of ValuJet Flight 592: A Case Study in State-Corporate Crime." *Sociological Focus*, 3, 281-298.

Matthews, R.A., M.O. Maume & W.J. Miller (2001). "Deindustrialization, Economic Distress, and Homicide Rates in Midsized Rustbelt Cities." *Homicide Studies*, 5, 83-113.

Matthews, R. & J. Young (eds.) (1992). *Issues in Realist Criminology*. London: Sage.

Mattley, C. & M.D. Schwartz (1990). "Living Under Tyranny: Gender Identities and Battered Women." *Symbolic Interaction*, 13, 281-289.

Maxson, C.L., G.D. Curry & J.C. Howell (2002). "Youth Gang Homicides in the United States in the 1990s." In W.L. Reed & S. Decker (eds.), *Responding to Gangs: Evaluation and Research* (pp. 107-137). Washington, DC: National Institute of Justice.

McCarthy, B., J. Hagan & T.S. Woodward (1999). "In the Company of Women: Structure and Agency in a Revised Power-Control Theory of Gender and Delinquency." *Criminology*, 37, 761-788.

McCorkle, R.C. & T.D. Miethe (2002). *Panic: The Social Construction of the Street Gang Problem*. Upper Saddle River, NJ: Prentice Hall.

McIntosh, M. (1975). *The Organization of Crime*. London: Macmillan.

McMillen, L. (1990). "An Anthropologist's Disturbing Picture of Gang Rape on Campus." *Chronicle of Higher Education*, 37, A3.

McQuaig, L. (1987). *Behind Closed Doors*. Toronto: Penguin.

McRobbie, A. & J. Garber (1975). "Girls and Subcultures." In S. Hall & T. Jefferson (eds.), *Resistance through Rituals: Youth Subculture in Post-war Britain* (pp. 209-229). London: Hutchinson & Co.

Mead, G.H. (1934). *Mind, Self and Society*. Chicago: University of Chicago Press.

Meier, B. (1992, June 15). "Bronco Accidents Pose New Questions for Ford on Safety." *New York Times*, A1.

Meier, R.F. & G. Geis (1997). *Victimless Crime?* Los Angeles: Roxbury.

Merton, R.K. (1938). "Social Structure and Anomie." *American Sociological Review*, 3, 672-682.

Messerschmidt, J.W. (1986). *Capitalism, Patriarchy, and Crime: Toward a Socialist Feminist Criminology.* Totowa, NJ: Rowman & Littlefield.

Messerschmidt, J.W. (1993). *Masculinities and Crime: Critique and Reconceptualization.* Lanham, MD: Rowman & Littlefield.

Messerschmidt, J.W. (1997). *Crime as Structured Action: Gender, Race, Class, and Crime in the Making.* Thousand Oaks, CA: Sage.

Messerschmidt, J.W. (2000). *Nine Lives: Adolescent Masculinities, the Body, and Violence.* Boulder, CO: Westview.

Messerschmidt, J.W. (2005). "Men, Masculinities, and Crime." In M.S. Kimmel, J. Hearn & R.W. Connell (eds.), *Handbook of Studies on Men and Masculinities* (pp. 196-212). Thousand Oaks, CA: Sage.

Messner, S.F. (1980). "Income Inequality and Murder Rates: Some Cross-national Findings." *Comparative Social Research*, 3, 185-198.

Messner, S.F. & J. Blau (1987). "Routine Leisure Activities and Rates of Crime: A Macro-level Analysis." *Social Forces*, 65, 1035-1052.

Messner, S.F., M.D. Krohn & A.E. Liska (1990). *Theoretical Integration in the Study of Deviance and Crime.* Albany, NY: SUNY Press.

Messner, S.F. & R. Rosenfeld (1997). "Political Restraint of the Market and Levels of Criminal Homicide: A Cross-national Application of the Institutional Anomie Theory." *Social Forces*, 75, 1393-1416.

Messner, S.F. & R. Rosenfeld (1999). "Social Structure and Homicide: Theory and Research." In D.M. Smith & M.A. Zahn (eds.), *Homicide: A Sourcebook of Social Research* (pp. 27-41). Thousand Oaks, CA: Sage.

Messner, S.F. & R. Rosenfeld (2001). *Crime and the American Dream,* 2nd ed. Belmont, CA: Wadsworth.

Messner, S.F. & K. Tardiff (1985). "The Social Ecology of Urban Homicide: An Application of the Routine Activities Approach." *Criminology*, 23, 241-267.

Michalowski, R.J. (1983). "Crime Control in the 1980s: A Progressive Agenda." *Crime and Social Justice*, Summer, 13-23.

Michalowski, R. (1985). *Order, Law, and Crime: An Introduction to Criminology.* New York: Random House.

Michalowski, R.J. (1991). "'Niggers, Welfare Scum and Homeless Assholes': The Problems of Idealism, Consciousness and Context in Left Realism." In B.D. MacLean & D. Milovanovic (eds.), *New Directions in Critical Criminology* (pp. 31-38). Vancouver: Collective Press.

Mihalic, S. & D. Elliot (1997). "If Violence is Domestic, Does It Really Count?" *Journal of Family Violence*, 12, 293-311.

Miliband, R. (1969). *The State in Capitalist Society: The Analysis of the Western System of Power.* London: Quartet.

Miller, D.L. (2001). "Poking Holes in the Theory of "Broken Windows" [Online]. Available at: http://www.chronicle.com

Miller, J. (2001). *One of the Guys: Girls, Gangs, and Gender*. New York: Oxford University Press.

Miller, J. (2003). "Feminist Criminology." In M.D. Schwartz & S.E. Hatty (eds.), *Controversies in Critical Criminology* (pp. 15-28). Cincinnati: Anderson.

Miller, J. & M.D. Schwartz (1995). "Rape Myths and Violence Against Prostitutes." *Deviant Behavior: An Interdisciplinary Journal*, 16, 1-23.

Miller, S.L. (1994). "Expanding the Boundaries: Toward a More Inclusive and Integrated Study of Intimate Violence." *Violence and Victims*, 9, 183-194.

Miller, S.L. & S. Simpson (1991). "Courtship Violence and Social Control: Does Gender Matter?" *Law & Society Review*, 25, 335-365.

Miller, W. (1958). "Lower-class Culture as a Generating Milieu of Gang Delinquency." *Journal of Social Issues,* 14, 5-19.

Miller, W. (1980). "Gangs, Groups and Serious Youth Crime." In D. Shichor & D. Kelly (eds.), *Critical Issues in Juvenile Delinquency* (pp. 115-138). Lexington, MA: Lexington Books.

Mills, C.W. (1959). *The Sociological Imagination*. New York: Oxford University Press.

Mokdad, A.H., J.S. Marks, D.F. Stroup & J.L. Gerberding (2004). "Actual Causes of Death in the United States, 2000." *Journal of the American Medical Association,* 291, 1238-1245.

Mokhiber, R. (2004). "Top 100 Corporate Criminals of the Decade" [Online]. Available at: http://www.corporatepredators.org/top100.html

Mooney, J. (2000). *Gender, Violence and the Social Order*. New York: St. Martin's Press.

Mooney, L., D. Knox & C. Schacht (2005). *Understanding Social Problems,* 4th ed. Belmont, CA: Thomson Wadsworth.

Moore, J. (1990). *Gangs, Drugs and Violence* (Rep. No. 103). Rockville, MD: National Institute on Drug Abuse.

Moore, J. & J. Hagedorn (2001). *Female Gangs: A Focus on Research*. Washington, DC: Office of Juvenile Justice and Delinquency Prevention.

Moore, J. & J. Hagedorn (2004). "What Happens to Girls in the Gang." In R. Petersen (ed.), *Understanding Contemporary Gangs in America: An Interdisciplinary Approach* (pp. 37-47). Upper Saddle River, NJ: Pearson.

Moore, M. (2003). *Dude, Where's My Country?* New York: Warner Books.

Morenoff, J.D. (1994). "Neighborhood Change and the Social Transformation of Chicago, 1960-1990." Working Papers Series, Vol. 2, No. 4. Center for the Study of Urban Inequality, University of Chicago.

Morenoff, J.D., R.J. Sampson & S.W. Raudenbush (2001). "Neighborhood Inequality, Collective Efficacy, and the Spatial Dynamics of Violence." *Criminology*, 39, 517-559.

Morgan, P. & K.A. Joe (1997). "Uncharted Terrain: Contexts of Experience Among Women in the Illicit Drug Economy." *Women and Criminal Justice*, 8, 85-109.

Morra, N. & M.D. Smith (1993). "Men in Feminism: Theorizing Sexual Violence." *The Journal of Men's Studies*, 2, 15-28.

Mosher, C. (2001). "Predicting Drug Arrest Rates: Conflict and Social Disorganization Perspectives." *Crime & Delinquency*, 47, 84-104.

Mouradian, V.E. (2004). *Abuse in Intimate Relationships: Defining the Multiple Dimensions and Terms* [Online]. Available at: http://www.vawprevention.org/research/defining/sthml

Muncie, J. (2001). "The Construction and Deconstruction of Crime." In J. Muncie & E. McLaughlin (eds.), *The Problem of Crime* (pp. 7-70). London: Sage.

Musto, D. (1988). *The American Disease: Origins of Narcotic Control*. exp. ed. New York: Oxford University Press.

National Clearinghouse on Marital and Date Rape (1998). *State Law Chart*. Berkeley, CA: Author.

National Commission on Product Safety (1974). "Perspectives on Product Safety." In D.A. Aaker & G.S. Day (eds.), *Consumerism: Search for the Consumer Interest* (pp. 31-322). New York: Free Press.

National Institute on Drug Abuse (NIDA) (2003). *Drug Use Among Racial/Ethnic Minorities: Revised* (Rep. No. 03-3888). Bethesda, MD: National Institute on Drug Abuse.

National Victims Center and the Crime Victims Research and Treatment Center (1992). *Rape in America: A Report to the Nation*. Arlington, VA: Author.

Nelsen, C. & L. Huff-Corzine (1998). "Strangers in the Night: An Application of the Lifestyle-Routine Activities Approach to Elderly Homicide Victimization." *Homicide Studies*, 2, 130-159.

Newman, O. (1972). *Defensible Space*. New York: Macmillan.

Newman, O. & K.A. Franck (1982). "The Effects of Building Size on Personal Crime and Fear of Crime." *Population and Environment*, 5, 203-220.

Nifong, C. (1999). "One Man's Theory is Cutting Crime in Urban Streets." In M. Fisch (ed.), *Annual Editions: Criminology, 99/00* (pp. 8-11). Guilford, CT: Duskin/McGraw-Hill.

Nisbett, R.E. (1993). "Violence and U.S. Regional Culture." *American Psychologist*, 48, 441-449.

Nisbett, R.E. & D. Cohen (1996). *Culture of Honor: The Psychology of Violence in the South*. Boulder, CO: Westview.

Notarius, C. & H. Markman (1993). *We Can Work It Out: Making Sense of Marital Conflict*. New York: Putnam.

Nye, I.F. (1958). *Family Relationships and Delinquent Behavior*. New York: Wiley.

Office of Juvenile Justice and Delinquency Prevention (1997). *1995 National Youth Gang Survey*. Washington, DC: Office of Justice Programs, U.S. Department of Justice.

Office of Juvenile Justice and Delinquency Prevention (2000). *1998 National Youth Gang Survey*. Washington, DC: Office of Justice Programs, U.S. Department of Justice.

Office of National Drug Control Policy (2003). *Drug Data Summary*. Washington, DC: National Drug Control Policy Information Clearinghouse.

Okun, L. (1986). *Woman Abuse: Facts Replacing Myths*. Albany: State University of New York Press.

Orenstein, P. (1994). *School Girls*. Garden City, NY: Doubleday.

Park, R.E. (1925). *Human Communities*. Chicago: Free Press.

Park, R.E., E.W. Burgess & R.D. McKenzie (eds.). *The City*. Chicago: University of Chicago Press.

Parker, K.F. & M.V. Pruitt (2000). "How the West Was One: Explaining the Similarities in Race-specific Homicide Rates in the West and South." *Social Forces*, 78, 1483-1508.

Parker, R.N. (1989). "Poverty, Subculture of Violence, and Type of Homicide." *Social Forces*, 67, 983-1007.

Passas, N. (1990). "Anomie and Corporate Deviance." *Contemporary Crises*, 14, 157-178.

Pateman, C. (1988). *The Sexual Contract*. London: Polity.

Paternoster, R. (1987). "The Deterrent Effect of the Perceived Certainty and Severity of Punishment: A Review of Evidence and Issues." *Justice Quarterly*, 4, 173-217.

Paternoster, R. (1991). *Capital Punishment in America*. Lexington, KY: Lexington Books.

Paternoster, R. & R. Bachman (2001). "Social Disorganization and Crime: Introduction." In R. Paternoster & R. Bachman (eds.), *Explaining Criminals and Crime* (pp. 113-123). Los Angeles: Roxbury.

Patterson, E.B. (1991). "Poverty, Income Inequality, and Community Crime Rates." *Criminology*, 29, 755-776.

Pattillo, M.E. (1998). "Sweet Mothers and Gangbangers: Managing Crime in a Black Middle-Class Neighborhood." *Social Forces*, 76, 747-774.

Pearce, F. (1976). *Crimes of the Powerful: Marxism, Crime and Deviance*. London: Pluto.

Pearce, F. (1989). *The Radical Durkheim*. Boston: Unwin Hyman.

Pearce, F. (1992). "The Contribution of 'Left Realism' to the Study of Commercial Crime." In J. Lowman & B.D. MacLean (eds.), *Realist Criminology: Crime Control and Policing in the 1990s* (pp. 313-335). Toronto: University of Toronto Press.

Pearce, F. & S. Tombs (1992). "Realism and Corporate Crime." In R. Matthews & J. Young (eds.), *Issues in Realist Criminology* (pp. 70-101). London: Sage.

Perkins, U.E. (1987). *Explosion of Chicago's Black Street Gangs: 1900 to the Present*. Chicago: Third World Press.

Peronne, P. & M. Chesney-Lind (1997). "Representations of Gangs in Delinquency." *Social Justice*, 24, 117.

Perry, B. (2001). *In the Name of Hate: Understanding Hate Crimes*. New York: Routledge.

Perry, B. (ed.) (2003a). *Hate and Bias Crime*. New York: Routledge.

Perry, B. (2003b). "Accounting for Hate Crime." In M.D. Schwartz & S.E. Hatty (eds.), *Controversies in Critical Criminology* (pp. 147-160). Cincinnati: Anderson.

Peterson, R.D. & L.J. Krivo (1993). "Racial Segregation and Black Urban Homicide." *Social Forces,* 71, 1001-1028.

Peterson, R.D. & L.J. Krivo (1999). "Racial Segregation, the Concentration of Disadvantage, and Black and White Homicide Victimization." *Sociological Forum,* 14, 465-493.

Pfhol, S.J. (1985). *Images of Deviance and Social Control: A Sociological History.* New York: McGraw-Hill.

Piquero, A. (1999). "The Validity of Incivility Measures in Public Housing." *Justice Quarterly,* 16, 793-816.

Pitts, V.L. (2003). "Crime and Embodiment." In M.D. Schwartz & S.E. Hatty (eds.), *Controversies in Critical Criminology* (pp. 121-132). Cincinnati: Anderson.

Polk, K. (1998). "Violence, Masculinity and Evolution: A Comment on Wilson and Daly." *Theoretical Criminology,* 2, 461-469.

Polk, K. (2003). "Masculinities, Femininities and Homicide: Competing Explanations for Male Violence." In M.D. Schwartz & S.E. Hatty (eds.), *Controversies in Critical Criminology* (pp. 133-146). Cincinnati: Anderson.

Pollard, C. (1997). "Zero-tolerance: Short-Term Fix, Long-Term Liability?" In N. Dennis (ed.), *Zero-tolerance Policing in a Free Society* (pp. 101-135). London: Institute of Economic Affairs.

Pratt, T.C. & T.W. Godsey (2003). "Social Support, Inequality, and Homicide: A Cross-national Test of an Integrated Theoretical Model." *Criminology,* 41, 611-643.

Pratt, T.C. & C.T. Lowenkamp (2002). "Conflict Theory, Economic Conditions, and Homicide: A Time-Series Analysis." *Homicide Studies,* 6, 61-83.

Prus, R.C. (1975). "Resisting Designations: An Extension of Attribution Theory into Negotiated Context." *Sociological Inquiry,* 45, 3-14.

Quinney, R. (1974). *Critique of the Legal Order.* Boston: Little, Brown.

Radford, J. (1987). "Policing Male Violence—Policing Women." In J. Hanmer & M. Maynard (eds.), *Women, Violence and Social Control* (pp. 30-45). Atlantic Highlands, NJ: Humanities Press International.

Random House (2003). Our Guys Reading Group Center [Online]. Available at: http://www.randomhouse.com/vintage/read/ourguys/

Rapaport, D. (1984). "Fear and Trembling: Terrorism in Three Religious Traditions." *American Political Science Review,* 78, 658-677.

Raphael, J. (2001a). "Public Housing and Domestic Violence." *Violence Against Women,* 7, 699-706.

Raphael, J. (2001b). "Domestic Violence as a Welfare-to-Work Barrier: Research and Theoretical Issues." In C.M. Renzetti, J.L. Edleson & R.K. Bergen (eds.), *Sourcebook on Violence Against Women* (pp. 443-456). Thousand Oaks, CA: Sage.

Raphael, J. & D.L. Shapiro (2004). "Violence in Indoor and Outdoor Prostitution Venues." *Violence Against Women,* 10, 126-139.

Rebovich, D. (1992). *Dangerous Ground: The World of Hazardous Waste Crime.* New Brunswick, NJ: Transaction.

Rebovich, D. & J. Layne (2000). *The National Survey on White Collar Crime.* Morgantown, WV: National White Collar Crime Center.

Reckless, W. (1961). "A New Theory of Delinquency and Crime." *Federal Probation,* 25, 42-46.

Reckless, W., S. Dinitz & B. Kay (1957). "The Self Component in Potential Delinquency and Non-delinquency." *American Sociological Review,* 22, 566-570.

Reiman, J. (2004). *The Rich Get Richer and the Poor get Prison: Ideology, Class, and Criminal Justice,* 7th ed. Boston: Allyn & Bacon.

Reiss, A. (1951). "Delinquency as the Failure of Personal and Social Controls." *American Sociological Review,* 16, 196-207.

Reiss, A.J. & J.A. Roth (1993). *Understanding and Preventing Violence.* Washington DC: National Research Council.

Renzetti, C.M. (1993). "On the Margins of the Malestream (or, They *Still* Don't Get It, Do They?): Feminist Analyses in Criminal Justice Education." *Journal of Criminal Justice Education,* 4, 219-234.

Renzetti, C.M. (1994). "On Dancing with a Bear: Reflections on Some of the Current Debates Among Domestic Violence Theorists." *Violence and Victims,* 9, 195-2000.

Renzetti, C.M. & D.J. Curran (2000). *Living Sociology,* 2nd ed. Boston: Allyn & Bacon.

Renzetti, C.M. & D.J. Curran (2002). *Women, Men, and Society,* 5th ed. Boston: Allyn & Bacon.

Renzetti, C.M., J.L. Edleson & R.K. Bergen (eds.) (2001). *Sourcebook on Violence Against Women.* Thousand Oaks, CA: Sage.

Renzetti, C.M. & S.L. Maier (2002). "Private Crime in Public Housing: Fear of Crime and Violent Victimization Among Women Public Housing Residents." *Women's Health and Urban Life,* 1, 46-65.

Reuters New Agency. (2002, September 30). "Music Companies to Pay $67.4 Million in Price-fixing Case" [Online]. Available at: http://wardsauto.com

Rogers, J.W. & M.D. Buffalo (1974). "Fighting Back: Nine Modes of Adaptation to a Deviant Label." *Social Problems,* 22, 101-118.

Rogness, M.M. (2003). *Toward an Integrated Male Peer Support Model of Marital/Cohabiting Rape in the United States.* M.A. thesis, Department of Sociology, Ohio University.

Rosenbaum, M. (1981). *Women on Heroin.* New Brunswick, NJ: Rutgers University Press.

Rosenfeld, R. (2000). "Patterns in Adult Homicide: 1980-1995." In A. Blumstein & J. Wallman (eds.), *The Crime Drop in America* (pp. 130-163). New York: Cambridge University Press.

Rosoff, S.M., H.N. Pontell & R. Tillman (2001). *Profit Without Honor: White-collar Crime and the Looting of America,* 2nd ed. Upper Saddle River, NJ: Prentice Hall.

Rubington, E. & M.S. Weinberg (1973). "Preface." In E. Rubington & M.S. Weinberg (eds.), *Deviance: The Interactionist Perspective,* 2nd ed. (p. vii). New York: Macmillan.

Rubington, E. & M.S. Weinberg (eds.) (2005). *Deviance: The Interactionist Perspective,* 9th ed. Boston: Allyn & Bacon.

Ruggiero, V. (1992). "Realist Criminology: A Critique." In J. Young & R. Matthews (eds.), *Rethinking Criminology: The Realist Debate* (pp. 123-140). London: Sage.

Russell, D.E.H. (1982). *Rape in Marriage.* New York: Macmillan.

Russell, D.E.H. (1984). *Sexual Exploitation: Rape, Child Sexual Abuse, and Workplace Harassment.* Beverly Hills, CA: Sage.

Russell, D.E.H. (1990). *Rape in Marriage,* exp. and rev. ed. New York: Macmillan.

Russell, D.E.H. (1998). *Dangerous Relationships: Pornography, Misogyny, and Rape.* Thousand Oaks, CA: Sage.

Russell, D.E.H. (2001). "Defining Femicide and Related Concepts." In D.E.H. Russell & R.A. Harmes (eds.), *Femicide in Global Perspective* (pp. 12-28). New York: Teachers College Press.

Russell, S. (2002). "The Continuing Relevance of Marxism to Critical Criminology." *Critical Criminology,* 11, 93-112.

SAMHSA (1993). *National Household Survey on Drug Abuse.* Washington, DC: U.S. Department of Health and Human Services.

SAMHSA (2005a). "Drugs of Abuse" {Online]. Available at: http://www.health.org/govpubs/rpo926/

SAMHSA (2005b). *National Survey on Drug Use and Health, 2002 and 2003.* U.S. Department of Health and Human Services [Online]. Available at: http://oas.samhsa.gov/nhsda/2k3tabs/toc.htm

Sampson, R.J. (1986). "The Effects of Urbanization and Neighborhood Characteristics on Criminal Victimization." In R.M. Figlio, S. Hakin & G.F. Rengert (eds.), *Metropolitan Crime Patterns* (pp. 3-26). Monsey, NY: Criminal Justice Press.

Sampson, R.J. (1987). "Urban Black Violence: The Effect of Male Joblessness and Family Disruption." *American Journal of Sociology,* 93, 348-382.

Sampson, R.J. (2002). "Transcending Tradition: New Directions in Community Research, Chicago Style—The American Society of Criminology 2001 Sutherland Address. *Criminology,* 40, 213-230.

Sampson, R.J. & W.B. Groves (1989). "Community Structure and Crime: Testing Social Disorganization Theory." *American Journal of Sociology,* 94, 774-802.

Sampson, R.J. & J. Lauritsen (1990). "Deviant Lifestyles, Proximity to Crime, and the Offender-Victim Link in Personal Violence." *Journal of Research in Crime and Delinquency,* 27, 110-139.

Sampson, R.J., J.D. Morenoff & F. Earls (1999). "Beyond Social Capital: Spatial Dynamics of Collective Efficacy for Children." *American Sociological Review,* 64, 633-660.

Sampson, R.J. & S.W. Raudenbush (2001). *Disorder in Urban Neighborhoods: Does It Lead to Crime?* Washington, DC: U.S. Department of Justice.

Sampson, R.J., S.W. Raudenbush & F. Earls (1997). "Neighborhoods and Violent Crime: A Multilevel Study of Collective Efficacy." *Science,* 277, 918-924.

Sampson, R.J., S.W. Raudenbush & F. Earls (1998). *Neighborhood Collective Efficacy: Does It Help Reduce Violence?* Washington, DC: U.S. Department of Justice.

Sampson, R.J., S.W. Raudenbush & F. Earls (1998). *Neighborhood Collective Efficacy: Does It Help Reduce Violence?* Washington, DC: U.S. Department of Justice.

Sampson, R.J., G.D. Squires & M. Zhou (2001). *How Neighborhoods Matter: The Value of Investing at the Local Level.* Washington, DC: American Sociological Association.

Sanday, P.R. (1990). *Fraternity Gang Rape.* New York: New York University Press.

Sandefur, R. & E.O. Laumann (1998). "A Paradigm for Social Capital." *Rationality and Society*, 10, 481-501.

Saville, G. & T. Clear (2000). "Community Renaissance with Community Justice." *The Neighborworks Journal*, 18, 19-24.

Saville, G. & G. Cleveland (1997). "Second Generation CPTED: An Antidote to the Social Y2K Virus of Urban Design." Paper presented at the Second Annual International CPTED Conference, Orlando, December.

Savolainen, J. (2000). "Inequality, Welfare State, and Homicide: Further Support for the Institutional Anomie Theory." *Criminology*, 38, 1021-1042.

Schaefer, D. (2004). "Perceptual Biases, Graffiti and Fraternity Crime: Points of Deflection That Distort Social Justice." *Critical Criminology*, 12, 179-193.

Schulman, M.A. (1979). *A Survey of Spousal Violence Against Women in Kentucky.* Washington, DC: Law Enforcement Assistance Administration.

Schur, E.M. (1973). *Radical Nonintervention.* Englewood Cliffs, NJ: Spectrum.

Schur, E.M. (1974). "A Sociologist's View: The Case for Abolition." In E.M. Schur & H.A. Bedau (eds.), *Victimless Crimes: Two Sides of the Controversy* (pp. 3-52). Engelwood Cliffs, NJ: Prentice Hall.

Schur, E.M. (1984). *Labeling Women Deviant: Gender, Stigma, and Social Control.* Philadelphia: Temple University Press.

Schwartz, M.D. (1990). "Work Status, Resource Equality, Injury and Wife Battery: The National Crime Survey Data." *Free Inquiry in Creative Sociology*, 18, 57-61.

Schwartz, M.D. (1991). "Humanist Sociology and Date Rape." *Humanity and Society*, 15, 304-316.

Schwartz, M.D. (2000). "Methodological Issues in the Use of Survey Data for Measuring and Characterizing Violence Against Women." *Violence Against Women*, 6, 815-838.

Schwartz, M.D. (2002). *Marital Rape.* Unpublished manuscript. Ohio University.

Schwartz, M.D. & W.S. DeKeseredy (1988). "Liberal Feminism on Violence Against Women." *Social Justice*, 15, 213-221.

Schwartz, M.D. & W.S. DeKeseredy (1991). "Left Realist Criminology: Strengths, Weaknesses and the Feminist Critique." *Crime, Law and Social Change*, 15, 51-72.

Schwartz, M.D. & W.S. DeKeseredy (1997). *Sexual Assault on the College Campus: The Role of Male Peer Support.* Thousand Oaks, CA: Sage.

Schwartz, M.D., W.S. DeKeseredy, D. Tait & S. Alvi (2001). "Male Peer Support and Routine Activities Theory: Understanding Sexual Assault on the College Campus." *Justice Quarterly*, 18, 701-727.

Schwartz, M.D. & S.E. Hatty (2003). "Introduction." In M.D. Schwartz & S.E. Hatty (eds.), *Controversies in Critical Criminology* (pp. ix-xvii). Cincinnati: Anderson.

Schwartz, M.D. & M.O. Maume (2003). "Preface." In M.D. Schwartz & M.O. Maume (eds.), *Teaching the Sociology of Deviance,* 5th ed. (pp. i-v). Washington, DC: American Sociological Association.

Schwartz, M.D. & D. Milovanovic (eds.) (1996). *Race, Gender and Class in Criminology.* New York: Garland.

Schwartz, M.D. & C. Nogrady (1996). "Fraternity Membership, Rape Myths and Sexual Aggression on a College Campus." *Violence Against Women,* 2, 148-162.

Schwartz, M.D. & V. Pitts (1995). "Exploring a Feminist Routine Activities Approach to Explaining Sexual Assault." *Justice Quarterly,* 12, 9-31.

Schwendinger, H. & J. Schwendinger (2001). "Defenders of Order or Guardians of Human Rights?" In S. Henry & M.M. Lanier (eds.), *What is Crime? Controversies Over the Nature of Crime and What to Do About It* (pp. 65-100). Lanham, MD: Rowman & Littlefield.

Schwendinger, J. & H. Schwendinger (1983). *Rape and Inequality.* Beverly Hills, CA: Sage.

Scully, D. (1990). *Understanding Sexual Violence.* Boston: Unwin Hyman.

Seis, M. (1998). "Five Types of Environmental Criminals." In M. Clifford (ed.), *Environmental Crime: Enforcement, Policy, and Social Responsibility* (pp. 255-280). Gaithersburg, MD: Aspen.

Sellin, T. (1938). *Culture Conflict and Crime.* New York: Social Science Research Council.

Sernau, S. (2001). *Worlds Apart: Social Inequalities in a New Century.* Thousand Oaks, CA: Pine Forge.

Sev'er, A. (2002). *Fleeing the House of Horrors: Women Who Have Left Abusive Partners.* Toronto: University of Toronto Press.

Shapiro, B. (1999). "The Crime Wavelet." In M. Fisch (ed.), *Annual Editions: Criminology, 99/00* (pp. 24-25). Guilford, CT: Duskin/McGraw-Hill.

Shaw, C.R. & H.D. McKay (1942). *Juvenile Delinquency and Urban Areas.* Chicago: University of Chicago Press.

Shelden, RG., S.K. Tracy & W.B. Brown (2001). *Young Gangs in American Society,* 2nd ed. Belmont, CA: Wadsworth.

Sheley, J.F. (1985). *America's "Crime Problem": An Introduction to Criminology.* Belmont, CA: Wadsworth.

Sheller, G. (2004, March 11). "Costly Lies: Martha Stewart Was Brought Down by Greed and Deception." *Columbus Dispatch,* A10.

Sherman, L., P. Gartin & M. Buerger (1989). "Hot Spots and Predatory Crime: Routine Activities and the Criminology of Place." *Criminology,* 27, 27-55.

Shoemaker, D. (2000). *Theories of Delinquency*, 4th ed. Oxford: Oxford University Press.

Short, J. (1997). *Poverty, Ethnicity and Violent Crime*. Boulder, CO: Westview.

Silverman, R. & L. Kennedy (1993). *Deadly Deeds: Murder in Canada*. Scarborough, Ontario: Nelson.

Sim, J., P. Scraton & P. Gordon (1987). "Introduction: Crime, the State and Critical Analysis." In P. Scraton (ed.), *Law, Order and the Authoritarian State* (pp. 1-70). Philadelphia: Open University Press.

Simon, D. (2002). *Elite Deviance*, 7th ed. Boston: Allyn & Bacon.

Simon, R.J. (1975). *Women and Crime*. Lexington, MA: Lexington Books.

Simpson, S.S. (2002). *Corporate Crime, Law and Social Control*. New York: Cambridge University Press.

Simpson, S.S., A.R. Harris & B.A. Mattson (1993). "Measuring Corporate Crime." In M.B. Blankenship (ed.), *Understanding Corporate Criminality* (pp. 115-140). New York: Garland.

Sinclair, R.L. (2002). "Male Peer Support and Male-to-Female Dating Abuse Committed by Socially Displaced Male Youth: An Exploratory Study." Doctoral dissertation, Carleton University.

Skogan, W.G. (1990). *Disorder and Decline: Crime and the Spiral of Decay in American Neighborhoods*. New York: Free Press.

Smandych, R.(1985). "Marxism and the Creation of Law: Re-examining the Origins of Canadian Anti-combines Legislation 1890-1910." In T. Fleming (ed.), *The New Criminologies in Canada: State, Crime, and Control* (pp. 87-99). Toronto: Oxford University Press.

Smith, A.B. & H. Pollack (1997). "Deviance as Crime, Sin, and Poor Taste." In P.A. Adler & P. Adler (eds.), *Constructions of Deviance: Social Power, Context and Interaction* (pp. 25-34). Belmont, CA: Wadsworth.

Smith, D. (1996). "Keynote Address." Presentation to the Western Association of Sociology and Anthropology, Kelowna, British Columbia.

Smith, M.D. (1986). "Effects of Question Format on the Reporting of Woman Abuse: A Telephone Survey Experiment." *Victimology*, 11, 430-438.

Smith, M.D. (1987). "The Incidence and Prevalence of Woman Abuse in Toronto." *Violence and Victims*, 2, 173-187.

Smith, M.D. (1990a). "Socioeconomic Risk Factors in Wife Abuse: Results from a Survey of Toronto Women." *Canadian Journal of Sociology*, 15, 39-58.

Smith, M.D. (1990b). "Patriarchal Ideology and Wife Beating: A Test of a Feminist Hypothesis." *Violence and Victims*, 5, 257-273.

Smith, M.D. (1994). "Enhancing the Quality of Survey Data on Violence Against Women: A Feminist Approach." *Gender and Society*, 8, 109-127.

Smith, W. & A. Smith (1975). *Minimata*. New York: Holt, Rinehart and Winston.

Snider, L. (1988). "Commercial Crime." In V.F. Sacco (ed.), *Deviance: Conformity and Control in Canadian Society* (pp. 231-283). Scarborough, ON: Prentice Hall.

Snider, L. (1993). *Bad Business: Corporate Crime in Canada*. Scarborough, ON: Nelson.

Spergel, I.A. (1995). *Youth Gang Problem: A Community Approach*. New York: Oxford University Press.

Spitzer, S. (1975). "Toward a Marxian Theory of Deviance." *Social Problems*, 638-651.

St. Jean, P.K.B. (1998). "Elaborating Collective Efficacy as it Relates to Neighborhood Safety." Unpublished manuscript, Department of Sociology, University of Chicago.

Stanko, E.A. (1990). *Everyday Violence: How Women and Men Experience Sexual and Physical Danger*. London: Pandora.

Stanko, E.A. (2001). "Women, Danger, and Criminology." In C.M. Renzetti & L. Goodstein (eds.), *Women, Crime, and Criminal Justice: Original Feminist Readings* (pp. 13-26). Los Angeles: Roxbury.

Starbuck, D., J.C. Howell & D.J. Lindquist (2001). *Hybrid and Other Modern Gangs*. Washington, DC: Office of Juvenile Justice and Delinquency Prevention.

Statistics Canada. (1993). *Violence Against Women Survey*. Ottawa: Author.

Sterk-Elifson, C. (2005). "Determining Drug Use Patterns Among Women: The Value of Qualitative Research Methods." In W.R. Palacios (ed.), *Cocktails and Dreams: Perspectives on Drug and Alcohol Use* (pp. 43-55). Upper Saddle River, NJ: Prentice Hall.

Straus, M.A. (1979). "Measuring Intrafamily Conflict and Violence: The Conflict Tactics (CT) Scales." *Journal of Marriage and the Family*, 41, 75-88.

Straus, M.A. (1998). "The Controversy Over Domestic Violence by Women: A Methodological, Theoretical, and Sociology of Science Analysis." Paper presented at the Claremont Symposium on Applied Social Psychology on Violence in Intimate Relationships, Claremont, CA, February.

Straus, M.A. & R.J. Gelles (1986). "Societal Change and Change in Family Violence from 1975 to 1985 as Revealed by Two National Surveys." *Journal of Marriage and the Family*, 48, 465-479.

Straus, M.A., R.J. Gelles & S.K. Steinmetz (1981). *Behind Closed Doors: Violence in the American Family*. New York: Anchor.

Straus, M.A., S.L. Hamby, S. Boney-McCoy & D.B. Sugarman (1996). "The Revised Conflict Tactics Scales (CTS2): Development and Preliminary Psychometric Data." *Journal of Family Issues*, 17, 283-316.

Sumner, C. (1994). *The Sociology of Deviance: An Obituary*. Buckingham, UK: Open University Press.

Sutherland, E.H. (1939). *Principles of Criminology*, 3rd ed. Philadelphia: J.B. Lippincott.

Sutherland, E.H. (1940). White-collar Criminality. *American Sociological Review*, 5, 1-12.

Sutherland, E.H. (1947). *Principles of Criminology*, 4th ed. Philadelphia: J.B. Lippincott.

Sutherland, E.H. (1949). *White Collar Crime*. New York: Holt, Rinehart & Winston.

Sutherland, E.H. & D. Cressey (1966). *Principles of Criminology*, 7th ed. Philadelphia: Lippincott.

Swidler, A. (1986). "Culture in Action: Symbols and Strategies." *American Sociological Review, 51,* 273-286.

Sykes, G. & F.T. Cullen (1992). *Criminology*, 2nd ed. New York: Harcourt Brace Jovanovich.

Sykes, G.M. & D. Matza (1957). "Techniques of Neutralization: A Theory of Delinquency." *American Sociological Review, 22,* 664-670.

Szasz, T. (1987). *Insanity: The Idea and its Consequences.* New York: John Wiley.

Szockyj, E. & N. Frank (1996). "Introduction." In E. Szockyj & J.G. Fox (eds.), *Corporate Victimization of Women* (pp. 3-32). Boston: Northeastern University Press.

Tallmer, M. (1987). "Chemical Dumping as a Corporate Way of Life." In S. Hills (ed.), *Corporate Violence: Injury and Death for Profit* (pp. 111-120). Totowa, NJ: Rowman & Littlefield.

Tappan, P. (1947). "Who is the Criminal?" *American Sociological Review*, 12, 96-102.

Tatum, B.D. (1997). *"Why Are All the Black Kids Sitting Together in the Cafeteria?* New York: Basic Books.

Taylor, C. (1993). *Girls, Gangs, Women, and Drugs.* East Lansing, MI: Michigan State University Press.

Taylor, C. (2001). "The Relationship Between Social and Self-Control: Tracing Hirschi's Criminological Career." *Theoretical Criminology, 5,* 369-368.

Taylor, I. (1992). "Left Realist Criminology and the Free Market Experiment in Britain." In J. Young & R. Matthews (eds.), *Rethinking Criminology: The Realist Debate* (pp. 95-122). London: Sage.

Taylor, I., P. Walton & J. Young (1973). *The New Criminology.* London: Routledge & Kegan Paul.

Taylor, R.B. (2001). "The Ecology of Crime, Fear, and Delinquency: Social Disorganization versus Social Efficacy." In R. Paternoster & R. Bachman (eds.), *Explaining Criminals and Crime* (pp. 124-139). Los Angeles: Roxbury.

Taylor, R.B. & A.V. Harrell (1996). *Physical Environment and Crime.* Washington, DC: National Institute of Justice.

Thio, A. (2004). *Deviant Behavior*, 7th ed. Boston: Allyn & Bacon.

Thornberry, T.P. & M. Farnworth (1982). "Social Correlates of Criminal Involvement: Further Evidence on the Relationship Between Social Status and Criminal Behavior." *American Sociological Review, 47,* 505-518.

Thornberry, T.P., M.D. Krohn & A. Lizotte (2003). *Gangs and Delinquency in Developmental Perspective.* New York: Cambridge University Press.

Thorne-Finch, R. (1992). *Ending the Silence: The Origins and Treatment of Male Violence Against Women.* Toronto: University of Toronto Press.

Thrasher, F. (1927). *The Gang: A Study of 1,313 Gangs in Chicago.* Chicago: University of Chicago Press.

Tittle, C.R. (1995). *Control Balance: Toward a General Theory of Deviance*. Boulder, CO: Westview.

Tittle, C.R. (1999). "Continuing the Discussion of Control Balance." *Theoretical Criminology*, 3, 344-352.

Tittle, C. (2000). "Theoretical Developments in Criminology." In *The Nature of Crime: Continuity and Change* (pp. 51-101). Washington, DC: U.S. Department of Justice, Office of Justice Programs.

Tjaden, P. & N. Thoennes (2000). *Extent, Nature, and Consequences of Intimate Partner Violence: Findings from the National Violence Against Women Survey*. Washington, DC: U.S. Department of Justice.

Toby, J. (1957). "Social Disorganization and Stake in Conformity: Complementary Factors in the Predatory Behavior of Young Hoodlums." *Journal of Criminal Law, Criminology and Police Science*, 48, 12-17.

Tong, R. (1989). *Feminist Thought: A Comprehensive Introduction*. Boulder, CO: Westview.

Tong, R. (1998). *Feminist Thought: A More Comprehensive Introduction*, 2nd ed. Boulder, CO: Westview.

Turk, A. (1975). "Prospects and Pitfalls for Radical Criminology: A Critical Response to Platt." *Crime and Social Justice*, 4, 41-42.

Uggen, C. & J. Manza (2002). "Democratic Contraction? Political Consequences of Felon Disfranchisement in the United States." *American Sociological Review,* 67, 777-803.

U.S. Bureau of Justice Statistics (2004). *Homicide Trends in the U.S.: Intimate Homicide*. Washington, DC: Author.

U.S. Consumer Product Safety Commission. (2004a, Fall). *MECAP News*, pp. 8-11.

U.S. Consumer Product Safety Commission. (2004b). "New CPSC Burn Center Reporting System Provides First Year of Data: Clothing-related Burn Injuries to Children Often Involve Gasoline" [Online]. Available at: http://www.cpsc.gov/

Vaughn, D. (1983). *Controlling Unlawful Corporate Behavior*. Chicago: University of Chicago Press.

Velez, M.B. (2001). "The Role of Public Social Control in Urban Neighborhoods: A Multilevel Analysis of Victimization Risk." *Criminology*, 39, 837-864.

Venkatesh, S.A. (1997). "The Social Organization of Street Gang Activity in an Urban Ghetto." *American Journal of Sociology,* 103, 82-112.

Venkatesh, S.A. (1998). "Gender and Outlaw Capitalism: An Account of the Black Sisters United 'Girl Gang.'" *Signs*, 23, 683-699.

Victim Policy Center. (2004). *When Men Murder Women: An Analysis of 2002 Homicide Data*. Washington, DC: Author.

Visano, L. (1985). "Crime, Law, and State: The Linkage Problem." In T. Fleming (ed.), *The New Criminologies in Canada* (pp. 43-61). Toronto: Oxford University Press.

Vold, G.B. (1979). "Group Conflict Theory as an Explanation of Crime." In G. Vold (ed.), *Theoretical Criminology*. New York: Oxford University Press.

Vold, G.B., T.J. Bernard & J.B. Snipes (1998). *Theoretical Criminology*, 4th ed. New York: Oxford University Press.

Wacquant, L. (2000). "The New 'Peculiar Institution': On the Prison as Surrogate Ghetto." *Theoretical Criminology*, 4, 377-389.

Walby, S. (1990). *Theorizing Patriarchy*. London: Blackwell.

Walker, S. (2000). *Searching for the Denominator: Problems with Police Traffic Stop Data and an Early Warning System Solution*. Washington, DC: National Institute of Justice.

Warr, M. (2002). *Companions in Crime: The Social Aspects of Criminal Conduct*. New York: Cambridge University Press.

Websdale, N. (1998). *Rural Woman Battering and the Justice System: An Ethnography*. Thousand Oaks, CA: Sage.

Weil, A. (1986). *The Natural Mind*. Boston: Houghton Mifflin.

West, C. (2001). *Race Matters*. New York: Vintage.

West, C.M. & S. Rose (2001). "Dating Aggression Among Low-Income African American Youth: An Examination of Gender Differences and Antagonistic Beliefs." *Violence Against Women*, 6, 470-494.

West, W.G. (1984). *Young Offenders and the State: A Canadian Perspective on Delinquency*. Toronto: Butterworths.

White, J. & M.P. Koss (1991). "Courtship Violence: Incidence in a National Sample of Higher Education Students." *Violence and Victims*, 6, 247-256.

Widom, C.S. (1989). "Child Abuse, Neglect and Violent Criminal Behavior." *Criminology*, 27, 252-271.

Wiersema, B. (2001). "Community Structure and Patterns in Criminal Homicide: Exploring the Weekend Effect" [Online]. Available at: http://www.ncjrs.org/pdf files1/nij/grants/187353.pdf

Wilkins, L. (1964). *Social Deviance*. London: Tavistock.

Williams, F. & M. McShane (1994). *Criminological Theory*, 2nd ed. Englewood Cliffs, NJ: Prentice Hall.

Williams, S. (2004, January 13). "Project to Address Racial Issues for Gays: YMCA Program Seeks to Foster Dialogue." *The Columbus Dispatch*, B3.

Wilson, M. & M. Daly (1985). "Competitiveness, Risk Taking and Violence: The Young Male Syndrome." *Ethology and Sociobiology*, 6, 59-73.

Wilson, M. & M. Daly (1992). "'Til Death do us Part." In J. Radford & D.E.H. Russell (eds.), *Femicide: The Politics of Women Killing* (pp. 83-98). New York: Twayne.

Wilson, M. & M. Daly (1994). *Spousal Homicide*. Ottawa: Canadian Centre for Justice Statistics.

Wilson, M. & M. Daly (1998). "Sexual Rivalry and Sexual Conflict: Recurring Themes in Fatal Conflicts." *Theoretical Criminology*, 2, 291-310.

Wilson, J.Q. (1985). *Thinking About Crime*. New York: Vintage.

Wilson, J.Q. & G. Kelling (1982). "Broken Windows." *Atlantic Monthly*, March, 29-38.

Wilson, W.J. (1987). *The Truly Disadvantaged: The Inner-City, the Underclass and Public Policy*. Chicago: University of Chicago Press.

Wilson, W.J. (1996). *When Work Disappears: The World of the New Urban Poor*. New York: Knopf.

Wolfgang, M.E. (1958). *Patterns of Criminal Homicide*. Philadelphia: University of Pennsylvania Press.

Wolfgang, M.E. & F. Ferracuti (1967). *The Subculture of Violence: Towards an Integrated Theory in Criminology*. London: Tavistock.

Wotherspoon, T. (1998). *The Sociology of Education in Canada: Critical Perspectives*. Toronto: Oxford University Press.

Wright, R.T. & S. Decker (1997). *Armed Robbers in Action*. Boston: Northeastern University Press.

Young, J. (1988). "Radical Criminology in Britain: The Emergence of a Competing Paradigm." *British Journal of Criminology*, 28, 159-183.

Young, J. (1997). "Left Realist Criminology: Radical in its Analysis, Realist in its Policy." In M. Maguire, R. Morgan & R. Reiner (eds.), *Oxford Handbook of Criminology* (pp. 473-498). Oxford: Clarendon Press.

Young, J. (1999). *The Exclusive Society*. London: Sage.

Young, T. (1981). "Corporate Crime: A Critique of the Clinard Report." *Contemporary Crises*, 5, 330-340.

Zahn, M.A. & P.L. McCall (1999). "Trends and Patterns of Homicide in the 20th Century United States." In D.M. Smith & M.A. Zahn (eds.), *Homicide: A Sourcebook of Social Research* (pp. 9-23). Thousand Oaks, CA: Sage.

Zielenbach, S. (2000). *The Art of Revitalization: Improving Conditions in Distressed Inner-city Neighborhoods*. New York: Garland.

Zimring, F.E. (1987). *Problems and Means of Measuring White Collar Crime*. Sacramento, CA: California Department of Justice.

Zimring, F. & G. Hawkins (1986). *Capital Punishment and the American Agenda*. New York: Cambridge University Press.

About the Authors

Tania Henvey

Walter S. DeKeseredy is Professor of Criminology and Justice Studies at The University of Ontario Institute of Technology. He has published close to 50 refereed journal articles and numerous book chapters on woman abuse, crime in public housing, and criminological theory. He is also the author of *Women, Crime and the Canadian Criminal Justice System*, and has authored and coauthored a variety of books on woman abuse, the role of male peer support, deviance, sexual assault on the college campus, and contemporary North American social problems. His most recent title is *Under Siege: Poverty and Crime in a Public Housing Community* (with Shahid Alvi, Martin Schwartz, and E. Andreas Tomaszewski). In 2004, DeKeseredy and Martin Schwartz jointly received the Distinguished Scholar Award from the American Society of Criminology's (ASC) Division on Women and Crime. In 1995, DeKeseredy received the Critical Criminologist of the Year Award from the ASC's Division on Critical Criminology and in 1993 received Carleton University's Research Achievement Award. Currently he serves on the editorial boards of several journals. He is currently publishing the results of an exploratory study of sexual assault during and after separation/divorce in three rural Ohio communities.

Desmond Ellis is a Senior Scholar at York University, Ontario, Canada. He has published a number of books and articles on deviance, crime, violence in prisons, violence against women who are separating/divorcing, and conflict and conflict resolution. As a professor at York University, he helped create the LaMarsh Research Centre on Violence and Conflict Resolution and created the York University Certificate Programme on Conflict Resolution. At present, he is involved in two research projects. The first one involves testing an instrument that assesses, predicts, and manages the risk of male partner violence against women who have decided to end the relationship. The second project involves an attempt to explain similarities in the amount and patterning of youth gang violence in Kingston, Jamaica, and Toronto, Canada.

Shahid Alvi is Associate Professor of Criminology and Justice Studies at the University of Ontario Institute of Technology. His research interests include masculinities, critical criminology, juvenile delinquency, crime and public housing, poverty and "welfare reform," the link between violence and culture, and violence against women. His recent publications focus on poor minority women's victimization by psychological and physical abuse, second-generation crime prevention through environmental design, women's victimization in public housing, feminist routine activities theory, and fear of crime. He is the author or co-author of numerous articles, book chapters, and three books, including the recently released *Under Siege: Poverty and Crime in a Public Housing Community* (with Walter DeKeseredy, Martin Schwartz, and E. Andreas Tomaszewski). He recently completed a research project examining the links between poor minority women's victimization and resilience in two St. Paul, Minnesota, public housing projects, and another on the social correlates of youth smoking. He is also the 2002 recipient of the Critical Criminologist of the Year Award from the American Society of Criminology's Critical Criminology Division.

Index

Entrepreneurial skills, teaching students, 274
Environmental crime, 175
Epstein, J., 171
Ermann, M.D., 170, 186
Esbensen, F.A., 256, 261-262
Estonia, homicide rates in, 127
Ethnic Cleansing, 16
Ethnicity, of gangs, 239-240, 261-263
Ethnographic studies, 60-61
Excusable homicide, 126
Experimenter drug users, 213
External containment, 251-252
Extralegal sanctions, 184
Exxon Corporation and Exxon Shipping, 176

F. Hoffmann-La Roche Ltd., 176
Fagan, J., 46, 277
Faith, K., 43
False advertising, 172, 174-175
False consciousness, 69
False statements, 175
Faludi, S., 292
Familial patriarchy, ideology of, 104, 110
Families of Homicide Victims and Missing Persons Inc., 154
Family, reducing violence in, 289-290. *See also* Woman abuse
"Family model of punishment," 55
Family socialization, 55
Farley, M., 4
Farnworth, M., 216, 250
FBI. *See* U.S. Bureau of Investigation (FBI)
FDA. *See* Food and Drug Administration (FDA)
Federal Bureau of Narcotics, 218-219
Federal Energy Regulatory Commission, 14
Fekete, J., 76, 89
Felony murder, 127. *See also* Homicide
Felson, M., 114, 116, 145
Female crime and deviance, 17-18, 43-46
Feminism, defined, 73-74
Feminist/male peer support model of sexual assault during and after separation/divorce, 116-118
Feminist routine activities theory, 114-116

Feminist theories, 73-77, 192
on drugs, 226-228
evaluation of, 76-77
feminist/male peer support model of sexual assault during and after separation/divorce, 116-118
five elements of, 73-74
liberal feminist, 74
Marxist feminist, 74-75
radical feminist, 75-76
socialist feminism, 75-76
Fenstermaker, S., 110
Ferenchik, M., 15, 15n7
Ferracuti, F., 138
Ferrell, J., 284, 284n12
Figlio, R.M., 64n15
Figueira-McDonough, J., 17
Financial crimes, 175
Finkelhor, D., 47, 100
Firestone tires, 169
First-degree murder, 127. *See also* Homicide
Fisher, G.A., 103n10, 128
Fisse, B., 185
Fitzpatrick, D., 87
Flavin, J., 76
Fleury, R.E., 100
Focal concerns, 245-246
Folk devils, 280
Food and Drug Administration (FDA), 186-187
Food and drug crime, 175
Ford Explorer, 169
Ford Pinto, 168-170
Foster Parents, 270
Fox, J.A., 127, 129, 131-133
Franck, K.A., 282
Frank, N., 160, 162-163, 170, 177-178, 181
Fraud, 175
Friedrichs, D.O., 9, 23, 49, 157-158, 160, 160n1, 163-164, 163n5, 168-169, 170n8, 171-172, 173, 177, 177n10, 181, 191, 193
Functional activities, 35
Functionalist approach, 37
Functional theory of crime and social control, 35-37
Funk, R.E., 285, 292
Furstenberg, F.F., 65

Gabor, T., 8-9, 11
Galliher, J.F., 218-219

Harney, P.A., 110, 115
Harper, T., 157
Harrell, A.V., 281
Harris, A.R., 128, 164
Harris, T., 20
Hartman, T., 158, 160, 172, 174
Hartnagel, T.F., 215
Hassel, William, 19-20
Hate crime, 79
Hatewatch, 300
Hatty, S.E., 67, 70, 79
Hawkins, D.F., 139
Hawkins, D.J., 254
Hawkins, G., 134
Hawkins, J.D., 240
Hawthorne, M., 7-8, 161
Hay, C., 254
Haysom, I., 149
Hayward, K., 135
Hazler, R., 286
Head Start, 270-271
"Heavy Electrical Equipment Antitrust Cases of 1961, The," 161
Hegemonic masculinity, 19. *See also* Gender; Men
Henry, S., 2n1, 72, 183
Henslin, J.M., 172
Herrnstein, R.J., 271
Hewett School's Department of Sociology web site on crime and deviance, 85
Hey, V., 109
Hidden curriculum, 272
Hierarchy of authority, 182-183
Hill, K.G., 254
Hill, R.H., 138
Hinch, R., 164, 169
Hindelang, M.J., 145
Hirsch, D.J., 128
Hirschi, T., 19, 32, 50-52, 54-55, 72, 140-141, 182-183, 217, 251
Hispanic drivers, 15
Hispanics
    number of, in United States, 165-166
    young men denied masculine status, 78-79
Hobbes, Thomas, 49-51
Hobbesian problem of social order, 56
Hobsbawm, E., 70
Hodgson, J.F., 4
Holsinger, A.M., 262
Holsinger, K., 262

Homicide, 125-154
    categories of, 126-127
    criminal, 127
    critical perspectives, 147-151
    defined, 126-127
    ecological theories of, 144-147
    excusable, 126
    extent and distribution of, 127-133
    gang, 243-244
    interactionist theories of, 141-144
    justifiable, 126-127
    "legally sanctioned," 126
    masculinities and, 149-151
    negligent, 127
    percentage of, by size of city, 132-133
    rate of, in New York City, 277
    rates as positively associated with income inequality, 137
    rates of, and income inequality, 137
    rational choice theories of, 134-136
    reckless, 127
    social control theories of, 140-141
    strain theories of, 136-138
    subculture theories of, 138-140
    theories of, 134-151
    trends in United States, 127-128
    type by race, 131
    victims by circumstances, 132
    See also Intimate femicide; Murder
Homicide Research Working Group, 154
Homicide-suicide, gender differences in, 130
Homicide Trends in United States web site, 154
Homophobia
    eliminating, 293-295
    and masculinity, 79
Hooker Chemical Company, 171
Hornosty, J.M., 292
Hotaling, G., 104
Howell, J.C., 239-241, 243-244, 254, 256
Hsieh, S., 217-218
Huff-Corzine, L., 145
Hughes, L.A., 255, 258
Huizinga, D., 256
Hull, J., 109
Human agency, 61
Human Ecology, School of, 61-62
Human ecology process model, 64-67
Hummer, R.A., 109

VAWS. *See* Violence Against Women
    Survey (VAWS)
Velez, M.B., 66
Venkatesh, S.A., 247, 256, 259, 263
Victim blaming, 272
Victim Policy Center, 98
Victim precipitation, 142
Victimization surveys, 163
Vieraitis, L.M., 138
Violence against consumers, 168-170
Violence Against Women Act (VAWA),
    290
Violence Against Women Office, U.S.
    Department of Justice, 123
Violence Against Women Survey
    (VAWS), 91-94
Violence against workers, 165-167
Violentization, 142
Virulency, 143
Visano, L., 190n15
VISTA. *See* Volunteers in Service to
    America (VISTA)
Vivendi's Universal, 173
Vold, G.B., 42, 57, 60, 76
Volunteers in Service to America
    (VISTA), 270
Vos, J., 135

Wacquant, L., 223, 225
Wald, M., 169
Walker, S., 15
Wallman, J., 277-278
Walton, P., 22, 32n1, 37, 68n18,
    73n25
Warner-Lambert, 176
Warner Music Group, 173
War on drugs, 200, 206, 226
    failure of, 223-224
    reasoning behind, 225
    social exclusion to, 225
    See also Drugs
War on gangs, 233
"War on Poverty," 270
"War on the Poor," 271
Warr, M., 39
Waste heat, 172
Webb, V.J., 235
Websdale, N., 117
Weil, A., 200
Weinberg, M.S., 186
Weitzer, R., 89n3, 146, 223, 259
West, C., 14, 103, 119n28
West, C.M., 80n31

West, W.G., 52
Westinghouse Corporation, 161-162
White, J., 103
White-collar crime, 158-159, 164. *See
    also* Corporate crime
Widom, C.S., 289
Wiersema, B., 131
Wildeman, J., 159
Williams, F., 32
Williams, K.R., 97
Williams, L.M., 95, 103, 119n28
Williams, S., 20
Wilson, J.Q., 52, 65, 85, 278
Wilson, M., 79, 97, 116-117, 150,
    165, 184, 281n10
Wilson, W.J., 70-72, 78-79, 111-112,
    111n19, 145, 222, 259, 271-275,
    286, 289
Winfree, L.T., 261-262
Wisniewski, W., 89, 103
Wolfgang, M.E., 138, 142
Woman abuse, 87-123, 283-284
    alcohol and, 109, 115
    defined, 89-96
    feminist theories, 113-116
    and feminist theories, 73
    incidence figures of wife abuse, 93-
        95
    incidents caused by psychological
        perspectives, 33
    integrated theories, 116-118
    intimate femicide, 96-99
    left realists and, 72
    lifestyle factors increasing women's
        suitability as targets of, 115
    male peer support theories, 106-110
    multidimensional nature of, 96
    nonlethal forms of, in intimate het-
        erosexual relationships, 99-104
    reducing, 290-292
    risk factors associated with lethal
        and nonlethal forms of, 103-104
    routine activities theories, 114-116
    social cohesion and, 286
    social learning theories, 105-106
    theories of, 104-118
    woman slain in front of police had
        court order on ex-husband, 88
    women's centers, 284
    See also Intimate femicide
Women
    cohabiting, 99-103, 117-118
    in gangs, 260-261